GHOST CRIMINOLOGY

The Gang's All Queer: The Lives of Gay Gang Members
Vanessa R. Panfil

Skateboarding LA: Inside Professional Street Skateboarding
Gregory J. Snyder

America's Jails: The Search for Human Dignity in an Age of Mass Incarceration
Derek S. Jeffreys

The Little Old Lady Killer: The Sensationalized Crimes of Mexico's First Female Serial Killer
Susana Vargas Cervantes

Ghost Criminology: The Afterlife of Crime and Punishment
Edited by Michael Fiddler, Theo Kindynis, and Travis Linnemann

Ghost Criminology

The Afterlife of Crime and Punishment

Edited by
Michael Fiddler, Theo Kindynis, *and* Travis Linnemann

NEW YORK UNIVERSITY PRESS
New York

NEW YORK UNIVERSITY PRESS
New York
www.nyupress.org

© 2022 by New York University
All rights reserved

References to Internet websites (URLs) were accurate at the time of writing. Neither the author nor New York University Press is responsible for URLs that may have expired or changed since the manuscript was prepared.

Library of Congress Cataloging-in-Publication Data
Names: Fiddler, Michael, editor. | Kindynis, Theo, editor. | Linnemann, Travis, editor.
Title: Ghost criminology : the afterlife of crime and punishment / edited by Michael Fiddler, Theo Kindynis, and Travis Linnemann.
Description: New York : New York University Press, [2022] | Series: Alternative criminology | Includes bibliographical references and index.
Identifiers: LCCN 2021011946 | ISBN 9781479885725 (hardback ; alk. paper) | ISBN 9781479842438 (paperback ; alk. paper) | ISBN 9781479848935 (ebook) | ISBN 9781479870493 (ebook other)
Subjects: LCSH: Criminology—Philosophy. | Violent crimes. | Ghosts. | Crime—Sociological aspects.
Classification: LCC HV6018 .G46 2021 | DDC 364.01—dc23
LC record available at https://lccn.loc.gov/2021011946

New York University Press books are printed on acid-free paper, and their binding materials are chosen for strength and durability. We strive to use environmentally responsible suppliers and materials to the greatest extent possible in publishing our books.

Manufactured in the United States of America

10 9 8 7 6 5 4 3 2 1

Also available as an ebook

CONTENTS

Ghost Criminology: A (Spirit) Guide   1
Michael Fiddler, Theo Kindynis, and Travis Linnemann

PART I. APPARITIONS AND THE (IN)VISIBLE

1. After the Fact: Spectral Evidence, Cultural Haunting, and Gothic Sensibility   35
Eamonn Carrabine

2. Ghost Method   67
Jeff Ferrell

3. The Specter of White Supremacy: Fugitive Justice and the Dead Body of US Racialized Politics   88
Michelle Brown

4. From Optograms to X-Rays: How to Conjure a Spectral Criminological Image   110
Michael Fiddler

PART II. THE NECROTIC AND (IN)CORPOREAL

5. (Dis)Posing of "Toxic Necro-Waste": Managing Unwanted Ghosts   135
Daniel Robins

6. Destroyed Records   155
Katherine Biber

7. Police: The Weird and Eerie   180
Travis Linnemann and Justin Turner

8. "Dripping from Head to Toe with Blood": Suffocation, Tentacles, Police, and Capital   202
Bill McClanahan

PART III. DEAD AND HAUNTED SPACES

9. The Time of Ghosts: Sites of Violence, Environments of Memory 227
Alison Young

10. Dark Diffractions: A Performative Hauntology of 10 Rillington Place 253
Elaine Campbell

11. Who's Been Sleeping in My Bed? Cheap Motel Rooms and Transgression 280
Carolyn McKay

12. Excavating Ghosts: Urban Exploration as Graffiti Archaeology 307
Theo Kindynis

Ghost Criminology: A Requiem 337
Michael Fiddler, Theo Kindynis, and Travis Linnemann

About the Contributors 345
About the Editors 349
Index 351

Ghost Criminology

A (Spirit) Guide

MICHAEL FIDDLER, THEO KINDYNIS, AND
TRAVIS LINNEMANN

There are specters haunting criminology. It is a discipline beset by voices from its troubled past, as well as a threatened future. Such "ghosts" manifest in ways that are quite different from the spectral forms familiar to us from supernatural fiction. The specters that we are describing here leave (in)visible traces in texts, images, and spaces. They radiate out from sources of trauma. "Absences" can linger and become inscribed in a location. More malevolent forces shroud themselves in black marks of redaction or render invisible those at society's edges. Some apparitions we must endeavor to exorcise. Others we must learn to listen to and attend to their demands. We must live with our dead.

In short, myriad ghosts haunt social life in myriad ways. Consider, for example, the following types of hauntings:

> *Boston. 1990.* Two men dressed as cops walk into the Isabella Gardener Museum. They steal 13 paintings, including works by Manet and Vermeer. Rembrandt's "Christ in the Storm on the Sea of Galilee" is cut from its frame. The works, valued at $500 million, are as yet still missing and the two cops, still at-large.

> *Boston. 2018.* Empty frames still hang in the gallery. "Hacking the Heist," an augmented reality app, reinstates the paintings within their frames. A flickering apparition of Rembrandt's "A Lady and Gentleman in Black" hovers on a tablet screen.

Or,

London. 1815. The Royal Bethlem Hospital opens. It is England's first hospital for the "mentally ill." Dogged by scandal, it soon becomes known colloquially as "Bedlam."

London. 1936. Formally the National War Museum, the Imperial War Museum opens in the buildings once occupied by the Royal Bethlem Hospital.

London. 2016. The artist Edmund Clark's collection—entitled "War of Terror"—opens at the Imperial War Museum. A centerpiece of the exhibition is "Control Order House." Blueprints of the house—a location in the UK where a suspected terrorist was held—mark the floor. Visitors "walk" from room to room. Hundreds of photos of its real-life interior line the walls. They depict the detritus of the everyday: a newspaper, a cup. The "terrorist" does not appear in any of the photos. A young girl plays hopscotch across the lines of the blueprint.

And finally,

Minneapolis. 1680. The Dakota Sioux are the sole inhabitants of the territory until European-American settlers arrive and begin to compete for resources with the indigenous population.

Minneapolis. 1787. The Northwest Ordinance is signed forbidding slavery in the Northwest Territory. This is not enforced. Human bondage continues.

By this point, the enforced assimilation, starvation, and internment have led to the exile of the Dakota Sioux from the territory.

Minneapolis. 2020. George Floyd is murdered. Derek Chauvin, a white police officer, is filmed kneeling on George Floyd's neck for 8 minutes and 46 seconds. In evident distress, George Floyd cries out that he cannot breathe.

Minneapolis. 2075. Rising temperatures across central America, gigafires across California and Oregon, rising water levels in Florida, increasingly numerous and severe storms across the Gulf of Mexico have driven vast swathes of the population north and east. Refugee camps encircle the city. Marginalized groups, made up of Black, Indigenous, and other people of color, are disproportionately excluded from the city's resources.

Something haunts these events. A presence lingers, as does an absence. Animating both those cherished things we wish to remember and the grim happenings we wish to forget (as well as the futures we hope to avoid) are revenant ghosts, moving in and out of recollection. In the gallery, we chase two thieves and their ill-gotten loot, and in the asylum, we conjure a prisoner denied a face and name. In a city, we see a societal trauma echo through time. But what of the lingering dead themselves? What does it mean to confront a ghost? Why do they unnerve us so?[1] We are, as Colin Davis puts it, "doubly angry" with the departed. "*How could they leave us and why do they not leave us alone?*"[2] In our vain attempts to transcend death we keep the dead near us, while also rejecting them for what they represent. Announcing this conflicted presence and absence, the ghost whispers *memento mori* and warns that some-*thing* is awry.

The key to understanding this particular sense of disquiet is to focus upon its temporal quality. Hamlet, when confronted by the ghost of his dead father, feels time slip "out of joint." We too get the sense that *our* time, "the living present," is scarcely as solid as it claims to be.[3] The seemingly firm periodicity of past, present, and future converge, yielding synchronicities *and* dissonances. As the twentieth-century cultural critic and philosopher Walter Benjamin phrased it, past and present come together in a flash as a constellation of connections is made between them. And once attuned to this slipping confluence of memory, time, and space, it may become difficult not to encounter a ghost with our every step and turn.

We should be clear that our title, "*Ghost* Criminology," does not profess a belief in ghosts or the supernatural. Rather, the title reflects our interest in those cultural forces that fashion or reveal our wavering present.[4] We conjure ghosts as conceptual metaphors, allowing us to *see* what we *feel* haunting us. Our efforts in this regard follow the "spectral turn" in sociology, specifically Avery Gordon's *Ghostly Matters*, as well as adjacent developments in psychoanalysis, geography, postcolonial studies, and literary criticism. We are also indebted to the work of the late cultural critic Mark Fisher.[5] In this weird, eerie, unmoored, and out-of-joint space, we find grounds upon which to confront the many crimes and wounds of the living. Straightforward enough, we aim to bring the spectral and hauntological—a term we will soon unpack—to bear on criminology's subject, to confront the ghosts to which we cling and those we wish to banish.

The writing in and out of criminology's ghosts, their very presence/absence, diagnoses a sense of uncertainty. They indicate a temporal dis-ease that is also—inevitably—felt with the discipline. There is, possibly, the implicit suggestion that the discipline has died and that this collection is a picking over of its mouldering corpse. We might say that we aim to make known a ghost *of* criminology, part of those spectral presences having always and already haunted the discipline. To paraphrase Fisher, ghost criminology seeks out the *no longer*, as well as the *not yet*.

We begin our investigation into ghost criminology by setting out our own specific focus and method—a magical working, if you will—for this particular project. It is one that builds upon the philosopher Jacques Derrida's notion of "hauntology." As such, we provide a brief overview of both the philosophical and psychoanalytic readings of ghosts, phantoms, and hauntings that underpin hauntology itself. We then hold a séance of sorts, calling forth those figures of criminology's past to show how they too used the language of haunting before examining the discipline's more recent "spectral turn." Finally, we conclude by providing the outline for this particular collection.

The Specter Comes Back

As we set off on our journey it is helpful to consider Wendy Brown's understanding of the ghost and specter:

> The specter begins by coming back, by repeating itself, by recurring in the present. It is not traceable to an origin nor to a founding event, it does not have an objective or "comprehensive" history, yet it operates as a force . . . We inherit not "what really happened" to the dead but what lives on from that happening, what is conjured from it, how past generations and events occupy the force fields of the present, how they claim us, and how they haunt, plague, and inspire our imaginations and visions for the future.[6]

We must attend to those forces of the past and future that act in the present. When time is "out of joint," we must consider the repeating eddies that radiate out across time from sites of trauma. We must convene with the passed and learn what "lives on" from that passing. Fundamentally, ours is an analysis of Weird temporality. However, as Steve Pile suggests, the spectral also requires a "particular type of seeing." In order to capture that which is out of joint, we must attend to those phenomena that flicker between presence and absence, visibility and invisibility. So, our attention is also drawn to the Weirding of spaces, as well as that which "inspirit[s] our imaginations."

Ghost criminology has, then, the ghost(ed) as its conceptual target. There are two aspects to this. First, we will examine how certain groups, individuals, cultural artifacts, and spaces have been rendered ghostly. We will explore how they have been subject to structural violence(s) and how the harms that they have suffered have been obscured or redacted. We are drawn, then, toward Gordon's framing of haunting as revealing "repressed or unresolved social violences" (Radway, ix). In this, we can access the "things behind the things" (Gordon 2008; Radway). Second, and this is where we extend the project beyond Gordon's framework, we see the ghost(ed) as an avenue to explore the fluidity between past-present-future. Drawing upon both Walter Benjamin and Jacques Derrida, we can explore the ways in which both past and future haunt the present. These are the looming shadows of the "no longer" and "not yet." To echo Gordon's (2008, p. 22) sentiment of calling up and calling out, ghost criminology sets out a framework to illuminate and make visible those who have been shadowed and give voice to those who have been silenced in a present haunted by both the past and the future.

So, let us return to the ghost(ed) that opened this chapter. We have three examples that are interruptions or eruptions of the past into the present; repressed traumas of social violence, as well as flickerings of simultaneous absence and presence. Let us trace them in turn. Bedlam became the site of the Imperial War Museum, which became the site of "War of Terror," an art exhibition documenting CIA "black sites" and secret prisons. The building, once a hospital and now an exhibition space, holds spectral traces. The constellation of past and present that Benjamin describes envisages connections within and between oppressive measures of state control, the "Great Game" of Imperial brinksmanship over Afghanistan, and the Royal Bethlem Hospital becoming known as Bedlam.[7] Likewise, the art exhibits that "return" as digital ghosts on tablet screens at the Isabelle Gardener museum speak to the neither/nor presence and absence of the spectral. They are at once visible and invisible. Finally, the unresolved racial violence and trauma of Minneapolis can be seen as an irruption of a past-present constellation. We inherit from the dead these "past" social injustices: These harms and violences are perpetual shadows in the present. Further, we can consider the "not yet" and the ways in which we are haunted and shadowed by future harms, as a climate crisis builds and disproportionately impacts on the lives of those who have been subject to structural violence for centuries.

In order to reckon with the ghost as social force, as described by Wendy Brown, it is helpful to go back to the work of psychoanalysts Nicolas Abraham and Maria Torok. The language of spectrality and haunting has been applied to social and cultural life at various different times and across various different disciplines (see Eamonn Carrabine's chapter in this collection for a comprehensive overview). Abraham and Torok offer a useful starting point since they applied this terminology to the experience of trauma. Commencing in the late 1950s and henceforth across a series of publications that culminated in *The Shell and the Kernel*,[8] the pair developed their influential understanding of the "phantom." In contrast to Brown, Abraham and Torok knew all too well their phantom's origin. For them, phantoms are born of the failure to properly mourn. If a person suffers the loss of something they love—a partner, a place, or even an idea—it provokes the process of *introjection*. Through this mourning process, the sufferer creates an inner psychic representation of loss, which they assimilate into their psyche. This process can, however, go awry and turn instead into *incorporation*. In his explication of the term, Jacques Derrida used words like "fantasmatic, unmediated, instantaneous, magical, sometimes hallucinatory."[9] As the term implies, incorporation describes a process that inters the love object within the psyche, enshrining it as though it were a living force in its own right. The incorporated and animated ghost speaks through or "ventriloquizes" a host who is unaware that they are haunted in their loss. The words and deeds of a failed mourning echo within an internalized "crypt." These are the "words buried alive" of which Derrida spoke.[10]

For psychoanalysts, incorporation is the mechanism by which haunting inherits across generations. It names the phenomenon that sees descendants of those who suffered a trauma carry the burdens of that same trauma. Incorporated, unspeakable loss is, in this way, transmitted inter- and intragenerationally and produces a mutual and "collective burial ground."[11] No mere family story, the phantom of incorporated loss, as Margery Kalb suggests, quite literally materializes as "inchoate, spectral, eerie, undead psychic imprints that colonize body and soul, resulting in highly phenomenologically disturbed states."[12]

From the position of Abraham and Torok and their followers, the phantom is a malignant presence. It dissembles and remains hidden, while returning again and again to repeat the trauma of its cause. Such an understanding has been utilized with great effect by literary critics who crack open texts in order to reveal the trauma within. Esther Rashkin (Rashkin 1992), for example, describes Poe's (1839/2003) *The Fall of the House of Usher* as a "text in distress" whose phantom is drawn out with close textual analysis. More explicitly, Art Spiegelman's (2003) graphic novel *Maus* sees the writer haunted by a brother who died during the Holocaust. As a "replacement child," Spiegelman struggles to live up to the memory of a sibling kept alive by his parents "in a nostalgic, almost hallucinatory presence that denies his actual death."[13] The 2019 HBO "remix" of Alan Moore and Dave Gibbons's graphic novel *Watchmen* illustrated transgenerational trauma by having its protagonist, Angela, take the in-world drug "Nostalgia" (Banwell, 2000). In the show, this drug allows the user to re-live their own memories, as well as those of others. Transgenerational trauma is given explicit visual and narrative form as we see Angela *re*-experiencing her father's traumatic childhood memory of the 1921 Tulsa race massacre and the subsequent racial violence that he suffered throughout the 1930s.

The philosopher Jacques Derrida wrote a foreword for Abraham and Torok's text *The Wolf Man's Magic Word*. Entitled *Fors*, Derrida plays with the meaning of the term "crypt" and the notions of introjection and incorporation that the psychoanalysts employ. While there are clear affinities, there are also important differences between Abraham and Torok's phantoms and the specter of Derrida. Where the phantom is a figure that returns from the past, the Derridean specter interrupts our present and prompts radical change. "Phantoms lie about the past," as

Davis put it, "while specters gesture toward a still unformulated future." Ghosts of the Derridean variety, then, are not mysteries to be solved, but rifts opened up "by the voices of the past or the not yet formulated possibilities of the future."[14] This might remind us of Walter Benjamin's framing of the passed and past. He rejected an understanding of time that imagined the present's relationship to the past as a linear, chronological series of events "like the beads of a rosary." Rather, as we have mentioned, past and present could be perceived as bursting into one another as a constellation. Within this framework:

> the potential for encounters between the living and the dead remains ever open; that such confrontations erupt at moments of crisis and may imply profound consequences; that the living have only partial control over these meetings. (Lincoln and Lincoln, 2014: 193)

To further understand Derrida's formulation of the ghost as a spectral force that troubles our present, we need to return to 1992 and the publication of Francis Fukuyama's *The End of History and the Last Man*.[15] Fukuyama famously argued that the victory of capitalism over communism ushered in the "end of history," marking the "end point of mankind's ideological evolution and the universalization of Western liberal democracy as the final form of human government."[16] In *Specters of Marx*, his response to Fukuyama's provocative thesis, Derrida began by asking, what precisely had come to an end? And, if history had indeed ended in the way in which Fukuyama proposed, then surely it had guaranteed a beginning or *a return*. Wendy Brown similarly asked,

> Are ghosts and spirits what inevitably arise at the end or death of something—an era, desire, attachment, belief, figure, or narrative? When we have arrived at the putative end of history, should it surprise us if history reappears in the form of a haunt? Put differently, when we cease to figure history in terms of laws, drives, development, or logic, are ghosts what remain?[17]

It is here that Derrida first introduces us to hauntology, his linguistic pun on ontology. If ontology is concerned with being and presence, hauntology disrupts those categories, denoting how presence and absence; life and death; past, present, and future exist simultaneously.[18] As such, the ghost operates within the gap between states and disrupts the familiar. It destabilizes any "neat compartmentalization of the past as a secure and fixed entity, or the future as uncharted territory."[19]

In its opening pages, Derrida's *Specters of Marx* offers two examples of this disruptive power. The first, of course, the ghost of Hamlet's father, and the second, "a specter is haunting Europe—the specter of communism," the famous opening line of *The Communist Manifesto*. A clue as to the nature of the second specter is found in the first. As Peter Buse and Andrew Stott remark, "Old Hamlet arrives from the past in order to make a demand on his son's future actions."[20] Wendy Brown makes this point as well, when she suggests "we inherit not 'what really happened' to the dead, but what lives on from the happening."[21] These lines are instructive for a couple of reasons. First, they suggest that we are indebted to what has come before or that there is some-*thing* to be inherited. Second, what "lives on" alludes to an ongoing persistence of ideas or events from the past. To be haunted, then, suggests a lack of resolution, a promise of future action, an indebtedness—or, relatedly—a ghostly inheritance. This is the force that casts time out of joint. What follows is the unravelling of "what lives on from the happening" of Old Hamlet's murder (prior to the start of the play) and the paying out of ghostly inheritance. Things of the past, when they appear, tend to make demands on the future. Again, the present is not quite as "solid" as it may appear. With nods to Abraham and Torok, and Derrida, Fisher distilled hauntology down to two strands:

> The first refers to that which is (in actuality is) *no longer*, but which *remains* effective as a virtuality (the traumatic "compulsion to repeat," a fatal pattern). The second sense of hauntology refers to that which (in actuality) has *not yet* happened, but which is *already* effective in the virtual (an attractor, an anticipation shaping current behaviour).[22]

While the first strand gestures toward intergenerationally transmitted trauma, the second is born of Derrida's treatment of the "specter of communism." For Marx, communism carried the sense of the "not yet ... but which is already effective." For Derrida, it provided the counterpoint to Fukuyama's end of history. In this framing, as Fisher writes, Europe and the world for that matter had been "haunted by events that had not actually happened, futures that failed to materialise and remained spectral."[23] Surely this was not the end of history then, but rather a return of the *no longer* and *not yet*.

Criminology's Ghosts

It is with the no longer and not yet in mind that we now beckon criminology's ghosts. In the vein of late nineteenth-century spiritualists, let us imagine ourselves holding séance with the ghosts of the discipline's past. Let us gather around a small table in a darkened room, place our hands together, and form a circle. Together, let us conjure the spirits that have haunted criminology, the ghosts that disrupt its present and call from its future.

While again we do not profess a belief in "real" ghosts, the language of spiritualism usefully frames our discussion, evoking its influence on nascent criminology and notably the work of Francis Galton, Cesare Lombroso, and Jeremy Bentham. The arcane imaginary of the séance, its superstition and pseudoscience, underlines our interest in disrupting the present, making known our attempts to call on or call out passed/past events. So, let us begin by again calling forward a spirit whose presence and absence lingers still.

Having discussed him in relation to Jacques Derrida, let us first bring forth a specter of Marx. In *The Eighteenth Brumaire of Louis Bonaparte*, Karl Marx refers to an 1814 children's story, titled *Peter Schlemihl's Wundersome Geschichte* (Peter Schlemihl's Miraculous Story). In the story, Peter sells his shadow to the Devil. Invoking Hegel's *Preface to the Philosophy of Right*, Marx writes, "If any section of history has been painted grey as grey, it is this. Men and events appear as Schlemihls-in-reverse, as shadows which have become detached from their bodies."[24]

In *The Criminal Spectre in Law*, Schlemihls-in-reverse becomes Hutchings's point of departure for divining the specter in the nineteenth-century subject. As he convincingly argues, "Ghostly, illusory powers; a pervasive taint of criminality: the nineteenth-century subject is haunted by crime, by its signs and stories and the shapes of institutions designed for its regulation."[25] It is that separated shadow, the specter, that becomes "the very form of law and the shape it seeks to control . . . jointly produced through the discourses of law, literature, psychiatry, aesthetics and criminology."[26]

We are reminded that Marx's Schlemihls-in-reverse accordingly haunts Foucault's critique of Bentham's style of "rationalist penology":

> At first a pale phantom, used to adjust the penalty determined by the judge for the crime, this character [the criminal] becomes gradually more substantial, more solid and more real, until finally it is the crime which seems nothing, but a shadow hovering about the criminal, a shadow which must be drawn aside in order to reveal the only thing which is now of importance, the criminal.[27]

For all of criminology's "positivist fantasies surrounding the criminal," as Hutchings comments, we are still haunted by the phantom, "because the question of the criminal is now no longer one of a body, but of a soul."[28] Of course, here is the inverse. In contrast with the "substantial shadow ... [within] the society of spectacle" of Marx's reading, "forensic psychiatry's founding illusion" posits not the shadow, but the centrality of the criminal. It is worthwhile highlighting a few examples of the discourses that constitute "the criminal," as they illustrate both the "imaginative engagement" and specter within the evidentiary.

And so, as Marx fades, Sir Francis Galton takes his place at the table. Charles Darwin's cousin, Galton was something of a polymath, but is now mostly associated with the eugenics movement, having first introduced the term. Galton's own articulation of the spectral Schlemihls-in-reverse appears in his efforts to develop the technique of composite portraiture in order to photographically capture the "criminal type." Using the same multiple exposure techniques as Victorian-era spirit photographers, Galton managed to call forth a "purely optical apparition," as Alan Sekula charged, an "empirically non-existent criminal face." Himself haunted by faith in the insidious "sciences" of "heredity and racial betterment," Galton's efforts to capture the shadow and give pictorial form to the imaginary were nevertheless at once the "most bizarre and the most sophisticated" efforts to employ photographic evidence in service of criminology.[29]

While Galton dabbled in spiritualism and attended a number of séances, Cesare Lombroso—along with Sherlock Holmes author Sir

Arthur Conan Doyle—considered spiritualism to be a scientifically verifiable, even if not a verified, phenomenon.[30] It is perhaps no surprise that Lombroso's late work, *After Death—What?*, includes chapters concerning "Phantasm and Apparitions of the Dead" and "Haunted Houses."[31] Likening the "spiritistic hypothesis" to a lost or submerged continent, he speculated that islands of knowledge and "undiscovered lands" could one day rise from the waves, revealing them to have always been part of a broader whole.[32]

It is from these undiscovered lands that our final spirit emerges. Jeremy Bentham, the eighteenth- and nineteenth-century philosopher, recounted his own encounter with the spectral in his 1843 memoirs. As a child, Bentham was teased and tormented by the servants of his household, later professing "it was a permanent source of amusement to ply me with horrible phantoms in all imaginable shapes."[33] One particular anecdote described the young Bentham as the victim of a prank by a coachman and footman. Tricked into thinking that he owed money to a local publican, a Mr. Palethorp, the footman would pretend to be a hunchback figure and the servants hung a picture of a "hobgoblin" (that they had named after the ominous publican) over the fireplace. Hutchings weighs this formative terror heavily on Bentham's later rationalism, writing,

> the young Bentham preyed upon by superstition and folk theatricals, led to commit the very confusion his later rationalizing of ontology and law will be at such pains to avoid: the confusion of a real and a fictitious entity, produced by the effects of a simple confusion upon a susceptible imagination.[34]

For Hutchings—and for us—the true potency of these experiences was more than teaching Bentham a fear of the supernatural.[35] Rather, "it had taught him the means *to haunt the social imagination*."[36] We need only look to that exemplar of phantom architecture—Bentham's Panopticon—to see how effective this has been. Within its central observation tower, the Panopticon was to house an unseen surveillant force—one that unknowably hovered between presence and absence, haunting the imaginations of those who were subject to its gaze. It is also phantom-like since it was never constructed per Bentham's instruction. The phantom of its physical and conceptual form haunts criminological thought. It has acted—and continues to act—as a force within criminological discourse, inspiring the discipline, acting as an attractor shaping both thought and action.

Gathering together the specters that hound the legacies of Cesare Lombroso and Francis Galton, among other proto-criminologists, ensures that we must not, for example, ignore the field's troubled and troubling relationship with race.[37] An analysis of the effects of returning memories of social violence must also take into account the discipline's own traumas and ghosts. Where Gordon forces a reckoning with sociology's ghosts, so too must criminology acknowledge its malignant inheritance. The discipline has its own practices that have been occulted just as it has rendered invisible individuals and groups. For instance, those working in the field of biosocial criminology tout a wholly (pseudo-)scientific, perhaps neo-Lombrosian understanding of race, which all but openly disavows social, cultural, and political power.[38] At the beginning of the twenty-first century, criminology remains troubled by modern ideas of race—an unwelcome presence in our midst that cannot merely be exorcised through ritualistic disavowal. A ghost criminology that looks to the practices of exploitation, marginalization, and exclusion; the disappearance(s) of people(s), practices, and concepts must—at the same time—recognise the broader discipline's complicity in those very practices. As Biko Agozino (2004: 346) phrases it, a foundational text for criminology—Beccaria's (1764) *On Crimes and Punishments*—was written, in part, in response to the wrongful execution in 1761 of a Frenchman whose son had died by suicide, but who was tried for his murder. And so,

> [t]he execution of a single Frenchman counts for more in the conventional history of the invention of criminology than the genocidal Trans Atlantic in which tens of millions of Africans were destroyed or the genocide against Native Americans and aboriginal Australians by European *conquistados*.

It is hard not to be reminded here of Walter Benjamin's notion that "the documents of civilization are at the same time documents of barbarism."[39] By taking the name "Ghost Criminology," we aim to situate ourselves as troubling critics within the academic criminology itself.

This approach follows a preference for "subversive readings of the past and of domains of knowledge" and those corners of our own discipline dismissed as unscientific or irrational.⁴⁰

The Ghost and the Gothic

As the candles gutter out from our séance, let us briefly discuss the ways that ghost criminology complements and diverges from uses of the Gothic by criminologists. Initiated by Horace Walpole's 1764 novel *The Castle of Otranto*, the Gothic tradition in literature counts Mary Shelley's 1818 *Frankenstein, or, Modern Prometheus*, Bram Stoker's 1897 *Dracula*, and of course the work of Edgar Allen Poe as its foundation. The term itself originates with the Visigoths and Ostrogoths tribes of northern Europe who sacked Rome in 410. During the Enlightenment, when Greek and Roman culture were revived and held as the standard of civilization, the "gothic" barbarians who brought the latter's downfall characterized a variety of regressive and transgressive cultural forms, becoming synonymous with the irrational superstition of the Dark Ages.⁴¹ Descending from Walpole, by the mid-eighteenth century, as Leila Taylor writes,

> a new form of romantic literature emerged that renounced the rationality of neoclassicism and embraced the phantasmagoric. The dull predictability of scientific reason did not have the same thrill that comes with the submission to uncertainty.⁴²

For us, this submission to uncertainty is best captured by the title of an etching made by Francisco Goya between 1797 and 1799: *The Sleep of Reason Produces Monsters*. As Goya suggests, the Gothic allows irruption of the unknown into our taught rational world, alerting us to the "presence of agencies we cannot explain."⁴³

In their efforts to establish an approach to criminology that attends to these themes, Caroline Joan Picart and Cecil Greek write that "Gothic criminology teaches its readers about the actual horrors that produce and prevail in the social construction of modernity" (Picard and Greek 2007, 13). The pair draw inspiration from Stanford Lyman, who advanced a Gothic perspective on capitalism and imperialism and the adjoining horrors of modernity, framing the work of Robert Park for instance, as an exploration of "vampiric capitalism."[44] Another criminologist, Keir Sothcott, speaking of late modern Gothic more broadly, makes the case that it provides "a mode by which transgressive behaviour is 'storied,' rendered into discourse and hence both directly and indirectly experienced as real and not merely improbable possibilities."[45] Sothcott's sketch bears some resemblance to David Garland's description of criminology as a project "of the self" and "of the other."[46] The former understands the criminal as a rational calculator, "ordinary consumers—'just like us,'" while the latter concerns itself with threatening strangers, the radical alterity that is at times hidden beneath a veneer of normality. Today the Gothic opens a doorway "to numerous fantasies and fears of horror, possession, zombification, alien invasion and serial killers."[47]

Gothic and ghost criminology are bedfellows, then, both concerned as they are with transgressions that confuse and stir boundaries. Where Gothic criminology is an "expression of dis-ease with the grand narratives of the Enlightenment,"[48] ghost criminology is concerned with a dis-ease of temporality. Where Gothic criminology questions the progress of Enlightenment, ghost criminology questions the linearity of that path.

Born in the same epoch, as twisted conjoined twins, the Gothic and criminology share the same shadow. In addition to his own interests and allusions to the spectral and supernatural, Nicole Rafter and Per Ystehede credit Lombroso with having invented the "criminological counterpoint to literary and visual Gothicism: the *born criminal*."[49] Indeed, when contemplating the skull of "born criminal" Giuseppe Villela, Lombroso's language is reminiscent of Stoker himself:

> This was not merely an idea, but a revelation. At the sight of that skull, I seemed to see all of a sudden, lighted up as vast plain under a flaming sky, the problem of the nature of the criminal—an atavistic being who reproduces in his person the ferocious instincts of primitive humanity and the inferior animals. There were explained anatomically the enormous jaws, high cheekbones, prominent superciliary arches, solitary lines in the palms, extreme size of the orbits, handle-shaped ears found in criminals, savages and apes, insensibility to pain, extremely acute sight, tattooing,

excessive idleness, love of orgies, *the irresponsible craving for evil for its own sake, the desire not only to extinguish life in the victim, but to mutilate the corpse, tear its flesh and to drink its blood.*[50]

Twisted conjoined twins indeed, Gothic literature and nascent Criminology. Recall in Stoker's Gothic masterwork, that Mina Harker informs Van Helsing that Dracula is *"of criminal type. Nordau and Lombroso would so classify him."*[51] Moving from literature in criminology, criminology in literature and back again, Rafter and Ystehede also locate degeneration theory woven throughout Lombroso's conception of the atavistic criminal. Degeneration theory—the notion that humans not only evolve but devolve—spread Lombroso's focus from exterior to the interior. The crumbling castles of the Gothic were now joined by crumbling psyches, the "manias and perversions that menaced Gothic figures from inside their own degenerating minds."[52]

To be clear, many of the chapters that follow pay close attention to the Gothic's aesthetics. This, however, is ghost criminology's point of differentiation from Gothic criminology. Where the Gothic landscape looks to "an external panorama or an internal landscape," the spectral places its emphasis upon the temporal dimensions of haunting, seeking to apprehend phantoms that emerge from past trauma and that haunt the present and inspirit the future. We are also acutely conscious of the problematic past, traumatizing the present and troubling future of criminology as a discipline that is complicit, or inseparable from state violence. Our task here then is to set out a guide, a set of workings with which to conjure that spirit. As such, it is important to map out for the reader these precursors that indicate that criminology has already been subject to a "spectral turn" to match that of other disciplines. These are works that take an examination of the ghost(ed) as their point of departure. To reiterate, the project of ghost criminology is—following Gordon—to call up and call out, to make visible the ghosting practices of exploitation, marginalization, and exclusion. Our principal analytical framework is informed by hauntology. It is a desire, influenced by Benjamin, to invoke "the past as a political and moral resource for present claims" while also looking to the influence of the "not yet" upon those claims (Lincoln and Lincoln, 2014: 192). We must, in short, "fight on behalf of the dead" (195). Further, as Brown writes, the ghost once called up can likewise be exorcised—shaping "both possibilities for and constraints on the future."⁵³

Criminology's Spectral Turn

Much of what we have outlined above has appeared or is beginning to appear within the confines of criminology proper.⁵⁴ From visual and intertextual analysis to psychogeography and phenomenology, there is an ongoing effort to reckon the things behind the things. These are works that wrestle with temporal dis-ease and spatial traces, and attempt to grasp the invisible.

Importantly, many of the contributions here attend to the way that violence lingers, or "sits in places," and how State power, through mastery of the (in)visible, both emboldens and disowns its own violence.⁵⁵ Consider, for instance, the way that the US state works to render its violence illegible. After US soldiers killed Osama bin Laden in Abbottabad, Pakistan in May 2011, global news media reported the United States had disposed of his body at sea, supposedly in accordance with Islamic traditions. Defending the controversial decision, a US spokesperson explained that "finding a country willing to accept the remains of the world's most wanted terrorist would have been difficult"—the logic being that any country that accepted the body would immediately become a destination or target for bin Laden's admirers and those sympathetic to al Qaeda's cause. By burying bin Laden at sea, the US state controlled and effectively eradicated a potentially problematic space and future, rendering bin Laden ungrievable, as Judith Butler might describe.

There is, however, another dimension above and beyond grievability and recognition detailed by the US state's treatment of bin Laden's mortal remains. Here it is useful to revisit Slavoj Žižek's resurrection of Jacques Lacan's two deaths.⁵⁶ Clearly the military mission to kill bin Laden was meant to remove him from the world of the living—the Lacanian Real—and thus eradicate a biopolitical threat. Yet by refusing to release the photos of his dead body and by denying him a publicly viewed burial and memorial gravesite, the US government effectively produced a second, symbolic death, working toward the goal of erasing bin Laden from the cultural register and symbolic order. We can say, then, that the US state engaged in an exorcism of sorts, attempting to rid cultural and political space of a certain kind of ghost. This is particularly the case if we understand exorcism as extending from its original Greek, *ex* or "out of" and *horkizein* "cause to swear an oath"—then exorcism is first directed toward the symbolic striking or "swearing" out, a particular understanding from the cultural record.[57] Along with bin Laden's physical and symbolic remains are exorcised the complicated histories of US empire, questions of blowback, and the bloody circumstance of an endless worldwide war on terror. What lingers, where bin Laden is concerned, is a spectral bogeyman, a mediated villain to stand in by name or in effigy in films and television such as *Zero Dark Thirty* and *Homeland* and the sloganeering of US political operatives.

While it is important to recognize attempts to harness and deploy the spectral from above, we might also enlist its critical sight and emancipatory powers in struggles from below. As Pilar Blanco and Peeren insist, rather than being exorcised, sworn out, or expelled, "the ghost should remain, be lived with," becoming "a figure of clarification with a specifically ethical and political potential."[58] Here we might ask how the politics of exorcism can underline a praxis for progressive change.

The summer of 2017—when white supremacists gathered in Charlottesville, Virginia to protest the proposed removal of a statue of Confederate General Robert E. Lee from Emancipation Park—the ghostly power of the dead again haunted public spaces and debates. Following the murder of nine people at the Emanuel African Methodist Church, in Charleston, South Carolina, by avowed white supremacist Dylann Roof, activists demanded the "swearing out" of the Confederacy's ghostly remains—monuments, iconography, discourse—from public spaces across the United States, including the park in Charlottesville. For the would-be exorcists, not only were the flags and monuments the residue of a hateful past, they were active and necessary constituents of a divisive politics of the present, forcefully characterized by the presidency of Donald Trump. As one critic observed, "obelisks don't grow from the soil, and stone men and iron horses are never built without purpose."[59] If we understand the removal of Confederate monuments as the attempt to exorcise public space of the ghosts of racism, chattel slavery, and the Jim Crow era in which most of the statues in question were erected, then the torch-lit rally of August 11, 2017—in which nearly one hundred white supremacists of various stripes surrounded the statue of Lee, chanting

"*Jews will not replace us*"—must also be understood as a ritual or séance, seeking to anchor certain ghosts in the realm of the living.

Both the symbolic erasure of bin Laden's gravesite and the unfolding "statue wars" demonstrate how "sites stained by blood and violence and covered by the ashes of tragedy," in the words of geographer Kenneth E. Foote, "pressure people, almost involuntarily, to begin debate over meaning" and to "face squarely the meaning of an event."[60] Foote's observations hint at how material and affective forces swirl together within the social imaginary, making the atmosphere of a particular place known. In his essay on Truman Capote's *In Cold Blood*, Travis Linnemann likewise demonstrates how the book perpetually conjures the specters of true crime—murderous drifters and helpless victims—into the affective and material landscapes of the everyday. He writes,

> Despite the attempts made to exorcise them, the spaces we travel through are alive with ghosts of the dead. Attached to homes, towns and people, the ghosts conjured by cultural production continue to make themselves known. So, if we are to "learn to live" we must confront these ghosts of past violence and reckon the force of haunting as a social phenomenon.[61]

From bodily encounters with the ethereal, secrets hidden within archives, and the lingering effects of violence and trauma, the specter's whispy trail spans contemporary cultural criminology. A growing body of work exploring the sensorial and atmospheric has clear thematic and conceptual overlaps with ghost criminology.[62] For instance, there is the presence of the incorporeal tendrils of the ghost in Alison Young's description of an atmosphere "as a phenomenon that is encountered: most obvious in the initial moments of an encounter, receding or diffusing as it becomes familiar or expected."[63] The spectral qualities of atmospheres are experienced phenomenologically as one's body moves through space, encountering "the structurally affective, poetic, spatial and material qualities of the scene."[64] Similarly, Jeff Ferrell's phenomenologically attuned "ghost ethnography" provides a method to attend to infinite possibilities of the unseen and intersecting spectral world of violence, oppression, and history.[65] Extending Ferrell's work, Theo Kindynis describes the out-of-time-ness of graffiti "ghosts." These fragments of past practice evoke a sense of uncanniness, urging "us to imagine an-other era—evoking an altogether different city: perhaps a kind of simulacratic nostalgia [. . .] of the 1970s, 1980s and 1990s, experienced—imagined?—vicariously through popular (sub)cultural representations."[66] Scribblings of graffiti written by a long-dead hand suggest—at once—the no longer *and* not yet, furnishing us "with the theoretical language necessary to explicate how memory and trauma become inscribed literally, symbolically, affectively and atmospherically in space and place."[67] Michael Fiddler has applied a psychoanalytically informed framework of trauma and haunting to a site-specific artwork in London's East End. He argues that "Die Familie Schneider" represents a "crypt" within which the traumatic repetition of the violences suffered within the local area can be located.

Katherine Biber's writing on the "afterlives" of criminal evidence is, also, inherently hauntological. Archives are, after all, haunted by what they contain as well as what they exclude. In a notion that we will see repeatedly in this collection, "history never effaces what it buries; it always keeps within itself the secret of kept secrets."[68] Indeed, the archive is spectral in that it is asynchronous *and* asymmetrical. As such, it can "willfully aggravate or interrogate the traumatic criminal circumstances from which the evidence arose."[69] To provide an example, Biber draws our attention to the clothing that Azaria Chamberlain was wearing in the summer of 1980 when she was taken by a dingo from her parents' tent while on a trip to Uluru in Australia's Northern Territories. Convicted for their daughter's murder, Lindy and Michael Chamberlain were then—six years after Azaria died—exonerated once the missing garment reappeared and made known a wholly different version of events.

An eerie mix of the Gothic and ghost appears in Janine Mary Little's writing on visual evidence in the case of Jill Meagher, who was abducted, raped, and killed in the Brunswick area of Melbourne, in September 2012.[70] Footage gathered from a bridal shop security camera shows Meagher as she is approached by her murderer on her walk home after a night out with friends. Like Biber, Little uses the language of spectrality, describing Meagher as "a ghostly persona," a "haunting presence filmed walking the liminal space between the material and the symbolic, in the minutes before her actual death."[71] Trapped in this virtual purgatory, the once-living woman is subsumed by a ghostly "Jill Meagher CCTV" and conjured again and again as legal and entertainment commodity. The CCTV footage, then, is a text haunted by both Jill Meagher *and* the gothic representations inscribed upon it.

Within criminology, these ideas have found presence within the "Black Feminist Hauntology" of Viviane Saleh-Hanna, which seeks to capture the expanding and repetitive nature of structural violence. Evoking the notion of hauntology as a means of conversing with the dead through an as yet inaccessible language, Saleh-Hanna captures this sense by calling for a "language to speak about the central, not just symbolic or theorized violence that is racial colonialism." There is a need to hear, to speak with the "ghosted," the silenced. It is worthwhile reiterating that spectrality is "a mode of historical attentiveness that the living might have to what is not present but somehow appears as a figure or voice, a 'non-living present in the living present' that is no longer or not yet with us" (Freccero, 2006: 69–70). Hauntology, as a response to that nonliving present/ce, "is then a way of thinking and responding ethically within history" (70). A "ghost criminology" is informed by this call to an ethical response to haunting, to the presence-absence of the spectral. It can hold séances with the past and passed, positing an ethical relationship with the traumatized pasts and subjects of structural violence.

A Spirit Guide

This collection, then, builds upon the spectral turn that the discipline has already been taking. It looks back to such "turns" that have occurred across other disciplines while also positing future trajectories. It draws upon the theoretical groundwork provided by—among others—Benjamin and Derrida, and situates it within the context that Gordon sets out. This is a discipline reckoning with its own troubled history with race and how that becomes a Benjaminian constellation with current practice.

The text itself is divided into three parts. Each of these seeks to capture or interrogate one of the aspects of spectrality discussed in the preceding pages. Part One looks to "Apparitions and the (In)visible." The opening chapter of the collection by Eamonn Carrabine provides an overview of spectrality across sociology, history, representation, and beyond to give us an understanding of how "haunting is a core feature of social life." Taking in Freudian unheimlich, a Lacanian analysis of Edgar Allen Poe, as well as the techniques and practices of communicating with the spirit realm, we see how ghosts have always been "a grave matter." We see this grave situation in Jeff Ferrell's chapter as he unpacks the lived—yet ghostly—experiences of undocumented migrants, ex-cons, registered sex offenders, nocturnal graffiti writers, homeless urbanites, and freight-hopping gutter punks. As Jeff states, this is not unfamiliar territory for him, having spent the last twenty-five years "working those shadows, attempting to understand the ghosts that inhabit them." Here he elaborates upon his "ghost method" and these ghostly encounters. These are populations who are subject to an enforced invisibility and who—if they are to survive this civil death—enfold themselves within the shadows. How, then, to study the invisible, the absent? One answer might be to excavate that very absence, to investigate traces. This has a future-looking orientation as well. We can anticipate future absences and invisibilities as populations are driven off land and out of communities. Michelle Brown brings together the un-visibility of the hyper-visible black body with the racial reckoning within the discipline of criminology and criminal justice. Here we come to learn of black men and women, murdered by the state, through a "mediatized visual and sonic death scene." Unpacking the white supremacist origins of both the discipline and criminal justice, Michelle questions whether—in attending to knowledges and criminologies that have been ghosted and made invisible—we might need to bring down the discipline as it is. There is a necessity to respond to what Saleh-Hanna (2005, cited by Brown) refers to as "the ghosted and ghosting essences of White scholarship." Brown identifies the potential for ghost criminology as lying in "its attention to a movement beyond the carceral state"; there are other ways of imagining and conceptualizing "justice," for eradicating the totalizing gaze of "white optics, ontologies and supremacies." What is required is a raising of the dead "as a commitment to an abolitionist politics of the living." Michael Fiddler looks to the constellation of past and present by drawing upon Walter Benjamin's notion of the "dialectical image." By bringing cultural artifacts of the "past" and "present" into alignment, we can produce a third, dialectical image that brings the constellation into focus. In this chapter, the dialectical image is a jumping off point from which to reflect upon earlier criminological visual systems that drew upon spectrality and the invisible. Here, Fiddler produces a dialectical image that looks at that which is to come, as well as the no longer. Referring to nuclear visuality and notions of slow violence, the chapter explores future ecological harms that are "not yet" and invisible yet which haunt the present.

Part Two, entitled "The Necrotic and (In)corporeal," further explores the uncanny co-mingling of presence and absence. Here we encounter bodies that house past traumas, the spectral remains of redacted or destroyed documents, the "shadow presence" of the police, as well as the Weird, tentacular nature of state violence. Daniel Robins opens this part with his chapter concerning the management of the dead body of the offender. The individual may be "no longer" but they remain(s). So, what do we owe to the dead and what do we inherit from them? Focusing upon the disposal of the body of Ian Brady—a figure that has haunted the UK imaginary, having been imprisoned in 1966 for the murder of five children—Daniel unpacks how a lingering toxicity endured even in death. Arguments arose as to what to do with this particular "necrowaste." The by-products of destructive state power are explored further in Katherine Biber's chapter. The ghosts of discarded or destroyed documents and evidence invoke "new spectralities, new fears." Biber draws upon the work of a range of artists, including: Jason File's artwork produced while working at the International Criminal Tribunal; Daniel Knorr's use of documents destroyed by the Stasi; Cornelia Parker's use of items seized and destroyed by Her Majesty's Customs and Excise in Cardiff, Wales; as well as Edmund Clark—who we referenced earlier in this chapter—and his works that focus on "negative evidence" and what hides behind the marks of redaction. Biber's analysis draws out the importance of the traces of destruction. As we sift through the "ruins left in Law's wake," we find that a haunting inevitably follows the destructive act. For their chapter, Travis Linnemann and Justin Turner take the "Weird-ness" of police as their point of departure. Drawing upon the work of Mark Fisher, they unpack how the Weird "exists outside typical boundaries of thought and crime." Police, within this framing, act as an "agency of the virtual" as they exist across both presence and absence. Simply put, they are never there when you need them and there when you don't. This formlessness is exemplified by the phenomenon of "ghost cars"—black police vehicles with greyed out identifying features and stripped of light bars—that can appear everywhere and nowhere. Linnemann and Turner extend this to the spectrality of a Blue Lives Matter movement and a "vengeful wraith of blue life [dragged] into the realm of the living." The Weird similarly seeps its tendrils into Bill McClanahan's chapter exploring the tentacular and police. Again, drawing upon this collection's haunting presence, Mark Fisher, McClanahan looks to the monstrousness of capital and the violences that flow from it. Indeed, horror is the most salient analytical framework to examine the conditions of contemporary capitalist subjectivity. And as China Miéville, quoted in the chapter, states, the tentacle is the "default monstrous appendage." McClanahan takes this uncanny assemblage of Weird, eerie, hauntological, and monstrous to examine the grasping, suffocating nature of both climate weirding and police violence. These are violences that claim "a penetrating territoriality over the internal vascular and respiratory function of the body."

Part Three, titled "Dead and Haunted Spaces," takes us to sites marked by the traces of past (and future) trauma. We begin in the early hours of June 14, 2017, and a fire engulfing Grenfell Tower, a 24-story residential tower block located in West London, England. This led to the deaths of an estimated seventy-two inhabitants. The fire was a result of multiple, overlapping failures and remains the worst fire in Britain since 1900. In the immediate aftermath, local residents "had to continue to live and work in close proximity to what was in effect a mass grave (and a crime scene)." Alison Young documents her visits to the site in 2018 and 2019. She describes the difficulty of being in a location where trauma is so *present*: "[T]he hundreds of memorial markers and the looming tower made the fire a continually present aspect of the place, not in any way a memory that was located in the past." The question of how to memorialize the site without it becoming a macabre tourist spot is a difficult one. Young details how the memorializing practice carried out by the local community is at once a "haunting of memory" and "haunted by memory." The following chapter, by Elaine Campbell, takes as its location 10 Rillington Place, in London's Notting Hill. This is the house where John Christie carried out eight murders between 1943 and 1953. The street has subsequently been re-named, the building demolished. Arguing that Derrida's "analytic is ill-equipped to probe the critical and political dynamics of haunting," Campbell instead makes a "quantum turn" to offer an alternative hauntological reading of both this space and Christie himself. Drawing upon the work of Karen Barad, the chapter uses "material-discursive entanglements, indeterminacies, agential cuts [and] intra-actions" to offer a "diffractive and performative" hauntology of 10 Rillington Place. Campbell takes the reader through the generation of the "material-cultural bricolage" of 10 Rillington Place through a nonlinear quantum enfolding. Place is also central in Carolyn McKay's chapter exploring the haunting of motel rooms by transgressive acts. The motel room is typified by its anonymity and the transience of its occupants. The room is at once an intimate and private space. Yet, a motel stay is typically fleeting, and that space is shared with its countless past and future occupiers. Focusing upon a series of sexual assaults that took place between 2001 and 2008 in Sydney motel rooms, McKay draws upon legal documents as well as her own visual arts practice to capture these spectral crime scenes. These uncanny spaces reveal evidentiary traces of "absent guests and lingering ghosts." Here, the author uses the camera's lens "to produce images of what was seen, while hinting at what was unseen." The chapter is accompanied by this "ghost photography," these documents of a "particular spatial ecology": an aesthetics of both banality and decay. There are similar ghostly encounters in this collection's final chapter. Here, Theo Kindynis sets out his encounters with "ghosts": "decades-old residual traces of graffiti." Further developing the method that we encountered earlier in the collection in Jeff Ferrell's chapter, Kindynis details his ghost ethnography through London's interstitial spaces. In locating and examining these "lost ecologies," these "architectural glitches," he frames them as an alternative to Marc Augé's (1992) "non-places." Rather, these are sites where "lingering material and atmospheric traces of the past" can be found. In this instance, they tell a subcultural history extending to the early 1980s in London. As we saw in Ferrell's chapter, it is these spaces that haunt the margins of everyday life and allow for encounters with those "living as ghosts." Given this, Kindynis emphasizes the importance of ghost ethnography as a "sensibility," one that embraces an "exploratory, situated, immersive, reflective, impressionistic and imaginative approach." This points towards a method that can be used to tap into "atmospheric traces, resonances or afterimages."

Having looked at time that is "out of joint," spaces that are haunted, and materials either necrotic or disappeared, this collection closes with a "requiem." It is our opportunity to reflect, to consider the "no longer" and "not yet" that haunt this particular project. We look to the events that have come to pass in the years-long process of drawing this text together and how they speak with and come into constellation with criminology's past. We also convene with the ghosts of the future, those figures and forces that haunt us from an anticipated "not yet." In drawing these spectral tendrils together, across and within a past-present-future, we set out a "Ghost Criminology."

NOTES

1 Slavoj Žižek, owing to Lacan, suggests that the dead return because "they were not really buried." There is a matter to be redressed. Alternatively, they have returned because the living present owes them a debt. They are returning in order to collect on their debt. Of course, the perception of the ghost as being in some way threatening is based in a eurocentric understanding of the spectral and haunting. Traditions within the Global South see the "ghost" as a playing many other, often positive, roles for those it haunts.
2 Davis 2007, 3.
3 Jameson 1999, 39.
4 Ibid.
5 See, for instance, Rashkin 1992, and María Del Pilar Blanco and Esther Peeren, 2013. *The Spectralities Reader: Ghosts and Haunting in Contemporary Cultural Theory*. London: Bloomsbury.
6 Brown 2001, 149–150.
7 The name "Bedlam" appears in *King Lear*. The character of Edgar feigns mental illness and becomes Tom o'Bedlam. Also known as Poor Tom, he is emblematic of the "madness" into which the world has descended.
8 Also, *The Wolf Man's Magic Word: A Cryptonomy* (1976), a literary analysis of Freud's case study of the Wolf Man.
9 Derrida 1986, xvii.
10 Derrida 1986, cited in Castricano 2001, 23.
11 Schwab 2010, 23.
12 Kalb 2016, 26.
13 Schwab 2010, 37.
14 Davis 2005, 378–379.
15 Francis Fukuyama, 2006. *The End of History and the Last Man*. New York: Simon & Schuster.
16 Fukuyama 1989, 4.
17 Brown 2001, 144–145.
18 Julian Wolfreys articulates this well by describing haunting as a "disruptive structure." Wolfreys 2002, 6.

19 Buse and Stott 1999, 14.
20 Ibid.
21 Brown 2001, 150.
22 Fisher 2014, 19.
23 Ibid., 107.
24 Karl Marx, "The Eighteenth Brumaire of Louis Bonaparte." Translated by Terrell Carver. In Marx's *'Eighteenth Brumaire': (Post)modern Interpretations*, Edited by Mark Cowling and James Martin, 1852. Cited in Hutchings 2001.
25 Hutchings 2001, 1.
26 Ibid. 2.
27 Foucault 1978, cited in Hutchings 2001, 6.
28 Hutchings 2001, 6.
29 Sekula (1986, quotes on p. 18). Hutchings, in potent phrasing, describes the specter as 'rational modernity's uninvited guest', suggesting that the surprising ties between the rationalists and spiritualists could, aside from photography, find a possible point of connection in "the emergent discourse of psychology which pathologized both the spiritualist and the criminal." Hutchings 2001, 6.
30 While Lombroso was careful to state that "in psychical matters we are very far from having attained scientific certainty," he certainly did entertain their likelihood. Hutchings 2001, 17.
31 Cesare Lombroso, 1909. *After Death, What?: Spiritistic Phenomena and Their Interpretation*. London: T. Fisher Unwin.
32 He was perhaps gesturing toward the notion of the lost continent of Lemuria that was popular in the mid-nineteenth century and picked up by the Theosophists in the latter part of the century.
33 Cited in Hutchings 2001, 29.
34 Ibid., 30.
35 Ibid., 43.
36 Ibid. Emphasis added.
37 Saleh-Hanna 2015.
38 Nicolas Carrier and Kevin Walby, "Ptolemizing Lombroso: the pseudo-revolution of Biosocial Criminology." *Journal of Theoretical & Philosophical Criminology* 7, 1: 2015.
39 Walter Benjamin. 2007. *Illuminations*. Translated by Harry Zohn. New York: Schocken Books, p. 256.
40 Ascari 2007, x.
41 Leila Taylor. 2019. *Darkly: Black History and America's Gothic Soul*. London: Repeater.
42 Ibid., 34.
43 James R. Kincaid. 2000. "Designing Gourmet Children or, KIDS FOR DINNER!" In *Victorian Gothic*, pp. 1–11. London: Palgrave Macmillan, 5.
44 Stanford M. Lyman. 1990. "Rereading Robert E. Park: Toward a Gothic Perspective on Capitalism and Imperialism." In *Explorations: The Age of Enlightenment*,

special series, volume 4, edited by Maurice W. duQuesnay. Lafayette: University of Southwestern Louisiana Foundation, pp. 29–108. Also Lyman, 1991, "Robert E. Park's Congo papers: A gothic perspective on capitalism and imperialism." *International Journal of Politics, Culture, and Society* 4, 4: 501–516.

45 Sothcott 2016, 432.
46 Garland 1996, cited by South 2017, 556.
47 South 2017, 556.
48 Picart and Greek 2007, 15.
49 Rafter and Ystehede 2010.
50 Lombroso-Ferrero 1911, xxiv–xxv, cited in Rafter and Ysteheda 2010, 275–276. Emphasis added.
51 Stoker 2009[1897], 456.
52 Botting 1996, cited by Rafter and Ysteheda 2010.
53 Brown 2001, 151.
54 See for instance: Linnemann 2015; Biber 2017; Kindynis 2019; Fiddler 2019; Young 2019.
55 Simon Springer. 2011. "Violence sits in places? Cultural practice, neoliberal rationalism, and virulent imaginative geographies." *Political Geography* 30, 2: 90–98.
56 Slavoj Žižek. 2000. *The Fragile Absolute*. New York: Verso, p. 30.
57 A. Hill 2015. "The bin Laden Tapes." In *Covering Bin Laden: Global Media and the World's Most Wanted Man*, edited by S. Jeffords and F. Al-Sumait. Champaign: University of Illinois Press.
58 Pilar Blanco and Peeren 2013, 7.
59 V. R. Newkirk. 2017. "Growing up in the shadow of the Confederacy," *The Atlantic*, August 22. www.theatlantic.com
60 K. E. Foote. 2003. *Shadowed Ground: America's Landscapes of Violence and Tragedy*. Austin: University of Texas Press, 3.
61 Linnemann 2015, 530.
62 K. J. Hayward. 2012. "Five spaces of cultural criminology." *British Journal of Criminology* 52, 3: 441–462; Bill McClanahan and Nigel South. 2020. "'All Knowledge Begins with the Senses': Towards a Sensory Criminology." *British Journal of Criminology* 60, 1: 3–23.
63 Young 2019, 267.
64 Ibid., 766.
65 Jeff Ferrell. 2016. "Ghost Ethnography: On crimes against reality and their excavation." Public lecture, University of Hamburg. In McClanahan and Linnemann 2018.
66 Kindynis 2019, 37.
67 Ibid., 39.
68 Derrida 1995, 21.
69 Biber 2017.
70 Little 2015.
71 Ibid., 398.

REFERENCES

Abraham, Nicolas. 1975. "Notes on the phantom: A complement to Freud's metapsychology." In *The Shell and the Kernel. Vol. 1*, edited by Nicholas Rand, 171–176. London: University of Chicago Press.
Abraham, Nicolas and Torok, Maria. 1972. "Mourning or melancholia: Introjection versus incorporation." In *The Shell and the Kernel. Vol. 1*, edited by Nicholas Rand, 125–138. London: University of Chicago Press.
Agozino, Biko. 2004. "Imperialism, crime and criminology: Towards the decolonisation of criminology." *Crime, Law and Social Change* 41: 343–358.
Ascari, Maurizio. 2007. *A Counter-History of Crime Fiction: Supernatural, Gothic, Sensational*. Basingstoke: Palgrave Macmillan.
Banwell, Stacy. 2020. "'Children of the enemy': Exploring the unresolved trauma of genocidal rape." Paper presented at Eurocrim 2020, online, September 10–11, 2020.
Benjamin, Walter. 1999. *The Arcades Project*. Cambridge, MA: Belknap Press of Harvard University Press.
Biber, Katherine. 2017. "The cultural afterlife of criminal evidence." *Oxford Research Encyclopedia of Criminology*. https://oxfordre.com/
Biber, Katherine. 2018. "Evidence in the museum: curating a miscarriage of justice." *Theoretical Criminology* 22, 4: 505–522.
Biber, Katherine. 2019. *In Crime's Archive: The Cultural Afterlife of Evidence*. Abingdon: Routledge.
Brown, Wendy. 2001. *Politics Out of History*. Princeton, NJ: Princeton University Press.
Buse, Peter and Stott, Andrew. 1999. "Introduction: A future for haunting." In *Ghosts: Deconstruction, Psychoanalysis, History*, edited by Peter Buse and Andrew Stott, 1–20. Basingstoke: Macmillan Press.
Castricano, Jodey. 2001. *Cryptomimesis: The Gothic and Jacques Derrida's Ghost Writing*. London: McGill-Queen's University Press.
Davis, Colin. 2005. "État présent: Hauntology, spectres and phantoms." *French Studies* 59, 3: 373–379.
Davis, Colin. 2007. *Haunted Subjects: Deconstruction, Psychoanalysis and the Return of the Dead*. New York: Springer.
Del Pilar Blanco, María and Peeren, Esther. 2013a. "Introduction: Conceptualizing spectralities." In *The Spectralities Reader: Ghosts and Haunting in Contemporary Cultural Theory*, edited by María Del Pilar Blanco and Esther Peeren. London: Bloomsbury.
Del Pilar Blanco, María and Peeren, Esther. 2013b. "The Spectral Turn/Introduction." In *The Spectralities Reader: Ghosts and Haunting in Contemporary Cultural Theory*, edited by María Del Pilar Blanco and Esther Peeren. London: Bloomsbury.
Derrida, Jacques. 1986. "Foreword: Fors: The Anglish words of Nicolas Abraham and Maria Torok." Translated by Barbara Johnson. In *The Wolf Man's Magic Word: A Cryptonomy*. Minneapolis: University of Minnesota Press, pp. xi–xlviii.
———. 1994. *Specters of Marx*. London: Routledge.

———. 1995. *The Gift of Death*. Chicago: University of Chicago Press.
Derrida, J. and Stiegler, B. 2002. "Spectographies." In *The Spectralities Reader: Ghosts and Haunting in Contemporary Cultural Theory*, edited by María Del Pilar Blanco and Esther Peeren. London: Bloomsbury.
Ferrell, J. 2015. "Looking for unknown others." The Other, International Cultural Criminology Conference, 25–26 June, Amsterdam, VU University Amsterdam.
Fiddler, Michael. 2019. "Ghosts of other stories: A synthesis of hauntology, crime and space." *Crime, Media, Culture* 15, 3: 463–477.
Fisher, Mark. 2014. *Ghosts of My Life: Writings on Depression, Hauntology and Lost Futures*. Winchester: Zero Books.
Freccero, Carla. 2006. *Queer/Early/Modern*. Durham, NC: Duke University Press.
Fukuyama, Francis. 1989. "The end of history?" *National Interest* 16, Summer: 3–18.
Gan, Elaine, Tsing, Anna, Swanson, Heather, and Bubandt, Nils. 2017. "Introduction: Haunted landscapes of the Anthropocene." In *Arts of Living on a Damaged Planet: Ghosts of the Anthropocene*, edited by Anna Tsing, Heather Swanson, Elaine Gan, and Nils Bubandt, G1–G16. London: University of Minnesota Press.
Gordon, Avery. 2008. *Ghostly Matters: Haunting and the Sociological Imagination*. Minneapolis: University of Minneapolis Press.
Hutchings, Peter J. 2001. *The Criminal Specter in Law, Literature and Aesthetics: Incriminating Subjects*. London: Routledge.
Jameson, Fredric. 1999. "Marx's purloined letter." In *Ghostly Demarcations: A Symposium on Jacques Derrida's Specters of Marx*, edited by Michael Sprinker, 26–67. London: Verso.
Kalb, Margery. 2016. "Ghosts in the consulting room: Reluctant ancestors." In *Demons in the Consulting Room: Echoes of Genocide, Slavery and Extreme Trauma in Psychoanalytic Practice*, edited by Adrienne Harris, Margery Kalb, and Susan Klebanoff, 19–45. London: Routledge.
Kindynis, Theo. 2019. "Excavating ghosts: Urban exploration as graffiti archaeology." *Crime, Media, Culture* 15, 1: 25–45.
Lincoln, Martha and Lincoln, Bruce. 2014. "Toward a critical hauntology: Bare afterlife and the ghosts of Ba Chúc." *Comparative Studies in Society and History* 57, 1: 191–220.
Linnemann, Travis. 2015. "Capote's ghosts: Violence, media and the spectre of suspicion." *British Journal of Criminology* 55, 3: 514–533.
Linnemann, Travis and Medley, Corina. 2019. "Black sites, 'dark sides': War power, police power, and the violence of the (un)known." *Crime, Media, Culture* 15, 2: 341–358.
Lippit, Akira Mizuta. 2005. *Atomic Light (Shadow Optics)*. London: University of Minnesota Press.
Little, Janine Mary. 2015. "Jill Meagher CCTV." *Feminist Media Studies* 15, 3: 397–410.
Mbembe, Achille. 2003a. "Life, sovereignty, and terror in the fiction of Amos Tutuola." *Research in African Literature* 34, 4: 1–26.
Mbembe, Achille. 2003b. "Necropolitics." *Public Culture* 15, 1: 11–40.
McClanahan, Bill and Linnemann, Travis. 2018. "Darkness on the edge of town: Visual criminology and the 'Black Sites' of the rural." *Deviant Behavior* 39, 3: 1–13.

McVarish, Maria and Leavitt, Julie. 2016. "Mourning in the hollows of architecture and psychoanalysis." In *Ghosts in the Consulting Room: Echoes of Trauma in Psychoanalysis*, edited by Adrienne Harris, Margery Kalb, and Susan Klebanoff, 156–180. London: Routledge.

Picart, Caroline Joan (Kay) and Greek, Cecil. 2003. "The compulsion of real/reel serial killers and vampires: Toward a Gothic Criminology." *Journal of Criminal Justice and Popular Culture* 10, 1: 39–68.

Picart, Caroline Joan (Kay) and Greek, Cecil. 2007. "Introduction: Toward a Gothic Criminology." In *Monsters in and Among Us: Toward a Gothic Criminology*, edited by Caroline Joan (Kay) Picart and Cecil Greek, 11–43. Madison, NJ: Fairleigh Dickinson University Press.

Pile, Steve. 2005. *Real Cities: Modernity, Space and the Phantasmagorias of City Life*. London: Sage.

Poe, Edgar Allan. 2003 [1839]. *The Fall of the House of Usher and Other Writings: Poems, Tales, Essays, and Reviews*. London: Penguin.

Radway, Janice. 2008. Foreword to *Ghostly Matters*, by Avery F. Gordon, vii–xiii. Minneapolis: University of Minneapolis Press.

Rafter, Nicole and Ystehede, Per. 2010. "Here Be Dragons: Lombroso and the Gothic, and Social Control." In *Popular Culture, Crime and Social Control*, edited by Mathieu Deflem, 263–284. Bingley: Emerald Publishing.

Rashkin, Esther. 1992. *Family Secrets and the Psychoanalysis of Narrative*. Princeton, NJ: Princeton University Press.

Saleh-Hanna, Viviane. 2015. "Black Feminist Hauntology: Rememory the ghosts of abolition?" *Penal Field*. https://journals.openedition.org/

Schwab, Gabriele. 2010. *Haunting Legacies: Violent Histories and Transgenerational Trauma*. New York: Columbia University Press.

Sekula, Allan. 1986. "The Body and the Archive." *October* 39: 3–64.

Sothcott, Keir. 2016. "Late Modern Ambiguity and Gothic Narratives of Justice." *Critical Criminology* 24: 431–444.

South, Nigel. 2017. Monstrous nature: A meeting of gothic, green and cultural criminologies. In *Routledge International Handbook of Visual Criminology*, edited by Michelle Brown and Eamonn Carrabine, 553–556. London: Routledge.

Spiegelman, Art. 2003. *The Complete Maus*. London: Penguin Books.

Stoker, Bram. 2009 [1897]. *The New Annotated Dracula*, edited by Leslie S. Klinger. New York: W. W. Norton.

Torok, Maria. 1968. "The illness of mourning and the fantasy of the exquisite corpse." In *The Shell and the Kernel*. Vol. 1, edited by Nicholas Rand, 107–124. London: University of Chicago Press.

Wolfreys, Julian. 2002. *Victorian Hauntings: Spectrality, Gothic, the Uncanny and Literature*. Basingstoke: Palgrave.

Young, Alison. 2019. "Japanese atmospheres of criminal Justice." *British Journal of Criminology* 59, 4: 765–779.

PART I

Apparitions and the (In)visible

1

After the Fact

Spectral Evidence, Cultural Haunting, and Gothic Sensibility

EAMONN CARRABINE

Haunting is a core feature of social life, mediating the borders between the thinkable and unthinkable, presence and absence, while speaking to the enduring human obsession with the remains of the dead. As the editors of this collection emphasize, ghost criminology is ultimately concerned with the politics of (dis)appearance. I suspect one reason why criminologists have begun to deploy spectral metaphors in their writing is that they provide provocative ways of drawing attention to issues of invisibility, marginality, and exclusion, as well as the processes of forgetting, repressing, and denial that feature in our subject matter. Although some will be skeptical of this focus, I begin by providing the key resources that have proved to be extraordinarily fertile in this turn to spectral politics. Avery Gordon's (1997/2008) now classic text on *Ghostly Matters* was an emphatic call for a new sociology, which could reveal and learn from subjugated knowledge. As she put it, the "ghost is not simply a dead or a missing person, but a social figure, and investigating it can lead to that dense site where history and subjectivity make social life" (Gordon 1997/2008, 8). Inevitably, Sigmund Freud features prominently in the book and the "return of the repressed" is a defining concept in psychoanalysis, while his essay on "The Uncanny" (1919/1958) addresses a form of haunting bound up with a frightening otherness. These ideas develop arguments from Freud's earlier *Totem and Taboo* (1913), where he maintains that the historical origins of a belief in ghosts is intimately connected to the divided, emotional impulses characterizing all close relationships, especially those between the living and the dead.

The insistence that haunting is an essential element in modern life and that to "study social life one must confront the ghostly aspects of it" was an argument conveying "the relevance of ghostly matters to the sociological enterprise" (Gordon 1997/2008, 7). With this thought in mind, it is instructive to look at the origins of classical social science to see how haunting and the afterlife played a significant role in the development of social theory, before addressing the ways in which historians have addressed the work of the dead. As will become clear, the figure of the ghost has been a haunting presence for a very long time, possibly forever, so that it is important to distinguish between the ghost as an actuality, a metaphor, and a concept (see Blanco and Peeren 2013, 2–10 for a concise summary of these efforts). Indeed, Freud's famous essay on the estranging experience of the uncanny or *unheimlich* (literally translated as "unhomely") is ostensibly a study of a literary genre and an aesthetic sensation, where he goes to considerable lengths to avoid any suggestion of the supernatural in his elaboration of the concept. The publication of Jacques Derrida's *Specters of Marx* (1993) was the catalyst for the recent turn to all things spectral across the academy, and while there are times when ghosts and haunting have been used excessively, granted too much explanatory force, there still remain "productive new roads to explore and old ones to revisit" (Peeren 2014, 13). Consequently, the chapter turns to the field of representation to explore how the ideas of spectral evidence and cultural haunting can shed light on things barely seen.

Sociology

Max Weber's (1930/1992) *The Protestant Ethic and the Spirit of Capitalism* is one of the most celebrated works in the social sciences, demonstrating an affinity between competitive, modern bourgeois individualism and the way of life embraced on religious grounds by ascetic Protestant sects in the past. The "spirit" was first published as a two-part article in 1904–1905; it sought to explain the historically specific emergence of this strange conjunction of the entrepreneurial drive to accumulate wealth combined with a disavowal of all the worldly pleasures money can buy. Puritanism not only inspired the sequence of change creating industrial capitalism, but also led to the eradication of all the specifically religious elements in the ethic that helped produce the modern economic order. Weber (1930/1992, 105) locates this as part of the "great historic process in the development of religions, the elimination of magic from the world," and the "basis for a fundamental antagonism to sensuous culture of all kinds." For Weber, such disenchantment lay at the heart of modernity and the renunciation of mystery meant that everything becomes subjected to the impersonal "interpretive schema of science and rational government" (Jenkins 2000, 12). His famous characterization of the "iron cage" in which we are compelled to live and the increasingly bureaucratic order from which the "spontaneous enjoyment of life" is brutally purged are distilled in his conclusion that the "Puritan wanted to work in a calling; we are forced to do so" (Weber 1930/1992, 181). Clearly, the "ghost of dead religious beliefs" is fundamental to Weber's sociological understanding of the "spirit of capitalism" (182).

Although they were contemporaries, Weber and Durkheim took little notice of each other's work (as far as we know), and while they are often presented as the polar opposites of classical social theory, there is an important sense in which "ghosts inhabit the work of Emile Durkheim just as much as Weber" (Hudson 2017, xi). To many sociologists Durkheim is the founding figure in sociology, defining the discipline as the study of social facts and highlighting the significance in all societies of binary categories, such as sacred and profane, pure and polluted, the individual and the collective. He was initially convinced that religion was coming to play a diminishing role in social life, but he later radically reversed his thinking, coming to see how modern, social institutions are deeply religious in character. Many secular beliefs are, he claimed, "indistinguishable from religious beliefs proper," and taking modern France as an example, he maintained that, like traditional societies, it had an unshakeable, shared faith:

> The mother country, the French Revolution, Joan of Arc, etc., are for us sacred things which we do not permit to be touched. Public opinion does not willingly permit one to contest the moral superiority of democracy, the reality of progress, and the idea of equality. (Durkheim 1899, 20, in Cladis 2001, xiii–xiv)

By the time of his last book, *The Elementary Forms of Religious Life* (1912/2001), which set itself the task of discovering the enduring source of human social identity, he was drawn to what he considered the most basic form of documented religion—totemism among the indigenous "tribes" of Australia and North America—to demonstrate how the most fundamental "collective representations" reflect past and present social organization. These collective representations are the concepts, images, symbols, myths, and stories through which a society comes to understand itself as such in a shared moral universe. Certain "sacred" collective representations (such as the totem) serve the purpose of giving members of a society a common identity and promoting allegiance to it.

Much of Durkheim's work on religion, especially on animism, the materialization of the dead, spirits, and the supernatural, can be seen as foundational to a sociology of ghosts. As he put it:

> the idea of the supernatural, as we understand it, is of a recent vintage: it presupposes its opposite, which it negates and which is not at all primitive. In order to call certain phenomena supernatural, one must already have the sense that there is a *natural order of things*, in other words, that the phenomena of the universe are connected to one another according to certain necessary relationships called laws. (Durkheim 1912/2001, 28, emphasis in original)

Such an approach encourages us to take the long view. Reverence for the "remains" of the dead goes back to the Palaeolithic and funeral customs are often less about grief and mourning than about providing a means to offer rituals and sacraments that will ease the dead gently out of this world, holding them securely in their graves because of an ingrained "terror of the ghosts of the unquiet dead" (Taylor 2001, 171). It was a student of Durkheim's, Robert Hertz (1907/1960) who made the crucial point that the dead have two lives: one in nature, another in culture. The relationship between these two conceptions—the dead as decaying organic matter, and as entities who have a social existence after death—is a variable one. How the "dead make social worlds" is the theme of Thomas Lacquer's (2015, 1) recent historical exploration of this cultural work and is indebted to this Durkheimian tradition, to which we will return in the next section.

The conjuring of ghosts and unseen forces features perhaps surprisingly in the writing of Karl Marx, not least since he advocated a materialist conception of history that took issue with the importance of ideas and consciousness in understanding the real conditions of worldly existence. He was a profound and subtle thinker, which has led to fundamentally conflicting interpretations of his project in and beyond Marxism. The doctrine of historical materialism was advanced most powerfully in *The Communist Manifesto*, which Marx co-authored with Friedrich Engels. Written in haste for a small club of exiled German workers in London, it was published in 1848 on the eve of the great revolutionary upheavals of that year, stretching from the Balkans to the Baltic, providing a highly distinctive and striking modernist vision of historical change and class struggle. The *Manifesto*'s impact was initially muted, but by the end of the nineteenth century it underpinned the creation of a global labor movement, eventually fueling the political conflicts and many wars that tore the world apart in the twentieth century. It remains an astonishing text, combining powerful slogans and crystal-clear exposition, switching from apocalyptic to ironic registers with blistering effect. The tone is established from the opening sentence, which memorably declares that a "spectre is haunting Europe—the spectre of Communism" (Marx and Engels 1848/2002, 218). Communism was indeed an apparition, a scattered network of barely more than a thousand people, yet one that spoke to a "mounting fear of mobs, of beggars, of violence during a decade of endemic economic crisis" (Stedman Jones 2002, 39). It has been said that Marx's distinctive ideas were a blending of German philosophy, English economics, and French politics and the *Manifesto* integrated these currents into an entirely novel history of class conflict.

The insight that the revolutionary process is a struggle between the past and future, new against the old, is developed in the exceptional commentaries Marx wrote in the early 1850s on the doomed French revolutions of 1848—*Class Struggles in France* and *The Eighteenth Brumaire of Louis Napoleon*. The latter essay contains some of his most important insights on historical repetition and the ghosts of the past, opening with this striking passage:

> Hegel remarks somewhere that all facts and personages of great importance in world history occur, as it were, twice. He forgot to add: the first time as tragedy, the second as farce . . . Men make their own history, but they do not make it just as they please; they do not make it under circumstances chosen by themselves, but under circumstances directly

encountered, given and transmitted from the past. The tradition of all the dead generations weighs like a nightmare on the brain of the living. (Marx and Engels 1968, 96)

In examining the weight of the past on the present, the piece addresses the relationship between Napoleon Bonaparte's imperial situation in the 1790s and the French Revolution of 1789 with that of his witless nephew's in the 1840s and 1850s. It is through reclaiming and "reassembling the fragments of the Napoleonic imageries and histories the new generation of 'petty' Napoleons would turn the tragic tales of the past into a farce" (Hudson 2017, 52).

More recently, Jacques Derrida (1994, 133) has detected in the "bereaved parody" of the *Eighteenth Brumaire* a "genealogy of ghosts" and thereby presents a radically new reading of Marx, in which he is understood to be obsessed with haunting, phantoms, and repetition. Derrida's (1994) *Specters* is not only a crucial addition to his philosophical project of deconstruction but is also a book preoccupied with the "death" of communism and how Marxism will continue to haunt capitalist societies long after its supposed demise. Indeed, his concept of "hauntology" is a pun on the more traditional concept of ontology, the philosophical study of what can be said to exist. Derrida's "rehabilitation of ghosts" as a reputable academic topic has been immensely influential, and hauntology offers a way of supplanting ontology by "replacing the priority of being and presence with the figure of the ghost as that which is neither present nor absent, neither dead nor alive" (Davis 2005, 373). There are parallels here with Judith Butler's (2004) examination of the politics of mourning, whereby some forms of grief become nationally recognized and other losses of life are ungrievable. Yet, sometime before Derrida's intervention Foucault criticized historians for what he called their "impoverished idea of the real" (cited in Burke 2008, 64), as they left no space for what is imagined. French historians have since responded to this accusation in significant ways and have developed a formidable history of the imaginary.

History

Until quite recently historians have been wary of dealing with ghosts and straying into the realm of the dead, treating the subject with "undue contempt" (Le Goff 1981/1984, 269). The wealth of the imaginary and the complexities surrounding it are explored in Jacques Le Goff's (1981/1984) *The Birth of Purgatory*, which traces the origins of the idea of a netherworld in the Middle Ages by connecting it to changing conceptions of space and time. He argued that the idea of a "third place" in the afterlife, along with heaven and hell, came into full bloom as a formal Catholic belief and doctrine rather late—in the twelfth century. It was gradually established as an intermediate space in which some lost souls were subjected to a trial that could be reduced through the prayers of perishable mortals. A distinct geography of the other world took shape in a detailed theology of retribution, sacrifice, penalties, pardons, and spiritual exchange between the living and the dead. A key function of the third place in the hereafter was the imprisonment of ghosts and confining the uncertain wanderings of suffering souls. Le Goff was also one of the first scholars to examine the history of dreams, so that studies of visions, ghosts, and the supernatural have become central to the new concern in cultural history with the active role of the imagination. Such studies have explored "apparitions of the ordinary dead, of everyday ghosts," and those occasions when the departed might return from the grave (Schmitt 1994/1999, 2). The very special dead—saints and martyrs—deserved extraordinary attention and it was beneficial for the ordinary dead to be buried near them (Brown 1981).

These groundbreaking French medievalists did not conclude that the dead were ubiquitous in the concerns of the living or that the living expected to see apparitions of their dead ancestors wherever they looked. Ghosts did not just appear to anyone, at any time, or anywhere. There is a fundamental anthropological point here:

> In medieval society, as in many other traditional societies, the specific type of existence attributed to the deceased depended on how the "rite of passage" of death occurred: the dead generally returned when the funeral and mourning rituals could not be performed in the prescribed way, for example, if the body of a drowning victim disappeared and could not be buried according to custom or if a murder victim, a suicide, a woman who died during childbirth, or a stillborn baby presented the members of the community with the danger of a blemish on their group. Such deaths were deemed unlucky. (Schmitt 1994/1999, 2–3)

This anthropological view is given historical specificity through the detailed examination of the mentalities and sensibilities of the period. It offers a history of the imaginary that is attuned to the very real social implications of the fantastic belief structures found in the tales and images, words and dreams of that distant time.

Others have built on historical anthropology to vastly broaden the ways that earlier systems of belief are now approached. Recent research has sought to further establish the nature of the relationship between living communities and the dead in Europe. Éva Pócs (1999) has explored the techniques and practices used to communicate professionally with the other world in the villages and towns of early modern Hungary. These shamanistic mediators were the magical specialists of everyday community life and they participated in gatherings of the dead when they were possessed by witches. Her account rests almost entirely on the records of witch trials, so the documents yield insights into several areas of witchcraft and reveal the communication techniques used by seers, sorcerers, and healers, but also the more general, everyday practices of ordinary people. She regards witchcraft both as an ideology that explains human misfortune and as an institution regulating communal conflict, yet the seers and sorcerers worked both inside and outside the system of supernatural witchcraft. Here she highlights the close relationship between the living and the dead, where the "dead, primarily individual or 'personal dead' *revenants*, that is, the returning dead, arrived and stayed according to various time frameworks" (Pócs 1999, 30, emphasis in original). The communal, or impersonal dead, also returned periodically during certain "death" periods and they were largely ambivalent about the fate of the living, though diverse forms of exchange relationships evolved between them.

The fact that ghosts were a grave matter in early modern Europe is an issue pursued by David Lederer (2002, 26) in a study of Bavaria, which demonstrates "just how dangerously politicized the supernatural had become in the sixteenth and seventeenth centuries." In his analysis, cases of shamanism, apparitions, and spirit possession graphically rendered explicit the confrontation between theological doctrine and popular belief. These beliefs and practices were not the product of backward medieval superstitions, rather they were given a new lease on life in the Renaissance, at the very dawn of the "rational" age. Nicole

Jacques-Lefèvre (2002) insists that the belief in witches, and in her analysis werewolves, has most often and mistakenly been tied to the Middle Ages and to peasants, but rather these beliefs were in fact elaborated with most conviction by Renaissance intellectuals. As a figure of disorder, a symbol of trouble that must be warded off, the werewolf that appears in these texts is rich in political allegory, tied to the most serious aspects of monstrous degeneration in the social body. Scholars since have "linked the idea of diabolic witchcraft developing in the fifteenth century to notions of a distinctly elite, learned form of demonic magic known as necromancy" (Bailey 2013, 11). Popular belief in witches, ghosts, and other supernatural forces persisted in Europe across all social groups well into the eighteenth century, troubling the authorities on a variety of levels. Both Catholic and Protestant reformers sought to impose a more rigid and disciplined social and political order during the sixteenth and seventeenth centuries, in their efforts to extinguish superstition and establish firm boundaries between licit and illicit action.

Appearances of ghosts that took conventional and unconventional forms increased in seventeenth-century Bavaria, where attempts to banish congress with the supernatural cost many their lives. In eighteenth-century Paris, "a series of trials of 'false witches' occurred during the beginning of the so-called Enlightenment, after the time when trials and penalties for witchcraft are perceived as being on the decline and some courts even declared that witches did not exist" (Edwards 2002, xix). The overall lesson from this scholarship is that there is considerable nuance in the levels of serious belief in supernatural or occult forces, and it cautions against interpreting the eradication of superstition or defeat of magic by the inexorable advance of modern rationality. Undoubtedly the most enduring overall narrative is the classic Weberian diagnosis of the progression from an "enchanted" premodern world rife with magic and superstitious thought to our "disenchanted" modern world governed by scientific rationality. The suggestion that these are two irreconcilable belief systems often misses the point. These transformations need not be linear or progressive, and while it may well be more useful to think of oscillating cycles of disenchantment and re-enchantment (Bailey 2013, 12), they can also unleash dangerous forces. Lederer (2002, 27) argues that such a volatile mix was to the fore in his analysis of ghosts and the treatment of mediums in sixteenth- and seventeenth-century Bavaria, where traditional and modernizing "attitudes mixed all too easily, concocting a heady cocktail of fear and repression and facilitated the worst stupor of witchcraft hysteria in European history."

Above all else what this historical work informed by anthropological and sociological themes points to is the importance of "deep time" in our understanding of how our species lives with the dead. This point is central to Thomas Laqueur's epic account of how the dead make civilization on a grand and intimate level. As he explains:

> the living need the dead far more than the dead need the living. It matters because the dead make social worlds. It matters because we cannot bear to live at the borders of our mortality. (Laqueur 2015, 1)

Death is not just a moment in time, it is also a ritualized process. It occupies a place in human existence that anthropologists describe as liminal, as it involves a threshold crossing, and such transitions (birth, puberty, marriage, and death) are fraught with peril. In fact, the "most dangerous person at a funeral," wrote Richard Cobb (1970, 8), an English historian of the French Revolution, "is the body in the coffin." Death is similar to birth in the sense that it is an event that cannot belong to us, but only to those who surround us, binding us into social relationships that take time to repair and rebuild. If society is pictured as a house, then people need permission to enter new rooms, and the threshold, or *limen*, was the key to their transition from one room (or state) to another (Van Gennep 1908/1960, 26). For a period of time, then, the person occupies an in-between status and liminality rituals are aimed at reducing this potential threat through securing the successful passage from one category to the next. Although the response to death and dying has changed dramatically over the last millennium, an abiding concern for some reassurance against the finality of death has endured, as Phillipe Ariès (1981) influentially argued and who inspired much of the literature and art that form our cultural heritage. He declared that death had become increasingly marginalized in contemporary culture, relegated to the secret, private space of the home or the anonymity of the hospital, yet representations of death remain absolutely central to it. In the next section we turn to how cultural representations have addressed death and how the ghostly offer "haunting reminders of lingering trouble" (Gordon 1997/2008, xix).

Representation

The rich variety of ways in which artists and writers have interpreted and invented ghosts further indicates a deep-seated fascination with the texture of death and the difficulty of confronting our own demise. As Hélène Cixous (1976, 542) has put it, there "is nothing more notorious and uncanny to our thought than mortality," so that the encounter between the human and ghost constitutes in literary form the "fiction" of our relationship to death. Ghosts have always been with us, but they are not what they used to be. It is, as we have just seen, possible to trace a history of ghosts, as well as to regard history itself as ghostly. Up until the eighteenth century the explicitly fictional appearance of ghosts was somewhat sporadic. Men and women may have "stopped seeing ghosts" not simply because ghosts came to seem "intellectually impossible" (though this was indeed the case) but because ghosts gradually lost their "social relevance" (Thomas 1971, 606) as the dead no longer exerted such a powerful influence over the living. This will now be a familiar sociological theme of modern disenchantment, but what is also clear is that the subsequent popularity of ghost stories throughout the nineteenth and for much of the twentieth centuries drew inspiration from the Gothic literary imagination flourishing in England from the 1760s onward.

The greatest work in the English language has a ghost at its heart. Shakespeare's *Hamlet* (1600–1601) draws on a revenge tragedy tradition and his plays feature more ghostly apparitions than those of any of his contemporaries. The range of his dramatic use of ghosts is perhaps an indication of an understanding that ghosts, real or imagined, make for good theatre (Greenblatt 2001). The vengeful ghost in *Hamlet* is an enigmatic manifestation, cryptic and elusive, eliciting the widest range of possible responses. Much has since been written on whether Shakespeare intended his ghosts to be subjective or objective: figments of overwrought imaginations or unremittingly corporeal realities grounded in theology and folklore. All these explanations are voiced in the play to such an extent that the ghost has an indefinable quality, a strangeness that cannot be contained by conventional thought. *Hamlet*, the prince of a rotten state, dwells on the problems of memory and forgetting, how the suppressed past rises like a terrifying revenant, manifest in bad dreams and hallucinations. Such themes are to the fore in psychonanalytic accounts of the play, which have given radically new interpretations of it. Rather than thinking *Hamlet* is about revenge—a familiar, safe subject—the real driving force of the drama is Oedipal desire. Jacques Lacan (1977) developed this controversial reading (in a seminar in 1959) and transforms the play into an allegory of phallocentric culture. According to Lacan all desire springs from a lack, which it strives continually to fill, so that in a more recent twist on this theme the play has been cast as a story about love and its many contradictions (Critchley and Webster 2013).

In contrast, Nicolas Abraham's (1988) ideas on transgenerational trauma and unspeakable secrets were developed through a close analysis of *Hamlet*. He notes how all the main characters appear to be driven by "some stranger within them" and the overwhelming sense of secrets taken to the grave, going so far as to say that "entire libraries of enigmas in literature would yield up their key, were we but to reconsider the 'supernatural element' responsible for them: to be precise, the manifestation of a Specter" (Abraham 1988, 3). Literature becomes then a place of ghosts, of what's unfinished, unhealed, and harboring secrets about which characters, and perhaps authors themselves, are largely unaware. These ideas are developed by Esther Rashkin (1992) in a nuanced analysis of literary texts and their phantom structures. She is careful not to overstretch the approach, insisting that not every text is possessed by phantoms, but rather she attends the specificity of each individual text and the distress that might be found in them. It is also worth recalling that in Derrida's (1994) account of Marx one of the most repeated phrases in it is from *Hamlet*, "the time is out of joint," and this theme of broken time is crucial to understanding his concept of hauntology.

Gothic fiction itself emerged somewhat suddenly as a popular form in the late eighteenth century, catering to a decadent appetite for all things gloomy, taboo, and medieval. The origins of the genre are usually traced to Horace Walpole's (1764) *Castle of Otranto*, the second edition of which was subtitled "A Gothick Story," that did much to establish narrative conventions that are revisited and reworked in subsequent writing. The emphasis on the returning past, transgression and decay, imprisonment and escape, the anticipation of the supernatural, usurpation and dynastic intrigue, are all present in *Otranto*. By the 1790s these trappings were famously elaborated in Anne Radcliffe's (1794) *The Mysteries of Udolpho*, which adopts the castle setting as well as the theme of inheritance and dreamlike wanderings through an oppressive Catholic landscape. If the fictional tempo in Radcliffe is somewhat meandering, then Matthew Lewis's (1796) *The Monk* opted for visceral sensation. Set in a Spanish monastery the plot revels in excess and corruption, where ambition, murder, and incest combine to provoke disgust and fascination in equal measure. Of course, the coherence (or otherwise) of gothic conventions (Sedgwick 1980) has received considerable attention, and the gothic novels of the 1790s can be read as a British reckoning with the carnage of the French Revolution and the stirring of guilty memories of the regicide of Charles I, which led to the founding of the Commonwealth some 150 years earlier. The eighteenth-century sense of British identity that came to replace the earlier ones of the home nations was forged in sectarian conflict so that to be "British was to be Protestant, with both identities drawing strengths from residual anti-Catholicism" (Miles 2007, 15) and the brutal repression of Irish, Scottish, and Welsh uprisings in the process of nation-building.

The early gothic novel mobilizes these tensions and hovers ambiguously between them, contrasting progressive and regressive forces, both implicitly (British and Protestant) and explicitly (European and Catholic). It feeds off a "Catholic" aesthetic, while taking its morality from its Protestantism. In the high camp theater of *The Monk*, for example, anyone who appears "to be more tolerant and possesses powers of rationality is really a closet Anglican" (McEvoy 1995, xxix). Gothic fiction also found an enthusiastic audience in North America, arriving in a completely different context from the old world and without a feudal past. Lacking all those ruins that furnished the European landscape—the castles, crypts, monasteries, and graveyards that evoked the fallen majesty and mystery of the Middle Ages—the new country seemed an unlikely place to establish a gothic literary tradition. Yet a distinctive set of factors were to prove decisive. These include the frontier mentality, the Puritan legacy, chattel slavery, political utopianism, and a migrant culture steeped in European folklore and importing literature from the thriving British and German publishing trade. It is this context that led Leslie Fielder to famously declare, in 1966, that American fiction was still "bewilderingly and embarrassingly, a gothic fiction, non-realistic and negative, sadist and melodramatic—a literature of darkness and the grotesque in a land of light and affirmation" (cited in Smith 2012, 165). Among the most celebrated exponents of such fiction was Edgar Allan Poe, and his legacy is considerable, introducing new dimensions to gothic tales.

Poe tended to use recognizably European settings for his stories in symbolic ways, most memorably in "The Fall of the House of Usher" (1839), which exudes claustrophobic menace. The crumbling mansion is home to incest and perversion, which becomes increasingly apparent as the story unfolds—the narrator explains that since time immemorial the inhabitants have practiced a bizarre form of intermarriage ensuring that the "entire family lay in the direct line of descent" (Poe 1839/2009, 172). When Roderick Usher prematurely buries his twin sister Madeline in the family vault, the decaying edifice finally collapses as she rises from the grave, emaciated and bloody. It is never clear whether the reader has been trapped by the ancient house or its disturbing inhabitants and their brooding secrets. The sense of past as burden is apparent in Poe's treatment of race and the haunting legacy of slaveholding, where the fears of insurrection and miscegenation are never far from the surface. In his story "Hop-Frog" (1849), for example, a much tormented dwarf court jester enacts his vengeance by persuading the king and his courtiers to dress up as chained orang-utans. Hop-Frog then strings them up to the ceiling and their tarred costumes are set on fire in what has been read as a grim parody of a Southern lynching. The dread of slave retribution also pervades his tale of "The Black Cat" (1843), where the narrator explains how he blinds and hangs his pet black cat in a drunken rage. Later he takes a shine to another cat that in time haunts him with memories of his cruelty. Determined to kill this cat too, he accidently strikes his wife dead with an axe. Seemingly unconcerned, he bricks her up behind a wall, where he inadvertently also seals in the cat who proceeds to feed on her decaying face. When the authorities eventually investigate his wife's disappearance, a wailing noise from the cat reveals the location of the corpse and the guilt of the narrator. Here the story invokes the impulsive character of the lynch mob and the dehumanization of slaves as pets. It also highlights the violent subordination of women that features so prominently in Poe's fiction.

In tales like "Ligeia" (1838), and especially "Berenice" (1835), the protagonists objectify and dismember the women they love. But they will not stay buried. By refusing to stay dead it can be argued that most of Poe's women refuse idealization. Moreover, his fiction reveals "the inalienable bond between the illusions of reverent attachment and the matter of human bondage" (Dayan 1994, 245). In making perverse desire the driving force of his central characters, the supernatural elements are usually explained by the narrator's insanity, so that he directs the sensationalism of European gothic toward inner conflicts while always suggesting "there is a dark impulse beyond understanding which wreaks havoc" (Smith 2012, 169). It was through his fiction that Poe transformed familiar and well-worn gothic plots, setting, and characters into the very stuff of modern literature, most evidently in the focus on the tortured mind suffering agonizing pressures, where the key idea is that "of the internally haunted self" (Brogan 1995, 152). The same can also be said of his invention of the detective story, which inspired a remarkable dispute over the meaning of language and truth that we will look at in more detail in the next section.

Purloining Poe

Poe's invention of the detective story introduced the crucial innovation of organizing the narrative around the intellectual genius of a detective hero, Auguste Dupin, who reconstructs the scene of a crime through the deductive powers of rationality to apprehend the guilty culprit through the clues left behind. In "The Murders in the Rue Morgue" (1841), the first of the Dupin stories, the detective reveals that the mysterious atrocities were committed by an escaped orang-utan. This explanation is totally rational in the context of the narrative, but at the same time bizarre and strange. It is this combination of reason and unreason that animates the detective story, which oscillates between the idea that modern life can be mastered and controlled, yet it is also dangerous, since that social order is delicate and vulnerable to the destructive forces of nature or premodern threats. In this rendering of urban modernity as gothic, he foreshadows how the city would become Other as the nineteenth century progressed, becoming an incomprehensible landscape frequently depicted as "labyrinth, jungle, swamp and ruin and described as blackened, rotten, shadowed and diseased" where, most significantly, this "city of dreadful night is populated by others who threaten to overrun or undermine the fabric of the imperial metropolis" (Warwick 2007, 34). Poe's final Dupin story, "The Purloined Letter" (1844), has also proven to be a remarkable site for textual interpretation and is worth looking at in more detail.

Set in modern Paris, the story begins with Dupin's invitation to solve a mystery concerning the theft of a letter from the royal apartments, the contents of which have the potential to jeopardize the Queen. The cunning "Minister D," sensing political advantage, steals the compromising letter before her very eyes, exchanging it for a worthless letter he happens to be holding, which she is unable to prevent owing to the King's presence. She is now open to blackmail, and every attempt by the police to discreetly retrieve the letter fails. Dupin is called upon to recover it. He makes an excuse to visit the Minister's house and manages to spot the letter openly displayed, hanging from the mantelpiece. Later Dupin returns and substitutes a copy for the original letter, rescuing the now doubly purloined letter for the Queen. Detective fiction is usually understood to have a highly conservative ideological form because its generic codes demand the restoration of the status quo. Yet what is particularly striking about Poe's story is not so much the way it inaugurates and reinforces these conventions, but how it opens up a range of paradoxes, sites of disruption and displacement.

The whole story is organized around the movement of letters from one place to another, and it was this sense of shifting signifiers that initially attracted Lacan to the text. Indeed, he chose his 1956 "Seminar on the 'The Purloined Letter'" to introduce the collection of his *Ecrits* (1966), whose essays otherwise appear chronologically. It is generally recognized that his interpretation of the story set off a radically new conception of psychoanalysis (by highlighting the dynamic of miss-seeing in the tale, thus offering an instance of how the gaze operates) and pioneered a type of reading unprecedented in literary criticism. Lacan (1956/1988, 28) situates his interpretation of the story in the Freudian problem of "repetition automatism" (the tendency of patients to mechanically repeat traumatic experiences) and a broader question over the nature of memory itself. His analysis hinges on two issues: the anomalous position of the letter, which while serving as the principal subject of the story, we come to know so little about it; and the pattern of intersubjective relationships and repetitions that arise in the tale.

It is striking that the story leaves us entirely ignorant of the nature of the letter, the sender, and the contents. Whether it is a love "letter or conspiratorial letter, letter of betrayal or letter of mission, letter of summons or letter of distress, we are assured of but one thing: the Queen must not bring it to the knowledge of her lord and master" (Lacan 1956/1988, 41-42). Thus, Lacan takes up the theme of lack in the symbolic order and makes it a key element in his analysis. Moreover, it is not the message in the letter, but the position of the letter within the group that determines what each character will do next. This is because "the letter does not function as a unit of meaning (a *signified*) but as that which produces certain effects (a *signifier*)" so that it becomes for Lacan "a kind of *allegory of the signifier*" (Johnson 1988, 217, emphasis in original). The letter generates a rotating pattern of human relationships and subject positions that different characters occupy in successive scenes. In Lacan's reading there are three subject positions in play: one subject sees nothing, so is "blind" to the situation (the King and the police); a second "sees" that the first subject sees nothing and thereby "deludes itself as to the secrecy of which it hides" (the Queen, then the Minster), that is, unaware of being "seen"; the third sees that "the first two glances leave what should be hidden exposed to whoever would seize it" (the Minister, and finally Dupin) and exploits the situation (Lacan 1956/1988, 32). The far-reaching claims about language and truth set out in Lacan's seminar have been influential and the source of fierce contention.

Among the most serious challenges to Lacan's interpretation of the story is Derrida's (1975/1988) critical deconstruction of it. Derrida's objections focus on the tacit assumptions and overall method deployed by Lacan. Although Lacan recognizes that the story is multiply narrated, he ignores the complexity of narration itself and the curious place of the narrator in the tale. For "once it is glimpsed, the analytic deciphering excludes this place, neutralizes it" and this neutralizing exclusion "transforms the entire Seminar into an analysis fascinated by content" (Derrida 1975/1988, 179). By overlooking the frame of narrative, Lacan misconstrues the entire structure of the text, missing the literary dimensions that make it Literature. Derrida also takes issue with Lacan's (and Freud's) use of fiction as a means of presenting the truth of psychoanalysis. To lay the ground for his critique Derrida (1975/1988, 175) begins by discussing how the structure of truth in Freud is based on familiar metaphors—exhibiting, denuding, undressing, unveiling—coordinated with "naked truth, but also with truth as nakedness," the concept is unwittingly problematized by Freud's own analysis of exhibitionism and neurotic dreams of nakedness. Derrida finds the very same problem at work in Lacan's use of the Poe story, so his critique is directed not only at what Lacan dispenses with in the text, but also at what he reads into the letter. By insisting that the letter's meaning is lacking, Lacan transforms this "lack into *the* meaning of the letter" (Johnson 1977/1988, 217, emphasis in original). As Derrida (1975/1988, 184) puts it, the "letter—place of the signifier—is found in the place where Dupin and the psychoanalyst expect to find it: on the immense body of a woman, between the 'legs' of the fireplace" and such "is its proper place, the terminus of its circular itinerary."

Deconstruction presupposes both a limit and a border, the careful teasing out of competing forces of signification within the text. "The deconstructive reading," as Barbara Johnson explains, "does not point out the flaws or weaknesses or stupidities of an author, but the *necessity* with which what he *does* see is symmetrically related to what he does *not* see" (1972, xv, emphasis in original). Nor does it imply complete interpretive license, but rather deconstruction demands considerable intellectual rigor and a forensic attention to detail. Later he would introduce the idea of "haunting into the very construction of a concept" (Derrida 1994, 161), bringing into focus the question of time that had been suppressed in his thought. The "conceptual function of spectrality" is to "call attention to and assign responsibility for social practices of marginalization and erasure, and for cultural and historical blind spots" (Peeren 2014, 13). The figure of the ghost is the trace of an absence that disturbs the taken-for-granted, suggesting that lurking beneath the surface lies another, untold story. Hauntology is not only an alternative theory (of ontology), but an ethical demand for responsibility and accountability. The usefulness of ghost stories to speak to repressed knowledge is at the core of Avery Gordon's (1997/2008) attempt to establish a new sociological imagination through attending to that which normally escapes attention. Her reckoning with that which modern history has rendered ghostly provides the starting point for the next section.

Cultural Haunting

It is significant that Gordon's (1997/2008) analysis of social haunting as a penetrating dissection of racialized capitalism and violent injustice is based on her remarkable reading of the authors Luisa Valenzuela and Toni Morrison. Both writers use imaginative fiction to see that which is usually hidden or thought to be dead and buried. Luisa Valenzuela is a prominent Argentine author and exponent of magical realism, through which she explores the violence and repression experienced in Latin America under authoritarian regimes. The military government exercised state power through disappearance and torture in clandestine detention centers where prisoners were kept in a constant state of imminent death. Few survived, and during the dictatorship (1976–83) it is estimated that thirty thousand mostly young students and workers were abducted and killed. In her book *He Who Searches*, Valenzuela (1977/79) explores this complex system of repression and the haunted society it produces. It is one "full of ghosts" and the narration of the story invokes a "kind of inverse colonization" that retraces the "steps of the initial conquest of Latin America" (Gordon 1997/2008, 98) and tells a story of the quest to find the disappeared.

The literary turn to the supernatural to recover a traumatic past is at the forefront in Toni Morrison's (1987) *Beloved*, which examines the destructive legacy of slavery and the unfinished project of Reconstruction. It is set in the mid-1800s and chronicles the life of a young mother, Sethe, who murders her child to save her from a life of slavery. Sethe and those who live with her are haunted by the memory of the dead child, who returns as a full-bodied and increasingly demanding ghost. It is a remarkable premise and shatters the void between the living and the dead:

> The ghost enters, all fleshy and real, with wants, and a fierce hunger, and she speaks, barely, of course, and in pictures and in a coded language.

> This ghost, Beloved, forces a reckoning: she makes those who have contact with her, who love and need her, confront an event in their past that loiters in the present. But Beloved, the ghost, is haunted too, and therein lies the challenge Morrison poses. (Gordon 1997/2008, 139)

The haunted narrative sees slavery living in the aftermath of its abolition, and how wrestling with a real ghost, who is also haunted, reflects the crisis of a larger social group. This attention to the repressive powers of silencing and premature closures is to focus on the "phantom subjects of history," and Gordon's (1997/2008, 196) book concludes with some reflections on what we learn of the world when we look at it through Valenzuela's and Morrison's fiction. Here she maintains they recover "the evidence of things not seen" (Baldwin 1985, viii), which was also the title of James Baldwin's searing indictment of the unsolved murders of twenty-eight black children in Atlanta in the early 1980s and the corrosive legacy of racism throughout the case. It is a powerful metaphor and compels us to see things and people who are barely visible, the trace of an absence, where haunting is both an individual and collective experience.

These stories of cultural haunting differ from earlier ghost stories for they "signal an attempt to recover and make social use of a poorly documented, partially erased cultural history" (Brogan 1995, 150). As such, they attest to the notion of "spectral evidence," which Ulrich Baer (2005) has deployed in a nuanced analysis of the photography of trauma. Taking as his point of departure the photograph's apparent immunity to time and the ghostly afterlife of every photograph's subject, Baer places the viewer in the role of bearing belated witness rather than innocent onlooker. The book concentrates on photographs that compel us to consider traumatic experiences that defy absorption into larger contexts or patterns of experience. An important chapter uncovers the complex and difficult relationships between memory and place by closely examining two contemporary photographs by the German photographer Dirk Reinartz and American Mikael Levin. The two photographs are quite different from most other postwar images of Holocaust sites, in that they address the almost empty landscapes in which Nazi concentration camps once stood. Although they were both unaware of each other's work and were pursuing quite separate objectives in their respective projects, the photographers deploy the same artistic conventions of Romantic landscape art to give absent memory a place.

Whereas most other images of former camps or killing fields are "oversaturated referents of ruin," decaying buildings once designed to kill are now maintained and "museumized," these two pictures instead "force us to see that there is *nothing* to see there; and they show us that there is something in a catastrophe as vast as the Holocaust that remains inassimilable to historicist or contextual readings" (Baer 2005, 66–67). Because they do not contain any physical evidence of the crimes committed at the scenes, the photographs seem to ask to be read on purely aesthetic terms, but such a formalist analysis is also exposed as equally insufficient to the task of achieving some comprehensive meaning or secure perspective. Instead, the photographs demand a new way of looking, which Baer offers as a mode of belated witnessing rather than a form of visual analysis. In doing so, he argues that these landscape photographs oblige us to rethink our relationships with memory, mourning, and remembrance:

> By creating an experience of place for areas designed to destroy the very possibility of experience, Reinartz and Levin show that Holocaust commemoration is not site-specific and that acts of secondary witnessing depend less on geographic or cultural positions than on becoming aware of our position as observers of experiences no one ever wanted to know about . . . Some former killing fields—sites such as Ohrdruf where thousands were murdered—were never marked on the itineraries of disaster tourism, are rarely mentioned in historical studies, and are likely to sink into complete oblivion once the survivors have passed away. When such sites are framed in terms of landscape art, we recognize the disappearance of the event as part of the intention of their Nazi creators, a recognition that might motivate us to halt the disappearance. (Baer 2005, 83)

The photographs are stark reminders of the contemporary subject's responsibility to the traumatic events, and they also manage to avoid lapsing into the triviality or kitsch that characterizes so many representations of the Holocaust (see Cole 2000; Eaglestone 2017; and Friedländer 1984, for work critiquing the modern tendency to mythologize Nazism).

It is significant that the ruin provides a point of departure for his reflections on the nature of spectral evidence and the experience of trauma. The attention to the spatial dimension of haunting was earlier raised by Anthony Vidler (1992) in a nuanced account of the nineteenth century's fascination with ruins, and especially with the ancient remains of Pompeii. The analogies between archaeology and psychoanalysis are many, not least in the uncovering of that which had long been buried, but also mirroring the uncanny itself: "To some people the idea of being buried alive is the most uncanny thing of all" (Freud, cited in Vidler 1992, 45). Hidden until the middle of the eighteenth century, the experience of visiting Pompeii was one of visceral contrasts—an ancient town, that had once been homely, domestic, teeming with life, was suddenly buried alive, entombed in volcanic ash and suspended in history. The unearthing of Pompeii inspired an erotics of the ruin, confirming not only the existence of a "dark side" of classicism, but also how living beauty was transformed into dead trace. The fascination with this buried city was bound up with an aesthetic that exalted ancient remains in the eighteenth century, revered testimony of a grand but lost heritage, and came to invest in the leftover fragment more than a fragmentary significance. The fragment as a "negative petrified sign of *nature morte* easily took its place among other similar fragments in literature and art that at once signaled an irretrievable past and evoked a desire for future plenitude: the Belvedere Torso, the Elgin Marbles, the Venus de Milo" (Vidler 1992, 50). This understanding of the place of the fragment in European culture has clear affinities with Walter Benjamin's attention to the transformations an object undergoes during its life and afterlife.

In *The Origin of German Tragic Drama*, Benjamin attempts to retrieve the baroque "mourning-play" (*Trauerspeil*) from the dismissive judgments of critics who viewed it as a crude and debased form of classical drama. In addressing this misinterpretation of minor German dramatists of the sixteenth and seventeenth centuries, Benjamin sets out an influential, if often esoteric, argument on the nature of allegory. Crucially, he sees an affinity between the literature and art of modernity and the earlier mourning play, with its ambiguity, multiplicity of meanings, and fragmentary representations. A key feature of allegory, as a form of signification, is its unpredictability, for any "person, any object, any relationship can mean absolutely anything else" and with "this possibility a destructive, but just verdict is passed on the profane world" (Benjamin 1928/1977, 175). As he goes on to write:

> Allegories are, in the realms of thoughts, what ruins are in the realm of things. This explains the baroque cult of the ruin ... That which lies here in ruins, the highly significant fragment, the remnant, is, in fact, the finest material in baroque creation. For it is common practice in the literature of the baroque to pile up fragments ceaselessly, without any strict idea of a goal, and, in the unremitting expectation of a miracle, to take the repetition of stereotypes for a process of intensification. (Benjamin 1928/1977, 178)

This idea of the "highly significant fragment" is fundamental to contemporary art. In his approach to allegory, Benjamin anticipates one of the most modern artistic means of dealing with a preceding tradition, which is through the practice of quotation, snatching a precedent out of context, effacing or obscuring an earlier meaning (Owens 1980). In the final section I will explore the relationships between allegory, landscape, and spectral evidence through the medium of photography.

Landscape, Memory, and the Unseen

Elsewhere I have described how some contemporary photographers have deliberately taken an anti-reportage position, slowing down the image-making process and arriving well after the decisive moment, yet still retaining a commitment to the social relevance of photography (Carrabine 2018). Here the use of allegory has become the means by which the enigmatic, partial, and unresolved traces of violence on the landscape ooze with repressed histories. This strategy can be found in Simon Norfolk's various studies of war and his efforts to challenge the oversimplification of much photojournalism. In his photographs of Afghanistan (Norfolk 2002) there is a deliberate attempt to understand the country's long struggle with colonialism; his images deploy a distinctive pictorial style, that invokes late eighteenth-century Western landscape painting and its portrayal of the decline of once-great civilizations. In this way, "the skeletons of bombed-out buildings are shown as romantic ruins on deserted plains" to make the critical point that it is because of the destruction inflicted through more than thirty years of war that "this ancient and culturally rich region has been returned to a premodern state" (Cotton 2015, 172).

This attention to the traces of time and how to visualize the complexity of human suffering is developed in his subsequent work. The failure of Western governments to intervene in the conflict in the former Yugoslavia is a theme explored in Norfolk's (2005) *Bleed*, which revisits the frozen landscapes of eastern Bosnia where thousands were massacred and the almost abstract images become powerful allegories for the secrets buried beneath the ice. For Norfolk it was crucial to know the exact location of the gravesites, to give the work a forensic credibility and visual power. As he explains, "it's even more important when the picture uses metaphors; if the detective work was poor then the whole project would unravel quickly. The only way you can come at it in such a symbolic way is if you are one hundred percent sure that here are the locations—otherwise it's a weak, feeble approach" (cited in Lowe 2014, 225). The tension between the arresting beauty of the images and the fact that something terrible is contained in them enables him to make a strong moral argument about the nature of guilt.

Since the 1980s, Willie Doherty has explored the representation of the conflict in his native Northern Ireland through his video and photographic work. He uses a combination of forms to explore the relationships between landscape, memory, and the legacy of trauma. His *Buried* (2009), for example, is an eight-minute film that takes the viewer on a disturbing journey through a dark forest. The creeping tension has been described as follows:

> Insects crawl in the rotting wood on the forest floor and the trees themselves leak an unidentified substance. The sound in the forest becomes increasingly threatening: thunder or a suppressed roar? Doherty plays with our expectations as he reveals traces of activity amongst the trees: a sleeping bag, a smouldering campfire, pieces of wire and plastic. Is this innocent litter or forensic evidence? As with most of Doherty's work the setting is Northern Ireland, however the pine forest suggests other European post-conflict landscapes. In Doherty's forest the event is left unspoken. (Bevan 2015, 42)

Throughout his work Doherty has addressed how the past haunts the present. It consistently addresses the politics of vision, and *Unseen* is the title of a retrospective that demonstrates the extent to which he has engaged with the tension between what is and what is not present in the visual field over the course of his career.

The powerful resonance of the "unseen" is exemplified in *Ghost Story* (2007), a fifteen-minute video installation that centers on an unsettling journey around Derry. The camera tracks slowly along a deserted country path, flanked by gloomy woods and ominous barbed wire fencing, intercut with close-ups of male and female eyes that look past the camera, witnesses to something that we never see. The video's narration, by the actor Stephen Rea, is a flat, impassive account of murder and violence, half-remembered yet potentially imaginary. He has described the underlying premise in the following way:

> The sense of the landscape being the scene of the crime, so to speak, and that it is also the source of a lot of the stories that perhaps need to be told. So that links back into using the landscape as a useful means to begin constructing *Ghost Story*. Then thinking about the spectral presence suggested by the camera's movement led me to doing some research into traditional Irish ghost stories. This has been a form that allowed people to both express grief and deal with ideas around superstition. In the ghost story there is often a kind of unhappy presence that needs to find a voice that conventional religion doesn't offer an outlet for—a sense of unresolved guilt or remorse or whatever ... In this post-Ceasefire context there are so many people still obviously traumatized by what happened to them. It also comes out of the sense that the relationship between the landscape and memory is very active and alive. (Doherty in Barber 2009, 196)

Doherty's approach dispenses with any narrative resolution, but the enigmatic tone does convey how complex political situations can be addressed outside the conventions of documentary photojournalism.

Another photographer who has consistently pushed the boundaries of documentary is Paul Graham. His early work includes *House Portraits* (1979–80), which concentrated on modern English suburban housing, followed by a deadpan study of the service stations and cafes that line the Great North Road, transposing the American road trip with the less glamorous terrain of Britain's A1 revealing its unexpectedly cinematic potential (Graham 1983/2020). His work took an explicitly political direction in the searing *Beyond Caring* (1986/2021), which examined the grim Social Security offices facing the unemployed under Thatcherism. His clandestine photographs of these spaces captured the boredom and despair of these spaces, epitomizing a nation in decline. But it was Graham's next project, *Troubled Land* (1987), that signaled a shift toward the elliptical, investing seemingly banal images with complex metaphorical and symbolic meanings. The series examined the condition of Northern Ireland at a time when the "Troubles" were at their most turbulent, but the images concentrate on what he terms the visual footnotes of the conflict. He has described how one photograph introduced this distinctive approach:

> A key image that helped locate the work was *Roundabout, Andersonstown, Belfast*, 1984, where you simply see a scruffy suburban fringe of Belfast, with everything looking quite banal, at least to anyone familiar with the topology of the British Isles, but then you realise all the lights have been smashed off the stands, the posters are placed very high so that nobody can interfere with them, the roundabout's all ripped up, there's nationalist graffiti on the railings. And then finally you see the soldiers, one running over the roundabout, others walking away on the extreme right, secreted into this everyday scene. So the inventory isn't actually correct, what appears to be ordinary is quite extraordinary, and perhaps more interestingly the opposite is also true, the adoption of the extraordinary into the ordinary fabric of the place. (cited in Wilson 1996, 13)

Graham's subsequent work has developed this open-ended strategy, and his pictures have become more oblique and enigmatic, examining how the echoes of local and regional history were playing themselves out across late twentieth-century Europe.

After moving to America, Graham published *American Night* (2003), which is his most ambitious attempt to use photographic aesthetics to explore social and political divides. It takes as its subject the invisibility of the poor. Many of the photographs are bleached-out and over-exposed images of roadsides and pedestrian walkways where the blinding whiteness of everyday life renders the solitary figures hard to distinguish in most cases. The technique is a striking comment on "the political invisibility and social blindness to poverty and racism in America" (Cotton 2015, 181) and is heightened by the juxtaposition with the vibrant, color-saturated pictures of wealthy suburban homes that punctuate the series. This work was the first of a trilogy that has become a major achievement in the history of photography, merging multiple layers of visual commentary on American society to create poetically charged vignettes of everyday life. Yet for all their artistry, these pictures are also about what cannot be seen. Indeed, Graham has recognized that this is a defining theme: "I realised that concealment . . . has run through . . . my work, from the landscape of Northern Ireland, and the unemployed tucked away in backstreet offices, to the burdens of history swept under the carpet in Europe or Japan. Concealment of our turmoil from others, from ourselves even" (Graham in Wilson 1996: Wearing interview). As such the work exemplifies the notion of spectral evidence that I see as crucial to the idea of cultural haunting, how it reminds us that each and every place has its own history that both haunts it and haunts us.

Conclusion

In this chapter I have sought to outline some of the ways in which the spectral has informed work in the social sciences and the humanities. I began with classical social theory, before addressing how historians and anthropologists have explored the relationships between the living and the dead, which provided a point of entry into the world of representation. The focus here was on gothic fiction, which has given voice and shape to hidden histories, proving itself to be open to all manner of political uses and interpretations—as the quarrel between Lacan and Derrida demonstrates. Other writers have used imaginative fiction to see that which is usually suppressed or thought to be dead and buried. While haunting can be a metaphor for less tangible anxieties and traumas associated with disappearance, Gordon (1997/2008) suggests it can also draw our attention to that which lingers, as in the impact of racial slavery and the failures of Reconstruction. These stories of cultural haunting differ from earlier ghost stories for they speak to the barely acknowledged erasure of history and memory, and in doing so they offer an instance of "spectral evidence" (Baer 2005). The final section concentrates on how photographers have sought to grapple with the traces of time and the power of the unseen in their images.

What unites these different projects is that they share a form of gothic sensibility, manifest in a preoccupation with lingering trouble and exploring dread through politicizing history. One of the appeals of ghost criminology lies in its "appreciation of the discontinuous, distorted and multiple temporalities" of social and cultural life (Kindynis 2019, 39–40). Another important theme here is the effort to make visible that which is inherently diffuse, abandoned, forgotten, overlooked, or deliberately concealed or hidden. Here, attention can be drawn to CIA "ghost" prisons and the hidden geography of state secrets (Paglen 2009) through to the money laundered in the "dead" spaces of speculative real estate and the lifeless dwellings of the super-rich (Atkinson 2019). We live in a world where power and wealth move ever farther out of sight and beyond the reach of law. In his account of the "offshore" practices of the rich and super-rich, John Urry (2014) reveals how their geographical mobility is at the heart of mammoth inequalities, which are sustained by a vast system of secrecy that damages not only democracy but the very future of the planet. There is not one secret world, but many: the offshoring of manufacturing work, of waste, especially e-waste, of energy, of torture, of leisure and pleasure, of CO_2 emissions, and of taxation.

The spectral turn in criminology can also enliven the discipline itself. On one level the study of deviance is in rude health, but on another it leads a "zombie existence" (Reiner 2016, 64). In the United States, some have noted that the sociology of deviance has lost much of its intellectual energy where the rapid growth of criminal justice as a vocational discipline had taken its toll, concluding that the concept was still alive, but not all that lively (Best 2004). Others speak of its "resurrection" (Dellwing, Kotarbe, and Pino 2014), suggesting just how helpful it is to "retain traditions while evolving with the times" (Anderson 2014, xviii). Among the many lessons one can learn from Marx is that those who are not prepared to learn from history are condemned to repeat the mistakes of the past, which still serves as an invaluable reminder as to how sociological criminology might proceed.

REFERENCES

Abraham, Nicolas. 1988. "The Phantom of Hamlet or the Sixth Act: Preceded by the Intermission of 'Truth.'" *Diacritics* 18, 4 (Winter): 2–19.
Anderson, Tammy. 2014. "Preface." In *Understanding Deviance*, edited by Tammy Anderson, xvii–xx. London: Routledge.
Ariès, Phillipe. 1981. *The Hour of Our Death*. New York: Knopf.
Atkinson, Rowland. 2019. "Necrotecture: Lifeless Dwellings and London's Super-Rich." *International Journal of Urban and Regional Research* 43, 1: 2–13.
Baer, Ulrich. 2005. *Spectral Evidence: The Photography of Trauma*. Cambridge, MA: MIT Press. Bailey, Michael D. 2013. *Fearful Spirits, Reasoned Follies: The Boundaries of Superstition in Late Medieval Europe*. Ithaca, NY: Cornell University Press.
Baldwin, James. 1985. *The Evidence of Things Not Seen*. New York: Holt, Rinehart and Winston.
Barber, Fiona. 2009. "Ghost Stories: Interview with Willie Doherty." *Visual Culture in Britain* 10, 2: 189–199.
Benjamin, Walter. 1928/2009. *The Origin of German Tragic Drama*. London: Verso Books.
Best, Joel. 2004. "Deviance may be alive, but is it intellectually lively? A reply to Goode." *Deviant Behavior* 25: 483–492.
Bevan, Sara. 2015. *Art from Contemporary Conflict*. London: IWM.
Blanco, Maria. and Peeren, Esther. 2013. "Introduction: Conceptualizing Spectralities." In *The Spectralities Reader: Ghosts and Haunting in Contemporary Cultural Theory*, edited by Maria Blanco and Esther Peeren, 1–27. London: Bloomsbury.
Brogan, Kathleen. 1995. "American Stories of Cultural Haunting: Tales of Heirs and Ethnographers." *College English* 57, 2: 149–165.
Brown, Peter. 1981. *The Cult of the Saints: Its Rise and Function in Latin Christianity*. Chicago: University of Chicago Press.
Burke, Peter. 2008. *What Is Cultural History?* Cambridge: Polity Press.
Butler, Judith. 2004. *Precarious Life: The Powers of Mourning and Violence*. London: Verso.
Carrabine, Eamonn. 2018. "Traces of Violence: Representing the Atrocities of War." *Criminology & Criminal Justice* 18, 5: 631–646.
Cixous, Hélène. 1976. "Fiction and Its Phantoms: A Reading of Freud's Das Unheimlichie (The 'Uncanny')." *New Literary History* 7, 3: 525–548.
Cladis, Mark. 2001. "Introduction." In Emile Durkheim, *The Elementary Forms of Religious Life*, vii–xxxv. Oxford: Oxford University Press.
Cobb, Richard. 1970. *The Police and the People: French Popular Protest 1789–1820*. Oxford: Clarendon Press.
Cole, Tim. 2000. *Selling the Holocaust*. London: Routledge.
Cotton, Charlotte. 2015. *The Photograph as Contemporary Art*. London: Thames & Hudson.
Critchley, Simon and Jamieson Webster. 2013. *Stay, Illusion!: The Hamlet Doctrine*. New York: Pantheon.

Davis, Colin. 2005. "État Présent: Hauntology, Spectres and Phantoms." *French Studies* 59, 3: 373–379.
Dayan, Joan. 1994. "Amorous Bondage: Poe, Ladies, and Slaves." *American Literature* 66, 2 (June): 239–273.
Dellwing, Michael, Joseph A. Kotarbe, and Nathan W. Pino (eds.). 2014. *The Death and Resurrection of Deviance: Current Ideas and Research*. London: Palgrave.
Derrida, Jacques. 1975/1988. "The Purveyor of Truth." In *The Purloined Poe*, edited by John P. Muller and William J. Richardson, 173–212. Baltimore, MD: Johns Hopkins University Press.
———. 1994. *Specters of Marx: The State of the Debt, the Work of Mourning, & the New International*. London: Routledge.
Durkheim, Emile. 1912/2001. *The Elementary Forms of Religious Life*. Oxford: Oxford University Press.
Eaglestone, Robert. 2017. *The Broken Voice: Reading Post-Holocaust Literature*. Oxford: Oxford University Press.
Edwards, Kathryn A. 2002. "Introduction: Expanding the Analysis of Traditional Belief." In *Werewolves, Witches and Wandering Spirits: Traditional Belief and Folklore in Early Modern Europe*, edited by Katherine Edwards, vii–xxii. Kirksville, MO: Truman State University Press.
Freud, Sigmund. 1919/1958. "The Uncanny." In *On Creativity and the Unconscious: Papers on the Psychology of Art, Literature, Love, Religion*. New York: Harper & Row.
Friedländer, Saul. 1984. *Reflections of Nazism: An Essay on Kitsch and Death*. New York: Harper & Row.
Gordon, Avery. 1997/2008. *Ghostly Matters: Haunting and the Sociological Imagination*. Minneapolis: University of Minnesota Press.
Graham, Paul. 1983/2020. *A1—The Great North Road*. London: MACK.
———. 1986/2021. *Beyond Caring*. London: MACK.
———. 1987. *Troubled Land: Social Landscape of Northern Island*. London: Grey Editions.
———. 2003. *American Night*. Göttingen: Steidl Verlag.
Greenblatt, Stephen. 2001. *Hamlet in Purgatory*. Princeton, NJ: Princeton University Press.
Harvey, Irene. 1988. "Structures of Exemplarity in Poe, Freud, Lacan, and Derrida." In *The Purloined Poe*, edited by John P. Muller and William J. Richardson, 252–267. Baltimore, MD: Johns Hopkins University Press.
Hertz, Robert. 1907/1960. "A Contribution to the Study of the Collective Representation." In *Death and the Right Hand*, trans. Rodney Needham and Claudia Needham. Aberdeen: Cohen and West.
Hudson, Martyn. 2017. *Ghosts, Landscapes and Social Memory*. London: Routledge.
Jacques-Lefèvre, Nicole. 2002. "Such an Impure, Cruel and Savage Beast . . . Images of the Werewolf in Demonological Works." In *Werewolves, Witches and Wandering Spirits: Traditional Belief and Folklore in Early Modern Europe*, edited by Katherine Edwards, 181–198. Kirksville, MO: Truman State University Press.

Jenkins, Richard. 2000. "Disenchantment, Enchantment and Re-Enchantment: Max Weber at the Millennium." *Max Weber Studies* 1, 1: 11–32.
Johnson, Barbara. 1972. "Translator's Introduction." In Jacques Derrida, *Dissemination*. Chicago: University of Chicago Press.
———. 1977/1988. "The Frame of Reference: Poe, Lacan, Derrida." In *The Purloined Poe*, edited by John P. Muller and William J. Richardson, 213–251. Baltimore, MD: Johns Hopkins University Press.
Kindynis, Theo. 2019. "Excavating Ghosts: Urban Exploration as Graffiti Archaeology." *Crime, Media, Culture* 15, 1: 25–45.
Lacan, Jacques. 1956/1988. "Seminar on 'The Purloined Letter.'" In *The Purloined Poe*, edited by John P. Muller and William J. Richardson, 28–54. Baltimore, MD: Johns Hopkins University Press.
———. 1977. "Desire and the Interpretation of Desire in Hamlet." *Yale French Studies* 55/56: 11–52.
Laqeur, Thomas. 2015. *The Work of the Dead*. Princeton, NJ: Princeton University Press.
Lederer, David. 2002. "Living with the Dead: Ghosts in Early Modern Bavaria." In *Werewolves, Witches and Wandering Spirits: Traditional Belief and Folklore in Early Modern Europe*, edited by Katherine Edwards, 25–53. Kirksville, MO: Truman State University Press.
Le Goff, Jacques. 1981/1984. *The Birth of Purgatory*. London: Scolar Press.
Lowe, Paul. 2014. "The Forensic Turn: Bearing Witness and the 'Thingness' of the Photograph." In *The Violence of the Image: Photography and International Conflict*, edited by Liam Kennedy and Caitlin Patrick, 211–234. London: IB Tauris.
Marx, Karl and Friedrich Engels. 1968. *Selected Works in One Volume*. London: Lawrence and Wishart.
———. 1848/2002. *The Communist Manifesto*. London: Penguin.
McEvoy, Emma. 1995. Introduction to *The Monk*, by Matthew Lewis, vii–xxx. Oxford: Oxford University Press.
Miles, Robert. 2007. "Eighteenth-century Gothic." In *The Routledge Companion to Gothic*, edited by Catherine Spooner and Emma McEvoy, 10–18. London: Routledge.
Norfolk, Simon. 2002. *Afghanistan*. Stockport: Dewi Lewis.
———. 2005. *Bleed*. Stockport: Dewi Lewis.
Owens, Craig. 1980. "The Allegorical Impulse: Toward a Theory of Postmodernism." *October* 12, Spring: 67–86.
Paglen, Trevor. 2009. *Blank Spots on the Map: The Dark Geography of the Pentagon's Secret World*. London: Penguin.
Peeren, Esther. 2014. *The Spectral Metaphor: Living Ghosts and the Agency of Invisibility*. Hampshire: Palgrave.
Pócs, Éva. 1999. *Between the Living and the Dead: A Perspective on Witches and Seers in the Early Modern Age*. Budapest: Central European University Press.
Poe, Edgar Allan. 1839/2009. "The Fall of the House of Usher." In *The Collected Works of Edgar Allan Poe*, edited by Michael Davis. Ware, Herts: Wordsworth.

Rashkin, Esther. 1992. *Family Secrets and the Psychoanalysis of Narrative*. Princeton, NJ: Princeton University Press.
Reiner, Robert. 2016. *Crime*. Cambridge: Polity.
Schmitt, Jean-Claude. 1994/1999. *Ghosts in the Middle Ages: The Living and the Dead in Medieval Society*. Chicago: University of Chicago Press.
Sedgwick, Eve Kosofsky. 1980. *The Coherence of Gothic Conventions*. New York: Arno.
Smith, Allan Lloyd. 2012. "Nineteenth-Century American Gothic." In *A New Companion to the Gothic*, edited by David Punter, 163–175. Oxford: Blackwell.
Smith, Philip. 2008. *Punishment and Culture*. Chicago: University of Chicago Press.
Stedman Jones, Gareth. 2002. "Introduction." In Karl Marx and Friedrich Engels, *The Communist Manifesto* 1848/2002. London: Penguin, 3–187.
Taylor, Alison. 2001. *Burial Practice in Early England*. Stroud: Tempus.
Thomas, Keith. 1971. *Religion and the Decline of Magic*. London: Weidenfield & Nicholson.
Urry, John. 2014. *Offshoring*. Cambridge: Polity.
Van Gennep, Arnold. 1908/1960. *The Rites of Passage*. London: Routledge & Kegan Paul.
Vidler, Anthony. 1992. *The Architectural Uncanny: Essays in the Modern Unhomely*. Cambridge, MA: MIT Press.
Warwick, Alexandra. 2007. "Victorian Gothic." In *The Routledge Companion to Gothic*, edited by Catherine Spooner and Emma McEvoy, 29–37. London: Routledge.
Weber, Max. 1930/1992. *The Protestant Ethic and the Spirit of Capitalism*. London: Routledge.
Wilson, Andrew. 1996. *Paul Graham*. London: Phaidon.

2

Ghost Method

JEFF FERRELL

"By 'modernity' I mean the ephemeral, the fugitive, the contingent," wrote Baudelaire (1964 [1863]: 13), famously, "the half of art whose other half is the eternal and the immutable." By ghostly, I mean the ephemeral, the fugitive, the contingent as well, the apparitional half of the contemporary world whose other half is the settled, the sedentary, and the sentries of social order.

Undocumented migrants, ex-cons, registered sex offenders, nocturnal graffiti writers, homeless urbanites, freight-hopping gutter punks—in the practice of their own lives and in the imagination of lawmakers, settled citizens, and the media, folks like these exist less as persons than as apparitions. Their presence is haphazard; between their own peripatetic movement and the ongoing attempts to exclude them from public space and public life, they float in and out of social experience more than they inhabit it. Constructed as threats to social order and public decency, they haunt the lives of the more secure, moving through the margins to seek shelter or beg for money, leaving vague reminders of their unauthorized presence in alleyways, on walls, along migrant trails. Ghostly also is their habit of standing in the shadows, moving through the night, spectral figures out there somewhere beyond the surveillance screens and mood lighting of late modern living.

For a quarter century I've been working those shadows, attempting to understand the ghosts that inhabit them. From lone buskers and street skaters to collectives like Critical Mass and Food Not Bombs, urban ghosts of all sorts deploy dis-organized, decentralized approaches that spawn mapless fluidity and uncertain visibility (Ferrell 2001). Urban trash pickers haunt the city's alleys and burrow in its trash bins, likewise taking care to maintain their own invisibility so as to avoid detection, confrontation, or arrest (Ferrell 2006). On the backroads of the

American West roadside shrines appear, ghostly memorials to those lost along the road—until such time as the shrines themselves are lost, too, decaying into the welter of roadside waste (Ferrell 2003). Spectral in its appearance and disappearance, contemporary graffiti exists as a series of urban apparitions, coming and going, its practitioners an ill-assembled army of nocturnal drifters (Ferrell 1996). When written on outbound freight trains, this graffiti gets cut loose from spatial context and becomes tangled up with other apparitions: the old graffiti monikers of hobos and train yard workers and the newer graffiti "sign-ins" of train-hopping gutter punks, all of them inked-in reminders of illicit identity.

These hobos and gutter punks constitute my latest ghostly encounters (Ferrell 2018). For a century and a half, hobos have been floating and fading, ghosts of the great American West and points beyond. "In the course of my tramping I encountered hundreds of hobos . . . who passed and were seen never again," recalled Jack London (1907, 71) in 1907. "On the other hand, there were hobos who passed and repassed with amazing frequency, and others, still, who passed like ghosts, close at hand, unseen, and never seen." Two decades later the hobo and wandering thief Jack Black (1926, 17) chronicled a similar life of invisibility and absence in which the illicit wanderer "shuns the bright lights, seldom straying far from his kind, never coming to the surface."

Like trash pickers and graffiti writers, hobos have long learned to make themselves disappear; melting into the machinery of the train at the moment of hopping aboard, camouflaging themselves inside dark clothes and railroad grime, the hobo negotiates an ongoing absence, a life of being there and not there. By the mid-twentieth century, writers like Jack Kerouac had come to see such hobos as "ghosts, spiritual guides circulating around the country" (Lennon 2014, 158). But spiritual guides or not, the train ghosts continue to roll today. Hanging out and hopping freights a while back with a gutter punk named Zeke, he told me stories about secretive groups like the Tramp Family Shadow People, and he reminded me of the old hobo creed: "You just want to be least visible as possible."

Then again, sometimes you don't have much choice but to be least visible as possible. Today, consumerist urban economies and aggressive urban policing combine to enforce invisibility on the homeless, herding them out of high-traffic areas, erasing them from public space, and sending them into perpetual motion, staggering zombie-like from place to place as they struggle to negotiate bulldozed encampments, banishment orders, and punitive park benches. As Kristina Gibson (2011, 3–4, 16) argues, when homeless street kids "are pushed out of public spaces around the city, their plight not only is worsened, it also is made invisible." Likewise, when contemporary graffiti writers haunt the nighttime urban margins, hiding in alleys and abandoned buildings, they do so not only out of a sense of nocturnal adventure, but because high-profile anti-graffiti campaigns have left them little else. The fluid identities and rhizomatic dynamics of street gangs likewise reflect the reality of urban street life, but also the adaptation to the aggressive criminalization of such gangs and imposed legal categorization of their members. And this is not to mention perhaps the most prominent contemporary example of imposed invisibility: the extra-legal lives of migrants and immigrants, stashed away in isolated refugee camps or traveling along back roads and hidden bivouacs, surreptitiously crisscrossing borders and serially moving away from and toward the wrong situation.

This dialectic between the enforced invisibility of ghosts and their own strategies for maintaining such invisibility points to a larger issue: the nature of the death that left them as ghosts in the first place. Twenty-five years into chasing ghosts, I would suggest that this death is distinctly social in nature—a *social death* whose pervasiveness identifies it as endemic to the contemporary social order. A social system built around economic inequality and exclusion systematically withdraws from its marginalized members the lifeblood of citizenship. Just as inclusive social life is defined by acceptance, mutuality, and shared respect, so this social death results from the enforced failure of such mutuality. Those who are today socially murdered are defined as outside the realm of warranted acceptance, stigmatized for their supposed failings, aborted in their attempts to gain and maintain cultural dignity, and erased from the spaces of shared social life. As a result, they live as social and cultural ghosts, dead to those who would condemn them, for others little more than specters sometimes glanced in a parking lot, beneath an overpass, or in a condemnatory headline. And you can indeed survive social death—survive as a ghost, that is—but only if you learn to enforce your own invisibility, to cooperate in your own exclusion. Perception intersects practice; all involved conspire in the construction of ghosts, in not seeing those who are not to be seen.

After all, we live in a time after time—a time of ghosts, aftermaths, and absences. The dying of the planet and the economic carcass of neoliberalism have left refugees, temporary workers, and the unemployed to wander from one lost opportunity to the next, zombies hidden away, crossing cities and continents and oceans in search of, well, something. Decades of mass incarceration have left millions of convicted felons to go about their lives "civilly dead" (Hernandez 2014, 418), disenfranchised and denied basic legal rights. Ghostly times indeed: aborted careers, dying planet, the ship of the nation-state dead in the water, apparitions aplenty. Undertaking to understand today's ghosts—for that matter, to find them in the first place—will require a new approach. Ghostly times will require ghostly method.

Accounting for Absence

One way to think about ghosts is to think about absence. Putting aside supernatural considerations for a moment, we can understand ghosts as embodying, if nothing else, the presence of absence. A deceased father who stays alive in the memories of a grieving daughter, a series of wartime horrors that rattle decades later in a veteran's head—these suggest that the absent and the missing remain with us. Put another way, these and other shared cultural experiences suggest that absence constitutes a phenomenon in its own right, a void as sensually immediate and emotionally present as any matter that might fill it; as the writer Wright Morris has said, "any house that's been lived in, any room that's been slept in, is not vacant anymore" (in Orner 2019, C19). For the dislocated, this is the case as well; by the nature of their dislocation, they are less likely to be present in any one place than to be absent from it—less likely to be here, that is, than to have been here, to have departed or disappeared altogether. The homeless shopping cart left under a bridge, the bus on the way out of town, the distant horn of a freight train and its transient human cargo—all denote the inevitability of absence. This absence shapes the experience of those who encounter the dislocated, and those who fear them, too. For them, dislocated populations seem mostly to offer up their absence, pending or accomplished, and with it the sort of apparitional uncertainty that discomforts those who seek stable circumstances, clear vision, firm understanding. Ghosts haunt the social worlds of these more sedentary citizens, present in their absence, visible in their invisibility.

As a researcher, my preferred method is ethnography—immersive, in-depth research with subjects of study—a method, I would argue, that is far more useful and humane than the abstracted, fetishized methods of conventional criminology. Where conventional methods are fixed before the research begins, ethnography tends to be supple and emergent, more an informed sensibility about what is being studied than a preestablished framework for inquiry; where conventional methods are designed for statistical abstraction and intellectual generalization, ethnographic methods are meant for attentiveness and fidelity to the situation under study. Yet for all its strengths, ethnography harbors a problem. Ethnography has traditionally been attuned to the careful study of definable groups and settled subcultures; it has also been dedicated to precise documentation of the people, objects, and interactions that the ethnographer finds to be present in certain settings. For ethnography and ethnographers, then, the problem arises when the subjects of study are ghosts, coming and going and mostly invisible, moving through settings more than occupying them—a problem once again of how to get near a ghost, or to find one in the first place. The problem is redoubled when ethnographers, trained to record what is present, are faced mostly with what is absent. Absence may be present, but knowing how to notice it, record it, and account for it is another matter.

A solution to this problem would retain the attentive sensibility of ethnography while reorienting it to the shape-shifting world of ghosts and drifters. Contemporary ethnographers have begun to consider such possibilities. "The ethnographic project has changed because the world that ethnography confronts has changed," argues Norman Denzin (1997, xii). "Everyone is a tourist, an immigrant, a refugee, an exile, a guest worker, moving from one part of the world to another." In this regard, I and others have begun to explore practices like "instant ethnography" and "liquid ethnography," with the goal of developing approaches that can account for ephemeral moments, unstable social circumstances, and the sorts of ceaseless movement that Denzin describes (Ferrell et al., 2015). Independent filmmaker Kelly Reichardt has likewise "made a career of silence and suggestion" while shooting a series of films about the lives of the sort of "lonesome, seminomadic searchers" we might call ghosts (in Gregory 2016, 37–38). She has done so by embracing the pain and hardship of such living, and by situating herself and her actors inside its sustained and often incommunicable discomfort. Following her lead and that of others, how might we study ghosts, and their absence?

Gary McDonogh (1993, 13) argues that "we must recognize and explore empty places as culturally created and socially meaningful zones rich in interest for our analysis of the city." McDonogh's notions of emptiness as being culturally constructed point to a critical analysis of absence—that is, an investigation of the social and cultural dynamics from which absence is built. By this logic, absence is neither natural nor inevitable; it is a residue of particular social conflicts and social arrangements. When for example nineteenth-century European settlers declared the Australian outback to be *terra nullius*—nobody's land—it was not of course because the land was absent inhabitants; it was because the settlers sought to eradicate the land's First Nations population, to erase their history and culture, and to render the First Nations People unseeable. Spaces of emptiness and absence are in this way often spaces of social death, sometimes the killing grounds on which citizenship and social visibility are exterminated, other times the spatial residues of such cultural violence. Emptiness is never fully emptied of its origins; absence is never absent the echoes of the forces that formed it. If we are to understand ghosts, our task is to find these origins, to listen to these echoes—to excavate absence for what remains present in it.[1]

As a starting point, absence can be excavated in search of those *not there*. This sort of excavation requires not only an ethnographic attentiveness to the particulars of absence, but an application of the sociological and criminological imagination—an ability to look past the overwhelming immediacy of presence to see those not allowed to be present, a willingness to unearth the residues of embedded exclusion. In contemporary exclusive society, and in the proliferating spaces in which such exclusion is enforced, far more people are denied access than are invited in. It's simple enough to notice those with invitations—but our job is to see those without access, and to glimpse the way their ghosts haunt the privileged pleasures of inclusion. A fine restaurant in a fine neighborhood, and a fine evening for those dining there as well—but notice that the undocumented immigrants preparing the meal are kept invisible in the kitchen, that those without the money for such a meal are absent altogether, and that homeless folks are carefully policed away from such places, left to circulate unseen in the city's darker districts. The first day of school, the bustle of students and teachers—but notice the refugees who aren't in attendance, lacking the official paperwork needed for registration, or excluded entirely by law, economy, or public condemnation. Televised coverage of a street protest somewhere around the globe, and the reporter's comments on the "thousands of citizens in the street"—but notice the enforced gender segregation by which all the "citizens" in the streets are men. Such situations are defined by who is absent as much as by who is present; in all such cases, the presence of absence is the politics of absence as well.

This absence of those not there often echoes the absence of those *no longer there*. Excavating this second sort of absence requires not only a sociological imagination, but an historical sensibility. If that fine restaurant sits in a recently gentrified neighborhood, then its presence also hides the absence of the little shops and low-rent apartments that once defined the neighborhood, and the absence of the homeless folks once allowed to congregate in it. The big box store out on the highway draws our attention, but in doing so it diverts our attention from the now boarded-up shops a few miles away on the town square and from all the nearby farms lost to foreclosure (Tunnell 2011). Over time, as cities enforce banishment and exclusion orders, the daily removal of street populations from public space accumulates into a history of removal—a history that hides the earlier vitality of such space, leaving it not only empty but emptied. As the wars on drugs and gangs drag on, generations of young Black men are pulled from their communities, such that these communities are increasingly haunted by those no longer present, shaped by those who are both in prison and out of the neighborhood; over time, villages in Central America likewise empty out and confront a recalibration of their social life as men and boys who were once there continue to migrate north in search of jobs that may be somewhere else. To be both not there and no longer there is to endure a double absence; it is to live as a ghost of circumstances changed and memory evacuated.

The absence of those not there and no longer there can coalesce into particular sorts of spaces as well, emptied spaces that Justin Armstrong (2010, 244) argues are amenable to a "spectral ethnography" attuned to the cultural resonances of past occupation. More generally, Michael Bell argues that "ghosts—that is, *the sense of the presence of those who are not physically here*—are a ubiquitous aspect of the phenomenology of place" across a range of locations (1997, 813, emphasis in original). If for Armstrong and Bell such places resonate with a mix of warmth and chill, a mélange of fond memories and sorrowful loss, for criminologists like Travis Linnemann and Mark Hamm there is often something more akin to cold sweat. Noting presidential assassination sites and Holocaust locations, exploring in particular the cultural residues of the *In Cold Blood* murders, Linnemann (2015, 517) has written of "the haunting power of human creation and indelibility of meaning—specters of remembrance that transmit and inherit across generations." Undertaking an "ethnography of terror," Hamm (1998, 115) tracked down the seedy Kingman, Arizona, motel room Timothy McVeigh had occupied a year earlier as McVeigh had prepared to truck-bomb the Murrah Building in Oklahoma City. McVeigh was by this time long gone, but Hamm moved in for a couple of nights anyway—and found his own distinctly terrifying, ghostly mélange of black auras and night panic.

A final sort of absence requires anticipatory excavation. The economic and political trajectories of the present suggest that the contemporary world consists not only of those not there, and those no longer there, but those who will soon not be there—those scheduled to be put adrift and made absent. The next corporate or university reduction in full-time staff, the next war and its forced refugees and bombed-out veterans, the next consumerist urban development plan—all will empty out social spaces, enforce absence, and cast lives adrift as surely as the ones before them. "Speculative emptiness," McDonogh (1993, 7) calls it—and excavating such speculative emptiness will mean decoding official pronouncements, watching carefully for the early signs of absence and emptying out, and confronting the insidious mechanisms of power by which such targeted absence is engineered, enforced, and forgotten. When graffiti writers were pushed out of lower downtown Denver, the anti-graffiti campaign that did the pushing was operating, we now know, as the forward edge of a long-term plan to clean the area in order to develop high-end housing and consumption. The plan was a success—and, save for a few critics like myself (Ferrell 1996, 2001), also a success in redefining these areas as an empty *terra nullius* all along, awaiting only developmental salvation. When my buddy Zeke was approached by a city cleanup crew near the Fort Worth railyards, and he persuaded the crew to wait while he ate breakfast, he wasn't just putting one over on the crew; he was seeing his own ultimate absence. I saw it too, hanging out with Zeke: the amassed bulldozers, the surveyor's stakes, portending—if you knew how to read them—the new toll road that would be built right over the to-be-razed hobo camps that had dotted that area for decades. Soon enough, speculative emptiness begets the presence of absence and amnesia.

Residues and Ruinations

In the aftermath of enforced absence, in the afterlife of social death, ghosts drift away to circulate along the shadow margins of social life. For them, the aftermath is an ongoing echo of the calamity by which they were initially made absent, a lingering reverberation of the social forces that conspired in their exclusion. This aftermath is itself a cultural and temporal space shaped by absence and ambiguity, a borderland "space of nonexistence" that "excludes people, limits rights, restricts services, and erases personhood," as Susan Coutin (2003, 172) writes in describing the lives of undocumented immigrants. To live inside it is to move about in a suspended state, to hide out in the temporal ruins of enforced non-being. Itself a ghost of the immediate, the aftermath is also the place where the ghosts of immediate injustice gather and disperse.

This aftermath is a residual phenomenon, powder burns after the explosion—and its residual dynamic doubles as ghosts and drifters move through it. Made to be always on the move, pushed out repeatedly by immigration policy or redevelopment plans, drifting ghosts have little choice but to leave behind residues of themselves. And so, just as they are more likely to be absent than present, they are more likely to be visible in the vestiges that remain than in the persons now departed. A woman or man *made* to travel, forced to move on time and again, has nothing but trouble in hanging on to what little is owned. So, if we want to get near ghosts, we had best reorient ourselves to their residues, and to developing a sociology of the residual.

Those who have tangled with ghosts can tell us something of residues, and of the ways they provide a lingering presence amidst human absence. Exploring the possibilities of spectral ethnography, Armstrong

(2010, 244, 247) has argued for a "form of ethnographic inquiry" in which "the traces, artifacts, and other resonances that people leave behind act as the focal point of an investigation of spectral ethnographic space." For Armstrong, this "archeology of hauntedness" has meant documenting disused sidewalks, boarded-up storefronts, and abandoned farm machinery to create an "archeology of the abandoned present." Noting the "ghosts of place," Bell (1997, 816) has likewise investigated the ways in which we mix "souls with things" and "souls with spaces," thereby imbuing long-held objects and well-worn environments with the residual ghosts of past relationships and experiences (see Linnemann 2015). In sorting through the cultural detritus of Timothy McVeigh's violent paranoia, Hamm (1998, 122) discovered a distinctively disturbing ghost. Immersed in McVeigh's music, books, and movies, Hamm found that he had summoned "the ghost of Earl Turner," the truck-bombing protagonist of *The Turner Diaries*—the book that had been McVeigh's inspirational blueprint for the attack.

Dorothea Lange and Paul Taylor (1969[1939]) pioneered their own sociology of the residual, and a visual sociology at that, during the Great Depression. Weathered, eroded, worn down—for Lange and Taylor, these were descriptions of the land and the people alike. Through Lange's photographs and Taylor's writings, they showed what was left of a farmer and a farm in the aftermath of ecological tragedy: emptied-out houses, domestic dilapidations, barbed wire twisted and splayed along a lost fence line in a way that no working farmer would countenance. And once that former farmer and his family, desperate to escape, gathered what little they had and took to the road: broken truck parts, abandoned alongside the highway; tin cans tossed away from improvised campsites; and in one of Lange's photos, captioned "Squatter camp on outskirts of Holtville," a foreground piled with discarded buckets, bottomless cans, meat tins. "A record of human erosion in the thirties," they subtitled *An American Exodus*, the book in which this all appeared, and as they well understood, that erosion inevitably left behind the worn-down vestiges of human misery. For those forced into hard traveling, the privilege of spatial stability and careful conservation of possessions is left behind; drift soon enough devolves into discards.

Perhaps the magnitude of a tragedy cannot be fully measured by its residues—but the ghosts of tragedy and the sensuality of suffering can certainly be glimpsed. Over the past few decades, countless undocumented migrants have undertaken the dangerous crossing of the Sonoran Desert of Arizona in an attempt to enter the United States. Hiking ahead at night, sleeping in hidden campsites, ducking the Border Patrol, they have remained not only undocumented but often unnoticeable. Yet along the journey they discard what they can no longer afford to carry, such that, over time, gullies near campsites fill with worn clothing and empty water bottles—to the point that "hundreds of thousands (if not millions) of water bottles, backpacks, shoes and other items have been left in the deserts of Arizona since the 1990s" (De Leon 2013, 327; 2015). More than this, these discards document a sensuality that otherwise remains itself undocumented: the profound suffering that accompanies those of little means as they illicitly cross a vast desert. As De Leon (2013, 321, 333) has shown, for example, their discarded shoes display holes worn through their soles, desperate on-the-fly repairs, menstrual pads inserted to cushion blistered feet, and cactus spines pushed through their sides. The vast, accumulated residues of generations of undocumented migrants suggest at least something of their sheer numbers; they also record what De Leon calls "the materiality of habitual suffering."

An exhibition based on De Leon's work, "State of Exception/Estado de Excepcion," accumulates and displays this materiality, presenting for example hundreds of discarded, dirt-encrusted backpacks (Cotter 2017). For artist and activist Ai Weiwei, the dirtiness of migrants' ghostly discards can likewise be read as a record of their vulnerable instability. With contemporary European refugees kept haphazardly on the move, Ai says, "there is no time to wash. They have to throw away dirty stuff"—and in this way "the migrants are there but they're not there" (in Pogrebin 2016, C18). But where De Leon, and Lange and Taylor before him, documented this displacement of possessions, Ai has staged an artistic intervention. Collecting the soiled clothes and blankets that migrants were forced to abandon as they were hustled from the Idomeni refugee camp along the Greek-Macedonian border, Ai has cleaned and washed them, paired them with a documentary on Idomeni and photos of the other refugee camps he has visited, and presented this as part of his "Laundromat" exhibition—all as a component of his broader focus on "uprootedness and displacement" (Pogrebin 2016, C18). For artists, anthropologists, and others attentive to ghostly drifters and their lives, their residues are indeed a text written by and about them, a trail of notes left behind—but, appropriately enough, it is a ghost text compiled in fragments, unsteady and unfinished, a moving absence whose lost passages are inscribed in invisible ink. Human erosion and material erosion, a discarding of personhood and possessions—each is a ghostly residue of the other. "Incoherence, in this sense, does not have to signal incomprehension," says Caitlin DeSilvey (2007, 420–421), "but may instead open a working space which respects the complexity of the historical subject we study."

Ruins offer up other sorts of residues. A beat-down abandoned building stands—and eventually falls—as the material aftermath of an economic and social moment now passed, a residue of long-ago commercial plans and structural accomplishments. Its emptiness is not only physical; inside its decaying walls is an absence of what once was, save perhaps for residual reminders encoded in faded wall advertisements or broken equipment. Because of this, temporal ruins and physical ruins demand once again an excavation of absence, and a critical inquiry into what is no longer there. The ruins of little stores and small businesses that dot Appalachia are, as Kenneth Tunnell (2011) has documented, also the ghosts of obliterated local economies; the regionally made merchandise that once filled their now deteriorating shelves is today globally manufactured and piled inside a nearby WalMart, at half the price and twice the social cost. The shells of shuttered Mid-American factories harbor the ghosts of Fordist jobs lost to globalization, with those who once held those jobs now out of work or drifting around the part-time service economy. Awaiting the bulldozer, boarded-up public housing in its emptiness anticipates the consumer-driven urban development that will replace it. So pervasive are such ruins amidst the predations of globalized late capitalism that the notion of "ruin porn" has emerged—the aesthetic appropriation of burned-out factory buildings and decaying shopping malls by photographers, urban explorers, and global tourists. Now, I'll admit, there can be something seductively pleasing in stylish photographs of such ruins, especially photographs of the big ruins—a visual confirmation that the past hubris of urban developers and corporate planners has now been humbled. Still, this isn't the real ruin porn; the real pornography of ruins lies in the obscenities of exploitation that they both hide and reveal, and in the absences that they hold.

For ghosts there is also a sad sort of circularity. Cast out from the local factory by the logic of neoliberalism, cut off from job or career, an unemployed ghost now returns to the factory's ruins in search of scrap metal or social invisibility; lacking the funds to purchase what the shopping mall sells, banished from the thriving commercial district, the urban ghost later finds in the now-boarded-up mall or the dying commercial district a bit of temporary shelter. Consigned to the social margins, made to conspire in their own invisibility, ghosts tend to gather in those spaces and structures that have themselves been rendered marginal; ruined social reputations tend to play out in ruined spaces. To put it in terms of Lange and Taylor, human erosion often accumulates, at least for a while, amidst physical erosion. "The thousand-and-one hiding holes of industrial night" to which Jack Kerouac (1960, 172) referred, and in which ghosts secret themselves away, have more often than not been carved out by long-flowing currents of economic erosion and spatial decay.

Little wonder, then, that the Timothy McVeighs of the world wash up in dilapidated flop motels, along with road hustlers, fugitives, runaways, and refugees; little wonder that they are joined there by those who suffer particularly thorough-going social death—ex-convicts, registered sex offenders, the mentally ill, families on welfare (Dum 2016). Actually, registered sex offenders are lucky if they can land a ruined motel; local residency ordinances often leave them with nowhere to reside but the shadows beneath bridges and viaducts. Amidst such ruined circumstances we can find yet another echo of Lange and Taylor, and their twined notions of human and physical erosion. Those made socially dead are often consigned to places of ecological death as well, to areas ruined not only by social and economic decay but by overcrowding, chemical contamination, or consumer waste.

Always a question haunts the world of ghosts: What was ruined, and what remains?

Spaces Between

The world of ghosts requires that we notice absence as much as presence, and that we explore ruins and residues rather than the obvious and the over-built. It also requires new ways of looking and seeing, inviting us to look sideways at the spaces in between one thing and another—and to think about the ways in which these spaces in-between constitute, like absence, ghostly phenomena in their own right. Keith Hayward (2012, 137) captures something of this with his notion of "parafunctional spaces"—"the abandoned, anonymous, and seemingly meaningless spaces within our midst." To understand the social lives of ghosts, we must theorize these "no places"—that is, those situations that have no place in the political economy of consumerist development, no place in the legal grid of the city, no place on conventional maps of meaning. Like the ghosts that traverse them, such situations exist in between; they are neither here nor there.

This interstitiality has long animated the lives of ghosts and drifters. Riding the rails from work site to work site, hobos lived much of their lives on the move between jobs and places. "The true hobo was the in-between worker, willing to go anywhere to take a job and equally willing to move on later," Nels Anderson (1923, p. xviii) concluded. The jungles in which hobos camped were themselves in-between spaces, wedged into derelict areas near railroad tracks or switching yards, generally not in the city itself but near enough to it, and so not rural either. The sedentary and the settled could hold a steady job, reside in one place; hobos by necessity moved between jobs, along the way camping in places that were officially no place at all.

Ruins constitute in-between places as well. They tenuously occupy the space spanning a structure's original construction and its ultimate destruction, hovering between past and future, between the assemblage of intentions through which the building initially came to exist and future possibilities for its location. Ruins are "terrain vague" and "interstitial spaces," Tim Edensor (2008, 126) concludes—and so are other absences that permeate contemporary social life. The "un-spaces" of absence that Armstrong (2010, 244) notes—"the abandoned and unseen locations that exist at the edges of everyday life and experience"—capture something of the hobo jungle, the shuttered factory, and the flop motel as well. All exist in the darkness at the edge of town, in the cracks that open when cities and economies collapse. Decorated by graffiti that itself floats specter-like somewhere between visibility and invisibility, occupied by a shifting cast of drifters and ghosts, such spaces hang in the air, ready always to evaporate into something else.

"Spectral housing," Arjun Appadurai (2000, 635–637) calls such living arrangements in Bombay, India—arrangements that embody the "experience of shortage, speculation, crowding, and public improvisation. . . . the absent, the ghostly, the speculative, the fantastic." For some in Bombay, "homes" of a sort are available in the form of outlying shantytown shacks, "unstable products—a bricolage of shoddy materials, insecure social relations, poor sanitation, and near-total lack of privacy." For occupants of these homes, the long train ride to work in central Bombay offers a sort of interstitial transformation, an opportunity to morph into the proper clerks and secretaries that they will be for the duration of the work day. For others, home is even less than this, a no-place that is interstitial in its entirety. As Appadurai reports, a large segment of Bombay's citizens "lives on pavements—or, more exactly, on particular spots, stretches, and areas that are neither building nor street. . . . Others sleep in the gray spaces between buildings and streets. Yet others live on roofs and on parapets, above garages, and in a variety of interstitial spaces that are not fully controlled by either landlords or the state."

This is indeed life lived in the spaces in-between—and of course such living is hardly confined to Bombay. When an inferno engulfed an old Oakland, California, warehouse known as the Ghost Ship, some three dozen people were killed—party goers and residents who had illegally colonized the warehouse as an alternative living/gathering space. The Ghost Ship, it turns out, was one of countless such illegal, patched-together living spaces in the city—so many that officials found themselves overwhelmed in their attempts to regulate them. Such spaces have proliferated in Oakland, San Francisco, New York, Seattle, and other cities due to increased economic inequality, and with it have come soaring rents, such that young, part-time workers and working-class families are effectively priced out of the legal housing market. As a result, an apparitional army floats between one Ghost Ship and another, caught in an ongoing netherworld between legality and illegality—since illegal housing, if legalized, quickly becomes unaffordable.

Those with even fewer resources suffer their own sort of interstitiality. Mitchell (2013, 67) argues that it is not only the old North American hobo jungles that were interstitial, but equally so today's self-organized tent cities that the homeless construct "under bridges, in abandoned lots still waiting development, on the grounds of old factories, in the scrub and silt of the rivers that run through town." Certainly these tent cities exist in the city's in-between spaces. A recent report noted that a San Francisco tent city had formed "between a food truck court ... and a vegetarian grocery co-op," and a nearby shantytown "along a narrow strip of concrete" between a busy street and a railway line (Duane 2016, 6). These encampments exist in between time as well. Like other ruins, the disused lot awaiting development and the old factory scheduled for removal offer a tenuous, temporary space in which to form a community, an indeterminate interregnum between one regime of urban development and the next. And for the residents of contemporary tent cities, the next legal and economic regime will be enforced soon enough; even if residents intend a degree of permanence, life in a tent city remains unsettled, suspended as it is between the fragility of present circumstances and the inevitability of outside interruption.

All of this grants a distinct materiality to the usual sense of a "subculture," and along the way highlights a further sort of space in-between. For ghosts and drifters, under is often the scene of the action—as much so for the homeless folks who camp in the storm drains beneath Las Vegas or live in a New York City train tunnel as for those sex offenders hunkering down below bridges. Across the bridge roll cars and buses, their occupants on the way to work or home; under the bridge gather the jobless and the homeless, at least for a while. The bridge is an obvious urban artifact; the space beneath it is uncertain, shadowy, and interstitial, a forgotten residue of construction plans and abutment specifications. Other of these little *lost ecologies* are scattered around city and country as well—triangles of land isolated between freeway ramps, streams channeled through concrete corridors, slivers of disused land overgrown between buildings—and these too are the in-between terrain of ghosts. Little more than the collateral damage of development for others, for ghosts they are islands of invisibility and survival. Over my years chasing ghosts, I've seen them time and again, stumbling upon a hidden homeless encampment burrowed into an embankment between a freeway interchange, finding other camps in floodplains or along railroad tracks.

The lives of past hobos and present Ghost Ship residents remind us that the spatiality of interstitial survival is in turn intertwined with what might be called occupational interstitiality. Hobos camped in jungles because they remained on the move between jobs; Ghost Ship residents resorted to one illegal warehouse or another because low wages and serial part-time work left them unable to afford legal housing. In the contemporary part-time service economy, millions likewise live occupationally in-between. At one time, being "between jobs" may have been, for some, little more than an interlude. Today, being between jobs—piecing together part-time work, moving always from one gig to another—constitutes its own liminal reality, its own endless interlude. To negotiate this sort of life is to traverse gaps in space *and* time, to remain in motion between memory and anticipation. The precarity of today's contingent arrangements doubles down—and so if we hope to find those trapped in these arrangements, we'd best look for them not on the job but between jobs, not at their non-existent home but on the move from one temporary living space to the next. In such a world, unemployment often means an indeterminate space between a job lost and the next one sought, and with it couch surfing or tent city survival. But even for those with jobs, there's the travel between them, the train car or automobile as rolling office, the hours lost waiting between split shifts, the netherworld of always being on call, the daily trips between day care, work, and temporary housing.

The contemporary mania for mass incarceration adds still other layers of interstitiality; those caught up in it traverse the spaces between prison and community. The pipeline that connects marginalized communities to imprisonment runs in both directions, with the flow of people both in and out of prison shaping individual and collective experience. Edward Green (2016) found that prisoners often occupy extended states of liminality, caught as they are between their pre-prison identities, their emerging circumstances in prison, and the anticipation of life post-prison. Jamie Fader (2013) spent three years with young Black men confined to reform school—young men who, once released, attempted to transition back into their old urban neighborhoods. She discovered that they must negotiate a double transition, between reform school and the community, and between adolescence and young adulthood. Now released from confinement, they must also conform to the demands of probation officers and reintegration workers, all while attempting to restore relationships with families and friends. As Fader (2013, 219–220) says, "they appeared to move back and forth between employment and unemployment, offending and conforming on an almost day-to-day basis." Family and friends of those still imprisoned navigate a similar string of interstitial experiences. Brett Story's (2016) poignant film *The Prison in Twelve Landscapes* documents these experiences. Waiting for the next visitation day, enduring the long bus rides to and from the prison once the day arrives, planning for a prisoner's eventual release and return home, the families endlessly navigate the lonesome distance between their lives and the lives of those imprisoned.

But, of course, it's not only prisoners who wait for their release, or their families who wait to visit; waiting pervades the lives of ghosts. Old hobos and young gutter punks wait for trains far more than they ride them. Trash pickers learn to wait, too—to wait for an event to end, or for objects to be discarded. Refugees wait interminably in isolated camps, wait to cross borders, wait to claim legal status. Waiting calibrates the degree to which those made to wait lack power and control. Waiting also constructs an absence of action, an experience of temporal interstitiality, an elongated moment that leaves its occupants suspended between what was and what may yet be. Interwoven with other forms of interstitiality—train hoppers waiting in the brush beside the track, trash pickers waiting not in the street but in the alley, contingent workers waiting out split shifts, migrants waiting in social and geographic borderlands—waiting grinds open one final gap, one further experience of absence, for those left with little but to live in between the spaces of social life.

Given all this, it seems to me that learning to look in between may be the most useful aspect of ghost method—the key to understanding and engaging with a world of ghosts. It may also offer a bit of hope. For progressive architects and urbanists, "a paradigm shift in thinking about planning and urbanism" is underway, a shift "from a primary focus on buildings to a focus on the spaces between buildings—public space" (Burney in Pogrebin 2015, C3). As regards democratized housing, Don Mitchell (2013, 82) argues that, "as a taking of land, as a non-commodified and cooperative form of property and social relations, as (potentially) an organization space, tent cities, and their progenitors like the hobo jungle, have much to teach us." Those interested in cultural activism might likewise learn the ways in which an interstice, as Andrea Mubi Brighenti (2013, xviii) suggests, can be "not simply a physical space, but very much a phenomenon on the ground," an interventionist "happening." As ghosts squat within the cracks in the social order, they sometimes widen them, at least for a while, with their own autonomous action.

Alongside the roads and amidst the ruins, beneath the bridges and between the viaducts, the ghostly denizens of social death remain on the move, perpetually absent and invisible, navigating the temporal and spatial residues of social life. To find them, to understand them—to learn from them—we must make their movements and their methods our own. Deleuze and Guattari (1987, 380) once proposed that "the life of the nomad is in the intermezzo"—that the nomad's knowledge of the world forms between and beyond the particularity of place. For ghosts also, intermezzos constitute the main performance. What kind of music emerges from their archipelago of intermezzos, and how might we learn to hear it?

NOTE

1 Similarly, Simon Hallsworth and Tara Young (2008, 131–132) argue, with regard to crime and silence, for "considering silence as the absent presence of crime," and for "a methodological approach for excavating silence," in order to understand the role of this "negative space'" in constituting crime and crime control.

REFERENCES

Anderson, Nels. 1961[1923]. *The Hobo: The Sociology of the Homeless Man*. Chicago: University of Chicago Press.

Appadurai, Arjun. 2000. "Spectral Housing and Urban Cleansing." *Public Culture* 12, 3: 627–651.

Armstrong, Justin. 2010. "On the Possibility of Spectral Ethnography." *Cultural Studies Critical Methodologies* 10, 3: 243–250.

Baudelaire, Charles. 1964[1863]. *The Painter of Modern Life and Other Essays*. London: Phaidon.

Bell, Michael. 1997. "The Ghosts of Place." *Theory and Society* 26: 813–836.

Black, Jack. 2000[1926]. *You Can't Win*. San Francisco: Nabat/AK Press.

Brighenti, Andrea Mubi, ed. 2013. *Urban Interstices*. Surrey, UK: Ashgate.

Cotter, Holland. 2017. "Things They Carried to the End." *New York Times*, March 4, C1, C2.

Coutin, Susan Bibler. 2003. "Illegality, Borderlands, and the Space of Nonexistence." In *Globalization Under Construction*, edited by Richard Perry and Bill Maurer, 171–202. Minneapolis: University of Minnesota Press.

De Leon, Jason. 2013. "Undocumented Migration, Use Wear, and the Materiality of Habitual Suffering in Sonoran Desert." *Journal of Material Culture* 18, 4: 321–345.

———. 2015. *The Land of Open Graves*. Berkeley: University of California Press.
Delueze, Gilles and Felix Guattari. 1987. *A Thousand Plateaus*. Minneapolis: University of Minnesota Press.
Denzin, Norman. 1997. *Interpretive Ethnography*. Thousand Oaks, CA: Sage.
DeSilvey, Caitlin. 2007. "Salvage Memory: Constellating Material Histories on a Hardscrabble Homestead." *Cultural Geographies* 14, 3: 401–424.
Duane, Daniel. 2016. "The Tent Cities of San Francisco." *New York Times*, December 18, 1, 6, 7.
Dum, Christopher. 2016. *Exiled in America*. New York: Columbia University Press.
Edensor, Tim. 2008. "Walking Through Ruins." In *Ways of Walking*, edited by Tim Ingold and Jo Lee Vergunst, 123–141. Aldershot, UK: Ashgate.
Fader, Jamie. 2013. *Falling Back*. New Brunswick, NJ: Rutgers.
Ferrell, Jeff. 1996. *Crimes of Style*. Boston: Northeastern University Press.
———. 2001. *Tearing Down the Streets*. New York: Palgrave/Macmillan.
———. 2003. "Speed Kills." *Critical Criminology* 11: 185–198.
———. 2006. *Empire of Scrounge*. New York: New York University Press.
———. 2018. *Drift: Illicit Mobility and Uncertain Knowledge*. Oakland: University of California Press.
Ferrell, Jeff, Keith Hayward, and Jock Young. 2015. *Cultural Criminology: An Invitation*, 2nd ed. London: Sage.
Gibson, Kristina. 2011. *Street Kids*. New York: New York University Press.
Green, Edward L. W. 2016. *Weight of the Gavel: Prison as a Rite of Passage*. PhD Thesis, Kansas State University.
Gregory, Alice. 2016. "The Precisionist." *New York Times Magazine*, October 16, 36–39.
Hallsworth, Simon and Tara Young. 2008. "Crime and Silence." *Theoretical Criminology* 12, 2: 131–152.
Hamm, Mark S. 1998. "The Ethnography of Terror." In *Ethnography at the Edge*, edited by Jeff Ferrell and Mark S. Hamm, 111–130. Boston: Northeastern University Press.
Hayward, Keith. 2012. "Using Cultural Geography to Think Differently about Space and Crime." In *New Directions in Criminological Theory*, edited by Steve Hall and Simon Winlow, 123–144. London: Routledge.
Hernandez, Kelly. 2014. "Hobos in Heaven: Race, Incarceration, and the Rise of Los Angeles, 1880–1910." *Pacific Historical Review* 83, 3: 410–447.
Kerouac, Jack. 1970[1960]. *Lonesome Traveler*. New York: Grove.
Lange, Dorothea and Paul Taylor. 1969[1939]. *An American Exodus*. New Haven, CT: Yale University Press.
Lennon, John. 2014. *Boxcar Politics*. Amherst: University of Massachusetts Press.
Linnemann, Travis. 2015. "Capote's Ghosts." *British Journal of Criminology* 55, 3: 514–533.
London, Jack. 1907. *The Road*. New York: MacMillan/Aegypan Press.
McDonogh, Gary. 1993. "The Geography of Emptiness." In *The Cultural Meaning of Urban Space*, edited by Robert Rotenberg and Gary McDonogh, 3–15. Westport, CT: Bergin and Garvey.

Mitchell, Don. 2013. "Tent Cities: Interstitial Spaces of Survival." In *Urban Interstices*, edited by Andrea Mubi Brighenti, 65–85. Surrey, UK: Ashgate.
Orner, Peter. 2019. "American Oddness, in All Its Glory." *New York Times*, July 19, C13, C19.
Pogrebin, Robin. 2015. "Pratt to Offer a Degree Focusing in Public Space." *New York Times*, March 30, C3.
———. 2016. "An Artist's Activism Turns to Migrant Misery." *New York Times*, October 21, C18.
Story, Brett. 2016. *The Prison in Twelve Landscapes*. Oh Ratface Films.
Tunnell, Kenneth. 2011. *Once Upon a Place*. Bloomington, IN: Xlibris.

3

The Specter of White Supremacy

Fugitive Justice and the Dead Body of US Racialized Politics

MICHELLE BROWN

My body was given back to me sprawled out, distorted, re-colored, clad in mourning in that white winter day. . . . All round me the white man, above the sky tears at its navel, the earth rasps under my feet, and there is a white song, a white song. All this whiteness that burns me.
—Franz Fanon, *Black Skin, White Masks*

[b]ut here, not earth
not heaven, we can't recall our white shirts
turned ruby gowns. here, there's no language
for officer or law, no color to call white.
if snow fell, it'd fall black. please, don't call
us dead, call us alive someplace better.
—Danez Smith, *Don't Call Us Dead*

Trayvon Martin. Michael Brown. Eric Garner. Rekia Boyd. Tamir Rice. Sandra Bland. Walter Scott. Freddy Gray. Philando Castile. Korryn Gaines. Alton Sterling. Pamela Turner. George Floyd. Breonna Taylor. Each, so singular, so collective, comes with their own mediatized visual and sonic death scene, murdered by the state. This is what we publicly come to know of them in life, in death. Each is not another who was also murdered. The body around which we most often organize for justice in the United States is a dead one. Poet Claudia Rankine insists that here, "the condition of black life is one of mourning," and the "killing of black people . . . an unending spectacle" (2015). Scholar Shatema Threadcraft insists similarly that "the body that receives the most attention in contemporary racial politics is a deceased one" (2017, 553; see also Balthaser 2016; Hayes 2015). The breach of Black death and white empathy materializes in "the endless replay" of racialized state killing as a kind of "cultural spectacle" (Cooper 2015). "A roll call of Black death and mourning," social media and news feeds make the visuality and sonic worlds of Black death intrusive, triggering, fetishized, ordinary (Carrington 2015). Christina Sharpe, in her poignant exposition of Black life lived in slavery's afterlife, refers to these as "orthographies of the wake—transmitted through Twitter timelines, Facebook feeds, websites, Tumblrs, Instagrams, and other online and traditional media, each organized to spectate the mothers bereft from the murders of their children, each mother forced to display her pain in public" (Sharpe 2016, 74). . . . "a dysgraphia of disaster . . . of Black social, material, and psychic death" (21). For her, the death-dealing violence of antiblackness is a kind of "Weather," ordinary, everywhere, the present that makes the future (21).

In this chapter, I offer a reading, one that challenges us—me—to rethink the white supremacist foundations of criminology and criminal justice. Relying upon literatures that are effectively silenced in the field, I take up the project and potential of a ghost criminology but one that necessarily is grounded in the speculative work of the Black radical tradition. It is this legacy that has transformed my own vantage point, rendering criminology and the idea of criminal justice illegible except as foundational forms of violence. Studying Black feminist modes of analysis directed toward the carceral afterlife of slavery—such classics as Christina Sharpe's *In the Wake*, Claudia Rankine's *Citizen*, and Saidiya Hartman's *Scenes of Subjection* and *Lose Your Mother* (see also Best 2018), I meditate on how these works rewrite criminology without criminology, insisting it into the space of an otherwise, one that has yet to take shape and may very well require criminology's destruction.

Antiblackness should be of utter importance to criminology—it is, of course, as common as the weather—and yet it is intentionally and intensively, foundationally, omitted. As anti-racism moves in as a key fulcrum for white intellectuals (and the liberal public) to attach themselves, terms such as white fragility and privilege dominate the pedagogies of diversity, but not white supremacy nor the coalitions that name and seek to destroy it. The erasure and disappearance of this violence leaves criminology not simply compromised but dangerous, unable to name the ways in which it replicates paradigms of racial regimes and necropolitics (Henne and Shah 2015; Lamble 2013). I take as foundational to this work Fanon's fact of Blackness, including the principle that "Antiblackness, while not representing the totality of the social, does constitute its essence or base. In short, politics from the vantage point of black existence offers the most radical potentiality for the creation of an entirely new world; justice remains unethical until and unless it is blackened, accountable to and authorized by the slave's grammar of suffering" (Saucier and Woods 2016, 17). Ultimately, these accounts necessitate that, while many kinds of deaths take shape in relation to state violence (white, Black, and beyond), there is no explanation—and certainly no transformation—of any death's conditions at the hands of the state without the foregrounding of epistemologies of Black life.

As I situate this reading in Afropessimist accounts of an inescapable antiblack formation at the foundations of the US carceral state, I also seek to draw our attention to the invention of race and racial regimes as socially constructed through whiteness and racial capitalism, including the important historical, material, and internationalist accounts that also make up the key tenets of the Black radical tradition—W.E.B. Du Bois (2017), Vincent Harding (1981), CLR James (2001), Cedric Robinson (Johnson and Lubin 2011), Robin DG Kelley (2002), and, of course, Angela Davis (2011). Both trajectories are, importantly, largely absent in criminology and sociology. This is evident in the ways that the terms white supremacy and racism are lost in the field's diffusions of disproportionality, disparity, inequality, and discrimination—the key vectors and variables of study. In that sense, white supremacy is always intentionally invisibilized, the ghost in the room whose powerful presence weighs on the past, present, and future.

In this account, I seek to elaborate various configurations of white supremacy in relation to a discussion of white visualities. As Mirzoeff (2011) argues, visuality is the ordering and visualization of history through the authority of the visualizer, who authorizes how we see history. For Mirzoeff, the slave plantation is visuality's first domain, monitored by the violent surveillance of the overseer, who occupies and produces the racialized vantage point of whiteness, power, and wealth accumulation. For Mirzoeff, this formation is attached as well to the complexes of imperialism: conquest and colonization, and the militarization of the present, with its global counterinsurgency against revolution. To think of visuality in relationship to the right to look—which is also the right to exist, to educate for emancipation, to not be disappeared—is one means by which to expose the spectrality of whiteness's exclusive claim on looking, which, importantly, is not only masculine and heroic, as Mirzoeff presents it, but white in its production and perpetual reinvention of racialized regimes. Insurgency, framed through the Black radical tradition, however, sees through the spectral, spiral of history: "move on, there is nothing to see here," demanding the right to look. As I was reminded by a thoughtful reviewer of this chapter, echoing Cedric Robinson, "racial regimes are inventions. As inventions . . . resistances are always leaving residues" (Camp and Heatherton 2017, 100).

As I trace it, white supremacy functions, then, in sociological terms, as the key formation that sustains white people's accumulation of wealth and power in cultural, economic, and political systems and in cultural and psychic ones as well. Embedded throughout social relations, white supremacy operates at the foundation of modernity's key institutions and knowledge forms. It is spectral precisely because it is invisible (naturalized, normative) and yet forceful in its shaping of the violence and terror of the world. It is pathological in its denial of its own terrifying presence and violence (colorblind, post-racial, etc.), in all the ways it refuses accountability and protects white prerogative (Christian 2019; Christian et al. 2019). It ignores emancipatory action, infrastructure, and coalition-building by commitments to ideas of negative freedom built upon liberal subjecthood singularly attentive to notions of white guilt, empathy, and shame. It is thus monstrous in its refusal to create an insurgent subject—an anti-racist or race traitor who is, echoing Malcolm X's question, an actual human being, capable of the very basics of collective and social thinking. White supremacy is at once invented, constructed, exclusive, negative, and spectral. Its production of whiteness, that naturalized vantage point and social position of white power in social hierarchies, as Christian (2019) argues, is deep, structural, malleable and global, rooted in historical struggles, but gravitating always back to fictional accounts, standards, and practices of equality and freedom. But it is alterable . . . or exorcisable, in its naming, contesting, and reckoning.

In this reading, I open with a discussion of the criminal legal system itself as a deathly archive, a record of dead time and disappeared bodies. I then follow how this violence is obscured by the specter of white supremacy which haunts any effort to view this archival effect. As an example, I interrogate how white supremacist optics are inescapably present in a recent exhibit that pictures Emmett Till's open casket. Here, the phantasmagoric is reversed: no longer fantasies of Black criminality, it is the murderous carceral state that takes shape in banal, daily repetitions of policing and imprisonment but still within the violence of white liberal empathy. As the commentary surrounding the performance makes clear, no mode of seeing, or empathy, is without the violent excess of white supremacy. A fugitive justice takes shape out of this, one that materializes most directly in the shadow of abolition and the concept of the captive maternal. Here, no mode of seeing, or empathy, is unaffected by the violent excess of whiteness. A kind of counter-public—a caring of and for the dead—takes shape out of and against the form of white liberal democracy in which these deaths occur. Here we are challenged to think relationally about our own positions within precarity and violence . . . and to do so in a manner that examines the white supremacist foundations of state forms of justice, a kind of living with and for the dead.

The Archive of Criminology and "Criminal Justice"

The many ways in which to understand social death in relation to Black social life under carceral regimes reveals that criminology and the criminal legal system itself is, in keeping with antiblackness, an archive of nonbeing. It is not unlike the archive of the hold, recorded only through the slave ship ledger that Hartmann describes as nothing more than "a death sentence, a tomb, a display of the violated body, an inventory of property, a medical treatise on gonorrhea, a few lines about a whore's life, an asterisk in the grand narrative of history" (2008b, 2). Criminal justice is a related mortuary in which the death count, those reified massive millions of the carceral state and unnamed numbers of police violence, leaves us with "a descriptive analytics of violence" (McKittrick

2014) found in the serialization of Black death (Williamson 2017). Here, as criminologists, we actively "subject the dead to new dangers and to a second order of violence" (Hartman 2008b, 5), a reproduction and reification of the grammar of death. And if there is no end to killing, then there is no end to counting and the question of mourning, for criminology, is transposed into one of haunting. As Martinot and Sexton write, "to merely catalogue these institutional forms marks the moment at which understanding stops" (2003, 180). In this moment, methodology borders on the uncanny as much as the empirical. Epistemic violence is deathly in a kind of archival loss that is anxiously reiterative: Think of the two million marker of mass incarceration where a world of (Black) social life comes into view only through its disappearance. As Best and Hartman write, "The incompleteness of redress is therefore related to the magnitude of the breach" (2005, 77).

Rarely does the question take shape of what it is to feel undone by such an archive. A field that has little recognition of the Black radical tradition, criminology remains without the vantage points to view—and interrupt—the violence it chronicles, what Saleh-Hanna calls "the ghosted and ghosting essences of White scholarship" (2015). With regard to a ghost criminology, we might think of this as a problem of the unseen or of blocked vision—we must work to see the things intentionally out of our line of sight (McClanahan and Linnemann 2018) and unsee others intentionally foregrounded, such as prisons and police as singular social solutions (Schept 2014). These processes are rooted in efforts to recognize the terror of a failure of non-appearance, of never making an appearance or of being disappeared, while other lives and appearances obstruct the horizon in their dominance. The impossibility of grief and mourning in relation to the political loss of life is well documented (Butler 2006; Woubshet 2015), even in relation to forms of white grievance (Hooker 2017); but little work explores how such endlessness—in its very disappearance of racialized life and death—its ordinary iterative missingness—becomes a kind of unnamed haunting that saturates, exhausts, and is fetishized within criminology, imbuing justice with spectral qualities. Death scenes serve as compulsive focal points of public (white) fascination, while leaving anti-black violence unended and unattended, as pervasive and unnamed as the weather. The dead beg for a listening, a "hearing" beyond the law, in which the complexities and singularities that precede their life as corpses might be named. Sharpe frames this as the foundational question of work in the wake or "wake work," a space where the living and the dead come together in the desire for a way "to inhabit and rupture this episteme with their ... knowable lives" beyond "an archive of hurt and death and destruction that reveals neither her name nor her sex nor any other details of her life" (2016, 51).

If we revisit this "scene" not simply as an empirical measure of chronic catastrophe and gratuitous violence (a criminology that is markedly politically unpersuasive in its own right) but as a site in which other things happen too, things that resist degradation and death, things beyond the frame—we find something still alive. Best and Hartman refer to this as a form of "black noise" that appears as a sonic presence across time and historical records where "claims for legibility before the state" continuously materialize, always present, always in the background (2005, 9).

> Black noise represents the kinds of political aspirations that are inaudible and illegible within the prevailing formulas of political rationality; these yearnings are illegible because they are so wildly utopian and derelict to capitalism (for example, "forty acres and a mule," the end of commodity production and restoration of the commons, the realization of "the sublime ideal of freedom," the resuscitation of the socially dead). Black noise is always already barred from the court. Black noise is defined primarily by virtue of its negative relation to the law.

Counter to criminology, what is most important to justice, then, is precisely that which can never be heard, that which is to be found in remnants, revenants that organize, infiltrate, refuse to die; hauntings that take shape when social violence can no longer be repressed, and out of which specters arise (Gordon 2008, 2011). To borrow from Linnemann's work on ghost criminology,

> Here we might say that we are concerned with the Hauntological—that which is neither present nor absent, alive or dead—the figure of the ghost (Derrida 2006) ... the ways in which the ghosts attached to people, places

and things, linger in the social imaginary. This sort of spectacularization, which moves from the specific singular case . . . to the generalized . . . is also productive of a disembodied, phenomenological residue—a spectre (Hutchings 1999). (2015, 517)

There are many ghosts in the archive of criminology. The specter that demands exorcism, however, is the one least discussed: white supremacy.

The Specter of White Supremacy

State-sanctioned racialized murder depends upon an order of white impunity and pathologies of whiteness that deny ways of seeing and render illegible the racialized dead. The recent Whitney Biennial controversy, in which Dana Schutz (a white artist) displayed her painting, "Open Casket" (2016), an abstract rendering of Emmett Till's death photo, enables us to see how dangerous white visualities take shape as "a pretext for white fascination that is grounded in a desire to see Black suffering," even, yes, if "well-intended" (Carrington 2015). In protest of its exhibition, artist activist Parker Bright positioned his body in front of the painting while wearing a shirt that read "Black Death Spectacle." Christina Sharpe wrote in response, "Where the viewer is positioned in Schutz's painting is looking into the casket. But what white people looked into Emmett Till's casket?" (Mitter 2017). Jared Sexton details how white supremacist optics are complicit in the violence of the showing, past and present, adding:

> Part of the difficulty of addressing the history of violence that killed Emmett Till is that there seem to be no stances that aren't implicated in the same violence, in some way or another. . . . There is, after all, no such thing as unalloyed looking or an image innocent of the violence it addresses. Can we tolerate, and negotiate, this sort of implication? (2017)

The specter of whiteness, its dangerous pathos of white grievance and racial resentment, is one born of complex forms of privilege, denial, passivity, and unreflexive positionality but also terror. Sexton lays out these dimensions when he writes, "This is not to say that Schutz is simply making indulgent autobiographical art, but rather that she cannot, in this work, simultaneously track her pathos and her positioning. She forgets that her interracial maternal empathy for Till-Mobley does not mitigate the fact that she is a white woman depicting a black boy killed, infamously, on the initiative of a white woman. Her empathy is entangled in that initiative" (2017). Here race—and, specifically, Blackness—as a kind of theoretical fetish fulfills an institutional (white) need for multicultural representation and diversity, while perpetuating colorblind logics where whiteness hides/haunts as invisible and depoliticized, a form of spectral power sustained through an intentional non-speaking of or about the everywhere-in-the-room of whiteness. In this way, the precarity of certain bodies and populations are made available (repeatedly) for maiming by way of liberal discourses of empowerment and visibility (2017; see also Puar 2017). White supremacist excess materializes in banality, in pervasive ordinariness. Outrage, as Carrington argues, "is beside the point when it comes to white people's gaze over Black death and Black violation" (2015). For Cooper,

> Black people's witness of racial atrocity is never believed on its own merits. Instead, white people need to be able to pull up a chair and watch the lynchings take place over and over again, to DVR them, fast forward and rewind through them, to smother Black pain and outrage and fear in an avalanche of cold, "rational" analysis. Meanwhile, minds rarely change. The endless analysis never seems to lead to an honest place. (2015)

Indeed, Juliet Hooker insists, "The dead black body was, then as it is now, the terrain on which white fears of loss of political rule and economic dominance were contested" (2017). Unabated Black death, for her, pivots upon an inability for whites to cope with political losses of unearned privileges and unjustified advantages, not a fragility as much as, again, a deadly pathos and pathology. Jefferson refers to this as a historical death-wage where "Nonwhite death induces a collective effervescence for a class that dimly senses itself in a state of ontological flux. The racialized death-wage restabilizes things," an arc spanning between wage labor and racialized police killings and lynchings (2016).

White supremacy then operates as what bell hooks calls "a terrorizing imposition, a power that wounds, hurts, tortures" (1992, 341). An "epistemology of ignorance" (Mills 2014), it is always a project of white will to intentionally misinterpret the world, an emptiness that, unlike the Black body, is the truer realm of deception, of the phantasmagoric.

> The inner dynamic of our attempts to understand its supposedly underlying meaning or purpose masks its ethic of impunity from us. White supremacy is nothing more than what we perceive of it; there is nothing beyond it to give it legitimacy, nothing beneath it nor outside of it to give it justification. The structure of its banality is the surface on which it operates. Whatever mythic content it pretends to claim is a priori empty. Its secret is that it has no depth. There is no dark corner that, once brought to the light of reason, will unravel its system. In each instance of repetition, "what is repeated is the emptiness of repetition," an articulation that "does not speak and yet has always been said" (Foucault 54). In other words, its truth lies in the rituals that sustain its circuitous contentless logic; it is, in fact, nothing but its very practices. (Martinot and Sexton 2003, 58)

Those practices, of course, include the repetition of violence that is, foundationally, the police, the prison, the law. This kind of intractability returns us to an unspeakable terror, one that "renders any real notion of justice or democracy on the map of white supremacy wholly alien and inarticulable" (ibid. 61). This gives way to a shift in the reading and practice of criminology and criminal justice, one that must be understood in the context of violence work (Seigel 2018). The murderous carceral state is grounded in spectral qualities of white, antiblack visuality. The ghost, then, is not the oft-cited specter of Black criminality but the ghosts and phantoms produced by white optics and a visuality rooted in colonization and conquest. As American Studies scholar Matthew Guterl argued in the aftermath of officer Darren Wilson's killing of Michael Brown, "the difficult work now is making sense of how Darren Wilson understands the phantasmagorical qualities of the black body—how all of our Darren Wilsons do. . . . We would illuminate the illogic of racial sight, and, in doing so, we'd acknowledge that we cannot police what we invariably see through the lens of the terrible and the fantastic" (Guterl 2014). Furthermore, state agents of violence present themselves through the optics of white supremacy as maligned, misunderstood, and self-identifying as the true victims. Here we see a "deadly self-pity" and political theater take shape within the police and the military which allows no room for analysis but is ready-made for racialized conflict and the deadly use of force (Chopra 2014; Guterl 2014; Salter 2014; Turner 2019).

The specter of white supremacy and antiblackness then is foundational to the criminal legal system and its diffusion of routinized, everyday forms of violence. It is, of course, especially insidious in its liberal forms. Or, as Claudia Rankine puts it, "Because white men can't police their imagination black people are dying" (2014, 135). Or, as Joseph Pugliese has written, "White supremacy is a priori the exercise of violence through the diffuse iteration of everyday practices that, precisely because of their quotidian status, render the violence unrepresentable to everyone but its targets" (2013, 79). And for Sciullo, "white supremacy is a ghostly regime of intolerance that serves as the justification for police violence and enables structural inequality" (2014, 1399). Furthermore, a small group of criminologists have related projects of policing and the carceral state to the spectral implications of whiteness. For instance, Linnemann et al. use the term *zombification*—the politico-cultural production of those who, in the words of Sharon Patricia Holland (2000), "'never achieve, in the eyes of others, the status of the living'—what we call the *walking dead*" in direct relation to "a long-standing practice of white supremacy and the walking dead, its product" (Linnemann et al 2014, 507, emphasis in original; see also Gamez 2013).

In these accounts, the biopolitical power of the state is a deathly logic. For Mbembé, necropolitics is an important corrective to biopolitical and Foucauldian understandings of race in its focus on surplus forms of life that are targeted for exclusion unto death, both social and physical, in specific ways, legitimized and authorized through the preservation/protection of others. The most original feature of this terror formation is its concatenation of biopower, the state of exception, and the state of siege. Crucial to this concatenation is, once again, race. Or, "in our contemporary world, weapons are deployed in the interest of maximum destruction of persons and the creation of death-worlds, new and unique forms of social existence in which vast populations are subjected to conditions of life conferring upon them the status of living dead" (Mbembé 2003, 39). Within the living conditions of the carceral state, this abjectness takes a potentially unlimited set of racialized forms: stop and frisk (Flacks 2020), arrest, police violence, pretrial detention, the monetization of fees and fines, in addition to its more apparent forms—mass incarceration, solitary confinement, and the death penalty. The stop, the hold, the wake, as Sharpe writes, like "the middle of Canfield Drive in Ferguson, Missouri is lit and filled with and by brutal imagination" (2016, 83). These practices are foundationally racialized in such a way that Gilmore's oft-cited definition of racism operates as a striking definition of the carceral state itself, as "the state-sanctioned or extralegal production and exploitation of group-differentiated vulnerability to premature death" (2007, 247). Similarly, we might think of this system as "the 'slow violence' of state organized race crime, where harms are more attritional, dispersed, and hidden" (Ward 2015, 300). It is also attuned to Lauren Berlant's definition of slow death as when "the physical wearing out of a population and the deterioration of people in that population . . . is very nearly a defining condition of their experience and historical existence" (2007, 754). Or, as Martinot and Sexton argue (2003, 179–180), this is white supremacy's "ethic of impunity, and the violent spectacles of racialization that it calls the 'maintenance of order' all of which constitute its essential dimensions. The cold, gray institutions of this society—courts, schools, prisons, police, army, law, religion, the two-party system—become the arenas of this brutality, its excess and spectacle, which they then normalize throughout the social field" (65).

As Rankine (and Sharpe 2016) write, criminal justice, then, is the space of white supremacist no's, a haunting that permeates the weather of Black life: "Though the white liberal imagination likes to feel temporarily bad about black suffering, there really is no mode of empathy that can replicate the daily strain of knowing that as a black person you can be killed for simply being black: no hands in your pockets, no playing music, no sudden movements, no driving your car, no walking at night, no walking in the day, no turning onto this street, no entering this building, no standing your ground, no standing here, no standing there, no talking back, no playing with toy guns, no living while black" (Rankine 2015). A structure of gratuitous violence, criminal justice can be nothing more than violence in excess for being Black and Black being ... in which case justice is always ghostly and fugitive.

Fugitive Justice

Defend the dead.
—Christina Sharpe (2016, 10)

[H]ow does one rewrite the chronicle of a death foretold and anticipated, as a collective biography of dead subjects, as a counter-history of the human, as the practice of freedom?
—Saidiya Hartman (2008b, 3)

One of the long-standing contributions of the Black radical tradition is its consciousness of and faithfulness to the impossibility of justice. Justice is always foundationally too late, its reparations only able to take shape within a failed and inherently unfinished abolition democracy. To that extent, we can imagine the end of prisons and police but not the irreparable harm they have committed. Justice, according to the black radical tradition, is a placeholder for impossible desires never fully achieved (Best and Hartman 2005). The Movement for Black Lives situates itself in the contours of this claim in its declarative form of love and remembrance: Black Lives Matter, itself a refusal to allow for the infliction of violence against Black bodies to be casually disappeared, and the reminder that those bodies count beyond the descriptives of violence. Out of this a particular conceptualization of the (im)possibility of justice takes shape that must be given account in criminology, a new baseline attuned to the specter of white supremacy and antiblackness—indeed, a kind of ghost criminology. As Vargas and James insist, "What happens when instead of becoming enraged and shocked every time a Black person is killed in the United States, we recognize Black death as a predictable and constitutive aspect of this democracy? What will happen then if instead of demanding justice we recognize (or at least consider) that the very notion of justice ... produces and requires Black exclusion and death as normative?" (2012).

The potential of a ghost criminology is found, in part, in its attention to a movement beyond the terms of the carceral state. There are other ways to conceptualize "justice" and other worlds that take shape in that imagining. For instance, in the time of serial and compounding loss of life, Black mourning, rooted in the legacy of slave narratives, songs, elegies, and spirituals, makes the paradigm of US law and criminal justice one of lamentation. Nowhere is this more evident than in the visuality of contemporary Black death, a kind of image work that summons the torture of slaves (Patterson 1982; Hartman 2008a, 2008b) and twentieth-century lynchings, a national iconography of unspeakable but deeply viewable brutality (Carrington 2015; Cooper 2015). And whether mourning seeks to be public, as with Mamie Till Mobley's remarkable decision to display her son's mutilated body and her own grief, or private as with Lesley McSpadden, clamoring in the August heat for her son's body to be removed from a Ferguson, Missouri street, Black maternal rage is always a kind of counter-public against the form of white liberal democracy in which these lives and deaths are considered ungrievable, vilified, and disprized in fearful white imaginaries. For Sharpe, this is a question of how we "join the wake with work in order that we might make the wake and wake work our analytic, we might continue to imagine new ways to live in the wake of slavery, in slavery's afterlives, to survive (and more) the afterlife of property" (Sharpe 2016, 18). As Sharpe insists, "We're all positioned by the wake, but positioned differently.... it's a way to think about continued precarity and violence, and where you're positioned in relation to it. And it can give people across race a way to understand the visceral responses to this work" (Mitter 2017).

Another way in which to think about this is, as Joy James (2016) names it, through a *captive maternal* politics dedicated to the life and memory of slain children and the construction of sanctuary practices rooted in life against death. This notion of the captive repurposes "the heteronormative category 'motherhood' . . . to reclaim ungendered generative powers to constitute black family, community, and society as a foundation for sanctuaries resisting repression" (James and Alves 2018, 360). In this account, "Sanctuary . . . means an inclusive, queered movement centered on the protection of black and other vilified lives . . . the locus for a unified hemispheric struggle to turn out of a continent sanctuaries securing black lives (ibid.). In James and Alves's account, we see a critical arc to discussions centered on the spectacle of Black death and mourning, one in which the womb itself, and life, not death, is invoked as a kind of "Maternal rage" that

> becomes the political resource for the dispossessed; the captive black maternal (ungendered) refuses death and defeat despite the inevitability of each. Black mothers have embraced the dead as "our" children beyond the criminalizing rhetoric of good victim/bad victim deployed by mainstream media and conservative movements. Relatedly, another strategy has been to "adopt" the forgotten dead as part of the denigrated black community. Mothering and maternal care reclaim the dead to forge community among the grieving and those who struggle. (360–361)

Such work models the possibilities of life's reclamation in its requirement for the utter destruction of white optics, ontologies, and supremacies. If, as Rankine writes, "We live in a country where Americans assimilate corpses in their daily comings and goings. Dead blacks are a part of normal life here. Dying in ship hulls, tossed into the Atlantic, hanging from trees, beaten, shot in churches, gunned down by the police or warehoused in prisons: Historically, there is no quotidian without the enslaved, chained or dead black body to gaze upon or to hear about or to position a self against" (2015), then that normality must be made visible in our daily practices, with the specter of white supremacy visible enough to demand its end, a world of insurgent, unending wake work. Sharpe imagines this space for us as a compelling multiverse:

> Wakes are processes; through them we think about the dead and about our relations to them; they are rituals through which to enact grief and memory. Wakes allow those among the living to mourn the passing of the dead through ritual; they are the watching of relatives and friends beside the body of the deceased from death to burial and the accompanying drinking, feasting, and other observances, a watching practiced as a religious observance. But wakes are also "the track left on the water's surface by a ship; the disturbance caused by a body swimming, or one that is moved, in water; the air currents behind a body in flight; a region of disturbed flow; in the line of sight of (an observed object); and (something) in the line of recoil of (a gun)"; finally, wake means being awake and, also, consciousness. (2016, 21)

Pivotal for Sharpe is the fact that amidst so much death, the wake is also the space in which a particular kind of life through labor and impossible joy develops: Black social life insists, against all odds, its own existence. Those who seek to survive the crisis of the carceral state do so via a call for transformation that has taken shape against the low, grinding hum of life lived for several decades under massification—mass criminalization, incarceration, and police and other forms of violence and premature death. Critical elements of this anti-prison work defy universalizing white epistemologies by what Gilmore describes as a shared grief at the loss of children, one that makes no judgments about innocence, and practices hope by coding crisis as an opportunity where analysis and action allow those targeted for premature death to make visible the ways in which prisons and police negatively organize their families and communities (2007). Against the logic of criminal justice and prisons, they asked instead what might it look like to build around the unimaginable tasks of abolition in practices of everyday life. James writes similarly of the essential vantage points of those directly affected by mass criminalization and the carceral state, where "Love and rage constitute the organizing force behind this gathering coordinated during expanding wars. Love for community, freedom, and justice, for the incarcerated and for the 'disappeared'—for those dying or surviving in war zones" (James 2013, 208; see also James 2005).

In these accounts, the work of fugitive justice originates in life-seeking resistance to violent and premature social and biological death, one in which no other space of existence is possible other than the struggle to end violence (Patterson 1982). These are spaces that foundationally destabilize whiteness as they are neither nostalgic nor universalizing; rather, they depend upon the utter destruction of a cultural formation that has eclipsed all possible futures other than that of white supremacy. A libidinal zone of rage, terror, and denial, the specter of white supremacy and the spectacle of Black death will not end until we address the white supremacist desire for both. Fugitivity relies upon hauntologies and spectralities with their emphasis upon tropes of absence and presence, being and nonbeing, inescapability and lines of flight. To un-think the spectral presence of white supremacy is to think across time and space about the terror of death and its correlates: gaslighting, disavowal, disqualification, and devaluation of knowledges and lives lived under racial capitalism. It is also to think in abolitionist terms, terms that necessarily engage efforts to see the unseeable, speak the unspeakable, and think the unthinkable—a confrontation and form of accountability of the life lived in loss and lamentation. Furtive social architectures, insurgent acts, and fugitive forms of Black social life have long served to threaten white nationalist power, hide insurrectionary activity, decommodify labor, and build communal and sacred spaces of stewardship (Dillon 2018; Neary 2017; Patel 2019; Roberts 2015; Saleh-Hanna 2015). They also foreground the practices of place and alternative figurations against the foundational projects of modernity: white supremacy, capital, and imperialism built upon the twin projects of conquest and slavery, a set of conditions that seek foundationally to dis-remember and dismember people from their own understandings of oppression, land, and community. In these liminal life spaces, counter-discourses of freedom take shape. As a number of contemporary Black feminist scholars lay out, it is the quotidian practices and micro-labors of Black subjects that are central to constructs of "fugitivity" or "taking flight"—that are central to Black futurity (Campt 2017).

The spectrality of white supremacy is linked to this problem of futures. In the time and space of collapsing horizons, we run up against terms like inexhorability, inevitability, exhaustiveness, the cruddy, chronic existences of survival, the noneventfulness of events. We cling to terms like the Gramscian interregnum between the birth of the new world and the death of the old, including the conjunctural and the contingent. Sharpe again offers cues: "What does it look like, entail, and mean to attend to, care for, comfort, and defend, those already dead, those dying, and those living lives consigned to the possibility of always-imminent death, life lived in the presence of death; to live this imminence and immanence as and in the 'wake'?" (2016, 38). We arrive at the possibility—the horizon of abolition—that exists only at the end of this world.

Conclusion

[H]aunting is an emergent state: the ghost arises, carrying the signs and portents of a repression in the past or the present that's no longer working. The ghost demands your attention. The present wavers. Something will happen. What will

happen of course, is not given in advance, but something must be done.
—Avery Gordon (2011, 3)

It is much too late for the accounts of death to prevent other deaths; and it is much too early for such scenes of death to halt other crimes. But in the meantime, in the space of the interval, between too late and too early, between the no longer and the not yet, our lives are coeval with the girl's in the as-yet-incomplete project of freedom. In the meantime, it is clear that her life and ours hang in the balance.
—Saidiya Hartman (2008b, 13)

If the racialized dead are foundational to and simultaneously erased from the project of criminology in various forms of premature, slow, and violent death, then an alternative project takes shape: the raising of the dead as a commitment to an abolitionist politics of the living. This fugitive line of flight assumes the dead have agency in the materiality of the body, engaging social and political processes with a particular kind of phantom ungovernability, interrupting the foundational violences of modernity: slavery and conquest. As corpses, memory, and unnameable affective attachments, the racialized dead do a continuous material work, legitimizing and resisting state authority, governing the living (Stepputat 2014). They connect the violence of their lives and deaths with the present violence of the afterlife—life in the wake. They never cease to point us to the prefigurative work of emancipatory projects, where the living and dead might permanently, publicly co-exist in productive struggle.[1] This is the tension in which multi-coalitions might take shape, built around those fissures, frayings, and moments when racialized regimes, as inventions, fall apart (Camp and Heatherton 2017), those moments when the regime reformulates its efforts to capture all that seek freedom. They mark the unending project of abolition as a visionary scape shaped by moments of refusal and ruptures: discourses of uprising, fugitivity, black futurity, and maroon culture in which Black life has always found ways to flourish amidst death; where interracial conspiracies of freedom are possible, albeit always within a temporal frame of ephemerality. Abolition is a continuous transformation of all that undergirds and structures antiblackness. Death worlds always also reflect a labor of aspiration beyond institutions, including the prison, police, law (Han 2015; Sexton 2011; Martinot and Sexton 2003), beyond societies. This requires a kind of faith that we share the same substance and are part of a political project of horizontal association and solidarity that is shared with the dead (Bennett 2009). It requires the overturning of all forms of non(being) in the unending question of what it would be to think liberation as unachieved and as a project in which we are all bound together, a vision that is foundational to the fugitive hallowed dreaming of the dead.

NOTE

1 For a remarkable set of cultural treatments of wake work, see the wink in Kendrick Lamar's smile in the aftermath of state murder (literally a white supremacist death wish) that concludes his video "Alright," or the Black joy in the savored deep breath (counterpoint to Eric Garner's "I can't breathe") of the dead/alive rapturous child from the front seat of his shared hearse in Flying Lotus's "Never Catch Me."

REFERENCES

Balthaser, B. 2016. "Racial Violence in Black and White." http://bostonreview.net/.
Bennett, J. 2009. *Vibrant Matter: A Political Ecology of Things*. Durham, NC: Duke University Press.
Berlant, L. 2007. Slow Death (Sovereignty, Obesity, Lateral Agency). *Critical Inquiry* 33, 4: 754–780.
Best, Stephen. 2018. *None Like Us: Blackness, Belonging, Aesthetic Life*. Durham, NC: Duke University Press.
Best, S., and Hartman, S. 2005. Fugitive Justice. *Representations* 92, 1: 1–15.
Butler, Judith. 2006. *Precarious Life: The Powers of Mourning and Violence*. London: Verso.
Cacho LM (2012). *Social Death: Racialized Rightlessness and the Criminalization of the Unprotected*. New York: New York University Press.
Camp, J. T., and Heatherton, C. 2017. The World We Want: An Interview with Cedric and Elizabeth Robinson. In *Futures of Black Radicalism*, edited by G. T. Johnson and A. Lubin, 95–107. New York: Verso Books.
Campt, T. M. 2017. *Listening to Images*. Durham, NC: Duke University Press.
Carrington Y. M. 2015. Trauma and Spectacle: Antiblack Violence and Media. *Model View Culture* (24). https://modelviewculture.com/.
Chopra, S. 2014. The Deadly Self-Pity of the Police. https://samirchopra.com/.
Christian, M. 2019. A Global Critical Race and Racism Framework: Racial Entanglements and Deep and Malleable Whiteness. *Sociology of Race and Ethnicity* 5(2): 169–185.

Christian, M., Seamster, L., and Ray, V. 2019. "New Directions in Critical Race Theory and Sociology: Racism, White Supremacy, and Resistance." *American Behavioral Scientist* 63, 13: 1731–1740.

Cooper, B. 2015. "Black Death Has Become a Cultural Spectacle: Why the Walter Scott Tragedy Won't Change White America's Mind," *Salon*, April 8, 2015. http://salon.com.

Davis, A. Y. 2011. *Are Prisons Obsolete?*. New York: Seven Stories Press.

Dillon, S. 2018. *Fugitive Life: The Queer Politics of the Prison State*. Durham, NC: Duke University Press.

Du Bois, W.E.B. (ed.). 2017. *Black Reconstruction in America: Toward a History of the Part Which Black Folk Played in the Attempt to Reconstruct Democracy in America, 1860–1880*. London, UK: Routledge.

Fanon, F. 2008. *Black Skin, White Masks*. New York: Grove Press.

Flacks, S. 2020. Law, Necropolitics and the Stop and Search of Young People. *Theoretical Criminology* 24, 2: 387–405.

Gamez, G. 2013. The Zombification of Formerly Incarcerated and Convicted People: Radical Democracy, Insurgent Citizenship, and Reclaiming Humanity. *Journal of Prisoners on Prisons* 22, 2: 50–75.

Gilmore, R. W. 2007. *Golden Gulag: Prisons, Surplus, Crisis, and Opposition in Globalizing California*, Vol. 21. Berkeley: University of California Press.

Gordon, A. F. 2008. *Ghostly Matters: Haunting and the Sociological Imagination*. Minneapolis: University of Minnesota Press.

Gordon, A. 2011. Some Thoughts on Haunting and Futurity. *Borderlands* 10, 2: 1–21.

Guterl, M. 2014. "Why Darren Wilson Is Driving You Mad." Opinion, *The Guardian*, November 30. http://theguardian.com.

Han, S. Y. 2015. *Letters of the Law: Race and the Fantasy of Colorblindness in American Law*. Stanford, CA: Stanford University Press.

Harding, V. 1981. *There Is a River: The Black Struggle for Freedom in America*. New York: Harcourt Brace Jovanovich.

Harney, S., and Moten, F. 2013. *The Undercommons: Fugitive Planning and Black Study*. Wivenhoe, UK: Minor Compositions.

Hartman, S. V. 1997. *Scenes of Subjection: Terror, Slavery, and Self-Making in Nineteenth-Century America*. New York: Oxford University Press.

———. 2008a. *Lose Your Mother: A Journey along the Atlantic Slave Route*. New York: Macmillan.

———. 2008b. Venus in Two Acts. *Small Axe: A Caribbean Journal of Criticism* 12, 2: 1–14.

Hayes, R. 2015. "Spectacles of Black Death and White Impunity," Op-Ed, Truthout, November 22, 2015. https://truthout.org.

Henne, K., and Shah, R. 2015. Unveiling White Logic in Criminological Research: An Intertextual Analysis. *Contemporary Justice Review* 18, 2: 105–120.

Holland, S. P. 2000. *Raising the Dead: Readings of Death and (Black) Subjectivity*. Durham, NC: Duke University Press.

Hooker, J. 2017. Black Protest/White Grievance: On the Problem of White Political Imaginations Not Shaped by Loss. *South Atlantic Quarterly* 116, 3: 483–504.
hooks, b. 1992. *Representing Whiteness in the Black Imagination*. New York: Routledge.
James, C. L. R. 2001. *The Black Jacobins: Toussaint L'Ouverture and the San Domingo Revolution*. London: Penguin UK.
James, J. 2005. *New Abolitionists: The (Neo)Slave Narratives and Contemporary Prison Writings*. Albany: SUNY Press.
———. 2013. *Seeking the Beloved Community: A Feminist Race Reader*. Albany: SUNY Press.
———. 2016. The Womb of Western Theory. *Carceral Notebooks* 12, 1: 253–296.
James, Joy, and Amparo, Alves J. 2018. States of Security, Democracy's Sanctuary, and Captive Maternals in Brazil and the United States. *Souls* 20, 4: 345-367.
Jefferson, B.J. 2016. "Policing, Whiteness, and the Death-Wage." Essays, *Society & Space*, August 16, 2016. http://societyandspace.org
Johnson, G. T., and Lubin, A. (eds.). 2017. *Futures of Black Radicalism*. London, UK: Verso.
Kelley, R. D. 2002. *Freedom Dreams: The Black Radical Imagination*. Boston, MA: Beacon Press.
Lamble, S. 2013. Queer Necropolitics and the Expanding Carceral State: Interrogating Sexual Investments in Punishment. *Law and Critique* 24, 3: 229–253.
Linnemann, T. 2015. Capote's Ghosts: Violence, Media and the Spectre of Suspicion. *British Journal of Criminology* 55, 3: 514–533.
Linnemann, T., Wall, T., and Green, E. 2014. The Walking Dead and Killing State: Zombification and the Normalization of Police Violence. *Theoretical Criminology* 18, 4: 506–527.
Martinot, S., and Sexton, J. 2003. The Avant-Garde of White Supremacy. *Social Identities* 9, 2: 169–181.
Mbembé, J. A. 2003. Necropolitics (trans. Meintjes, L.). *Public Culture* 15(1): 11–40.
McClanahan, B., and Linnemann, T. 2018. Darkness on the Edge of Town: Visual Criminology and the "Black Sites" of the Rural. *Deviant Behavior* 39, 4: 512–524.
McKittrick, K. 2014. Mathematics Black Life. *Black Scholar* 44, 2: 16–28.
Mills, C. W. 2014. *The Racial Contract*. Ithaca, NY: Cornell University Press.
Mirzoeff, N. 2011. The Right to Look. *Critical Inquiry* 37, 3: 473–496.
Mitter, S. 2017. "'What Does It Mean to Be Black and Look at This?' A Scholar Reflects on the Dana Schutz Controversy." Art, Interview. *Hyperallergic*. http://hyperallergic.com
Neary, J. 2017. *Fugitive Testimony: On the Visual Logic of Slave Narratives*. New York: Oxford University Press.
Patel, L. 2019. Fugitive Practices: Learning in a Settler Colony. *Educational Studies* 55, 3: 253–261.
Patterson, O. 1982. *Slavery and Social Death: A Comparative Study*. Cambridge, MA: Harvard University Press.

Puar, J. K. 2017. *The Right to Maim: Debility, Capacity, Disability.* Durham, NC: Duke University Press.

Pugliese, J. 2013. *State Violence and the Execution of Law: Biopolitical Caesurae of Torture, Black Sites, Drones.* London, UK: Routledge.

Rankine, C. 2014. *Citizen: An American Lyric.* Minneapolis, MN: Graywolf Press.

———. 2015. "The Condition of Black Life Is One of Mourning." Magazine, *New York Times*, June 22, 2015. http://nytimes.com.

Roberts, N. 2015. *Freedom as Marronage.* Chicago: University of Chicago Press.

Saleh-Hanna, V. 2015. Black Feminist Hauntology. Rememory the Ghosts of Abolition?. *Champ pénal/Penal field*, http://journals.openedition.org/.

Salter, M. 2014. Toys for the Boys? Drones, Pleasure and Popular Culture in the Militarisation of Policing. *Critical Criminology* 22: 163–177.

Saucier, P. K., and Woods, T. P. (eds.). 2016. *On Marronage: Ethical Confrontations with Antiblackness.* Trenton, NJ: Africa World Press.

Schept, J. 2014. (Un)Seeing Like a Prison: Counter-visual Ethnography of the Carceral State. *Theoretical Criminology* 18, 2: 198–223.

Sciullo, N. J. 2014. The Ghosts of White Supremacy: Trayvon Martin, Michael Brown, and the Specters of Black Criminality. *West Virginia Law Review* 117: 1397.

Seigel, M. 2018. *Violence Work: State Power and the Limits of Police.* Durham, NC: Duke University Press.

Sexton, J. 2011. The Social Life of Social Death: On Afro-Pessimism and Black Optimism. *InTensions Journal* 5: 1–47.

———. 2017. "The Rage: Some Closing Comments on 'Open Casket.'" Special Features, *Contemptorary*, May 21, 2017. http://contemptorary.org

Sharpe, C. 2016. *In the Wake: On Blackness and Being.* Durham, NC: Duke University Press.

Stepputat, F. (ed.). 2014. *Governing the Dead: Sovereignty and the Politics of Dead Bodies.* New York: Manchester University Press.

Threadcraft, S. 2017. North American Necropolitics and Gender: On #BlackLivesMatter and Black Femicide. *South Atlantic Quarterly* 116, 3: 553–579.

Turner, J. 2019. "It All Started with Eddie": Thanatopolitics, Police Power, and the Murder of Edward Byrne. *Crime, Media, Culture* 15, 2: 239–258.

Vargas, J. C., and James, J. 2012. Refusing Blackness-as-Victimization: Trayvon Martin and the Black Cyborgs. In *Pursuing Trayvon Martin: Historical Contexts and Contemporary Manifestations of Racial Dynamics*, edited by George Yancy and Janine Jones, 193–204. Lanham, MD: Rowman & Littlefield.

Ward, G. 2015. The Slow Violence of State Organized Race Crime. *Theoretical Criminology* 19, 3: 299–314.

Williamson, T. L. 2017. Why Did They Die? On Combahee and the Serialization of Black Death. *Souls* 19, 3: 328–341.

Woubshet, D. 2015. *The Calendar of Loss: Race, Sexuality, and Mourning in the Early Era of AIDS.* Baltimore, MD: Johns Hopkins University Press.

4

From Optograms to X-Rays

How to Conjure a Spectral Criminological Image

MICHAEL FIDDLER

A small glass cube rests on the floor. Measuring 20cm across each of its sides, it contains swirls of aquamarine within greys and blacks. We see trapped air bubbles and floating impurities. Taking a step back, we see the room within which the cube sits. There is a window high in the wall. Light strikes the cube, refracting into a milky white across its edges. It is seemingly lambent with an unseen interior light. The floor is covered in a rust-colored dust. Water appears to have seeped in between the large grey tiles on the walls. The room looks dis-eased. We preemptively wheeze when we see it; it feels as though we breathe in the dust and the mold, take both into the body. What is this exposure doing to the viewer?

Trevor Paglen's site-specific artwork entitled *Trinity Cube* (2015) can be found within the Fukushima Exclusion Zone. In March 2011, an earthquake forced the automatic shutdown of active reactors in the Fukushima Daiichi Nuclear Power Plant. The earthquake caused a 15m tsunami that then disabled the plant's emergency power supply. The cores of three of the reactors subsequently melted. Radioactive material was vented into the atmosphere and surrounding seawater in order to reduce gas pressure within the containment vessels. Iodine-131 and Caesium-137 were released in levels that were "roughly 10% and 20% of those in the Chernobyl accident" (Sato and Lyamzina 2018, 2). As with Chernobyl, it was classified as a "level 7" major accident on the International Nuclear and Radiological Event Scale for its impact on the environment and population (ibid.). An evacuation took place and, as of March 2018, 49,492 people had not been able to return to their homes (Lewis 2018). Prohibited zones exist around the plant itself, while some 15.2 million cubic meters of contaminated soil have either been buried or secured in large black plastic sacks. Paglen's work was part of a site-specific exhibition entitled *Don't Follow the Wind*. The title was taken from the advice given to those fleeing the area in the immediate aftermath of the disaster. The show—something of a misnomer—will not be seen until the exclusion zone is lifted. The cube itself was made from irradiated glass collected from the site with a core of Trinitite; this is the oceanic green man-made mineral that was formed by the melting of sand at the detonation of Trinity, the first nuclear bomb tested near Alamogordo, New Mexico.

My interest in *Trinity Cube* lies in its fusing of differing aspects of the hauntological. A key element of hauntology is the notion of time being "out of joint." In this instance, Fukushima calls to mind other such disasters. This repetition speaks to a failed nuclear utopianism, the literal and figurative fallout of which contaminates a collapsed past, present, and future. This nuclear hauntology is, as Bloom (2018, 226) describes it, a "present [that] is troubled by a traumatic past in a dreaded future." From its irradiated core to its unseen exhibition, it evokes the invisible nature of this specter. It resonates with Buck-Morss's (1989, cited in Hetherington 2001, 26) sense of the spectral inhabiting "the ruined object—in the rubble of history where utopian wishes have been expressed and then suppressed but not fully swept away." I intend to use this particular image of *Trinity Cube* as a jumping off point for a counter-visual that can capture harms that have either been obscured or occulted. Specifically, we will focus on "haunting" ecological harms that span time and cross borders. In order to do so, I will reconfigure Walter Benjamin's "dialectical image" to produce a spectral image that makes those harms visible. This will involve us first taking a journey through the history of early criminological visual systems. The final dialectical image, making use of *Trinity Cube*, will, in turn, be "haunted" by these earlier techniques.

I have spoken about the traumatic effects of harm "haunting" space in earlier work (Fiddler 2018). What I intend to do in this chapter is to set out a framework to understand the *occluded* effects of harm. In that earlier piece, I drew upon spectrality in psychoanalysis and literary criticism to present a method of "reading" spatialized trauma. My focus in this chapter is to explore spectrality within visual systems. So,

Figure 4.1. *Trinity Cube*, Installation view as shown in the exhibition, *Don't Follow the Wind*, Fukushima Exclusion Zone, 2016. Inkjet print on archival paper 11 × 17 in. Copyright: Trevor Paglen. Courtesy of the Artist and Metro Pictures, New York.

we will tie threads between techniques of both capturing and projecting imagery.

Before we proceed to those visual systems, it is important to first revisit the terminology of hauntology itself to see how it—in turn—can inform our understanding of criminological image-making. Fisher (2014, 19) described hauntology's two central elements:

> The first refers to that which is (in actuality is) *no longer*, but which *remains* effective as a virtuality (the traumatic "compulsion to repeat," a fatal pattern). The second sense of hauntology refers to that which (in actuality) has *not yet* happened, but which is *already* effective in the virtual (an attractor, an anticipation shaping current behaviour).

That first element—capturing the compulsion to repeat—is a phenomenon that I explored by tracing the "phantoms" of trauma echoing its effects in space (Fiddler 2018). The second, within the broader framework that Fisher (2014) sets out, establishes the ghost as a figure of "clarification with a specifically ethical and political potential" (Del Pilar Blanco and Peeren 2013, 7). They provide "a productive opening of meaning" and the opportunity to see anew (Davis 2005, 377). Yet, what *do* we see? Let us clarify what is meant by "invisibility" so as to better "see" the spectral going forward.

Following Derrida (2008), we can differentiate between in-visibility and the invisible visible. The former is that which is kept "secret while remaining within what one can call exteriority" (ibid., 90). For example, the body contains organs that may become visible through accident or surgery, but which are ordinarily hidden behind a visible exterior. The latter, the invisible visible, speaks to the temporal aspect of haunting outlined above. Here it refers to "the visibility of a body which is not present in flesh and blood" (Derrida and Stiegler 2002, 38). This is what separates hauntology from ontology. Rather than being and present, the ghost is "neither present, nor absent, neither dead nor alive." Its importance lies in "repetition and the triggering of memory" (Bloom 2018, 228). This fluid interplay between presence and absence are inherent to the image. For example, to capture one's presence in a photographic image or to be caught on film draws attention to our own death, our future absence. As Lippit (2015, 48) puts it, "[b]y capturing single moments in time, all photographs suggest future anniversaries." And, future absences: "we are already haunted by this future, which brings our death. Our disappearance is already here" (Derrida and Stiegler 2002, 38).

In examining these presences and absences, we can begin to capture the unseen or hidden effects of crime and social harm. We will do so by looking at visual systems that have touched upon the invisible and imagination: the phantasmagoria, the optogram, spirit photography, and nuclear visuality. Each of them possesses a "screen" (either physical and external to the viewer or internal and within the viewer) upon which the imaginary is projected. As we shall see, they each illustrate an aspect of the criminological imaginary and spectrality. Each of them contains an aspect of the spectral. In exploring their relationship to the criminological imaginary, they offer the potential to *see* anew. The phantasmagoria of the eighteenth century; the optogram and spirit photography of the nineteenth; and the nuclear in-visible of the twentieth and twenty-first centuries can be used to explore the overlapping of the real and illusory, the secret interiority and visible exteriority. Drawing these concepts together, we will conclude by returning to *Trinity Cube* and generating a "dialectical image." This will see us conjure a specter to inform our understanding of harms that—in Fisher's (2014) phrasing—have the traumatic "compulsion to repeat." We turn first to the phantasmagoria to establish the core concepts of "screen," "image," and "imagination" that we will revisit in the coming pages.

The Phantasmagoria, the Optogram, and Spirit Photography

Derived from the earlier mechanism of Athanasius Kircher's magic lantern, the phantasmagoria was a popular entertainment throughout Europe in the late eighteenth century. Images of performances show audiences huddled in appropriately Gothic catacombs lit by candlelight while a (hidden) lantern projects images onto a diaphanous screen or billowing wall of smoke. The imagery projected in these early shows was predominantly supernatural in tone. Buck-Morss (1992, 22) sees the term itself—phantasmagoria—as "describing an appearance of reality that tricks the senses through technical manipulation." For the audience, the phantasmagoria collapsed seeing and imagining into a singular, thrilling, and spectacular effect.

If the structure of the camera obscura can be seen as analogous to the mind and eye, the phantasmagoria can be read as an externalization of imagination itself. To put this differently, audiences at the performances saw the ghosts and spirits of their imagination taking on form outside of themselves in what was a shared experience. Castle (1988) traces the way in which the term phantasmagoria became latterly associated with internal and subjective experience. Empiricists, for example, would liken the operation of the mind to the phantasmagoria or magic lantern through the projection of "image-traces of past sensation onto the internal 'screen' . . . of the memory" (30). Phantasmagoria then became the term to describe a dream or nightmare-like procession of images. This is what Castle (1988, 29) refers to as the "spectralization or 'ghostifying' of mental space": "[g]hosts were not exorcized—only internalized and reinterpreted as hallucinatory thoughts." The viewing experience was also a *collective* one. This was a shared "hallucination." Buck-Morss (1992, 22) goes further in arguing that the collective experience, where "[e]veryone sees the same altered world, experiences the same total environment" meant that "the phantasmagoria assume[d] the position of objective fact." I have spoken elsewhere of the phantasmagoric nature of nineteenth-century prison architecture (Fiddler 2011). To reiterate, the phantasmagoria consisted of a hidden projector, Gothic imagery, and a screen all combining to elicit a "collective hallucination." So, the prison façade, infused with culturally Gothic meaning, obscured its meaning and prompted a shared imaginative response in those who saw it. We similarly see imagery, mechanism, and imagination intermingle with especial potency with the optogram.

With a nod to Poe's "The Tell-Tale Heart," Campion-Vincent (1999) refers to the optogram as the "tell-tale eye." Simply put, the optogram was an idea first espoused in mid-nineteenth century newspaper reports and fiction (and latterly brought under forensic analysis) that the retina—like a photographic plate—could capture an image. Specifically, it was claimed that the interior of the eye could contain an image of the last thing an individual had seen. For example, the physiologists Franz Christian Boll and Wilhelm Kühne explored these "natural photographs" and claimed to have captured the dying visions of rabbits. This led to the ghoulish idea that an examination of the retina of a murder victim could reveal the identity of that individual's killer. So, akin to a beating heart beneath the floorboards, evidence could reside hidden away within the optical "equipment" that had captured it. In this seemingly diabolical act of image creation, the eye became a medium, transmitting information from beyond the grave to help the living and bring closure to the dead.

Decades after the dismissal of Kühne's findings, the optogram was sufficiently burned into the social imaginary that "the general public and mass media continued to press for the examination of the retinas of murder victims" (Lanska 2013, 55). There was a residual appeal to this Gothicized idea and the potential for a hidden mystery to be revealed. This takes us back to the specter that is also, "among other things, what one thinks one sees, and which one projects—on an imaginary screen where there is nothing to see" (Derrida 1994, 125).

There is something of a literal cadence to this and the optogram. We see this after-image of the Gothic appear in the work of one of criminology's early pioneers. As Rafter and Ystehede (2010, 265) argue, Cesare Lombroso's criminal anthropology was "a Gothic science and . . . Gothicism was essential to its nature." This posited the Gothic as the Enlightenment's "double . . . its dark underbelly" (ibid., 277). Lombroso's (1909) text on spiritism entitled *After Death—What?* featured photographs of "spirits." These images, including a close-up of "the imprint spirit of fingers . . . made due to the soul's radioactive qualities," demonstrate the integral nature of the Gothic to his work (Rafter and Ystehede 2010, 277). Our interest lies in the commingling of imagination, those labeled as "the criminal," and harm within these new representational regimes. It is here then that we can see the importance of spirit photography to late nineteenth- and early twentieth-century Western society. The camera acted as a medium, conversing with an unseen world, materializing it onto a photographic plate. The invisible was being made visible as "ghosts" were captured on film. So, in turn, a criminological imaginary was concurrently materialized by Sir Francis Galton as he employed the techniques of spirit photography to conjure "the criminal."

To contemporary eyes that can easily detect the use of image-editing software like Photoshop, the spirit photography of the turn of the century appears, well, absurd. Simplistic photographic composites depict the departed hovering in mid-air behind mourning loved ones. Some practitioners of the time did suggest that these images were not intended to be seen as capturing the spirits themselves. Rather, they were representations of how the departed had looked in life: "the once recognizable image of a now invisible presence" (Smith 2013, 12). These were to be perceived as "afterimages" of the living. Sir Francis Galton—a prolific Victorian-era polymath perhaps most keenly remembered for developing the "field" of eugenics—employed the technique in order to render visible the criminal type. He achieved this by compositing the headshots of multiple "criminals" to produce a face that represented criminality. In Sekula's (1986, 19) phrasing, Galton engineered a *"purely optical* apparition" (emphasis in original). The portraits were of an imagined Other. In attempting to produce the image of the criminal type, Galton literally effaced those whose images constituted the collective portrait. Their individuality was occluded as they were pushed into illegibility. While derived from a world of empiricism, the act of compositing saw the camera and photographic plate act as a medium to invoke the criminal "Other" from the social imaginary rather than from the Summerland of the spiritual realm. In France, Arthur Batut further developed Galton's composites, referring to his portraits as "images of the invisible" (cited in Hamilton and Hargreaves 2001, 99).

This takes us to our final visual system. Where we have seen the phantasmagoria externalize imagination, the optogram internalize the "screen," and the composited image produce the "virtual," the next example sees the body's interior become the photographic plate. It is there that the effects of social harms persist beyond the level of unaided perception. In a thematic return to *Trinity Cube*, the image that opened this chapter, we will focus our attention upon "nuclear visuality": the visual systems that have emerged around differing applications of radiation and nuclearity. We will look at the intersection of radiation and the image before exploring the body-as-screen. This will frame the discussion that then follows of violences that are slow and obscured. This will help us to generate a dialectical image in the concluding section.

The "Slow Violence" of Radiation and the Body as a Photographic Plate

Alexander Kupny, a health physics technician for Chernobyl's reactor 3, began to take radiation readings in the ruined maw of reactor 4 after starting work at the plant in 1989. Once the concrete sarcophagus encased the ruins, Kupny ventured within, taking his camera with him. It is a curious feature of radiation that—depending upon wavelength—it both occludes and exposes. As we will discuss later, X-rays penetrate tissue, revealing Derrida's in-visible interior. Still photography and film footage taken at the sites of nuclear accidents, by contrast, depict bright comet-like trails or a milky clouding. If Galton's composites were effacing, Kupny's photographs are "cesium, plutonium, and uranium self-portraits" (Brown 2017, G41). Those trails hint at penetrations of the body of the camera operator as well. As Nixon (2011, 6) observes,

> radiological violence [...] is driven inward, somatized into cellular dramas of mutation that—particularly in the bodies of the poor—remain largely unobserved, undiagnosed, and untreated.

The bombings at Hiroshima and Nagasaki first unleashed a monstrous atomic visibility. Victims of the blasts became "photographic effects" (Lippit 2005). The body itself became a photographic plate as patterns of clothing seared onto flesh. They were photograms: "images formed by the direct exposure of objects on photographic surfaces" (Lippit 2005, 94). The body was subject to a "catastrophic light," losing materiality and becoming a visual effect of this "dark atomic room" (ibid.). Interiority and exteriority fused into pure surface: shadows scorched upon walls and stairs. Following the excess visuality of the atomic age, Masco (2006, 4) points to a "nuclear uncanny" that has arisen following the end of the phantasmagoria of nuclearity: "a spectral fascination that distracts attention from the ongoing daily machinations of the U.S. nuclear complex." The uncanny has replaced the spectacular, existential threat of a phantasmagoric nuclear conflict. Specifically, the nuclear uncanny "exists in the material effects, psychic tension, and sensory confusion produced by nuclear weapons and radioactive materials" (28).

This reading of "excess visuality" places primacy upon damage that is spectacular and *instantaneous*. My argument here is to look at prolonged harms and consider a counter-visual to demystify that which has been hidden. This counter-visual will be the spectralized dialectical image of the section that follows. For now, let us focus upon the long-lasting impacts of these trails of caesium, plutonium, and uranium as they create their self-portraits, streaking not simply into camera film, but cells. The corruption that follows prolonged exposure can be difficult to parse. As Masco (2006, 32) puts it, "those exposed to iodine-131 from atmospheric fallout in the late 1950s, for example, may have experienced the first signs of thyroid cancer only in the 1980s." An inability to know of the impact upon one's body is the very stuff of the uncanny. A paranoia follows this "assimilation to a radioactive space (real or imagined)" (ibid.). It haunts the imagination.

To give a clear articulation to this idea of a divine light whose shadow seeds decades- long, generation-spanning cellular aberration, it is useful to return to the example of Chernobyl. Save for distant, long lens shots of exhaust chimneys or the hurried motion of individuals in emergency equipment, this was not a "spectacular" event in the normative sense. Rather, there was an imposed asymmetry of vision. The Soviet state occluded sight. Efforts to represent the disaster were hidden, diminished, and punished. What occurred in the days, months, and years following was the *"production of invisibility"* (Kuchinskaya 2014, 2; emphasis in original). The State-authored representations of the event and its aftermath served to obscure what had occurred: "imperceptible hazards [were] made publically invisible" (ibid., 10). This led, to use Proctor and Schiebinger's (2008 cited in Kuchinskaya 2014, 2) phrase, to the "social construction of ignorance." The schema to understand and make sense of the events were refracted to obscure both what had occurred and what would come to pass. In a simple fashion, this can be illustrated by two voices taken from Alexievich's (2006) oral history of the Chernobyl disaster. A soldier who took part in the cleanup in the aftermath recalled being "warned that in the interests of the State, it would be better not to go around telling people what we'd seen" (ibid., 51). This can be compared with a later re-settler in the area who boldly stated, "I don't think there was any Chernobyl, they made it up . . . Just fairy tales! Stories and more stories" (52–53).

This has a resonance with the ghostly presences that exist behind redacted text. What Kuchinskaya describes was a reduction *and* refraction of imagination. The events of the disaster were State-authored in the social imaginary. They provided a second order of opacity, further obscuring the lingering invisible physical effects of exposure. Biber (cited in McClanahan and Linnemann 2018, 515) describes the "bureaucratic creativity" that produces "social, legal or material barriers" (ibid.). This (visible) black mark of redaction "enable[s] us to glean the existence of the secret, but not its contents" (Biber 2018, cited in McClanahan and Linnemann 2018, 515). It lets us know that a text exists, in the same way that an image exists beyond the frame of a cropped image. This too is Derrida's in-visible. Or, to draw upon phrasing from elsewhere in his work, it is "the secret of kept secrets" (Derrida 2008, 100). This is the jumping off point for a counter-visual that seeks to illuminate the enshrouded and refocus. This is a reaction to disappearance, to *occulting*.

Beck's (1992 cited in Nixon 2011, 62) notion of a "shadow kingdom" is also useful here. The term followed from his 1986 essay "Anthropological Shock" in which he described the "cultural blinding" following the Chernobyl disaster. This blinding referred to the inability of laypeople to ascertain or understand the risk of exposure to radiation. Simply put, "human senses register nothing when exposed to increased levels of radiation danger" (Kuchinskaya 2014, 65). Therefore, we are reliant upon the data of exposure that has been mediated. We emerge, then, into a "shadow kingdom." In an evocative turn of phrase, Beck (1992 cited in Nixon 2011, 62) describes it as

> comparable to the realm of gods and demons in antiquity, which is hidden behind the visible world and threatens human life . . . Dangerous, hostile substances lie concealed behind the harmless façades. Everything must be viewed with a doubled gaze, and can only be correctly understood and judged through this doubling.

Beck's conjuring of the uncanny here speaks to the threat to (unseen) interior states from (unseen) exterior forces. Nixon argues that we pay attention to the temporal gap between the gazes: "beyond the optic façade of immediate peril, what demons lurk in the penumbral realms of the *longue durée?*" (Nixon 2011, 62).

This is an inversion of the phantasmagoria. That saw imagery upon a screen—exterior to the self—"spectralize" interior/mental space. In this instance, the body is the screen containing and surrounded by the monstrous of the imagination *and* intangible. Instead, it is more closely analogous to the optogram. Yet, rather than capturing the moment of death, the body contains the traces, the slow accretions of the violent act. The harms enacted upon body and landscape emerge together from the shadow kingdom: a corrupting toxicity concealed behind those harmless façades.

A valuable framework to further develop this can be derived from Nixon's (2011) notion of slow violence. This speaks to an obscured violence of the longue durée. Nixon (2011) refers to "slow violence" as an alternative to phenomena that are sudden, spectacular, and spatially limited. Rather, a slow violence can capture the impact of events that *slowly* accrete, their borders spreading and indeterminate, their effects prolonged. With the spatial dispersal of both actors and catalysts for slow violence, the destructive, harmful effects may not be felt for generations. As Davies (2018, 1538) puts it, it can be "difficult to epidemiologically and geographically locate blame." It follows, then, that a "major challenge is representational: how to devise arresting stories, images, and symbols adequate to the pervasive but elusive violence of delayed effects" (Nixon 2011, 3). In order to see or make visual the effects of slow violence, we must radically shift our systems of representation to account for these prolonged temporal periods.

The body itself is a marker of forces that transcend and expand beyond human timescales. To give an example once more from Chernobyl, Nixon (2011, 49) describes the "different timelines of mutation—international, intranational, inter-generational, bureaucratic, and semantic" as the radiation plume corrupted both bodily integrity and traversed national borders. It is within the interiority, in Derrida's invisible, that the accretion of these harms accrued. How then to capture that which has been let die across the longue durée? Davies (2018) calls for "slow observations" to capture the experiences of those living within ecological death-worlds. It requires a doubled gaze to determine the harms experienced and being done. In the final section, I will make use of Benjamin's dialectical image as a basis to capture this slow observation. Generating a dialectical image—within a hauntological framework—allows us to read harms that are "out of joint."

Walter Benjamin and the Dialectical Image

To reiterate, so far we have seen how differing visual systems reveal "hidden" dimensions of criminality, punishment, and the criminal, be it the phantasmagoric prison, the retinal burn of the optogram, or the composite's optical apparition. These relied upon a commingling of mechanism, image, and imagination. Likewise, a nuclear visuality evokes the notion of the body itself as a photographic plate. Benjamin's work provides a seam through these elements while also pointing toward the potential for radical change that the image contains. Benjamin saw in both still photography and the moving images the capacity for the visual to capture and reveal heretofore unseen aspects of existence. For example,

> [w]ith the close-up, space expands; with slow motion, movement is extended. The enlargement of a snapshot does not simply render more precise what in any case was visible, though unclear: it reveals entirely new structural formations of the subject. So, too, slow motion not only presents

familiar qualities of movement but reveals in them entirely unknown ones. (Benjamin 1935, cited by Lippit 2005, 62)

This refers, in part, to what Benjamin termed the optical unconscious. There was a fluidity to his use of the term, but the elements that are relevant to our discussion here include its ability to capture unseen phenomena and the revelation of the unconscious drives of a given culture. It could reveal, make visible, that which was unseen or unseeable. It offered a second sight. Benjamin saw the potential for photography to "defamiliarize and denaturalize seeing" (Smith 2013, 220). To clarify, Benjamin was not simply suggesting that the camera could capture phenomena that had gone unnoticed. Rather, it allows us to see things that the eye could not perceive unaided. This takes us to the second aspect, the unconscious drives of culture. Benjamin saw the potential of the image and camera to reveal psychic structures. More specifically, this was part of his

> theory of mass communication that is centred on the notion of the unconscious rather than rationality or reason. Here photography becomes a key medium for the circulation of a culture's unconscious desires, fears, and structures of defense. (Smith and Sliwinski 2017, 9)

Benjamin suggests that a means to reveal these structures could be found in the stereoscope. A stereoscope involves two slightly different images being separately presented to each eye. The viewer's perceptual system then produces a three-dimensional rendering of the image (or, at least, an appearance of planes indicating depth). The image that is perceived with a stereoscope is virtual. It exists solely within the viewer's perceptual system. The resulting image, with the suggestion of depth, has no materiality of its own. Benjamin expanded upon this to develop the notion of the "dialectical image." As the stereoscope produces the virtual from the doubled, so the dialectical image is derived from a juxtaposition of texts. To be more precise, a fragment/image of the past could be brought together with an artifact/image of the viewer's present to produce the dialectical image. As the stereoscope produced the perception of depth, the dialectical image would reveal the "depths of historical shadows" (Benjamin 1999, cited in Smith and Sliwinski 2017,

9). This pulls the "what-has-been" and "now" together in a "flash." This "flash" produces the dialectical image or "constellation." This would see "fragments of the past... surge into the present as the new" (Conty 2013, 474). That shock of the constellation forming is intended to wake the viewer from the "dream state" into which they had sunk. In so doing, they could develop a "new form of critical memory and a new conception of the images of historical time," having had their understanding of "continuous, chronological time" disrupted (Pensky 2004, 188, 192).

The vision would push to one side the gossamer-thin screen of the social phantasmagoric that swirled around the viewer to reveal that which lay beneath. The mechanisms of capitalism, obscured, would be rendered bare. But there must first be the "*imaginative interaction* between reader and text" (Smith and Sliwinski 2017, 11; emphasis added). My aim here is to re-frame the dialectical image. There are certain resonances between Benjamin's virtual dialectical image and Derrida's specter. I want to harness its capacity to examine time out of joint. Simply put, I use it in the coming pages as a medium to conjure the Derridean specter. I see hauntological qualities to the dialectical image in a manner not found in Benjamin's work. Where Benjamin saw it as a way of awakening the viewer from a dream state to view the constellation of past and present, I hope to present it as capturing the "no longer" (but still effective) *and* the "not yet." To be clear, the aim of the remainder of this chapter is not to elucidate the similarities or differences between Benjamin's and Derrida's reading of time (for this, I would direct the reader to Ware 2004 and Conty 2013). At the risk of being reductive, Benjamin is backward looking in generating the constellation of past and present. As Conty (2013, 481) notes, Benjamin "redeems the future by returning to the past, as if the already and the not yet alone could level the trauma of the past." Derrida, by contrast, draws upon the future-to-come, as well as the no longer. It is *this* that I wish to call up.

Using the Dialectical Image to Conjure a Specter

Wilhelm Röntgen discovered X-rays while working in the laboratory at his university in Bavaria in November 1895. Taking what would be the first medical X-ray, Röntgen captured the image of his wife Berthe's hand. *Hand mit Ringen* (hand with ring) provides a close-up of Berthe's left

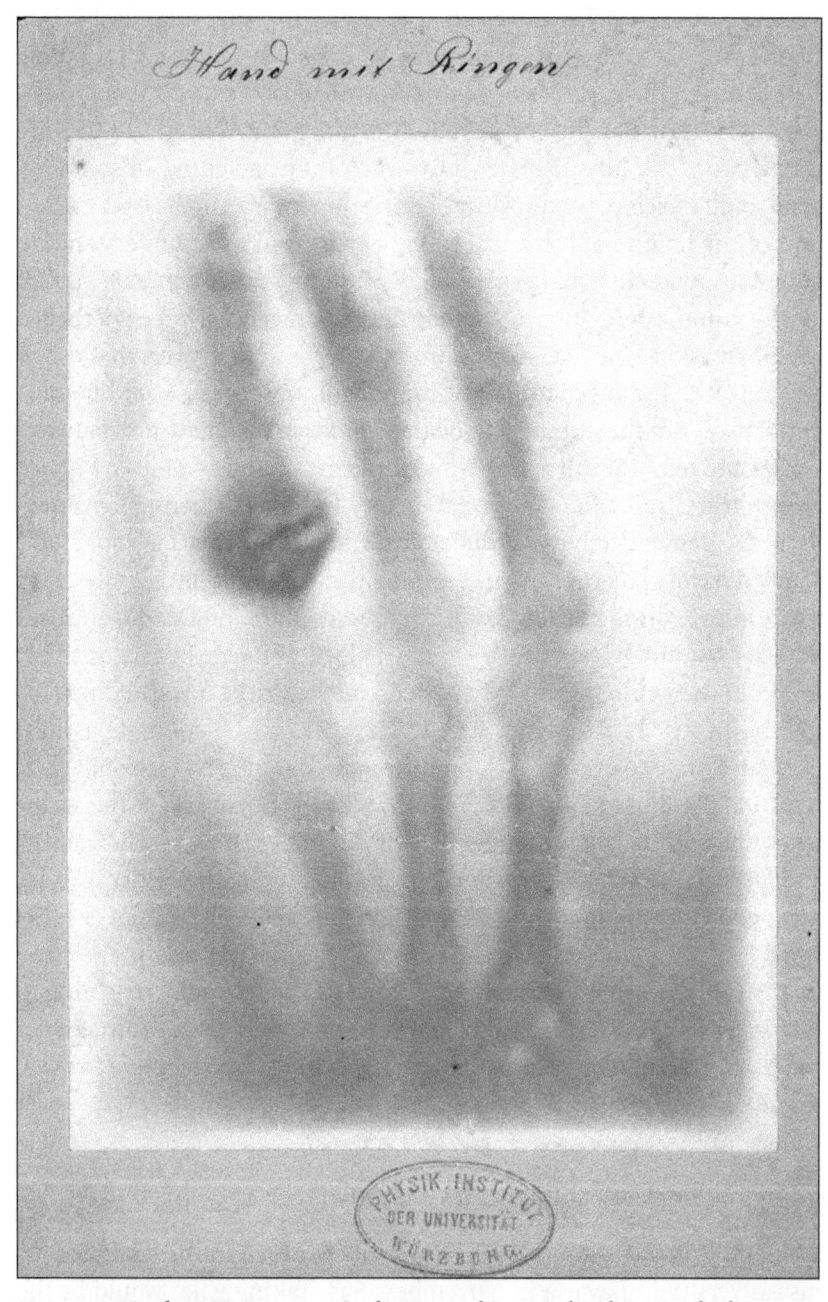

Figure 4.2. *Hand mit Ringen*, 1895. Credit: Pictorial Press Ltd / Alamy Stock Photo.

hand. Or, rather, it depicts the bones of her left hand. In sepia tones, the spindly metacarpals and proximal phalanges of her four fingers seem to coalesce from a milky fog. The fingers of the hand have been degloved, the flesh of the palm melted away under the insistent penetration of the X-ray. Upon seeing the image, Berthe is reported to have said that it brought a "vague premonition of death" (Lippit 2005, 46).

There are two particular aspects of this X-ray I wish to point out. First, Berthe's reaction was prompted by the fragile bones being rendered suddenly obscene in their visuality. In this instance, the thanatotic quality is self-evident: "Berthe peers into the depths of her own body and sees the future, sees her own death" (Lippit 2005, 46). Recall that every photo anticipates an anniversary and the passing of its subject. Second, Lippit draws attention to the "flattening" that occurs with X-ray imagery. Within the X-ray image there is a "simultaneous view of the inside and outside" (ibid., 42). Surface and interiority occupy the same plane; everything is surface, everything is interior.

I aim to use this as our prompt toward producing a dialectical image in the Benjamian mold. Let us juxtapose this image from 1895 of Berthe Röntgen's hand with that of Trevor Paglen's *Trinity Cube* that opened this chapter. In doing so, I am echoing Benjamin's juxtaposition of two images or artefacts to produce a third, virtual image.

My suggestion here is to take this virtual image and use it to channel the spectral, and, in doing so, begin to capture the ethical and political potential of the specter in relation to slow violence enacted upon an ecology "let die" (see Mbembé 2003). It is an intertwining of the "image-making medium within" that Benjamin describes with Castle's spectralization of mental spaces. It is a product of imagination. As such, by focusing upon the imaginary, I also owe a debt here to Haraway's (2016, 12) call for "speculative fabulation in the scholarly mode." In trying to capture something of the social imaginary, it pays to think imaginatively. And so this virtual image will, of course, be a "fabulation." As we have seen repeatedly in this chapter, the spectral featured centrally in the visual systems used in criminology's early decades. From the "tell-tale eye" of the optogram to both Lombroso's and Galton's use of the techniques of spirit photography, these visual systems have been touched by both the otherworldly and imagination. My interest lies in the ways in which they "spectralized" mental processes. In short, they were intimately bound up with the haunting of the criminological imagination. Galton's optical apparitions fed into the imaginary of the criminal "look." The optogram drew upon the Gothic to inform popular understandings of criminality. My use of the spectral in generating this virtual image is intended to echo this relationship with the criminological imagination while also evoking Derrida's reading of the specter. Rather than mirroring Galton's composites that erased differences, I see this dialectical image as drawing out the temporal, haunted constellation of connections between them. Recalling Fisher's (2014) framing of the hauntological, this virtual image captures that which is no longer, but remains effective. We can employ this technique to examine harms that are out of joint as they ebb and flow across time and space. This resonates with Brown's (2001, 149–150) reading of the ghost:

> We inherit not "what really happened" to the dead but what lives on from that happening, what is conjured from it, how past generations and events occupy the force fields of the present, how they claim us, and how they haunt, plague, and inspirit our imaginations and visions from the future.

As I have alluded to above, there are already spectral dualities within these images. If hauntology is centrally concerned with repetition and memory, we can be reminded of that image of the imprint of spirit fingers—caused, according to Lombroso, by the *radioactivity* of the soul—as an echo of *Hand mit Ringen*, making text out of subtext regarding the latter's "premonition" of death. Recall too that *Trinity Cube* consists of a fusing of Trinitite and materials from Fukushima. It is already something of "the past as yet unfulfilled or unfinished" (Bloom 2018, 226). It is "no longer," yet it is also effective as a virtuality as it "colors and shapes the present" (ibid.). I see this dialectical image as generating the spectralized constellation of what "lives on from the happening" *and* provides glimpses of "visions from the future." So, given these spectral traces within the two separate images, what is the virtual image that is produced when we combine them?

Let us first "flatten" the X-ray of Berthe Röntgen's hand onto Trevor Paglen's cube. Let the in-visible bones coalesce with the unseen art display. The two images merge. The flash occurs and a constellation begins to materialize. We can focus first on that element that is no longer, but that lives on in the compulsion to repeat. *Hand mit Ringen* pre-echoes the ulcerations, the excarnation, and eventual amputation of the digits and hands of the early X-ray operators. Hands withered over the decades following prolonged exposure to materials that were *known* to cause biological decay. This was an optogram made real; the killer was contained within the body all along. Then, we begin to see the repetitions. The silence that cloaked the corruption of the bodies of those operators folded itself first around Chernobyl and then, later, Fukushima. This was the secret of kept secrets fashioned by a certain bureaucratic creativity. It was the social production of ignorance. The reader will recall both Kuchinskaya's (2014) description of the occulturation that followed the disaster at Chernobyl, as well as the testimony of those who suffered its effects in Alexievich's (2006) oral history. We can see the constellation connecting with Paglen's "ruined object" that carries within the acts of silencing that surrounded the disaster at Fukushima. Perrow (2014), for example, describes the phenomenon of the "nuclear village" in Japan: "the incestuous relationship between the national government, the utilities and the press." This facilitated a pall of silence. This was subsequently allied with an act passed by the National Diet in 2013 that "provides jail terms for a variety of offenses, including independent helicopter surveillance of the reactors and publishing negative information regarding Fukushima's nuclear power station" (ibid.). What "lives on from the happening" can begin to reveal to us the effects beneath the black marks of redaction.

What then of the "visions of the future"? *Hand mit Ringen* provides us with the shiver at the sense of our mortality. Juxtaposing it with *Trinity Cube* projects that premonition of death and populations "let die" into the longue durée. What I mean by this is that the contamination within and surrounding *Trinity Cube*—the dangerousness of the hostile substance, to paraphrase Beck—will continue. It extends into the future. It suggests future anniversaries where the hazard will endure. The sense of an obscured threat commingling with time out of joint is well summarized by Bloom (2018, 228):

> This threat of intrusion of the past into the future (our present) effects a play with time, reprovoking the feelings of dread of future environmental disasters and failed apprehension captured in the hindsight of what haunts documentation and display.

Hand mit Ringen and *Trinity Cube* are both examples of these haunted and ruined objects. They are monuments to failed utopian futures. These are the "visions from the future" described above. In Gan, Tsing, Swanson, and Bubandt's (2017, G2) phrasing, "Anthropogenic landscapes are . . . haunted by imagined futures." Ecological traumas are inflicted and their effects are out of joint. They transcend time. Flesh is ruined, land is poisoned; all for "'dreamworlds' of progress" that are built upon the ashes of colonized peoples, decimated species, and a corrupted atmosphere. The ghosts of the Anthropocene haunt a future yet to come. Theirs is the double death of fatalities in the present preceding on-going and future death. They birth ghosts of an extinguished future.

I recognize that this is all—at best—a little abstract. We can ground the discussion somewhat by pointing to specific examples of work that juxtaposes imagery and begins to capture "what lives on from the happening." To give concrete examples among this abstraction, we can turn to the work of Goldsmith University's Forensic Architecture team. They investigate State crimes through the forensic analysis of visual data. A recurrent technique across their projects is to patchwork together still images and video footage to establish accurate timelines as well as the spatiality of events. Weizman (2017) refers to this as the "architecture" of an event. Forensic Architecture also refers to "dialectic montage"—Sergei Eisenstein's term to refer to "a juxtaposition in which the meaning lies not in the images, but in the tension or discord between them"—which has self-evident echoes of Benjamin's dialectical image (ibid., 98). They draw upon "before" and "after" satellite imagery as evidence. These act as baselines establishing that which was "normal" and the impact of the "abnormal" event or act. The resolution of commercially available satellite imagery cannot capture a human scale, nor—because of orbit time—can it capture events unless through pure happenstance. It is the opposite then of "time-bound incidents of spectacular violence" (ibid.). Instead, these before and after images reveal an impact that is beyond easy human perception. They illuminate the shadowed time between. Similarly, McClanahan (2019, 11) describes "decoupling" a dialectical image to illustrate a "before" and "after" of the violent extractive processes enacted upon the Appalachian landscape. Although, in that example, the violence was far from slow with the destruction wrought in a matter of days.

In this chapter, we have looked at screens, both corporeal and imaginary. We have sought to trace the presence/absence of the spectral and considered the spectralization of mental spaces. Our journey through visual systems has taken us from eyes containing imagined scenes to imagined figures derived from composited photographs, and bodies haunted by traumas of slow violence. This compilation of visual materials acts as "doorways to other photographs; that is to say, we look at images *through* images" (Weizman 2017, 100; emphasis added). The "tension and discord" of the dialectical image/montage reveals that which was hidden. My use of the dialectical is more abstract. Owing a debt to both Benjamin and Derrida, I see it as means to look *through* and, in so doing, conjure a specter that regards us from the past and haunts our future. To echo Haraway (2016, 12) once more, "it matters ... what descriptions describe descriptions." This is a counter-visual that uses images imagining images.

REFERENCES

Alexievich, Svetlana. 2006. *Voices from Chernobyl: The Oral History of a Nuclear Disaster* (trans. Keith Gessen). London, UK: Picador.

Benjamin, Walter. 1999. *The Arcades Project*. Cambridge, MA: Belknap Press of Harvard University Press.

Bloom, Lisa E. 2018. "Hauntological Environmental Art: The Photographic Frame and the Nuclear Afterlife of Chernobyl in Lina Selander's Lenin's Lamp." *Journal of Visual Culture* 17, 2: 223–237.

Brown, Kate. 2017. "Marie Curie's Fingerprint: Nuclear Spelunking in the Chernobyl Zone." In *Arts of Living on a Damaged Planet: Ghosts of the Anthropocene*, edited by Anna Tsing, Heather Swanson, Elaine Gan, and Nils Bubandt, G33–G50. London, UK: University of Minnesota Press.

Buck-Morss, Susan. 1992. "Aesthetics and Anaesthetics: Walter Benjamin's Artwork Essay Reconsidered." *October* 62: 3–41.

Campion-Vincent, Véronique. 1999. "The Tell-Tale Eye." *Folklore* 110: 13–24.

Castle, Terry. 1988. "Phantasmagoria: Spectral Technology and the Metaphorics of Modern Reverie." *Critical Inquiry* 15, 1: 26–61.

Conty, Arianne. 2013. "They Have Eyes That They Might Not See: Walter Benjamin's Aura and the Optical Unconscious." *Literature & Theology* 27, 4: 472–486.

Davies, Thom. 2018. "Toxic Space and Time: Slow Violence, Necropolitics, and Petrochemical Pollution." *Annals of the American Association of Geographers* 108, 6: 1537–1553.

Davis, Colin. 2005. "État Présent: Hauntology, Spectres and Phantoms." *French Studies* 59, 3: 373–379.

Del Pilar Blanco, Maria and Peeren, Esther. 2013. "Introduction: Conceptualizing Spectralities." In *The Spectralities Reader: Ghosts and Haunting in Contemporary Cultural Theory*, edited by Maria Del Pilar Blanco and Esther Peeren, 1–28. London, UK: Bloomsbury.

Derrida, Jacques. 1994. *Specters of Marx* (trans. Peggy Kamuf). London, UK: Routledge.

———. 2008. *The Gift of Death*, 2nd ed. (trans. Davis Willis). London, UK: University of Chicago Press.

Derrida, J. and Stiegler, B. 2002. "Spectographies." In *The Spectralities Reader: Ghosts and Haunting in Contemporary Cultural Theory*, edited by Maria Del Pilar Blanco and Esther Peeren, 37–52. London, UK: Bloomsbury.

Fiddler, Michael. 2011. "A 'System of Light Before Being a Figure of Stone': The Phantasmagoric Prison." *Crime, Media, Culture* 7, 1: 83–97.

———. 2018. "Ghosts of Other Stories: A Synthesis of Hauntology, Crime and Space." *Crime, Media, Culture*. doi.org/10.1177/1741659018788399

Fisher, Mark. 2014. *Ghosts of My Life: Writings on Depression, Hauntology and Lost Futures*. Hants, UK: Zero Books.

Foucault, Michel. 1990. *The History of Sexuality*, vol. 1 (trans. Robert Hurley). New York: Vintage Books.

Freccero, Carla. 2006. *Queer/Early/Modern*. Durham, NC: Duke University Press.

Gan, Elaine, Tsing, Anna, Swanson, Heather, and Bubandt, Nils. 2017. "Introduction: Haunted Landscapes of the Anthropocene." In *Arts of Living on a Damaged Planet: Ghosts of the Anthropocene*, edited by Anna Tsing, Heather Swanson, Elaine Gan, and Nils Bubandt, G1–G16. London, UK: University of Minnesota Press.

Hamilton, Peter and Hargreaves, Roger. 2001. *The Beautiful and the Damned: The Creation of Identity in Nineteenth Century Photography*. Hampshire, UK: Lund Humphries.

Haraway, Donna. 2016. *Staying with the Trouble: Making Kin in the Chthulucene*. Durham, NC: Duke University Press.

Hetherington, Kevin. 2001. "Phantasmagoria / Phantasm Agora: Materialities, Spatialities and Ghosts." *Space & Culture* 11 and 12: 24–41. https://sites.ualberta.ca/

Kuchinskaya, Olga. 2014. *The Politics of Invisibility: Public Knowledge about Radiation Health Effects over Chernobyl*. London, UK: MIT Press.

Lanska, Douglas J. 2013. "Optograms and Criminology: Science, News Reporting, and Fanciful Novels." *Progress in Brain Research* 205: 55–84.

Lewis, Robin. 2018. "Fukushima's Nuclear Exclusion Zone: 7 Years On." Social Innovation Japan. *Medium*. http://medium.com

Lippit, Akira Mizuta. 2005. *Atomic Light (Shadow Optics)*. London, UK: University of Minnesota Press.

Lombroso, Cesare. 1909. *After Death—What?*. Boston, MA: Small, Maynard and Company.

Masco, Joseph. 2006. *The Nuclear Borderlands: The Manhattan Project in Post-Cold War New Mexico*. Oxford, UK: Princeton University Press.

Mbembé, Achille. 2003. "Necropolitics." *Public Culture* 15, 1: 11–40.

McClanahan, Bill. 2019. "Earth-World-Planet: Rural Ecologies of Horror and Dark Green Criminology." *Theoretical Criminology* doi.org/10.1177/1362480618819813

McClanahan, Bill and Linnemann, Travis. 2018. "Darkness on the Edge of Town: Visual Criminology and the 'Black Sites' of the Rural." *Deviant Behavior* 39, 4: 512–524.

Nixon, Rob. 2011. *Slow Violence and the Environmentalism of the Poor*. London, UK: Harvard University Press.

Pensky, Max. 2004. "Method and Time: Benjamin's Dialectical Images." In *The Cambridge Companion to Walter Benjamin*, edited by David Ferris, 177–198. Cambridge, UK: Cambridge University Press.

Perrow, Charles. 2014. "Five Assessments of the Fukushima Disaster," Nuclear Risk, Nuclear Energy, *Bulletin of the Atomic Scientists*. https://thebulletin.org/

Rafter, Nicole and Ystehede, Per. 2010. "Here Be Dragons: Lombroso and the Gothic, and Social Control." In *Popular Culture, Crime and Social Control*, edited by Mathieu Deflem, 263–284. Bingley, UK: Emerald.

Sato, Akiko and Lyamzina, Yuliya. 2018. "Diversity of Concerns in Recovering after a Nuclear Accident: A Perspective from Fukushima." *International Journal of Environmental Research and Public Health* 15, 2: 350.

Sekula, Allan. 1986. "The Body and the Archive." *October* 39: 3–64.

Smith, Shawn Michelle. 2013. *At the Edge of Sight: Photography and the Unseen*. Durham, NC: Duke University Press.

Smith, Shawn Michelle and Sliwinski, Sharon. 2017. "Introduction." In *Photography and the Optical Unconscious*, edited by Shawn Michelle Smith and Sharon Sliwinski, 1–31. London, UK: Duke University Press.

Ware, Owen. 2004. "Dialectic of the Past/Disjuncture of the Future: Derrida and Benjamin on the Concept of Messianism." *Journal for Cultural and Religious Theory* 5, 2: 99–114.

Weizman, Eyal. 2017. *Forensic Architecture: Violence at the Threshold of Detectability*. New York: Zone Books.

PART II

The Necrotic and (In)corporeal

5

(Dis)Posing of "Toxic Necro-Waste"

Managing Unwanted Ghosts

DANIEL ROBINS

With this collection focusing on what the ghostly figure offers to the study of criminology, it's fitting that this chapter concentrates on the management of the dead body. The dead are where the ghost so often comes from; a haunting specter of something or someone now gone, be it as a shadowy figure at the end of the hallway, or as a memory from times since passed. The ghost reminds us that our dead are seemingly no longer present in the way that they were, but also ensures us that they are not entirely absent either. It flickers as a reminder of our loved ones. However, there are cases where the deceased has committed so much harm and depravity that their presence is not wanted, and their ghostly apparition must somehow be managed in public life as unwanted excess. In keeping with this idea, the chapter focuses on the death and disposal of UK serial killer, Ian Brady, to assess how British society contended with and attempted to control the emergence of his "ghost" in public life.

Brady died of a chronic pulmonary obstruction in May 2017 in Ashworth High Security Psychiatric Hospital, where he had been imprisoned since 1986. He had been transferred there from Durham High Security Prison, where he was originally incarcerated for his crimes in 1966. Along with his partner, Myra Hindley, Brady murdered five children—torturing and raping four—before burying them on the Saddleworth Moor in Northern England. The crimes were shocking and, while they were committed back in the 1960s, the scars they left on British culture remain. I was born nearly thirty years after the murders, and Brady and Hindley had long been behind bars as I spoke my first words. Yet, their mugshots have retained a sense of power as they echoed throughout British culture, reinforcing the heinousness of Brady and Hindley, and haunting the public imagination (Glancey 2002). It would turn out that Brady, even in death, would maintain a haunting presence.

Given his notoriety, it is of no surprise that Brady's death was headline news. When the immediate publicity had died down, it was not long until attention turned to how his corpse would be managed. It was reported that Christopher Sumner, the coroner charged with holding the body after its transport from Ashworth Hospital, refused to release it from his care until two assurances had been met. First, there had to be confirmation that Brady's ashes would not be spread on the Saddleworth Moor where four of the victims had been buried and one is thought to still lie. Second, there had to be a funeral director and crematorium willing to take control of the body (Robins 2017). By October 2017, there was still no verified authority willing to handle the body by choice. In these situations, the Public Health Act 1984 requires the local authority to take control of the disposal, and they then contracted a funeral director and crematorium to handle the discard. In the end, Brady would be cremated without a funeral and his ashes would be deposited into the sea in a biodegradable urn. Throughout, there was an intention to distance the remains, and this final discard showed certain similarities to Osama bin Laden's burial at sea, which was underpinned by the drive to make the remains disappear from social life through the depthless abyss of the sea (Schrift 2016).

While media attention turned quickly toward what would happen to Brady's corpse, academic attention on this type of subject has been relatively minute. This is especially surprising as wider literature has noted how significant the dead body is for studying the death process (Walter 2002). For instance, Tarlow (2002) has argued that the dead body is imbued with meaning and that, as social scientists, we should use it as a vehicle to inform wider understandings of the social world that are generated through a study of the social (dead) body. Brady's corpse is a valuable focal point of study as it is imbued with meaning. It's a potential marker for understanding the more intricate details of death disposal as it is what the process revolves around (Young and Light 2016). Therefore, in this chapter, Brady's corpse is used as a focal point to assess how UK death disposal practices contend with a "monstrous other" (Troyer 2008) through the management of his remains.

There remains a gap in criminology for this sort of exploration. Whilst attention has been paid to human remains in criminology and its surrounding disciplines (Moon 2014; Shute 2014), this focus is limited. Explorations have provided a strong foundation for the corpse's value in criminology, but these have often been removed from the death disposal process. For example, Penfold-Mounce (2016) has analyzed what the consumption of the image of criminal celebrity means for public reactions to death. Moreover, Troyer (2008) has assessed how the corpse could provide challenges for the legal system when it is a victim of a crime. The corpse is difficult to contend with in the legal system as it cannot stand trial or be a credible witness. As such, a rich criminological discussion can be had on the management of the human remains, which is, as of right now, incomplete.

A "ghost" criminology provides a means to achieve this as it offers a conceptual tool for exploring how Brady is dead in the physical sense, but very much alive in a symbolic one. He is no longer present in the same way as the living, breathing, talking person; but neither is he absent from social life. He exists as an unwanted ghost. While alive, he was segregated in Ashworth High Security Psychiatric Hospital. His body was being controlled by a medico-legal space, becoming a subject of the criminal justice system (Foucault 1991), as well as a "medical personage" (Foucault 2001, 213). A conflict emerged as, when he died, Brady's body was no longer subject to this medico-legal control, but the level of his notoriety (Penfold-Mounce 2016) and heinousness of his crimes meant that death did not release his identity either (Denham 2019). It will therefore be argued that Brady's remains continue to embody his criminal identity, which underpins the problems it poses for UK death disposal practices as it seeps out of control despite still requiring it.

Methods of control are used to make sure that the remains enter into the "right" place and are handled by the "right" people. It is suggested that these management techniques reveal the symbolic "toxicity" of Brady's remains, which must be kept at a safe, symbolic distance (Douglas 1966/2002). Part of this distancing is to conceptualize Brady as a monster, whereby the only way that his ghost can be safely present in society is through its manifestation as something other than human. If he was considered as human, the symbolic distance closes, and his toxicity seeps into public life, as he becomes not so different from you or me. Of course, since his arrest this has always been the case. The only difference now is that he leaves the walls of the institution and falls into uncharted territory as a non-living body retaining the identity of his living self. The dynamic has shifted and new techniques are required to present the ghostly figure of Brady as monstrous.

The argument is that these techniques are contained within the process of disposal, which is considered as a procedure for organizing the meaning of Brady's ghost (Munro 2001). The toxicity of Brady's remains affects how his image is arranged throughout disposal as work is done to ensure that it does not seep back into the realms of the living. It is this toxicity of the remains that informs a process of their (re)ordering. There is an attempt to order them by maintaining and emphasising the distance of their "humanity" by reinforcing their "monstrosity" through management techniques designed to combat the harms of this toxicity. After a process of reordering, the ghost of Brady is (re)presented as a monster in death, as much as he was in life. This organization is explored through four particular spaces of disposal, otherwise known as "conduits of disposal" (Hetherington 2004, 164). These conduits are where Brady's meaning flows and changes, and this work of designing an acceptable version of his ghost takes place. They are battlegrounds for managing Brady's (re)emergence into public life as a ghostly figure. The four conduits of disposal are: Ashworth Hospital, the "Monster" Morgue, the crematorium, and the sea where the ashes were discarded. The chapter concludes that ghost criminology provides a unique insight into the management of the criminal dead as it draws attention to how the state accounts for, and is not held accountable by, the management of the toxicity entangled within the remains of heinous criminal actors.

Brady's Remains: "Toxic Necro-Waste"

The corpse is a vehicle for understanding wider death practice as it is something that the death disposal process can be considered to revolve around (Walter 2002). As Olson (2016) argues, there are many different ways of knowing a corpse, and each of these provides different insights into wider management practices governing the work of death professionals and public understanding. For clarity, the corpse can be known in almost countless ways, a few examples being as a source of contamination

(Douglas 1966/2002), as sacred (Davies and Rumble 2012), or as an ecological entity (Plumwood 2008). If the corpse is known as sacred, the moral underpinnings of disposal methods, such as burial or cremation, may be drawn into focus. Specifically, Saad (2017) has noted how cremation by fire is morally inadequate for Muslim families. In Muslim culture, the body must be carefully disposed of as a whole vessel, with the face pointed toward Mecca. Reducing the body down to an ash would be undignified as it means that this ritual would not be achieved.

A different analogy, and one arguably more important to this chapter, is the analogy of human remains as material waste, otherwise known as "necro-waste" (Olson 2016, 327). Necro-waste is a conceptual methodology that can be used to explore the ways that the death disposal process accounts for excess materials in cremation or burial. For example, there are significant waste management issues emerging from death disposal technologies. In 2012, an initiative was introduced into the UK whereby 50% of crematoria emissions would need to be filtered due to concerns over mercury emissions from dental amalgam polluting the atmosphere (Rumble et al. 2014). A waste methodology draws attention to how these mercury emissions are policed, or indeed recycled, as part of a wider environmental initiative to reheat crematoria.

In order to explore the management of Ian Brady's corpse, this chapter has taken a few of these conceptual methodologies forward to create a new one called "Toxic Necro-Waste" (Robins 2017, 40). Olson's (2016) notion of necro-waste underpins this since toxic necro-waste aims to provide more depth to the particularly toxic aspects of waste management that disposal presents. Waste is a very open term that can be subject to a variety of different meanings. As much as one could know waste as abject, contaminating, and generally unwanted, it can also be a term used to think about the reuse of waste materials. An example of this is found in natural burial. The culture of natural burial is concerned with using the dead body to give back to the natural environment (Davies and Rumble 2012). As the decomposing body is the means for achieving this, the classifications of decomposing flesh are positive as these waste materials are recyclable and in many ways valuable (Krupar 2018). Thus, how waste is known varies across cultures of disposal.

Toxic necro-waste is specifically used as a concept to overcome this openness of waste, drawing attention to the strategies for managing its horrifying particulars. It builds on Mary Douglas's (1966/2002) work on *Purity and Danger*, where she argues the significance of studying "dirt." Dirt is matter that is categorized as something that doesn't belong, falling out of accepted boundaries. It is not absolute, but rather is relational to culture. Dirt, for Douglas, is culturally specific. It falls through classification as "matter out of place" (Douglas 1966/2002, 44), causing pollution to social life. Her example of this is the book of Leviticus from the Bible. In this book, safe categories of food for consumption are established, which have more or less informed the eating habits in Western cultures. They are generally found in three categories: land animals, which have four legs; air animals, which have two legs and wings; and sea animals, which have no legs, but do possess gills. Animals such as spiders and snakes are not deemed safe to eat in Western cultures as they defy these classifications. In the West, they are not eaten and are seen as polluting to the dinner plate. Matter frequently slips outside of boundaries and it is a task of social life to (re)order this dirt and to (re)figure its pollution.

Toxic *necro-waste* is a conceptual methodology that has been created to explore issues of managing the particularly harmful, contaminating surplus that emerges from the dead body and defies classification (Douglas 1966/2002). Contaminating means both physical and social but, in Brady's case, there is more significance in the social contaminating that the remains cause. The argument is that by conceptualizing Brady's remains as "toxic," more can be gathered from the management techniques used to police where the remains can go and who can control them. Specifically, this social contaminating can be observed through the efforts taken by the state to ensure that the remains would not pollute public life. As established, the coroner for Brady's case, Christopher Sumner, refused to release the remains from the morgue. One of the reasons for this included concerns that the ashes would be spread on Saddleworth Moor, a space synonymous with the crimes as it was where many of the victims were buried. Vital to this anxiety was that there was no verified authority ready to take control of the remains as no death professional was willing to work with them and, as such, there was no certainty that the remains would stay away from Saddleworth Moor. The ashes were not contaminating in the sense that they would destroy any of the local wildlife, or physically poison the ground to stop things from growing there. As far as it's known, they were not radioactive, nor did they contain any harmful chemical combinations that could survive a cremation. The contamination was a purely social one as it is thought that one of the victims, Keith Bennet, is still buried on the Moor, and any scattering of Brady's remains would affect the dignity of the families of all of the victims and arguably of broader society by polluting Bennet's burial site.

This conceptualization of Brady's remains as toxic necro-waste therefore shows how harmful they can be when not properly controlled. The remains still embody his criminal identity as somebody evil, heinous, and monstrous. The managing of him as symbolically toxic is a reflection of this monstrous character. If his corpse were just an empty vessel, these extra lengths used to manage him would be unnecessary. He has arguably always been toxic since his arrest, but that toxicity has now left a space designed to combat it. Leaving this space, but also retaining that symbolic toxicity, means that new management techniques must be adapted by an authority that is not used to containing this sort of toxicity. These authorities of the coroner, funeral director, crematorium staff, as well as wider local authority staff, must work to contain this pollution, stop it from seeping back into public life, and infecting the rest of the population. This is where the absence/presence of Brady's monstrous image comes into sharper focus.

The key contention for this chapter is that this toxic necro-waste seeps into public life when the image of somebody like Brady is presented as human. The problem from this would be that the symbolic distance between Brady and the public is closed in these cases. He becomes more like us, revealing the uncomfortable reality that a fellow human being is capable of killing and torturing children. Therefore, work must be done by death professionals to ensure that this image of humanness is not communicated and, when his presence does inevitably seep through the cracks of the disposal process, he must be presented as a monster, with his ghostly figure presented as being as distant from human as possible. In this sense, the analogy of Brady's remains as toxic necro-waste reveals unique insights into his disposal and how exactly his ghostly manifestation was controlled. Disposal becomes a process of symbolic ordering, whereby the meaning of Brady's remains is tightly controlled, and (re)presented in a less dangerous form (Douglas 1966/2002). Not as human, but as monster (Grixti 1995).

Disposing of "Toxicity"

The death disposal process is therefore a way of (re)ordering the disordered, from "dirty" and chaotic to "clean" and ordered. This (re)ordering is the doing of work to maintain a monstrous image. Disordered and dirty in Brady's case would be if he was (re)presented as human. "Clean" and orderly is if he is (re)presented as monster. He fits into a symbolic order that negates some of his threat if he is (re)presented as monster since he is further distanced; keeping human beings away from the pollution of his acts. We can rest assured that a significant distance separates him, the monster, and us, the human.

The significance of disposal as a process is vital to this. That is, disposal is the process of meaning management that distances Brady and attempts to stop his toxicity from seeping into public life. Ideas such as these have been reflected by Munro (2001). For Munro, disposal is about managing a thing's meaning; particularly any kind of excess in meaning that it may have. He largely works from Mary Douglas's (1966/2002) *Purity and Danger*, to argue that a thing's relation to order and safety is dependent on the management of its meaning during the process of its disposal. Neutralizing the danger of dirt is achieved through its ability to be displaced from disorder and into a category of order. In this case, any residues of humanness are displaced with monstrosity.

This reflects Cohen's (2007) argument that the monster frequently disappears and (re)emerges, as it is not easily classified. It is a hybrid of things that come from different classifications. Cohen's point is that its distortion as parts of the many means that the monster emerges at times of crisis, incorporating a variety of parts into one. Drawing on Cohen's notion of the monster, this chapter leans in the direction that the monster emerges to contend with materials having a classificational crisis. It is a patch that is made from differently classified fragments and placed onto materials that defy order. Essentially, with Brady's remains, attempts are made to patch the wide residues of humanness tied to his dead body. These specks of the *human* are toxic as they fall out of the classifications of *loved* and *missed* that underpin how the dead human being is culturally understood. Brady's remains mock and challenge these discourses by being a material not physically distinct from other human remains, while at the same time being the remnants that committed inhuman, evil acts. By classifying the remains as monstrous, the varying out-of-place notions of humanity can be brought together into a parallel image that crafts them as something not quite like us. Therefore, displacing humanity with monstrosity is a way to deal with the classificational crises entangled within toxic necro-waste. The monster is a classificational tactic used to mediate a distance between Brady and the population.

Yet, Brady had been disposed of from public life as a monster while alive and, since he already was a monster, some of those patches of humanity have been drawn together pre-death. His death strengthens his monstrosity as his classificational crisis only worsens and more fragments of humanity must be absorbed into the monstrous sign. The role of disposal is in maintaining this sign of the monster post-life. To do this, a concession is made; media and state institutions only (re)order and clean Brady by making him into a monster. Rather than shift Brady's humanity, attention is instead turned to displacing the sign of "monster" into one of cleanliness by emphasizing the distance that it has from human beings. Thus, "monster" puts him in his place. Through being monstrous, he becomes the ordered haunting figure. He is far enough removed that any residue of humanness will not seep into public life. The mission of Brady's disposal is therefore to ensure that he only manifests as the monster to cease his pollution from leaking into public life.

The problem is that the ghostly figure of Ian Brady is an absent presence, manifesting at certain moments in the death disposal process. He cannot be fully neutralized and made fully absent, which is why his manifestation as monster occurs in the first place. His ghost is a constant reminder that his disposal may never be fully complete. The only compromise that is made is an attempt to maintain him as a distant being. This discussion resonates with Hetherington's (2004) work on disposal, where he conceptualizes it as a process for managing the absence of a thing. Hetherington (2004, 163) states that disposal prompts "a question of how we account for or are held accountable by that which we have tried to dispose of but have left unfinished." Thus, Brady's ghost also asks us to consider how we are held accountable by our attempts to cease his pollution. Who are these people that design the manifestation of his ghost? How does it take place? Why is it necessary? The rest of this chapter will focus on these questions by exploring four significant "conduits" (Hetherington 2004, 164) of disposal. It is in these spaces that Brady's pollution is tackled and his status as monster is most clear. These conduits of disposal are battlegrounds where his meaning is pulled into contention and the work of maintaining his monstrosity takes place. They are Ashworth High Security Psychiatric Hospital where he died; the "Monster" Morgue where he was held alongside the Manchester Bomber, Salman Abedi; the crematorium where his body was turned into ash; and the sea where those ashes were discarded.

Conduit 1: Ashworth High Security Psychiatric Hospital

The disposal of Brady's body starts at the place where he died: Ashworth High Security Psychiatric Hospital. This space is suited to controlling the toxicity from the living being. A place with bars and security, its space fulfills a carceral role for housing those who commit dangerous acts. Yet, it's also a medical space. It's seemingly a space to control the toxicity emanating from those who are not solely bad, but also mad (Foucault 2001). It therefore fulfilled a role in keeping Brady's toxicity from seeping into public life while he was alive. However, after his death, it's no longer a space that can contain him.

The challenge for this conduit is whether punishment necessarily ends at death. In Brady's case, his remains do not cease holding his criminal identity. They are bound together; the body being a marker for this long after his death (Shilling 2005). The body was the vessel that carried out the crimes and, as such, has just as much of a role in the crimes as the character of Brady does. In this way, the body carries on being a marker for the acts committed by Brady after death. It is a symbolically powerful entity that must be managed as being a part of Brady, rather than being separated from his actions after his life has ended.

This retaining of criminal identity only complicates the practicalities of disposing of a corpse. The corpse is an entity that must be disposed of for legislative reasons and care must be taken to ensure that it is handled in accordance with the Public Health Act (1984). It is of course a potential source of disease; it can decompose and begin to leak. Places like Ashworth Hospital are not designed for the long-term management of the dead body and so it must be transported to an institution that is designed to contain decomposition. In this transport, however, there is a trade-off. Ashworth Hospital is a state-sanctioned acceptable place to keep the public safe from Brady's toxicity, but cannot hold the deceased for a long period of time. Various death disposal spaces, such as the crematorium grounds or cemetery, are where the deceased are kept for long periods of time, but would not be designed to house and keep the public safe from Britain's most monstrous criminals. It is in this moment of transport between the hospital and the next space, the morgue, where the ghostly figure is at its quietest.

Underpinning this is that the corpse is an uncertain entity at this point, which problematizes its mobility. Troyer (2008) has discussed the uncertain status that the corpse has in legal cases and how this uncertainty can prove problematic for exercising the law in cases involving the corpse. The same can be said for the transport of Brady's body. In this moment, the corpse is an uncertain entity as it goes from a controlled living space to a controlled dead space. This uncertain movement is compounded by risks of Brady's toxic residue seeping out of the transition of control as the body changes institutional hands. This, I would suggest, is why little about any details of the corpse are heard at this time. There is only silence as we would prefer not to think about how Brady's dead body moves between spaces. Any details could, after all, reveal that his movement is quite similar to our own, drawing him into the realm of human.

In the end, Brady's remains transition into the morgue, which is for legislative reasons stipulated in the Coroner's and Justice Act (2009). The act states that bodies can be retained in the morgue for three reasons. That is, the deceased died a violent or unnatural death, there was an unknown cause of death, or the deceased had died in custody. Dying in custody meant that Brady's remains were subject to a coroner's judgment. This is significant as the morgue is the closest symbolic space to Ashworth Hospital since it is both a medical and a legal space, but rather than being for the living, it is a space for the dead, albeit only a temporary one. It is therefore the logical destination for this transport if the toxicity of Brady is to be contained.

Conduit 2: The "Monster" Morgue

The morgue arose to public attention when the news reported that Brady was housed in the same morgue as the Manchester bomber,

Salman Abedi. Abedi had detonated a bomb in Manchester Arena a week after Brady's death at Ashworth Hospital. Due to both perpetrators dying in close proximity, the local morgue was required to house both corpses. The importance of this was the symbolic use by the media of the term "the monster morgue" to describe a morgue that could house the remains of two of the most heinous killers in the UK (Robertson 2017). It is argued that this use of "monster" mediates Brady's (re)presentation through media. As Abedi enters into the morgue, Brady's pollution is drawn back into contention, symbolically leaking back into public life. His heinousness reinforces Brady's, furthering the risk of it seeping back into personhood. In an attempt to recalibrate the space, Abedi's monstrous nature is also drawn upon to reclassify the morgue as symbolically different to others; it is a particular symbolic space for monsters: the monster morgue.

Grixti (1995) has argued that the use of "monster" when referring to the serial murderer is particularly significant as it serves to place a barrier between "us" and "them." What is being argued here is that the public media discourse used to generate the *"monster"* morgue reinforces the separation of Brady from the wider public. It further removes him from being human. The use of the term "monster" serves to order him and neutralize his toxicity in this way. Essentially, the barrier shielding the human from the monster formulates Brady into a supernatural figure that could not be confused for a member of the civilized population. Yet, there is an extra layer to this monstrosity, as Brady is also corpse. Corpses have a rich backing in being considered as supernatural, too. This is evident in Penfold-Mounce's (2018) work, where she argues that the undead have a role in allowing the public to safely engage with ideas of otherness. These ideas are found with Brady's body as it lies in the *monster* morgue. His classification of "monster," using Penfold-Mounce's (2018) argument, is a way to engage with his otherness as "matter out of place" (Douglas 1966/2002, 44). It is a term used to grapple with his material remains being entangled within a classificational crisis; the monster is a tool that is able to draw many distinctly classified aspects into one, shaping him into some form of ordered classification of "monstrosity." This is a way of rendering his inevitable presence in public life somewhat safer and more distant from humanity.

Therefore, the meaning of Brady's remains is rearranged in this conduit through the use of discourse to construct him as a supernatural being. Supernaturalizing Brady serves to place him farther away from public life, behind a symbolic lockbox in a space where no other person could go. Indeed, the monster morgue is a special, symbolic place as it symbolically distances Brady from being able to exist in any other morgue where other people lie. Yet, it is also a place that no other person could enter. Other deceased may lie in the same physical morgue, but not necessarily in the "monster morgue." In this way he's separate from our dead loved ones. He's his own type of dead: a monstrous dead, symbolically segregated from the non-monsters.

No matter how symbolically powerful the monster morgue is in containing Brady's toxicity, it must contend with the physical aspects of the dead body. The dead body is, after all, something that must be discarded, and the Public Health Act (1984) states that the local authority are required to dispose of it if no one else is able to do so. As such, the local authority contracted a funeral director and crematorium, bringing Brady into the third conduit of disposal, the crematorium.

Conduit 3: The Crematorium

The crematorium is a particularly important conduit of disposal as it is argued to be the vital transformative site, where the tangible, fleshy remains of Brady are turned into a set of cremated ash. This is significant as it transforms the manifestations of his presence. No longer is Brady physically humanoid, with two arms and two legs, physically relatable as a member of the human race. He is now a form of dry ash: a powder that does not share the human shape. Thus, the crematorium makes Brady present in a different way than he had been before by adapting his physical appearance.

The act of this transformation itself is also vital to understanding how his toxicity is controlled. The use of fire and extreme heat has been notorious in the killing of bacteria. The physical pollutant of his dead body, its risk of decomposing and poisoning those around it, is neutralized through the use of extreme temperature. Moreover, it was later reported that the crematorium subjected the body to further measures of control. The cremation itself was conducted after dark, at 10 p.m., outside of the crematorium opening hours; the coffin did not enter any public space, being brought directly into the back, staff-only areas; and the cremator machine used was professionally cleaned afterward (BBC 2017).

While the use of temperature may serve to halt any potential of physical toxicity in the crematorium, the rest of these management techniques may be seen as acts of symbolically distancing Brady's body from the broader public. Conducting the cremation after hours meant that there would be no chance that Brady's cremation would be happening at the same time as a service or cremation of somebody else. Second, his denial of entry into any of the public areas is significant as there is little risk of his trace residually haunting any of the public areas of the crematorium, where others would be having their service. Third, this deep cleaning of the cremator also ensures that nobody else's ashes would have any risk of containing a speck of Brady. After the cremation, an operator can never ensure that 100% of the remains are removed from the cremator as some of these remains can be as small as grains of sand. The deep cleaning serves to neutralize this risk, removing any of these potential residual grains of Brady. However, it also removes the micro-organisms, any particles that may not be seen. To quote Douglas (1966/2002, 2), it "purifies" the machine on a symbolic level. It wholly ensures that there is no essence of Brady in the chamber. Any evidence of monster from the cremator is removed, ready for the next person to be cremated within it, without the risk of coming into contact with micro-Brady materials. These practices limit the possibilities of his physical presence contaminating others.

Thus, great efforts are made during the cremation to limit any toxicity from Brady residually haunting the crematorium. However, the nature of cremation in transforming the remains from humanoid to ash also opens up Brady to new forms of agency. As Young and Light (2016) have argued, a dead body possesses many different qualities, which means that it slides from category to category. For example, it was a fleshy, humanoid figure, but is now ash. The way the dead body is materialized sets limits for its agency and affects how its personhood is manifested in public life. For example, the transformation from fleshy body to ash opens up new avenues for touch-based interaction. The bereaved can hold and run their fingers through the cremated remains of a loved one (Mathijssen 2017). Yet, weaving fingers through the fleshy corpse, particularly those involved in traumatic incidents where the body may be open or in pieces, is generally not an option. Furthermore, in these cases, the bereaved may even be warned against viewing the body (Parsons 2003).

Returning to Douglas (1966/2002) and her categories of order, there's something to be said about the relationship between these interactions and the order tied to the remains. The physically ripped, shredded, and opened corpse may be of fascination to some (Seltzer 1998), but that fascination always takes place behind a barrier. The openness of the corpse closes interactions because our insides can trouble those nearby. They can be unpleasant to look at and potentially full of bacteria. Quigley (1996) has reaffirmed this by drawing attention to some of the troubles that medical students have faced when encountering the opened cadaver; particularly through the smells, sights, and feelings that the insides of the body draw. The presence of the opened corpse is therefore one of danger, closing avenues of communication and affecting its agency. The cremated remains are, on the other hand, pacified. There's nothing wet or fleshy about them. Importantly, they have been subject to incineration and any potentially troubling bone fragments are ground up. It's viewed as safe to communicate with in a variety of ways. For example, some place these cremated remains into tattoo ink, and mix them with their own bodies (Heesels, Poots, and Venbrux 2012). In this way, cremated remains are seen as safe and are physically ordered. The crematorium is therefore a conduit for everyday death disposal practice as it helps to arrange the meaning of the dead through this adapting of the body's material form.

The problem that Brady poses, however, is that his deeper criminal meaning is still present within the corpse's changing form. While the ash form usually orders the remains, I would suggest that this makes Brady's cremated remains even more problematic. Further work must be done to separate them from the now non-humanoid being. It's not enough to categorize him as a monster, when the human barely resembles what we know as a human. When our deceased are ash, the fact that Brady would be ash too draws him further into similarity. The symbolic distance is in some ways lessened, making his manifestation potentially more toxic as he could be dispersed just as anybody else would.

Rather than solely forming new opportunities for agency vis-à-vis Young and Light (2016), I would argue that this new material form presents new opportunities for Brady's contamination. In ash form, he can be dispersed over a landscape in a similar manner to anthrax. Essentially, Brady could end up anywhere and, as a result, policing the cremated remains is thought of as being just as important as policing the fully formed dead body. This was evident in Glasgow council's decision to restrict any form of Brady's scattering on their lands. The significance of this is that Brady was born in Glasgow. Glasgow council wanted to divorce the area from his relation. Even in ash form, he is deemed so socially poisonous that he could infect the area, making it dirty by proxy of his scattering (Robins 2017). It is clear that the transformation of Brady's body into ash exposes new physical avenues for his contamination, while at the same time problematizing the amount of symbolic distance between him as monster and us as human. This becomes clearer when it is considered that his ashes ended up being deposited into the sea.

Conduit 4: The Sea

The significance of the sea is, first, its makeup. To deposit Brady into the sea is to deny him being scattered on the lands of Britain. To be scattered on land means that there's a place that people can come to memorialize. The sea, by contrast is almost endless and, as such, extraordinarily difficult to identify the resting place of anybody deposited in it. This was remarkably similar to the disposal of bin Laden's remains at sea. In this case, the sea was used as a depthless abyss in an attempt to make him disappear from social life (Schrift 2016). These efforts of removal, disappearing, and distancing are certainly reflected in the discarding of Brady's ashes in the sea.

The use of the sea was not entirely unexpected as there had been earlier restrictions regarding the geographical spreading of Brady's ashes. As mentioned, Glasgow council said that they would not allow Brady's ashes to be scattered in their jurisdiction. Of course, there was also the coroner's statement that the body would not be released to a funeral director until it was confirmed that the ashes would not be spread on Saddleworth Moor. To remove any and all possibility of the remains poisoning a specific British area, they were deposited into the sea. Significantly, the ashes were not scattered over the sea, which meant that there would be less risk that they would be carried through the air, covering a larger section of the sea or inadvertently being carried by the wind onto land. They were instead placed inside a biodegradable container, which only opened and scattered after the remains were submerged in water. It is perhaps an unpleasant thought to know that Brady's *resting* place is not far from where we rest. This use of the sea might be considered as a further bracketing of him away from public life, an attempt to ensure that the ghost of Brady does not manifest without consent.

The sea acts as a barrier; the water blocks out the symbolic pollution of the toxic necro-waste. As his ashes disappear into the water, the best effort possible is made to force Brady to be as symbolically distant from human as possible. Indeed, how would one know where Brady is in the sea? The ashes could be in any number of locations and carried through currents. He essentially has no final resting spot. Instead, he is in a continuous state of fluidity, being carried across the seabed. If his location is anonymous, he becomes more akin to a myth; somebody that once existed, but no longer does.

Conclusion: A Ghost Criminology of Death Disposal

It is clear from this discussion that Ghost Criminology offers a unique lens for exploring the disposal of the particularly heinous, criminal dead body. The idea of Brady's remains as "toxic necro-waste" provides a way to observe how this process of disposal is underpinned by an effort to limit his pollution from seeping back into public life. In an attempt to distance him from ourselves, his ghost is designed to be one of a monstrous being, classifying him as a different species to the human being, which is closer to myth than reality. Through the process of disposal, this design takes place and efforts are taken to ensure that Brady is symbolically contained. It was within this idea that the chapter considered how we account for and are held accountable by the disposal of toxicity which is left *unfinished* (Hetherington 2004, 163). Four conduits of disposal where Brady's meaning is most prominently arranged were used to assess this in more detail. Each of these conduits told a story of the manifestation of Brady's fluidic ghost, detailing the attempts to distance its manifestation from public life.

The value of Ghost Criminology has been its ability to explore the relationship that toxic necro-waste has with disposal. It provides a way to unpick attempts to account for and, not be held accountable by, the unfinished management of the toxic dead. In this way, studying the threshold between absence/presence reveals attempts to halt or even control the pollution of toxic necro-waste, lending a new way of conceptualizing UK death disposal practices. However, given that these ideas of toxicity are culturally mediated (Douglas 1966/2002), it is argued that a lens of Ghost Criminology could provide a useful tool for assessing how the criminal dead are managed cross-culturally. The sites of contention would be where and how the ghost of the toxic dead manifests. In a Western context, Ghosts may manifest as monsters because the sign of monstrosity provides a way to address materials having a classificational crisis by drawing a variety of classifications together. Yet, monsters are also a source of fascination and profit in Western capitalism (Jarvis 2007). This society is one where monsters are distant enough to be a source of fascination, but close enough to still be thrilling (Grixti 1995). The same may not be said for another culture where the sign of the monster may mean something else entirely. I argue that the ghost of the toxic dead would likely manifest in a different way across the globe, with each manifestation providing information about these varying cultural approaches to disposal (Munro 2001). It's clear that, as of now, the ghostly manifestation of a criminal character after death provides a platform for further consideration.

REFERENCES

BBC. 2017. "Moors Murderers: Ian Brady's Ashes Disposed of at Sea," Manchester, *BBC*, November 3, 2017. http://bbc.co.uk

Cohen, Jeffery. J. 2007. "Monster Culture (seven theses)." In *Gothic Horror: A Guide for Students and Readers*, edited by Clive Bloom, G198–G217. Basingstoke: Palgrave Macmillan.

Davies, Douglas and Rumble, Hannah. 2012. *Natural Burial: Traditional-Secular Spiritualities and Funeral Innovation*. London: Continuum International.

Denham, Jack. 2019. "Collecting the Dead: Art, Antique and 'Aura' in Personal Collections of Murderabilia." *Mortality*, 1–16.

Douglas, Mary. 1966/2002. *Purity and Danger*. London: Routledge.

Foucault, Michel. 1991. *Discipline and Punish*. London: Penguin Books.

———. 2001. *Madness and Civilisation*. London: Routledge.

Glancey, Jonathan. 2002. "Image that for 36 Years Fixed a Killer in the Public Mind." UK News, *The Guardian*. November 16, 2002. http://theguardian.com

Grixti, Joseph. 1995. "Consuming Cannibals: Psychopathic Killers as Archetypes and Cultural Icons." *Journal of American Culture* 18, 1: 87–96.

Heessels, Meike, Poots, Fleur, and Venbrux, Eric. 2012. "In Touch with the Deceased: Animate Objects and Human Ashes." *Material Religion* 8, 4: 466–488.

Hetherington, Kevin. 2004. "Secondhandedness: Consumption, Disposal, and Absent Presence." *Environment and Planning D: Society and Space* 22: 157–173.

Jarvis, Brian. 2007. "Monsters Inc.: Serial Killers and Consumer Culture." *Crime, Media, Culture* 3, 3: 326–344.

Krupar, Shiloh. 2018. "Green Death: Sustainability and the Administration of the Dead." *Cultural Geographies* 25, 2: 267–284.

Mathijssen, Brenda. 2017. "The Ambiguity of Human Ashes: Exploring Encounters with Cremated Remains in the Netherlands." *Death Studies* 41, 1: 34–41.

Moon, Claire. 2014. "Human Rights, Human Remains: Forensic Humanitarianism and the Human Rights of the Dead." *Social Science Journal* 65, 1: 215–221.

Munro, Rolland. 2001. "Disposal of the Body: Upending Postmodernism." *Ephemera* 1, 2: 108–130.

Olson, Philip R. 2014. "Flush and Bone." *Science, Technology, & Human Values* 39, 5: 666–693.

———. 2016. "Knowing 'Necro-Waste.'" *Social Epistemology* 30, 3: 326–345.

Parsons, Brian. 2003. "Conflict in the Context of Care: An Examination of Role Conflict Between the Bereaved and the Funeral Director in the UK." *Mortality* 8, 1: 67–87.

Penfold-Mounce, Ruth. 2016. "Corpses, Popular Culture and Forensic Science: Public Obsession with Death." *Mortality* 21, 1: 19–35.

———. 2018. *Death, the Dead and Popular Culture*. Bingley: Emerald Publishing.

Plumwood, Val. 2008. "Tasteless: Towards a Food-Based Approach to Death." *Environmental Values* 17, 3: 323–330.

Quigley, Christine. 1996. *The Corpse: A History*. Jefferson, NC and London: McFarland & Company.

Robertson, Alexander. 2017. "The Monster Morgue: Bodies of Ian Brady and Manchester Bomber Salman Abedi STILL Lie in the Same Mortuary Because Undertakers Refuse to Touch Them." *MailOnline*, July 25, 2017. http://dailymail.co.uk

Robins, Daniel. 2017. "Toxic Necro-Waste." *Social Epistemology Review and Reply Collective* 6, 10: 39–41.

Rumble, Hannah, Troyer, John, Walter, Tony, and Woodthorpe, Kate. 2014. "Disposal or Dispersal? Environmentalism and Final Treatment of the British Dead." *Mortality* 19, 3: 243–260.

Saad, Toni. 2017. "The Moral Inadequacy of Cremation." *New Bioethics* 23, 3: 1–12.

Schrift, Melissa. 2016. "Osama's Body: Death of a Political Criminal and (Re)birth of a Nation." *Mortality* 21, 3: 279–294.

Seltzer, Mark. 1998. *Serial Killers: Death and Life in America's Wound Culture*. London: Routledge.
Shilling, Chris. 2005. *The Body in Culture, Technology and Society*. London: Sage.
Shute, J. 2014. "Moral Discourse and Action in Relation to the Corpse: Integrative Concepts for a Criminology of Mass Violence." In *Human Remains and Mass Violence: Methodological Approaches*, edited by Jean-Marc Dreyfus and Élisabeth Anstett, 81–105. Manchester: Manchester University Press.
Tarlow, Sarah. 2002. "The Aesthetic Corpse in Nineteenth-Century Britain." In *Thinking Through the Body*, edited by Yannis Hamilakis, Mark Pluciennik, and Sarah Tarlow, G85–G97. Boston: Springer.
Troyer, John. 2008. "Abuse of a Corpse: A Brief History and Re-Theorization of Necrophilia Laws in the USA." *Mortality* 13, 2: 132–152.
———. 2016. "'Owning' Necro-Waste." *Social Epistemology: A Journal of Knowledge, Culture, and Policy* 5, 3: 59–63.
Walter, Tony. 2002. *Revival of Death*. London: Routledge.
Young, Craig and Light, Duncan. 2016. "Interrogating Spaces of and for the Dead as 'Alternative Space': Cemeteries, Corpses and Sites of Dark Tourism." *International Review of Social Research* 6, 2: 61–72.

6

Destroyed Records

KATHERINE BIBER

> HAMLET: Remember thee!
> Yea, from the table of my memory
> I'll wipe away all trivial fond records,
> All saws of books, all forms, all pressures past,
> That youth and observation copied there;
> And thy commandment all alone shall live
> Within the book and volume of my brain
> (Shakespeare, *Hamlet*: Act I, Scene V)

Destroying records, documents, and evidence is a commonly used administrative and legal technique for mitigating the potential dangers of their dissemination. This chapter examines criminal evidence and records destroyed or damaged as legitimate practices of the state and its agents. These destructive state practices invoke ghosts, in the form of the traces of dead records, documents, and evidence, things that were killed in the administration of justice. What remains of these destructive practices are ghostly apparitions, specters of crime, and these generate new spectacles and new fears. Critical writing about crime, from Foucault to Derrida, Benjamin to Garland, has employed the language of ghosts and shadows and faceless figures. Whether invoking crime's perpetrator, crime's victim, crime's nemesis, or crime's records, this language is enormously provocative, confirming the criminal law's imagination of itself as formless, frightening, and everywhere. Much of this writing responds directly to Shakespeare's creation of the Ghost of Hamlet's father, thus drawing a clear connection between the spectral and the ethical. Hamlet's father was the rightful king, killed by his brother; in death he returns as a ghost, urging Hamlet to avenge his murder and restore legitimate sovereignty. By linking the ghost with a

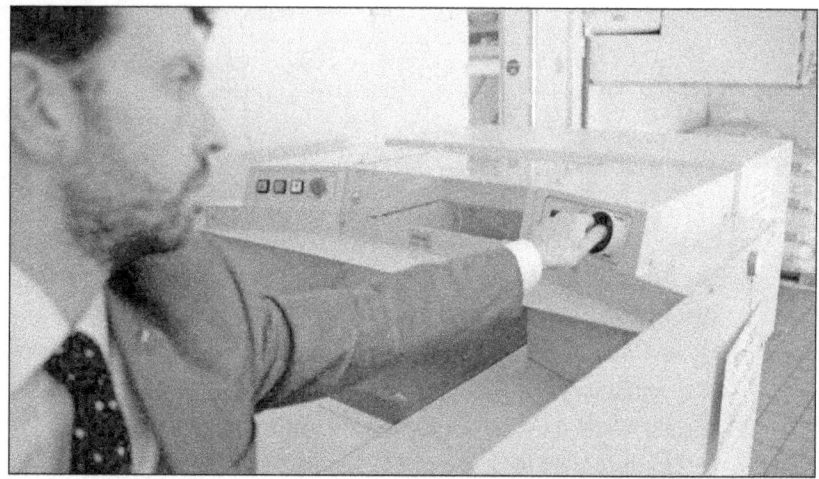

Figure 6.1. *Erasing a Classified Military Document* (2013), video still. Credit: Jason File. Reproduced with permission.

conception of justice, the ghost's return serves as a threshold moment and the ghost's demand as a decisive challenge. In this chapter, the spectral remainder of destroyed evidence issues its own challenge, and several contemporary artists respond. In their responses, with the specters they summon, we learn to see the entanglement of sovereignty with violence.

Erasing a Classified Military Document (2013) is a limited-edition video documentation of a performance executed on May 27, 2013. (See figures 6.1 and 6.2.) With a duration of 1 minute 39 seconds, this is an artwork by Jason File, in which the artist, wearing a suit and tie, turns a knob on a beige metallic industrial shredding machine before inserting a sheet of paper. The artist described the work as a "readymade performance," in which a "real and consequential event" is transformed into an artwork (File 2015). An important fact about Jason File is that this artwork was made during the course of his day job; at the time of the performance, File was an international war crimes prosecutor at The Hague, and he destroyed this classified military document during his service in the International Criminal Tribunal for the former Yugoslavia (ICTY). We don't see the document before it is destroyed; that it needed to be destroyed by a legal professional tells us that this document contained something powerful and secret, and that the administration of justice demanded we should not know.

Jason File's work points to the banality of administrative destruction and urges us to pay attention to the specters of crime that are hiding in plain sight. In office garbage bins, in industrial compactors, in biohazardous waste disposal containers, linger the ghosts of criminal acts, criminal investigations, and criminal prosecutions. Drawing upon materials found in the ICTY, File's work is made from hole-punch waste, photocopied paper, taped-over video recordings, and drawn-out trial footage in which he cross-examines a witness against a transcript of their earlier evidence while multiple language translators are heard to speak over each other.[1] He calls forth ghosts from this evidentiary garbage and clutter.

File's subsequent work *In Black and White* (2018) comprises several sheets of artist-made paper produced from the shredded remains of classified military, intelligence, and legal documents. (See figures 6.3 and 6.4.) The sheets of paper demonstrate that, with different degrees of destruction—from coarse shredding through to fine pulping—the remains of the destroyed records could be rather easily discerned. Some sheets of paper contain the remnants of legible text; some are smooth and almost entirely monochromatic. For File, the work implicates

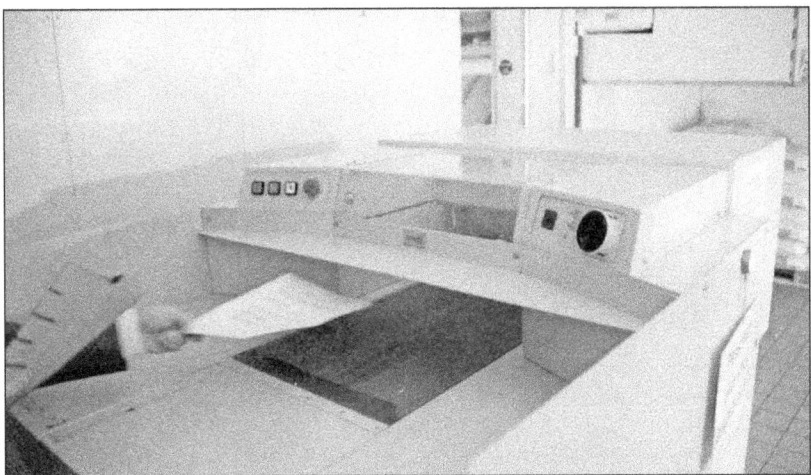

Figure 6.2. *Erasing a Classified Military Document* (2013), video still. Credit: Jason File. Reproduced with permission.

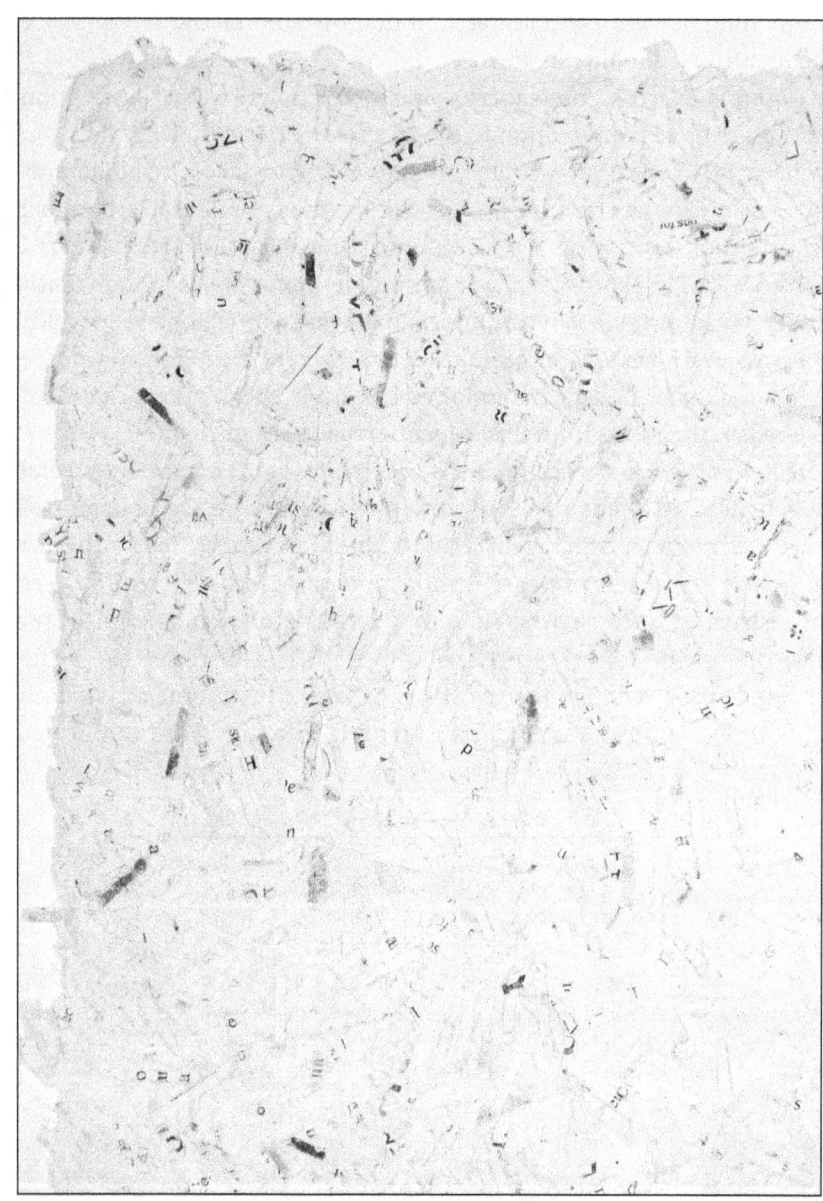

Figure 6.3. *In Black and White* (2018), detail view. Credit: Jason File. Reproduced with permission.

"longstanding associations between text on paper and ideas of legal certainty, historical clarity, or archival veracity" (File 2018). The sheet of paper is a synecdoche for law. The paper chase, the paper trail, and mundane paperwork provide evidence of legal labor. By attending to File's smooth sheet of paper, with all evidence of crime almost entirely effaced, we are forced to reckon with the impassivity with which law's destructive work is done. This chapter argues that, by attending to the materials that have been destroyed by and through crime, we can visualize the violence of law's processes, and the spectacles it generates with its violence.

In philosophy, destruction has been associated with nihilism and epistemological failure, following Nietzsche (1967), and also with a productive, interrogative quest for authenticity, after Heidegger (Crowe 2006); both were influential in Derrida's concept of deconstruction and

Figure 6.4. *In Black and White* (2018), installation view, NARS Foundation, Brooklyn, NY. Credit: Jason File. Reproduced with permission.

hauntology (1995). For economists, destruction is a necessary process for the functioning—and ultimately also the anticipated end—of capitalism (Elliott 1980, 55; Schumpeter 1950, 83). Marx and Engels explicitly characterized this process as the exorcism of a specter (1888/1977). Among art historians, there are various motivations for destruction: iconoclasm, repression, protest, vandalism, aesthetics (Walden 2013a). Historians of architecture and the built environment distinguish slow decay from sudden acts, studying destroyed monuments, attempts to destroy culture, and the role of war and conflict in these practices (Bevan 2016; Bresnahan and Mancini 2015; Connor 2017). A significant body of scholarship has formed around the study of ruins, and ruination, and the symbolic, analytical, aesthetic, and affective potential for ruins to point to the sociocultural conditions in which they were produced (DeSilvey and Edensor 2012; Hell and Schönle 2010; Stoler 2013). The growing fields of environmental humanities and sciences take account of the destruction wrought by, and upon, the natural environment, and the entangled ecology of humans, industry, and climate in the contemporary escalation in destructive environmental disasters (Brisman and South 2014; Wright and Nyberg 2015; Tsing 2015). This literature reveals that what destruction is, and what it means, continues to demand investigation and attention.

Whether sustaining Derrida's concept of hauntology (2006), or Žižek's notion of the apparition as the ultimate horizon of ethics (1999, 79), or Fisher's notion of lost futures (2014), the ghost appears at a moment of cataclysm, issuing what Žižek termed an "inexorable ethical injunction" (2001, 14). Whether arriving or returning, the ghost issues a demand that we pay attention to something that is difficult to visualize, or in danger of being forgotten. These are the perpetual responsibilities of the legal practitioner, conjuring causes of action from past harms, and generating documentation to sustain a file. This chapter draws attention to the materials that are damaged and destroyed in pursuit of law's objectives, and to the specters called forth by acts of lawful violence.

The destruction of legal documents implicitly elevates their significance. Documents are destroyed when they are important; insignificant documents are left behind, forgotten, or thrown in the garbage. In many jurisdictions, legislation related to biosecurity, biodiversity, environmental protection, weapons, and customs requires the destruction or disposal of various things. Biohazardous substances such as blood, or contaminants such as asbestos, are routinely destroyed. Non-native animals found on state land by a ranger can be destroyed. Live animals and plants seized in the context of smuggling, or perishable animal and plant materials, narcotics, weapons, unseaworthy vessels, and goods that pose a danger to public health or safety, or to biosecurity; all of these may be lawfully destroyed by the state. In some jurisdictions, the destruction is carefully documented, often visually. In most places this destruction occurs without scrutiny, in banal administrative contexts, which implicitly conceal the bureaucratic inventiveness they demand.

A creative imagination could conjure myriad ways by which the legal professional might destroy her records. They might be incinerated by dragon's breath or consumed by maggots or cast off a precipice or crushed in a vise. Of course, much evidence destroyed by legal professionals is done so wrongfully. Evidence and records might be destroyed in criminal acts, spoliation, negligence, neglect, error, or oversight. In the wake of a Royal Commission into Trade Union Governance and Corruption, some union officials in Australia set their records on fire. Fearing the flames would attract emergency services, they doused the fire, hired an excavator, and took them to a garbage dump. They destroyed the records but saved the receipt for the truck hire, and their explanation that they were engaged in an innocent office cleanup was not accepted, resulting in a rare criminal conviction for destruction of records (Attorney General's Department 2015; AAP 2018; Sibson 2018). In the so-called big tobacco litigation, and again in the wake of the exposure of Enron's corporate fraud, revelations were made about concealment and warehousing of evidence—literally placing it in a jurisdiction beyond the court's reach. These practices frustrated the fair administration of justice and resulted in new jurisprudential principles and laws, which compelled preservation of records and outlawed some of these destructive corporate practices.

The legal scholar Cornelia Vismann, in her book *Files* (2008), traced the immense innovation practiced by record makers and record keepers within the long history of administration and paperwork. Contemporary practices of record destruction have their origins in the early techniques of cancellation and effacement that Vismann examined. Traced back to the thirteenth-century chancery, cancellation was the drawing of latticed lines or bars on a document, indication it was no longer the "original" version and was not to be copied again (Vismann 2008, 26). As Vismann wrote, "Crossing out, it seems, is more elementary than the more productive act of writing down. Deleting rather than writing establishes the symbolic order of the law" (ibid.). Cancellation is a form of document destruction that leaves a trace. We know that something has been removed, because evidence of its removal survives, visibly and tangibly upon the surface of the record.

In her history of the *déchiqueteuse*, or paper-shredder, Immi Tallgren explores the early patents of machines intended to cancel or mutilate records (2018). First patented in 1909 by the American inventor Abbot Augustus Low, it wasn't until the 1930s that a German inventor, Adolf Ehinger, actually developed the first model, which he based on a hand-cranked pasta maker, later modified with an electric motor (Tallgren 2018, 206). For Tallgren, legal documents have a "life-cycle," and the déchiqueteuse is an object of "epistemic hygiene" that regenerates the cycle (213). The paper-shredder is simply "a handy instrument that supports the normality of the birth, life, and death of international law. Standing next to the gestational objects (printer and copy-machine), it tactfully takes care of the life-cycle's end" (212). However, shredded documents were vulnerable to reincarnation via reassembly—Tallgren writes of the Iranian carpet weavers hired after the 1979 revolution to manually reconstruct documents destroyed by the US embassy in the final hours before the fall of the old regime (206). In Tallgren's history of the paper-shredder, pulverizing, pulping, and chemical decomposition were used to augment shredding, to protect destroyed records from subsequent reconstitution (ibid.). For this reason, the US Department of Homeland Security now prescribes methods and standards for the destruction of records, and these include "burning, cross-cut shredding, wet-pulping, mutilation, chemical decomposition, or pulverizing" (ibid.).

Following the fall of the East German regime, multiple attempts were made to reassemble documents that had been torn up by hand by Stasi staff executing destruction orders in the final weeks of the regime. The manual destruction of the records was arduous labor: "Destroying paper is shit work. After two days your joints hurt. They ripped for two months," a government archivist Stephan Wolf recalled (Curry 2008). After the regime fell, in the first frenzy of document rescue, surviving records and fragments were salvaged instinctively: "We didn't have time to look at it. We had no idea what it would mean," volunteer David Gill recounted (ibid.). These records filled 16,000 bags which, when the Stasi Records Agency (BStU) took custody of them, were transferred into hand-numbered brown paper sacks, filling the steel shelves of a three-story, 60,000- square-foot warehouse on the outskirts of Magdeburg, a former industrial town west of Berlin. Initially the reconstruction work was undertaken manually—including outsourcing to refugees in Zirndorf (Bavaria)—and 1.5 million pages were manually reconstructed, indexed, and archived (Federal Commissioner, n.d.; Oltermann 2018). The rate of work was approximately one bag per worker per year (Curry 2008). From this reconstruction work, information was revealed about the GDR's persecution of individual dissidents, surveillance of peace activists, doping practices in sport, the GDR's investigations into a Nazi war criminal, and its provision of sanctuary for certain members of the Red Army Faction (Federal Commissioner, n.d.).

From 2007, the Stasi records agency offered grants to competitors who could meet the challenge of digitally reconstituting the manually destroyed records. The successful bid came from the Fraunhofer Institute, a research non-profit. With an investment of €8m, twenty-three bags of torn records were reconstructed using digital methods. They digitally scanned each torn fragment and classified it according to paper stock and color, typewriter font, the shape of the torn remnant, and its location and layering in the original bag. However, the ePuzzler algorithm is unable to reconstruct records that were reduced to tiny snippets, (Federal Commissioner, n.d.; Oltermann 2018) and without further technological innovation, the remainder of the project cannot be completed (Federal Commissioner, n.d.). These records are what Tallgren describes as "walking-deads"; in a limbo state between death and resurrection (Tallgren 2018, 207).

The post-Stasi records administration acknowledges the futility of attempting to summon ghosts from most of the destroyed records. Several thousand bags of paper scraps were retrieved, having been shredded by machine into tiny pieces in 1990. Tearing records by hand only occurred after mechanized methods of destruction had failed. Initially, trucks filled with records were destroyed by *Papierwolfs* and *Reisswolfs*— paper-wolves and rip-wolves—and also office shredders, many of whose motors burned out from overuse (Curry 2008). Many of these records were reduced to confetti, "largely unrecoverable," and by 1991, the BStU had inspected and itself destroyed them, using a method that was not disclosed (Federal Commissioner, n.d.; Curry 2008).

The artist, Daniel Knorr, has exhibited a collection of "file stones" produced by Stasi agents' attempts to destroy records in Leipzig. Using a *feuchtschredder*, or wet shredder, papers, microfilm, audio tapes, and polaroids were combined with oil and water, and then pulverized. This produced cellulose lumps which, when dried, resembled stones. Some of these were buried, and some were flushed into the Leipzig municipal sewer system, which became blocked, causing flooding. Knorr describes his series *The State of Mind* (2007) as a "readymade"; he sees the East German state as the "sculptor," with his role being simply to display the stones (Pangburn 2016). The stones are masses made from destroyed records—their colors are grey, blue, and pink, corresponding with the color-classification system used by the Stasi—and they look like lumpy excreta, piled into a Plexiglass gallery box (Schwartz 2016; Biber 2018). Tallgren might contrast these inadvertent monuments with international law's perpetual production of "monuments." By this she means that a great deal of document destruction is motivated by political and diplomatic objectives, "sorting out who will look good, who bad, and on what basis," so that destruction is a type of camouflage, and the paper-shredder is a "suspect instrument of tailoring histories," "tampering with them," "creating holes" (Tallgren 2018, 208). Tallgren describes the déchiqueteuse as "a spectral object, busy trying to silence the ghostly cries that resonate" (207). These records are simultaneously monuments and ruins, the ghostly remnants of a destroyed regime and also the looming specter of its supreme authority.

The artist Cornelia Parker has created a series of works made from items seized and destroyed by Her Majesty's Customs and Excise in Cardiff, Wales. Made between 1995 and 2006, these works include *Exhaled Cocaine* (1996), in which Parker displayed a small mound of ashes remaining after smuggled cocaine was forensically incinerated, and *Pornographic Drawing* (1995–2006), a series of works made from pornographic videotapes intercepted and shredded by state agents. Parker extracted the ferric oxide from the shredded tapes by suspending them in a solvent. Once liquefied, she used this ink to print abstract shapes onto paper, resembling Rorschach blots. Parker drew a direct link between the appearance of these blots and their status as somehow carrying a psychological residue of the unconscious desires of the patient under psychoanalysis (Blazwick 2013, 100). Despite being shredded and liquefied, the destroyed evidence of confiscated pornography nevertheless remained haunted by erotic content; the un-dead specter of illicit commodities of desire. Parker describes herself as being drawn to found objects, things that already exist in the world, but which may have been "killed off symbolically and then resurrected" (Wagstaff 2018, 33). She said, "I've always loved found objects but for me it's important to do something to them: I have to kill them off, so that I can remake them" (Tickner 2003, 368).

Parker's work, *Cold Dark Matter: An Exploded View* (1991), saw her collaborate with a British Army ammunition unit to explode a garden shed; she gathered the burned fragments left behind and suspended them from wires in a gallery, like floating ghosts of their former selves. This was followed by *Hanging Fire (Suspected Arson)* (2000), which she made from the charred remains of a suspicious fire on the outskirts of London, an installation of suspended pieces of blackened wood hanging by 12-foot strands of wire and string from a gallery ceiling (Edgers 2006). Parker described her interest in making "calm installations about destructions," which have been described as "a charcoal drawing in space" (Morgan 2000, 37); "as if a campfire has been painstakingly dissected and then recreated by an obsessive-compulsive physicist" (Edgers 2006).

In her work *Mass (Colder Darker Matter)* (1997), she gathered and then suspended the shards of burned charcoal left behind after a Texas church was struck by lightning. In *Anti-Mass* (2005), she retrieved and suspended shards of burned charcoal remaining after a racist arson attack upon a Kentucky church. She said: "I'm drawn to these tropes, these violent ends to things, and then I like the act of reconstruction, building something new that is quiet and contemplative" (Wagstaff 2018, 31). Whilst the materials from which the work is made convey death and violence, for Parker, once suspended in the air they are "reanimated" and somehow revived (Tate online). The latter work is literally the specter of a crime; these blackened shapes hang in the air from invisible threads, oscillating gently. For Avery Gordon, haunting is "an animated state in which a repressed or unresolved social violence is making itself known" (1992, xvi). Although burned to cinders, in Parker's work, the blackened shards of these Baptist churches are ambient evidence of their former selves. For Gordon, haunting occurs "when the over-and-done-with comes alive, when what's been in your blind spot comes into view" (1992, xvi). Parker works with the notion of "an avoided object," in which an otherwise-recognizable object is "presented as something other and unfamiliar" (Morgan 2000, 7). For Imogen Racz, in Parker's work "the previous life of each object still speaks in its transformed state" (Racz 2013, 47). Transformation is also important to Parker; Morgan tracks Parker's interests: "from vast to minute, ethereal to worldly, spectacular to mundane" (2000, 5). Parker examines—and sometimes exerts—transformations upon objects, whether material or conceptual, and finds ways to visualize these. Her works are the spectral remains of earlier acts of violence, some of them criminal, and by resurrecting these destroyed materials she is in dialogue with these ghosts.

Anti-Mass is the evidence left behind following of a crime; *Mass (Colder Darker Matter)* is what remains of a naturally destructive event. That they are visually indistinguishable is part of their power; both works invite spectral analysis. For Derrida, the specter returns from the place in which it was repressed; it marks the arrival (*avenir*, yet to come) of ethics. Like Hamlet, confronted with the ghost of his dead father ("*Remember me!*"), our response to the specter provides a measure for our character. For Ari Hirvonen, "To live more justly is to live with ghosts. This *with* is most important. Without *with* there is no being-with, no society" (1998, 204). The Ghost has urged Hamlet to take responsibility for an injustice, to avenge a crime, and to restore legitimate sovereignty. For Hirvonen, when summoned by the Ghost, "Hamlet is chosen, addressed, made responsible, summoned, charged" (199). The specter has returned and issued an ethical call to justice. For Derrida, it is important that the ghost comes *first*, or rather, that it *returns*, and the ethical response is inaugurated by its arrival (Hirvonen 1998, 199–200). Where artists work with destroyed criminal records, they are conversing with crime's specters. Whether their work displays, critiques, or transforms these acts of legal destruction, theirs is a response to the ethical injunction inaugurated by a ghost: *Remember me!*

The socialization of ghosts, recognizing them as the ordinary personnel of social life, is an important project for the humanities. Particularly for scholars of law, schooled in the black letter, the document, the instrument, and the book, it is necessary also to acknowledge the trace of what has been removed: the redacted, the inadmissible, unavailable, confidential, privileged, classified, secret, the lost, and the dead. The implicitly destructive nature of legal practice is not much examined, buried as it is beneath doctrines disguising this violence as the everyday work of law. Through many of the artworks under discussion here, we become able to visualize some of the usually hidden, ghostly practices of legal destruction.

Taryn Simon's series, *Contraband* (2010), comprises 1,075 photographs she took during one week she spent at John F. Kennedy International Airport in New York.[2] Her photographs document items seized at the US Customs and Border Protection Federal Inspection Site and the US Postal Service International Mail Facility. Portraying prohibited, contaminated, biohazardous, and counterfeit items, the majority of these items were later destroyed. Simon's beautiful photographs recorded these items before they were killed, and they now serve as haunting specters of this illicit contraband. Simon has classified these materials by type and exhibited them alphabetically—Anabolic Steroids (Illegal); Animal Corpses (Prohibited); Animal Parts (Prohibited); Animal Skeletons (Prohibited); Animal Specimens (Prohibited)—and this taxonomy and the careful framing of these images represent her endeavor to bring a bureaucratic sensibility to the inexhaustible traffic in contraband. The critic Hans Ulrich Obrist draws attention to Simon's list-making, with its repetitions and volume serving as markers of our social urge to accumulate, but also our affinity for the disposable; a "time-capsule" of our current historical moment, characterized by the unrelenting illicit global traffic in foods, pharmaceuticals, toys, fakes, plants, and animals (2010, 4). For Obrist, *Contraband* is "playful and absurd," revealing "disorder and chance," and serves as a monument to Simon's self-discipline and endurance (2010, 3). Her documentation of the bizarre, extraordinary, and humdrum items people have tried to smuggle into the United States is set against what Obrist describes as "an unchanging grey backdrop, the colour of administration and neutrality" (2010, 4). Yet *Contraband* is also a last glimpse at a monumental criminal archive; the careful classification of objects destined for destruction. Susan Sontag drew the analogy between photography and death, calling it "a soft murder, appropriate to a sad, frightened time" (1971, 15). Sontag compared the "trace" of the photograph with a death mask, for capturing something real at the moment of its death (153). Simon's photographs are a type of ghost photography, capturing things no longer in the world; things that it might confound us to believe were ever in the world. That these items were ever real, ever desired, seems confounding. As evidence of crimes, they are compelling and strange. As criminal objects captured photographically in the moments before their destruction, their death becomes poignant. *Contraband* functions as an exemplar of Roland Barthes's *punctum*, the affective prick that pierces us when we look at a formally beautiful photograph: These objects are going to die. They document a death in the anterior future because by the time we see these images, we know that this contraband has been forensically destroyed. As Barthes wrote, after looking at a photograph of his mother when she was a child: "I shudder ... *over a catastrophe which has already occurred*. Whether or not the subject is already dead, every photograph is this catastrophe" (1981, 96).

Scholarship into state secrecy offers us a plethora of sites that might augment an inquiry into destruction and creativity. Secrecy begets obfuscation, redaction, concealment, and obliteration; it also begets leaks, whistleblowers, and the entire discourse of transparency. The legal scholar Mark Fenster explains that, in the digital age, the neoliberal state can pursue boundless opportunities for obfuscation and destruction (2012; 2014). With new opportunities to destroy come new opportunities for visualizing this destruction. In the work of criminologist Travis Linnemann, we see that state agencies, particularly police, are motivated to produce sensational visual spectacles of their acts of destruction. For Linnemann, what he calls police "trophy shots" feed the voyeuristic impulses of information-starved citizens, producing images of seized weapons or drugs set on fire or pulverized in a crusher, producing icons of destruction as evidence of the effective operation of state power. In addition, Linnemann reminds us that each trophy shot signifies—in the public imagination—the prevention and elimination of crimes. Each seized asset represents a murder or a robbery or a drug deal that didn't occur, and this is what he calls the "unknowable death and destruction" that frames and legitimizes these spectacles of sovereignty (2017, 62). For Linnemann, these images represent the narcissism or "gloating" that accompanies police power (59–63). These police, like customs officers, forensic officers, legal officers, and others, in their destructive duties enact creative interventions upon criminal records and materials. Unnamed, unknown, and usually unrecognized, these bureaucratic ghosts conjure the artistry of the state. Perhaps they are solo spirits, perhaps they work in collaboration with other specters; they might act independently, or they may be ghostwriting for others. We will probably never know. But they have visibly, lawfully, creatively intervened to damage or destroy records, and it is through the work of contemporary artists that we begin to appreciate the imaginative legal labor of destruction.

In recent decades, but increasing exponentially since the terrorist attacks of 9/11, artists have been responding to redacted legal and government records. "Redaction" refers to the concealment of data in official records. The function of redaction is to enable a declassified document to be released with modifications—usually deletions—as an alternative to withholding or permanently destroying it. Redaction is a tool of both secrecy and transparency; it is visible evidence of something unseen. It demands a destructive act: the wilful withholding, concealing, obfuscating, and deleting of part of the official record; it appears before us as a specter looming over an unreadable document. Some writers have observed that redaction is itself an art form, with its black marker, opaque tape, sharp razors, or photocopiers; more recently redaction may be undertaken digitally, using software applications (Powell 2010). The redactors themselves are secretive, spectral agents of bureaucratic destruction, purposefully removing facts from official records. In the digital age, and in the freedom-of-information era, in which records are formless, immaterial, or redacted, artists have generated new ways of visualizing ghostly legal facts.

The American artist Mariam Ghani has undertaken multiple projects responding to the redaction of declassified documents by the US government.[3] She describes herself as working with the themes of "visibility and invisibility, forgetting and wilful amnesia" (Frizzell 2017, 56). Her video work *The Trespassers* (2011) is made from redacted records; it examines the erasure from the official record of the anonymous translators used in prisoner interrogations. These sources are now freely available online, and are official records declassified and released following freedom-of-information applications by the American Civil Liberties Union or other applicants (Ghani 2011). Making *The Trespassers*, Ghani asked different translators, speaking Dari or Arabic, each with different degrees of connection to these events, to "translate" the redacted documents by drawing their own inferences about "what might belong in the blank spaces" (ibid.). With multiple voices speaking simultaneously, the work is deliberately hard to comprehend. Ghani was attempting to echo the conditions of an interrogation room where, she wrote, "important information is being volleyed back and forth between multiple codes and languages and no single person—not even the translator—fully understands everything that is going on" (ibid.).

Ghani's collaboration with Chitra Ganesh is titled *Index of the Disappeared* (2004–) and it uses redacted records to draw attention to US policy since 9/11, and the removal of facts from official records relating to disappearances, deportations, renditions, and detention, as well as techniques of interrogation and torture (Ganesh and Ghani 2011). In pursuit of what they call "ghost prisoners" (Ganesh 2016), they are interested in exposing "the human cost" of policies of disappearance; both the removal of people from specific jurisdictions and also the constraints upon legal and media professionals in representing these actions (Ghani and Ganesh 2005, 161). The project has created artworks, installations, web-based resources, and textual works, and also aims to engage its audience in a dialogue. The work re-presents redacted records, but it also makes humane interventions upon them; often these are hand-written, hand-drawn; watercolor portraits of file subjects might appear in place of official photographs, or marginal comments are written in response to file notes, and some of these are in the form of poetry. Different data from different records might be reassembled into a new narrative, or redactions might be replaced with new material, and the results might be simultaneously touching and absurd, or starkly critical. Aesthetically, the work aims to "mine the rich possibilities of the visual" at a site of disappearance (Ghani and Ganesh 2005, 161). But politically, they are seeking evidence of lives, individual and collective stories, that are "disappeared" through US policy, and that also "disappear" beneath the surface of voluminous "unquantifiable data"; ibid.). Ghani described this project as one of "radical archiving" (2015, 58). While this term operates in different registers, for Ghani and Ganesh, it relates to activating an archive in the present moment, rather than pushing it to the past or future. For Ghani, "archives can be crime scenes in the present" (62). Summoning them *now* issues a spectral demand for an ethical dialogue: How should we respond to these acts of violence against records? How should we remember them?

Ghani described her own trajectory toward this project, in the face of accumulating official policy instruments of disappearance. These began at the end of 2001 with the FBI's identification of 760 "special interest" detainees, who Ghani said "then disappeared into the secret files, courts and cells erased from the public eye by a Department of Justice gag order" (Ghani 2009). Next came a Special Registration program, with the detention and deportation of men from "terror watch list" countries (ibid.). Ghani describes reading the legal instruments and reports, noticing that the law's language and classifications were designed to "enclose and exclude," and that the documents themselves were "full of absences—redactions, erasures, censorships" that were mirrored in immigrant communities impacted by these acts of detention and deportation (ibid.). Another of Ghani's humane interventions into redacted records, which she described as an "empathetic leap," is what she calls "'warm' data" (ibid.). With Ganesh she produced a "warm database" titled *How Do You See the Disappeared?* (2005). By warm data, they refer to the extraction of information that provides "a portrait, not a profile"; warm data is "the opposite of cold, hard facts. Warm data is subjective" (Ghani 2009). Warm data is also in opposition to erasure or removal. Ghani described the questionnaire she designed, in collaboration with affected communities, and that was intended to elicit answers that were "specific and personal"; "public, not secret"; "voluntary" (ibid.). This included questions such as "What place do you see when you close your eyes at night? Describe an offhand remark that someone once made to you that you've never been able to forget" (ibid.). In gathering warm data, Ghani is also drawing our attention to the data-gatherer and data-manager. Usually these are assumed to be invisible specters in the vast machine of the state, but Ghani reminds us that these are human subjects exercising judgment. Whereas in official records, these specters enact the violence that sustains state sovereignty, Ghani shows us that this is neither natural nor inevitable.

Other artists present redacted records in a manner that highlights the aesthetic achievement of this administrative act of violence. Jenny Holzer, in her series, *Redaction Paintings* (2006–), made paintings from heavily redacted declassified documents about the war in Iraq, extraordinary rendition from Afghanistan, torture at Abu Ghraib, and interrogation techniques at Camp X-Ray.[4] Her work drew attention to the official origins of these documents as well as their pre-release redaction, and was simultaneously abstract and political. In the work's reliance upon aesthetic formalism and Realpolitik, Holzer sustained an ironic dialogue between the techniques for achieving secrecy and the horrors that are being hidden. For some critics, her canvases portraying documents almost entirely obscured by blocks of black were aesthetic citations of Cold War paintings by Mark Rothko or Robert Motherwell, prompting a reassessment of those earlier paintings, with their paint-soaked blocks, blotches, and stains, as foundational artworks about secrecy and paranoia (Slaughter 2010).

That Holzer's work has these forebears points to the longer narrative in which formalism appears in political art. But it also draws attention to the brazenness of contemporary bureaucracy, which deploys such traditional abstract devices as cubes, lines, and blocks of color in the concealment of such materially real and embodied practices of state-sanctioned deprivation and violence. The literary scholar Joseph Slaughter described Holzer's 2009 exhibition *Protect Protect* as featuring what he called some of the "infamous masterpieces" of the Bush administration's circumvention of the Constitution and international treaties, alongside what he called "lesser known works of criminal activity, intent and investigation" (Slaughter 2010, 207). Slaughter was gesturing at the immense creativity that enables state criminality to be effaced by the impassivity of bureaucracy, where the artistic meets the artful. The Bush administration was not a machine. It comprised creative individuals, endlessly reimagining and reinterpreting, and taking pleasure in their mastery of abstract formalism, with its respect for structure, balance, and harmony, all in the service of concealing official state practices that bore none of these attributes.

In 2004, the American Civil Liberties Union attempted to obtain documents held by the Pentagon relating to prisoner abuse in American offshore detention centers, and in 2016 received 198 out of 2,000 extant photographic images taken at Abu Ghraib. Prior to their release, the images were redacted. The artist Edmund Clark, in his work *198/2000* (2018), projected these onto a gallery wall "at odd intervals [. . .] calibrated [. . .] to raise questions about what's missing" (Backman 2018).[5] His work *Negative Publicity* (2011–16), in collaboration with the counterterrorism investigator, Crofton Black, is a compilation of photographs and documents that "confront the nature of contemporary warfare and the invisible mechanisms of state control" (Clark, *Negative Publicity*). Clark and Black confronted "negative evidence," because no public records were available that would enable them to document the CIA's incarceration of people in a global network of secret prisons (Clark, *Negative Publicity*). Instead, they attempted to establish a paper trail "via the weak points of business accountability: invoices, documents of incorporation, and billing reconciliations produced by the small-town American business enlisted in prisoner transportation" (Clark, *Negative Publicity*). Clark also took a series of super-realist photographs of prison sites, the homes of those detained, and other government locations, in an effort to document activities related to black sites (Clark, *Negative Publicity*). Described as "artefacts of extraordinary rendition," the work also includes "a largely redacted CIA handbook of interrogation techniques [. . .] with sub-sections that include 'stiff brush and shackles' and, more infamously, 'water-board techniques'" (Slessor 2016).

In *Letters to Omar* (2010), Clark presents a selection of letters and cards received by the prisoner Omar Deghayes during his six-year detention at Guantanamo Bay Detention Camp. The correspondence had been sent by family members and strangers, and Deghayes only received it after it had been "scanned for dangerous substances, redacted and copied or scanned—including the backs of envelopes and blank sheets of paper—officially stamped and/or given a unique reference number" (Clark, *Letters*). For Clark, "these degraded, abstracted gestures of support became complicit in the control process exercised over Omar and ultimately contributed to his paranoia and disorientation" (Clark, *Letters*). In all of this work, we are presented with an array of methods by which the state destroys records, and also the function of that destruction within the work of sovereignty. Destroying these records is purposeful and productive; it regenerates and reanimates the power of the state. In most of this work, we are able to perceive the hand of the destroyer, or their tools, following lawful directions to materially gouge or tear apart records.

A new challenge arises in our contemporary moment. Now evidence destruction takes advantage of the affordances of digital technologies, making it difficult to draw the line between lawful and unlawful destruction and also presenting challenges for artists seeking to visualize it. Techniques of redaction, removal, and destruction no longer need to leave any traces of their occurrence. Digital records can be altered in a way that only experts can perceive. Or records might be destroyed with nobody noticing: How would we know? Real secrets stay off the record. Knowing that the documents used by the artists examined here recorded the terrible secret facts of policies of violence, coercion, and control, we now might wonder about how much worse are the secret-secrets, too dreadful to record.

Deleting files and software, deleting social media posts or accounts (*Torres v Lexington Ins. Co*; *Katiroll Co v Kati Roll & Platters Inc.*; *Allied Concrete Co v Lester*), clearing caches (*United States v Kernell*), moving files onto a USB (*United States v Keith*), over-writing data (*FTC v DirecTV Inc.*), not using version-control software (*Coalition America Inc v Arlotta et al*), altering meta-data (*Krumwiede v Brighton Assocs. LLC*), syncing data across devices and destroying devices, and the burgeoning market for ephemeral data (*Waymo LLC v Uber Techs. Inc*)—are all digital methods of evidence destruction that have demanded judicial attention. These are merely the methods that the law has already noticed. Beyond these are a gathering army of specters who operate out of our view, and whom we may never see. In the digital age, law's destructive work might never be known, and those who undertake it never unidentified.

In her history of files as instruments of legal authority, Cornelia Vismann realized, "In cultural memory . . . these techniques of effacement have themselves been effaced" (2008, 26). Contemporary records are digital. Declassifying digital documents is done using computer software. The US National Security Agency distributed a guide called "Redacting with Confidence" (2008). The guide replaces the term "redaction" with "sanitization"; other organizations use an even more invisible term: "data loss prevention." The production of new forms of abstraction—in which language no longer conveys meaning—points to the ongoing creativity of institutions. The logic of data loss prevention is that information is "lost" when it is disclosed. The data itself it not lost; it is shared. What is lost is institutional control of the data: where it goes, how it is used, and how it is understood. Data control is preserved by keeping information secret, and so loss prevention demands concealment and effacement. The challenges posed by digital data storage are seized upon by information managers as new creative opportunities. The black boxes are digitally drawn, but the guidelines prefer that the boxes be grey, or that they are not boxes at all; sensitive text is replaced with innocuous text, and the replacements should all be of uniform size so that we cannot speculate upon the amount of text that was there before. The hidden data in digital documents needs to remain hidden, and the replacements are encrypted, so that different users with different access rights might be able to see more or less data. Whereas redaction draws attention to the document's sensitivity by visually indicating the portions of it that are missing, a sanitized document hides sensitive content in a way that conceals its own hiding. Legal discourse and legal consciousness in the twenty-first century remain as obsessed as ever with record-keeping and the tensions between disclosure and concealment. But the affordances of the digital age have overwritten the binary: Preserve or destroy. Today, sovereign power no longer relies upon destruction, instead relying upon coercive practices of concealment and obfuscation. The state continues to hoard its secrets, and to modify, redact, or hide its records. It has turned its spectacular violence upon transparency activists—those who leak sensitive information. Meanwhile, innocuous and barely perceptible tools are deployed as the state wields its power through endless acts of bureaucratic imagination.

In this chapter, by drawing attention to the ruins left in law's wake, we can visualize law's violence through its destructive spectacles. Each of the artists whose work is made from or about destroyed records is addressing themselves to the question: *How should we remember the dead?* Destroyed evidence, redacted documents, shredded papers, they all leave traces. Often incomprehensible, these traces nevertheless tell us that something powerful has been withheld from us. We return to Hamlet, recalling that the Ghost appeared at a threshold moment. He embodied sovereignty, legitimacy, violence, and secrecy, and he challenged Hamlet to respond with justice. Hamlet was indecisive and driven mad by the impossibility and futility of his task. Despite mounting evidence of injustice, the state perseveres, and its endurance is achieved through perpetual acts of destruction, denial, and obfuscation. As the curtain falls, we bear witness to the corpses strewn across the stage, including Hamlet's. These are evidence of the violence and destruction wrought by lawful state actions. Amid the hollow ceremonies of mourning—marching, gunshots, music—comes an important message: "Speak loudly for him" (*Hamlet*: Act V, Scene II)—urging us to maintain vigilant attention to the spectral remains of law's destruction. Look at them, remember them, speak up against them.

NOTES

1 See Jason File. 2015. "A Crushed Image (20 years after Srebrenica)." Program, Stroom Den Haag, http://stroom.nl; File. 2018. "In Black and White," Jason File, http://jasonfile.com.
2 See Taryn Simon. 2010. "Contraband," Works, *Taryn Simon*, http://tarynsimon.com/.
3 See Mariam Ghani. "Work > Photography + Prints," Work, *Mariam Ghani*. www.mariamghani.com.
4 See Jenny Holzer. "Jenny Holzer Mass MoCa." Exhibitions, *Jenny Holzer*. https://projects.jennyholzer.com/.
5 See Edmund Clark. "Work," Work, *Edmund Clark*. https://edmundclark.com.

REFERENCES

Cases
Allied Concrete Co v Lester [2013] 285 Va. 295; 736 S.E.2d 699; Va. LEXIS 8.
Coalition America Inc v Arlotta et al [2008] U.S. Dist. LEXIS 129820.
FTC v DirecTV Inc. [2016] U.S. Dist. LEXIS 176873.
Katiroll Co v Kati Roll & Platters Inc. [2011] U.S. Dist. LEXIS 85212.
Krumwiede v Brighton Assocs. LLC [2006] U.S. Dist. LEXIS 31669.
Torres v Lexington Ins. Co [2006] 237 F.R.D. 533; U.S. Dist. LEXIS 64458.
United States v Keith [2011] 440 Fed. Appx. 503; U.S. App. LEXIS 20231.
United States v Kernell [2010] 667 F.3d 746; U.S. App. LEXIS 1690.
Waymo LLC v Uber Techs. Inc [2018] U.S. Dist. LEXIS 16020.

Secondary Sources
Attorney General's Department. 2015. Royal Commission into Trade Union Governance and Corruption, Final Report (Vol. 4). Canberra: Commonwealth of Australia.
Australian Associated Press (AAP). 2018. "Former Union Boss Convicted of Destroying Tonnes of Evidence to Pre-Empt Royal Commission." *The Guardian* (Australia), December 17.

Backman, Marjorie. 2018. "Photographs Trace US Government Abuses, from Manzanar to Guantánamo." *Hyperallergic*, March 5. www.hyperallergic.com

Barthes, Roland. 1981. *Camera Lucida: Reflections on Photography*. New York: Hill and Wang.

Bevan, Robert. 2016. *The Destruction of Memory: Architecture and War*. London: Reaktion Books.

Biber, Katherine. 2018. "The Art of Bureaucracy: Redacted Readymades." In Desmond Manderson (ed.), *Law and the Visual*. Toronto: University of Toronto Press.

Blazwick, Iwona. 2013. *Cornelia Parker*. London: Thames & Hudson.

Bresnahan, Keith and J. M. Mancini. 2015. *Architecture and Armed Conflict: The Politics of Destruction*. London: Routledge.

Brisman, Avi and Nigel South. 2014. *Green Cultural Criminology: Constructions of Environmental Harm, Consumerism and Resistance to Ecocide*. London: Routledge.

Chitra, Ganesh, 2016. "Codes of Conduct, 2016." www.chitraganesh.com

Clark, Edmund, 2010. "Letters to Omar." www.edmundclark.com

———. "Negative Publicity." www.edmundclark.com

Connor, Andrea. 2017. *The Political Afterlife of Sites of Monumental Destruction*. London: Routledge.

Crowe, Benjamin D. 2006. *Heidegger's Religious Origins: Destruction and Authenticity*. Bloomington and Indianapolis: Indiana University Press.

Curry, Andrew. 2008. "Piecing Together the Dark Legacy of East Germany's Secret Police." www.wired.com.

Derrida, Jacques. 1995. "Archive Fever: A Freudian Impression." *Diacritics* 25 (2): 9–63.

———. 2006. *Specters of Marx: The State of Debt, the Work of Mourning and the New International*. Abingdon: Routledge.

DeSilvey, Caitlin and Tim Edensor. 2012. "Reckoning with Ruins." *Progress in Human Geography* 37, 4: 465–485.

Edgers, Geoff. 2006. "Picking Up the Pieces; Cornelia Parker Strung Up Hundreds of Charred Wood Fragments to Install 'Hanging Fire'. (Hint: She had a cheat sheet)." www.archive.boston.com

Elliott, John. 1980. "Marx and Schumpeter on Capitalism's Creative Destruction." *Quarterly Journal of Economics* 95, 1: 45–68.

Federal Commissioner for the Records of the State Security Service of the Former German Democratic Republic. "The Reconstruction of Torn Documents," Archives, *Stasi Records Archive*. http://bstu.ed.

Fenster, Mark. 2012. "Disclosure's Effects: WikiLeaks and Transparency." *Iowa Law Review* 97: 753–807.

———. 2014. "The Implausibility of Secrecy." *Hastings Law Review* 65: 346.

File, Jason. 2015. "Erasing a Classified Military Document, 2013." In *A Crushed Image (20 Years After Srebrenica)*. [Exhibition catalogue] Stroom Den Haag, March 22–April 12, 25.

———. "In Black and White, 2018." www.jasonfile.com

Fisher, Mark. 2014. *Ghosts of My life: Writings in Depression, Hauntology and Lost Futures*. Winchester: Zero Books.
Frascina, Francis. 2016. "Redaction." *Art Monthly* 393: 1–4.
Frizzell, Deborah. 2017. "Seeing the Unseen: An Interview with Mariam Ghani." *Cultural Politics* 13, 1 (March): 48–57.
Ganesh, Chitra. 2016. "Codes of Conduct," Portfolio, *Chitra Ganesh*. http://chitraganesh.com.
Ganesh, Chitra and Mariam Ghani. 2011. "Introduction to an Index." *Radical History Review* 111: 110–129.
Ghani, Mariam. 2009. "Divining the Question: An Unscientific Methodology for the Collection of Warm Data [proof for Conversation Pieces exhibition reader]." www.mariamghani.com.
———. 2011. "The Trespassers: FAQ, Notes, Interview, Transcripts." www.mariamghani.com
———. 2015. "What We Left Unfinished: The Artist and the Archive." In Anthony Downey (ed.), *Dissonant Archives: Contemporary Visual Culture and Contested Narratives in the Middle East*. London: I.B. Tauris.
Ghani, Mariam and Chitra Ganesh. 2005. "Notes on the Disappeared: Towards a Visual Language of Resistance." *Sarai Reader* 05: Bare Acts: 154–161.
Gordon, Avery. 1992. *Ghostly Matters: Haunting and the Sociological Imagination* (rev. ed.). Minneapolis: University of Minnesota Press.
Hell, Julia and Andreas Schönle. 2010. *Ruins of Modernity*. Durham, NC: Duke University Press.
Hirvonen, Ari. 1998. "After the Law." In *Polycentricity: The Multiple Scenes of Law*. London: Pluto Press.
Linnemann, Travis. 2017. "Proof of Death: Police Power and the Visual Economies of Seizure, Accumulation and Trophy." *Theoretical Criminology* 21, 1: 57–77.
Marx, Karl and Friedrich Engels. 1977[1888]. *The Communist Manifesto*. Middlesex: Penguin Books.
Morgan, Jessica. 2000. "Matter and What It Means." In *Cornelia Parker* [exhibition catalogue], Institute of Contemporary Art, Boston, February 2–April 9. Boston: ICA.
National Security Agency, Information Assurance Directorate. 2008. *Redacting with Confidence: How to Safely Publish Sanitized Reports Converted from Word 2007 to PDF*. http://citeseerx.ist.psu.edu/
Nietzsche, Friedrich. 1967. *The Will to Power: A New Translation* (trans. W. Kaufman and R. J. Hollingdale). New York: Vintage Books.
Obrist, Hans. 2010. "Taryn Simon, Contraband, 2010," Essays/Videos, *Taryn Simon*. www.tarynsimon.com.
Oltermann, Philip. 2018. "Stasi Files: Scanner Struggles to Stitch Together Surveillance State Scraps," Germany, *The Guardian*, January 3, 2018. http://theguardian.com.
Pangburn, D. J. 2016. "Shredded Spy Agency Documents Become Readymade Art." www.vice.com.

Powell, Michael G. 2010. "Blacked Out: Our Cultural Romance with Redacted Documents." *The Believer*, June. www.believermag.com

Racz, Imogen. 2013. "Cornelia Parker's Thirty Pieces of Silver." In Jennifer Walden (ed.), *Art and Destruction*, 45–56. Newcastle Upon Tyne: Cambridge Scholars Publishing.

Schumpeter, Joseph A. 1950. *Capitalism, Socialism and Democracy*, 3rd ed. New York: Harper Torchbooks.

Schwartz, Robert. 2016. "Art Made of Destroyed Stasi Documents Displayed in Berlin." www.DW.com.

Sibson, Ellie. 2018. "Dave Hanna, Ex-Union Boss, Found Guilty of Destroying Papers Sought by Royal Commission." www.abc.net.au.

Slaughter, Joseph R. 2010. "Vanishing Points: When Narrative Is Not Simply There." *Journal of Human Rights* 9: 207–23.

Slessor, Catherine. 2016. "Black Sites: Torture's Hidden Infrastructure." www.architects journal.co.uk.

Sontag, Susan. 1971. *On Photography*. London: Penguin.

Stoler, Ann Laura. 2013. "The Rot Remains: From Ruins to Ruination." In *Imperial Debris: On Ruins and Ruination*, 1–38. Durham, NC: Duke University Press.

Tallgren, Immi. 2018. "Dechiqueteuse (Paper-Shredder)." In Jessie Hohmann and Daniel Joyce (eds.), *International Law's Objects*, 203–213. Oxford: Oxford University Press.

Tate online. "The Story of Cold Dark Matter." www.tate.org.uk.

Tickner, Lisa. 2003. "A Strange Alchemy: Cornelia Parker." *Art History* 26, 3: 364–391.

Tsing, Anna L. 2015. *The Mushroom at the End of the World: On the Possibility of Life in Capitalist Ruins*. Princeton, NJ: Princeton University Press.

Vismann, Cornelia. 2008. *Files: Law and Media Technology* (trans. G. Winthrop-Young). Stanford, CA: Stanford University Press.

Wagstaff, Sheena. 2018. "A Conversation with Cornelia Parker." In *Transitional Object [Psychobarn]*. London: Royal Academy of Arts.

Walden, Jennifer. 2013a. "Introduction." In *Art and Destruction*. Newcastle Upon Tyne: Cambridge Scholars Publishing.

———. 2013b. *Art and Destruction*. Newcastle Upon Tyne: Cambridge Scholars Publishing.

Wright, C. and D. Nyberg. 2015. *Climate Change, Capitalism and Corporations: Processes of Creative Self-Destruction*. Cambridge: Cambridge University Press.

Žižek, Slavoj. 1999. "The Spectre of Ideology." In Elizabeth Wright and Edmond Wright (eds.), *The Žižek Reader*, 53–86. Oxford: Blackwell.

———. 2001. *Did Somebody Say Totalitarianism? Five Interventions in the (Mis)use of a Notion*. London: Verso.

7

Police

The Weird and Eerie

TRAVIS LINNEMANN AND JUSTIN TURNER

There is a saying: The police are never around when you need them, but always around when you don't. Though we aren't sure of its origin, this adage returned to us as we read the late Mark Fisher's (2017) final work, *The Weird and the Eerie*. In his most basic phrasing, Fisher describes the weird as the out of place—*the conjoining of two or more things which do not belong together*—a sense of wrongness, the not quite right (Fisher 2017:10–11). By its very nature, the weird manifests as unease, but it may also signal a shock of the new, an outmoding or radical departure from our existing frameworks of understanding. To encounter the weird in this regard is to stand with bewilderment in the presence of that which exists *outside* typical boundaries of thought and sight.

Alongside the *unwelcomed* intrusions of the weird, Fisher positions the eerie, denoting an equally untoward sense of presence or absence. It is here that we might ask ourselves, *Why is there something here where there should be nothing? Or, why is there nothing here when there should be something?* (Fisher 2017:12). Fisher's efforts of course should not be confused with an imaginative attempt to revive late nineteenth-century spiritualism. Rather, as an extension of his earlier work on hauntology,[1] *The Weird and the Eerie* continues the search for ways to grasp the "agency of the virtual," of those things that act upon the realms of the living without actually existing. By way of example, he notes that "capital is at every level an eerie entity: conjured out of nothing, capital nevertheless exerts more influence than any allegedly substantial entity" (Fisher, 2017:11). Borne of, inseparable from, and necessitated by capital, the police power is also at every level eerie. In fact, so interwoven are police with the mundane pace of life under late capitalism, that they often go eerily unnoticed—that is, *until they don't*. Such is the point made by Walter Benjamin in his famous essay "Critique of Violence" (Benjamin, 1978:286). In setting out distinctions between lawmaking and law-preserving violence—twin forces that produce and preserve bourgeoise order—Benjamin finds in police a "spectral mixture" of both. Simply put, rather than enforcing law on behalf of the state or public, police and their attendant violence emerge from and mark the precise point at which the state's power begins to wane. For "security reasons" then, police choose to intervene in the lives of subjects in countless instances where crime and law are of no particular concern, fabricating social order through the "brutal encumbrances" of haphazard and unequal regulation, supervision, surveillance and, above all, violence. Driven by capacious discretionary privileges, the police power is then as Benjamin thusly described "formless"—everywhere and nowhere—a "ghostly presence in the life of civilized states" (Benjamin 1978:287). Picking up on this eerie presence, in his article "In Baltimore, Police Seem Everywhere and Nowhere at Once," journalist Scott Beyer writes, "Baltimore is suffering from a contradiction of sorts. On the one hand the city is known for tough cops and citywide camera surveillance. On the other hand, it can seem at times like there are hardly any police around" (Beyer 2018:1). Despite this astute observation, Beyer dismisses policing's formlessness as a symptom of corruption rather than as evidence of the invariably uneven application of the police prerogative. Misrecognition of this sort is not terribly surprising, as policing's broad discretionary powers are among its most closely guarded secrets.[2]

Well ahead of Benjamin and Beyer, in 1715, Benard le Bovier de Fontenelle, an early French police commander remarked similarly,[3] "to be everywhere, without being seen; finally, to move or to check at will a vast and tempestuous multitude and to be the ever active and nearly unknown soul of this great body; these are the duties of the police magistrate" (Brodeur 2010:225-226). "The ever active and nearly unknown soul of this great body" being "everywhere without being seen" and intervening "at will a vast and tempestuous multitude" certainly allies with the formless nature of discretionary violence identified by Benjamin. But in developing secret, political or so-called high police in order to thwart the gathering revolution, Fontenelle and his contemporaries revealed another of policing's weird and eerie dimensions. As opposed to what they called "base" or "low" police tasked with producing order through their physical presence and quotidian commands, "Haute" or high police were said to operate in the background in the interests of "national security" as "*shadow police*, thwarting coalitions and conspiracies."[4] Of course, subsequent thinkers were quick to note that the ability to evade detection to "catch" lawbreakers, hide their identities in order to infiltrate groups, and lie to obscure their true intentions are skills required of all police. Even more to the point, detractors argued that the high police is not so much a different form of police as it is an obvious political activity operating through the medium of police.[5] Rather than upholding an unhelpful high/low dichotomy, we might simply state the obvious: Police are not only inherently political, but the key point at which abstract politics meets the flesh and blood of the population. While a theoretical non sequitur, discussions of high/low police are necessarily productive for our purposes, as they draw out further the ways that the police themselves understand, distinguish between, and play upon their own presence and absence.

From the apparent trend of white women calling the police, for no reason, on their black neighbors, to instances of lethal police violence that began as routine contact, for many individuals, particularly black Americans, the police are quite often around when you don't need them. With upwards of 800,000 sworn cops, or roughly 1 cop for every 400 of its citizens, the United States stands as a uniquely and perhaps over-policed society when compared to its counterparts.[6] In the United States, you will find police assigned to schools, universities, hospitals, housing developments, parks, airports, train stations, and you'll find them in their private forms, guarding banks, malls, convenience stores, even churches. Never confined to the corporeal realm, the police power has of course colonized the cavernous, rhizomic spaces of the Internet.[7] Switched on in the background, listening to our conversations, the police power outlines and animates a boundless yet invisible—should we say spectral—assemblage. With more than 100 million smart speakers standing by as potential witnesses, and the doorbell security camera company Ring partnered with hundreds of departments nationwide to provide police-monitored "neighborhood portals," it seems now more than ever that police power is everywhere and nowhere simultaneously.

Despite their looming presence in public life, police quite often perform the trick of being conspicuously absent. In the thick of the violent clash at the "Unite the Right" protests in Charlottesville, Virginia, those who stood in opposition to right-wing groups reckoned first-hand the absence of police. In a prelude to the larger event planned for Saturday, a group of more than one hundred white nationalists marched through the University of Virginia campus Friday night. With faces glowing from the flames of their torches and chants of "Blood and Soil" filling the air, the men encircled a small group of counter-protestors linked around a statue of Thomas Jefferson. Behind the unsettled faces and the flickering shadow cast by their torches stood riot-geared police who were content, it seemed, to allow the violence of the protests to work itself out. Recalling the scene and inaction of police, Cornell West said that without the intervention of anti-fascist protestors, the gathering of clergy of which he was a part "would have been crushed like cockroaches."

Beyond apathy and inaction, other grim circumstances outline the occluded parameters of police duty. Following the shooting at Marjory Stoneman Douglas High School in Parkland, Florida, courts again considered the duty of police to protect the public, after it was learned that police present that day failed to engage the shooter Nikolas Cruz. One cop, Scot Peterson, was particularly reviled, after video emerged showing him hiding at a distance, as Cruz killed seventeen people and wounded seventeen more.[8] In a suit brought against the school district, Broward Sheriff's Office, and Peterson himself, US District Judge Beth Bloom affirmed prior rulings from higher courts, finding that police in fact bear no legal obligation whatsoever to defend the public.[9] The decision cited a 2005 Supreme Court case where Colorado police failed to enforce a no-contact order against a man who later abducted and murdered his three children.[10] In this case, as with Parkland later, the court ruled that since the killer was not in the custody of the police (i.e., an escaped prisoner), they could not be held liable, even for gross inaction. Of course, our suggestion here is not that police invariably shirk their duties. Our point, rather, is this: *Despite what we are led to believe, despite what we know to be true, police offer no real protection and, in most instances, are under no legal obligation to do so.*

While obvious and well established, neither policing's omnipresence nor its empirical limits and failures quite fit Fisher's weird and eerie.

Joining the effort to illuminate the agency of the virtual and that which is *outside*, our aim in this chapter is to direct attention to a few ways that the ghostly power of police enters into and acts upon the realms of the living.[11] Such observations not only present a novel way to analyze police, but lead to an important conclusion: The very concept of police, and the attitudes and actions of those who occupy the role, are nothing if not horrific, eerie, and just plain weird.

Now You See Them, Now You Don't

As the suggestive dread of the music from Carl Orff's *O Fortuna* rises, so too wispy tendrils of fog passing a full moon, signaling an eerie night. This is not, however, a trailer for the latest in Hollywood horror flick, but the opening moments of a promotional video produced by the North Carolina State Police to introduce their newest innovation, so-called ghost cars designed specifically to evade the detection of speeding motorists.[12] Painted black, stripped of rooftop light bars and other obvious giveaways, the cars' scant markings glow with otherworldly luminescence when shown in the headlights of a passing car. As the ominous score concludes, the message is clear—lawbreakers beware, "with the ghost car, you won't even see us coming."[13]

Let us briefly imagine an instance in which the ghost car operates as intended. A dark roadway, a passing motorist's headlights catch the iridescent graphics, causing them to glow. More literally than Benjamin likely ever imagined, police emerge from the ether, a ghostly power invading the world of human relations. Of course, since the advent of the automobile, police have hidden alongside roads, behind billboards, and in other nooks and crannies hoping to catch speeding motorists, making ghosts cars hardly novel.[14] Without the aid of ghost cars, several departments in Michigan recently ran the aptly named "Operation Ghost Rider" using unmarked vehicles to spot texting drivers.[15] Yet given the desire to advertise their newly acquired spectral powers to, as one cop put it, "put the scare into speedsters," ghost cars are apparently a point of pride for departments that deploy them.[16] Moving between the registers of the visible and invisible, they are, in the words of one cop, "the best of both worlds."[17] Maintaining a presence when presumed absent and absent when perhaps expected, ghost cars demonstrate how police produce and play upon the eerie by being *in* place and *out* of place, at once. From ghost cars and ghost operations, to untraceable "ghost guns" and "ghost warrants" that refuse to be cleared, it is evident that the police and the spectral, two things that should not belong together, continue a weird marriage.[18] Such is the lesson of the ghost car: *The police power is spectral power.*

Powers Invisible

However spectral, the police power is not primordial. It is a power borne of the demonic relations of man. As Mark Neocleous (2016) convincingly argues in his book *The Universal Adversary: Security, Capital and "The Enemies of All Mankind,"* for the apparitional power of police to have ever intervened in the worlds of the living, it must have first been called forth by the threats and dangers of an equally formless enemy. Returning to the origins of contract theory and hence the origins of police, Neocleous notes how in *Leviathan*, Hobbes paid close attention to the imaginative realms ordered and inhabited by "Powers Invisible," "Invisible Powers," "Spirits Invisible," "Invisible Agents," and "Invisible Spirits." For Hobbes, fear of things invisible—a demonic spirit, a vengeful god—forms the basis of religious authority and, importantly for those inclined "to nourish, dresse, and forme it into Lawes," the basis of political power also.[19] Fear of death, fear of other humans, and fear of an invisible, unknown, yet-to-arrive enemy produces obedience, permitting sovereign power to organize security and social order as it wishes. Here, against a perpetual universal adversary rises, as he puts it, the "permanent ghostly presence of the police power, that all-pervasive power that lies at the heart of the state." And so, it is through the political/theological sorcery that summons enemies once invisible, that police—this "ghostly presence in the life of civilized states"—enters the realms of the living.

For the initiated, these spectral powers invisible abound. Consider the antagonisms between Black Lives Matter, which rose to international prominence following the killings of Trayvon Martin and Michael Brown, and the various offshoots of a loosely adhered "Blue Lives" movement animated by portents of disorder and insurrection following the murders of NYPD officers Rafael Ramos and Wenjian Liu. Just five months after the late 2014 murders of Ramos and Liu, President Obama signed the "Blue Alert Act of 2015," surrounded by members of the slain officers' families. After coming under fire for limiting the Pentagon's 1033 "police militarization" program, the "Blue Alert" act—which established a nationwide communication network to share information regarding threats to police—was an important symbolic move to "back the blue." Lost in the political theater surrounding the dead cops was that the shooter, Ismaaiyl Brinsley, had murdered his girlfriend Shaneka Thompson before driving from Baltimore to Brooklyn, killing Ramos and Liu and then himself. *Four lives lost, not two.*

Nevertheless, the "Blue Alert Act" joined a swell of similar legislation aimed at safeguarding police and punishing those who do them harm. One such provision, predictably named the "Blue Lives Matter law," passed first in Louisiana and then in Kentucky and Mississippi, extending hate crime protections to police. Not to be outdone, Arizona legislators went further, covering any "peace officer" on duty or off with hate crime protections. At the federal level, the yet-to-pass "Protect and Serve Act" seeks to do the same. Obviously, it is always a crime to harm police. The redundancy of these laws therefore reveals the obvious—the whole Blue Lives coalition is a petulant reaction to a perceived attack on police, which is to say an attack on the established order.

While Black Lives Matter, like the Black Panther Party before it, emerged as retort to the violence police have long visited on black people and the black body politic, the sad and perverse irony is that a reactionary and imaginary blue life now openly demands and enjoys legal protections that blacks themselves have never fully received. Against the "unique authority, impunity and power" of the police uniform, as Natasha Lennard rightly argues, "Black skin is marked with the opposite." Now, with the move to recognize blue life with new legal protections, lawmakers have "affirmed a willingness to hold black life in America in even lower standing."[20] The emergence of blue life as a distinct subject position, one accorded special rights and protections, particularly in direct opposition to Black Lives Matter, usefully demonstrates the breadth of support for police, the extent to which that support is *white* support,[21] and just how quickly that support can be transformed into concrete political action and policy.

While it may be the most recent and most visible enemy to raise the vengeful specter of police power, Black Lives Matter is certainly not the first. Three decades before the murders of Ramos and Liu, another dead New York cop helped bolster a rising political order. As Justin Turner's (2018) account of the 1988 murder of NYPD officer Edward Byrne documents, violence against police provides a useful avenue for sloganeering, retaliatory violence, and political initiatives. In the case of Byrne, a rookie cop murdered by members of a Queens drug gang, venomous calls from the NYPD, George H. W. Bush, Rudy Giuliani, and others to "take back the streets" fit perfectly within a rising-order maintenance and broken windows policing campaign that ramped up violence against poor people across the city under the banner of "quality of life." Extending beyond the temporal and spatial boundaries of 1980s New York City, the Department of Justice, Edward Byrne Memorial Justice Assistance Grant program, the nation's largest funding opportunity for local and state police, still carries the dead officer's name. Byrne's murder and its ghostly afterlife lingers in memoriam, evident not just in the revanchist policies of the so-called New York Miracle but in the multi-jurisdictional task forces, buy and bust programs, asset forfeiture, and no-knock raids of the indefatigable war on drugs.

All of this, of course, continues. In July 2016, days after a man named Micah Johnson killed five Dallas cops, former Milwaukee County Sheriff David Clarke, who gained national prominence as a vocal and notably black critic of Obama, took to Fox News to shore up an imaginary link to Black Lives Matter, writing:

> Stand up to Black Lives Matter. Show you don't kowtow to the liberal pressure exacted to achieve their political goals on the backs of the suffering of black Americans due to crime and the dissolution of their communities. It is the hard road to sow in our culture where the right thing is shamed and the wrong thing is held up, but as a law enforcement officer I can tell you this is the time for choosing: law and order, justice, the American way or anarchy, division, hate, and authoritarianism. Black Lives Matter has shown their hand in Dallas: they choose the latter.[22]

Long before Clarke and other conservatives began focusing on Black Lives Matter, the War on Cops was part of a broader narrative advanced by prominent right-wing think tanks and activist groups. Continuing in the tradition of the John Birch Society, Manhattan Institute affiliate Heather MacDonald has, since the early 1990s, advanced a militant pro-cop agenda, writing two books and dozens of articles decrying liberal challenges to law and order. Now with a visible enemy to name and challenge, MacDonald's work has been reinvigorated. In the first pages of her aptly titled *The War on Cops: How the New Attack on Law and Order Makes Everyone Less Safe*, she blames Black Lives Matter for a rise in violent crime (later called the Ferguson Effect). She writes:

> Fueling the rise in crime in places like Baltimore and Milwaukee is a multipronged attack on law enforcement. Since last summer 2014, a protest movement known as Black Lives Matter has convulsed the nation. Triggered by a series of highly publicized deaths of black males at the hands of police, the Black Lives Matter movement holds that police officers are the greatest threat facing young black men today. That belief has spawned riots, "die-ins," and the assassination of police officers.[23]

MacDonald, like Clarke, sees Black Lives Matter, not as a righteous response to police violence but as the vanguard of an ongoing war—an attack on civilization itself. Describing the killings of Ramos and Liu as "assassinations" and the first shots in a "wrenching attack on civilization," MacDonald directly and powerfully endorses a Hobbesian understanding of social order utterly dependent on the violence of police.[24] The mythical "War on Cops," discredited "Ferguson Effect," and attendant claim "Blue Lives Matter" are nonetheless potent ideological vehicles that help imagine and solidify the vocation of police, as a unique identity and subject position, worthy not only of respect and sympathy, but protection.

In *The New Inquiry*, Nijah Cunningham and Tiana Reid comment similarly, arguing that the reactionary incantation brings an apparitional blue life into being, "giving flesh to the ghostly presence of police power."[25] To see this sorcery at work, they write, is to bear witness to the ways that police power summons the specter of the very enemy it seeks to destroy. "By producing and then gesturing towards an amorphous hatred," they add, "'Blue Lives Matter' constitutes an uninhabitable legal identity out of a repertoire of fear, dread, and trepidation." As a moral claim and performance of vulnerability, the claim transforms nearly any action—feelings, utterances, mindsets, opinions, fantasies—into an attack on blue life, making protest into aggression, collectivity into a riot, and self-preservation into resisting arrest.[26] In the case of Brinsley, as his identity dissolved into the monstrous category *cop killer*, he became metonymic of the broader and incalculable threat of black political solidarity. In a double move, Blue Lives Matter names its own enemy and bolsters its own power, while simultaneously exorcising and rendering invisible the violence and terror that police bring into being. Calling forth an ethereal and wholly virtual blue life to act on the realms of the living—martialing reactionary support, while also occluding its own misdeeds and history—the police power is formless, present *and* absent. It is here that we ask, again, *why is there something where there should be nothing? Why is there nothing where there should be something?*

These questions again sharpen our focus on the occulted powers that bring "the blue" into being. In their book by the same name, Karen and Barbara Fields use the term *racecraft* to describe the complex yet unseen thicket of background forces that constitute race and racial differences and that render the adjoining practices of racism, for some, somehow rational.[27] Drawing comparisons to folk witchcraft practices, the pair describe how race is constituted by a similar system of rituals, circular reasoning, negation of contradictory evidence, and by a disciplinary system fashioned of gossip, exclusion, scapegoating, and coercion.[28] Like the superstitious and unscientific rituals and practices that make devotees of witchcraft believe the implausible and impossible, race, racial difference, and racial hierarchy are borne of an equally pernicious set of practices. Long tasked with producing and upholding racial categories and enforcing the color line, police power runs through and is mutually constitutive of racecraft. Indeed, in the United States, police is one of the key ways liberal subjects come to know the supposed realities of race and racial difference and, importantly, act on them. In one particularly grim instance, the pair recall the killing of Omar Edwards, a young black NYPD rookie mistaken for an armed criminal and shot and killed by a fellow (white) officer. Noting other incidents of its kind, they ask, "Why do black officers not mistake white officers for criminals and blaze away?" Of course, everyone has a skin color, but not everyone's skin color is read as a mark of danger and criminality. As Barbara Fields explained elsewhere, the power of racecraft transforms the action of the perpetrator into a characteristic of the target—*transferring one's action into another's being*.[29] From the slave patrol, criminal anthropometry, lynchings, and the Klan, eugenics, early crime statistics, drug panics, gang sweeps, right on through to stop and frisk and numerous spots along the way, police have been at the center of the deep historical, occulted practices that brought blackness into being and merged it with threat, danger, and criminality.

In the well-known NYPD killing of Amadou Diallo, Fields and Fields note again that it is an incorrect assumption to suggest he was simply killed "because he was black" as much of the mainstream news media had reported. Regardless of how Diallo thought of himself, Guinean, Malinké, immigrant, or simply a New Yorker, the police power "controlled the moment," and with the forty-one shots that took his life, forever solidified him as a *black man* murdered by trigger-happy cops. This is one of the defining features of racism, as they put it, "even though the targets may imagine that their race is their identity, and it is an identification they can choose to identify with as others identify them, racism determines that one can override the other."[30] Similarly, when a Dallas cop named Amber Guyger attempted to enter her neighbor's apartment, mistaking it for her own, and then shot and killed its rightful occupant, assuming he was an intruder, the skin color or race of the murdered man, Botha Jean, was not to blame, but instead the racist sorcery that in an instant turned blackness to danger. As with the death of Omar Edwards, Fields and Fields conclude, "racism did not require a racist. It required only that, in the split second before firing the fatal shot, the white officer entered the twilight zone of America's racecraft."[31]

The sorcery that gives human flesh to the ghostly matter of police power, constituting it not just as an occupation, but as a singular identity demanding of respect and protection, seems to work in similar ways. As Cunningham and Reed put it, blue life is the "byproduct of a spirit possession ritual in which the formless authority of police power momentarily inhabits the body and poses as a form of life." Brought into being with the rallying cry to "stand up to Black Lives Matter," blue life always exists in opposition to blackness, its adversary, even when possessing and haunting the words and deeds of a black cop like Clarke.

Often gone before we know it, policing's powers invisible nevertheless abound. When, in May 2018, NYPD Commissioner James O'Neill issued a statement condemning the parole of Herman Bell, who in 1971, along with several other members of the Black Liberation Army (BLA), murdered NYPD officers Joseph Piagentini and Waverly Jones, he raised the specter of blue life. Orchestrating a séance of sorts, O'Neill called on the ghosts of the dead officers to make known Bell's depravity and reaffirm the position of police as the heroic, albeit overmatched, arbiters of social order. Although Bell had served nearly five decades in prison, O'Neill lamented lack of a "permanent" form of punishment and begged for justice for the officers who, because of their "blue uniforms," could "never be paroled from death." Like claims that Edwards, Jean, and others were killed simply because they were black, the incantation—these men were *"targeted solely for the blue uniform they wore"*—chanted by the NYPD's high priest, drags the vengeful wraith blue life into the realms of the living once more, reaffirming its fiction. Vanishing along with the spell is all political and historical context, the grievances of the Black Liberation Army, and the unbroken record of police terror endured by Herman Bell and his kind. Like the equally potent spell "they hate us for our freedom," the BLA and BLM are reduced to monstrous cop killers, savage terrorists, "black identity extremists" who simply hate cops, while blue life manifests and is affirmed as the righteous protectors of all that is good.

The Police in Our Heads

For the title of the third of his four-part BBC documentary series *The Century of the Self*, filmmaker Adam Curtis appropriated a phrase apparently popular among the 1960s counterculture, "There Is a Policeman Inside All Our Heads; He Must Be Destroyed," which gestured toward a growing recognition of the many ways consumer culture, cold-war paranoia, and the buttoned-down conservatism of the postwar United States and United Kingdom had seeped into and arrested the minds of the young. Not specific to the uniformed police, Curtis's concern is those market forces that police, broadly, the attitudes and actions of modern subjects, what we might plainly call neoliberalism. But what of the actual police inside our heads? As we have seen from eerie roadways stalked by ghost cars to political landscapes haunted by blue life, the police power assumes myriad forms and spans myriad terrains. Taking Curtis's speculative lead, we now consider how policing's powers invisible set in on the mind, to goad, coerce, and craft a uniquely policed subject.

Commenting on anti-black violence following the death of Michael Brown, Afro-pessimist writer and critic Frank Wilderson insisted, "the world is not ready to think about policing the way that it affects black people. We are policed all the time and everywhere."[32] Though it might come as a discretionary ghost to some, Wilderson's point is that for black people, the police power has always been inescapable and totalizing. One of the ways we might think about how policing's powers invisible unevenly haunt the minds of black people, helping to produce a distinct form of racialized political subjectivity, is to attend to some of the morbid symptoms that have emerged in the post-Ferguson moment. One such symptom, "the police talk" or "the talk"—the conversations black parents and guardians have with their children to prepare them for encounters with police—reveals the distinct ways black people are dogged and violated by policing's spectral power.

For instance, in the video *How to Deal with the Police, Black Parents Explain*,[33] several pairs of parents and children discuss the safest procedures for police encounters. One parent, speaking to her child whose hands are already in the air, instructed, "If you've got to go to your wallet to get your ID out, say can I reach in my back pocket to get my ID out?" Each of the parents stressed that a key component of a successful police encounter is display of a sufficiently polite and subservient demeanor. As another parent warned, "Don't get upset, don't get sassy, why did you pull me over, just follow instructions and stay calm," and another advised, "If he tells you to be quiet, be quiet, do everything you can to get back to me." While critical of the talk, our aim is not to adjudicate its practical necessity. It emerges from the acute and inarguable dangers posed by police to people of color.[34] Beyond this, however, the talk also offers a particularly powerful example of the ways that a uniquely racialized, policed subject is formed. As radical police critics David Correia and Tyler Wall suggest, the talk, like so much of what police demand, might be better understood as an insidious *rehearsal for domination*. They write,

You must always be courteous, and always let the officer do the talking. Be polite. "Yes, officer." "No, officer." "Thank you, officer." Don't ask questions or talk back or challenge the cop's understanding of the encounter. It is a rehearsal of and for domination. If you break out of the polite decorum by asking questions, acting the smart ass, slow in response to what is commanded, or if you make any movement the officer later calls "furtive," well, the full force of the state can make itself known. *And sometimes, even when you do exactly as you are told*, as Philando Castile did, *you still might end up dead.*[35]

While limiting "furtive movements" and cultivating a submissive demeanor are two bits of advice that most parents would endorse, the video further demonstrates how the police talk is a uniquely racialized practice. In one particularly emotional segment, a parent asks her young daughter, "Why would a police officer assume that you did something bad?" To which the child timidly responds, sobbing, "maybe because of my skin color?" Reckoning the weight of the talk, another parent confided in her child, "I see it weighing on you and I don't want it to weigh on you." Important here is the prefigured and uneven "weight" of police violence.

Writing on the broader context of gun violence, Madison Armstrong and Jennifer Carlson frame the talk as a form of anticipatory trauma, in which black parents and guardians, in grim resignation, teach their children to expect violence and to practice a form of contingency planning in order to minimize potentially lethal outcomes. They write,

> Black parents must explain to their children that danger is not particularly unlikely, and that in order to maintain safety, children must "self-police" their behaviors. The responsibility for safety, rather than being placed in the hands of authority figures near the children, is placed with the children themselves. Authority figures are not a source of comfort but a primary source of potential danger. A parent's wish to maintain a child's feeling of safety is necessarily eclipsed by the need to make children aware of the persistent potential for deadly violence.[36]

Understood as anticipatory trauma, the talk demonstrates that even when they are physically absent, the police power is a violent force stalking the background, patrolling the head, demanding the racialized practice of self-policing.[37] Here, only the whisper of violence—a news media account, a social media post—is necessary for police power to enter the realms of the living. From such a view, then, direct corporeal violence is not the chief, or only, concern. As Frank Wilderson insists, the problem for black people is not police brutality, but "one of complete captivity from birth to death, and coercion as the starting point of our interaction with the state and with ordinary white citizens."[38] Perhaps in some agreement, Shannon Malone Gonzales suggests that the police talk signals a Du Boisian "lifting of the veil," a moment when "black children are socialized to understand their vulnerability by seeing themselves as the police view them—through stereotypes of criminality—and learning how to protect themselves from police violence."[39] Again, while not dismissive of the talk's practical aims, care must be taken to ensure that it does not perform the trick of reducing police violence to simply the outcome of anti-black racism and in doing so, following Fields and Fields, reaffirm blackness as a concrete, totalizing, and inescapable category.

Focusing explicitly on its ends, we instead understand the talk as training in resilience, a political technology that, while seemingly proactive and positive, nevertheless produces and organizes depoliticized subjects in accordance with the overriding and established neoliberal order. As outlined above, the politics of security and police power are raised and enacted through the threat of a new or yet-to-arrive enemy. Key to the production, organization, and mobilization of policed subjects, then, is the political imagination of fear and anxiety—fear of death, fear of other humans, or the general, objectless anxiety of an unknown and unknowable future. Of course, revealed by the talk are the jagged edges of trauma, a bloody wound ripped open by the unending and public litany of human beings killed by police. As one young woman confirms, "But it's all you see on the news and in the newspapers it keeps happening, it's just in a different way. People are like, you should forgive so and so, but they keep doing it to me, I forgave them, but they keep doing it to me, it gets harder and harder to forgive them." Married to the trauma of overwhelming and unforgivable police violence is the fear and anxiety of it entering your life. As the same young woman tearfully explained, "I'm just worried about [her cousin] Donovan, I'm worried about him now, I don't want him to be shot, I don't want him to go to jail." Offering explicit instructions to assuage very real fear and anxiety, the talk is nothing if not training in the procedures necessary to plan for and minimize a potential catastrophe. This sort of anticipation and management has become, in Neocleous's words, "a way of mediating the demands of an endless security war: a war whose permanence and universality has been established to match the permanence and universality of our supposed desire for security."[40] Which is to say, the needs of the insecure subject are those that only the state and its police can meet. And so, odd as it might seem, the trauma, fear, and anxiety generated by police violence, and the training in resilience offered by the talk, doubles back to reaffirm the police power and mold the subjectivity of a uniquely policed subject.

While the experts who trade in the discourses of resilience frame their work in only positive terms, insisting they aim to help individuals and communities overcome trauma, underlying plans to triumph over and "bounce back" from the disasters to come is the reminder of one's own inherent vulnerability. "To be able to become resilient," as Brad Evans and Julian Reid put it, "one must first accept that one is fundamentally vulnerable."[41] Rather than challenging the broader conditions that contribute to social insecurity, political subjects are encouraged to adapt and overcome, to manage social problems as individual rather than collective phenomena. Individuation, as such, turns inward as anxious self-policing, conjuring, and nurturing "the policeman in our heads." Driven by the demand for resilience, our insecurities as parents, as children, as subjects, play out in the mind, as a rational risk-calculating technology of the self. This, as Neocleous puts it, "is police power at its most profound."[42]

Planning for catastrophe and cultivating resilience, so that we might move past and "get over" trauma, stifles the political imagination and forecloses possibilities for alternate futures. Such a foreclosure is evident in the discourses of the talk, whose wrenching, fearful tenor proves that, even among presumed critics, there remains an undying faith in police as the wellspring of security. Indeed, as one parent pleaded, "Don't always assume that all of them are bad." While another insisted, "there are great police officers out there, there is also some police officers who are not so good, and my fear is that you run across one of those bad ones." Subsumed by the demonic figure of the "bad cop" is the long history of policing's wicked deeds, of racist terror, violence, and murder. Here, the talk not only reminds each child of their own racialized vulnerabilities but constructs a system of thinking where future trauma is ultimately determined by chance encounters with the *wrong* cop, rather than the social structures that enable, in fact rely upon, the violence of *all* cops. Foreclosed then is a revolutionary political imagination—a politics of anti-security—that might refuse a pledge of fealty to "good cops" and the false promise of security.

No Future

In the summer of 2019, police in Galveston, Texas, responding to a report of loitering near a Merrill Lynch Financial Services building, arrested a mentally ill homeless man named Donald Neely, for misdemeanor criminal trespass. The two arresting officers, part of a mounted horse patrol, apparently could not raise a squad car to taxi Neely to the jail, so they decided instead to attach a rope to the handcuffed man and lead him some eight blocks down blistering Texas streets to rendezvous with transport. Bystanders were understandably aghast at the sight of two white cops donning white cowboy hats, on horseback, leading a handcuffed black man down the street by a rope. Even the cops themselves understood the optics of their decision, as their body-worn cameras recorded one of them repeating "it's gonna look so bad." The scene did indeed *look bad*, and once images were shared on social media, widespread outrage and condemnation ensued. Characterizing the criticism, Texas politician and presidential candidate Beto O'Rourke chimed in on social media, stating, "A black man, dragged with a rope by police officers on horses, in 2019, demands accountability, justice, and honesty—because we need to call this out for what it is: racism at work." Galveston Police Chief Vernon Hale responded to the "negative perception" generated by the arrest, halfheartedly disavowed his officers' "poor judgment," and promised to suspend what had previously been a "trained technique."[43] Yet, as O'Rourke's comment hinted, no doubt fueling the outrage was how the images of Neely's arrest echoed the vile history of chattel slavery. Underlining the present, the president of the local chapter of the NAACP James Douglas likewise remarked, "This is 2019, not 1819. I am happy to know that Chief Hale issued an apology and indicated that the act showed poor judgment, but it also shows poor training. Even though the chief indicated that the technique would be discontinued, he failed to address the lack of respect demonstrated by the officers in the episode."

Neely's arrest and the accompanying commentary, such as this, open space for the final point we would like to make regarding policing's weird, eerie, and spectral qualities. First, there is stubborn refusal to see policing's misdeeds as anything but the consequence of human error and lack of training. Following Fisher's brand of hauntology, we also see in it future traces of what could have been. As he put it, "the future is always experienced as haunting: as a virtuality that already impinges upon the present, conditioning expectations."[44] The future captured in the images of two cops on horseback, leading a restrained black man to a cage, upends assumptions of progress, civility, and justice, inviting instead recognition that "time is out of joint" and the protestations of incredulous onlookers who insist that the year is indeed 2019! But what of the future that could have been? Is time really out of joint? Or does Neely's arrest simply reaffirm a present that is more horrific than haunting, a system of police power that since its inception has offered its subjects *no future* at all?

Over the past decade or so, as Linette Park reports, police in California have arrested anti-police violence demonstrators who have attempted to intervene in or "de-arrest" their comrades and charged them with the arcane crime of "self-lynching." On the books for more than a century, the self- or "felony-lynching" statute was meant to punish members of lynch mobs who wrestled an arrestee from police custody. Park argues that "self-" and "felony-lynching" cases "aver the uncanniness of anti-black racism by way of a structural perversion," approximating the Freudian sense of witnessing something familiar *as if* unfamiliar. Such a description reminds that the police power is as timeless as it is formless, "always having been present in the collective unconscious of racial slavery's formations of horror."[45] Neely's arrest does not reveal a revenant of a bygone era, or the reemergent symptom of that which is repressed. It is, as it has always been, a spectral ghost haunting this order, bound forever to the terrains, politics, and subjects of racial capitalism. Yet, by gesturing to its morbid symptoms, the police power performs its most diabolical trick, having us believe that its darkness and horror are things of the past.

Tied together figuratively and literally by the same murderous rope, yesterday's lynched and today's prisoner are held captive in the same space. This is the "unbroken line of police violence" that, as Angela Davis suggests, transports us to, or traps us in, the "days of slavery, the aftermath of slavery, the development of the Ku Klux Klan."[46] This "strange simultaneity" implicates a future that is nothing more than a continuation of the present, a haunted future that has long since ceased to offer any alternative in which the police don't exist. And so, returning to Fisher once more, we might say that we are collectively haunted both by the police of our past who continue to be "around" when we don't need them and equally by an as-yet unimagined future where we might.

NOTES

1 Fisher defines hauntology: "[t]he first refers to that which is (in actuality is) *no longer*, but which *remains* effective as a virtuality . . . The second sense of hauntology refers to that which (in actuality) has *not yet* happened, but which is *already* effective in the virtual (an attractor, an anticipation shaping current behaviour)."
2 As Tyler Wall and Travis Linnemann insist, "what needs to be said more clearly, it would seem, is that there is no police without violence, and the discretionary powers of police is always a violent prerogative." Wall and Linnemann, forthcoming.
3 One of the first attempts to systematically describe emergent police systems, *Traité de la Police* (Treaty of Police), was written by a French magistrate and later police commissioner Nicolas Delamare over a period of several years, with the final of four volumes published in 1729.
4 L'Heuillet, *Basse politique, haute police*, p. 16.
5 Brodeur 1983; Von Hentig 1919.
6 In the UK, for instance, the ratio is 1:508.
7 Hayward 2012.
8 David Fleshler and Megan O'Matz, "New video shows school cop Scot Peterson hiding as gunman shoots Parkland students," *South Florida Sun Sentinel*, September 5, 2018. www.sun-sentinel.com/.
9 Also see *Warren v District of Columbia* (444 A.2d. 1, DC Ct of Ap. 1981); *Balistreri v Pacifica Police Department* (August 23, 1988); *DeShaney v Winnebago County* (February 22, 1989).
10 *Castle Rock v Gonzales* (545 US 748, 2005).
11 Ibid., p. 8.
12 Gallager 2018.
13 Ibid., April 30. The next time you get pulled over, it might be by a glow-in-the-dark 'ghost' police car. *The News & Observer*. www.newsobserver.com/.
14 Battles 2010.
15 Operation Ghost Rider 2019.

16 J. Ferguson, Road Runner: 'Ghost cars' used by Pima County and state DPS are tough to spot, October 1, 2018. Tuscon.com. https://tucson.com.
17 Ibid.
18 Operation Ghost: www.southcoasttodaysom; Ghost guns: www.thetrace.org; Ghost warrants: www.themarshallproject.org.
19 Hobbes, *Leviathan*, p. 75; cited in Neocleous 2016, p. 16.
20 Lennard 2018.
21 Singh 2014.
22 Clarke 2016.
23 MacDonald 2016, p. 3.
24 Ibid., p. 41.
25 Cunningham and Reid 2018.
26 Ibid.
27 Fields and Fields 2014.
28 Ibid., p. 198.
29 Denvir 2018.
30 Ibid.
31 Fields and Fields 2014, p. 27.
32 Wilderson 2014, p. 5.
33 How to Deal with the Police, Black Parents Explain. https://www.youtube.com/watch?v=coryt8IZ-DE.
34 As one study recently found, black men and boys are nearly two and a half times as likely to be killed by police as their white counterparts. Edwards, Esposito, and Lee 2018.
35 Correia and Wall 2018, p. 76. Emphasis in original.
36 Armstrong and Carlson 2019.
37 As law professor Bryan Adamson explained, "the code of racial self-policing is a deplorable fact of life for men of color. In the most perverse sense, it is one side of a social contract. Put bluntly, if I behaved a certain way and made no 'furtive moves,' then I would not be shot." B. Adamson, 2013. "The Racial Self-Policing that African-American Men Already Do." *Seattle Times*. http://old.seattletimes.com
38 Ibid., p. 6.
39 Malone Gonzalez 2019, p. 365.
40 Neocleous 2012.
41 Evans and Reid 2013, p. 84.
42 Neocleous 2015.
43 Galveston Police Department, August 5, 2019. Press release. www.facebook.com/galvestonpolice.
44 Fisher 2012, p. 16.
45 Park 2019, p. 691.
46 S. Jeffries. 2014. "Angela Davis: 'There is an unbroken line of police violence in the US that takes us all the way back to the days of slavery.'" *The Guardian*. www.theguardian.com

REFERENCES

Armstrong, Madison and Jennifer Carlson. 2019. "Speaking of Trauma: The Race Talk, the Gun Talk, and the Racialization of Gun Trauma." *Palgrave Communications* 5, 112: 7.
Battles, K. 2010. *Calling All Cars: Radio Dragnets and the Technology of Policing.* Minneapolis: University of Minnesota Press.
Benjamin, W. 1978. "Critique of Violence." *Reflections* 14, 3: 277–300.
Beyer, Scott. 2018. In Baltimore, Police Seem Everywhere and Nowhere at Once. www.governing.com/
Brodeur, J. P. 1983. "High Policing and Low Policing: Remarks About the Policing of Political Activities." *Social Problems* 30, 5: 507–520.
Brodeur, J. P. 2010. *The Policing Web.* Oxford: Oxford University Press.
Clarke, David. 2016. "Sheriff David Clarke: It's Time to Stand Up to Black Lives Matter." www.foxnews.com/
Correia, D. and T. Wall. 2018. *Police: A Field Guide.* Brooklyn, NY: Verso Books.
Cunningham, Nijah and Tiana Reid. 2018. Blue Life. https://thenewinquiry.com
Denvir, Daniel. 2018. Beyond "Race Relations": An Interview with Barbara Fields and Karen Fields. www.jacobinmag.com
Edwards, F., M. H. Esposito, and H. Lee. 2018. "Risk of Police-Involved Death by Race/Ethnicity and Place, United States, 2012–2018." *American Journal of Public Health* 108, 9: 1241–1248.
Evans, B. and J. Reid. 2013. "Dangerously Exposed: The Life and Death of the Resilient Subject." *Resilience* 1, 2: 83–98.
Fields, K. E. and B. J. Fields. 2014. *Racecraft: The Soul of Inequality in American Life.* Brooklyn, NY and London: Verso Trade.
Fisher, Mark. 2012. "What Is Hauntology?" *FILM QUART* 66, 1: 16–24.
———. 2017. *The Weird and the Eerie.* London: Repeater Books.
Gallager, Ron. 2018. The Next Time You Get Pulled Over, It Might Be by a Glow-in-the-Dark "Ghost" Police Car. www.newsobserver.com/
Hayward, Keith J. 2012. "Five Spaces of Cultural Criminology." *British Journal of Criminology* 52, 3: 441–462.
Lennard, Natasha. 2018. Call Congress's "Blue Lives Matter" Bills What They Are: Another Attack on Black Lives Retrieved. https://theintercept.com
L'Heuillet, Hélène. 2001. *Basse politique, haute police. Une approche historique et philosophique de la police.* Paris: Fayard 2001, p. 16. Cited in Nowotny and Raunig, "On Police Ghosts and Multitudinous Monsters." *European Institute for Progressive Cultural Policies*, June 2008. http://eipcp.net/transversal/
MacDonald, Heather. 2016. *The War on Cops: How the New Attack on Law and Order Makes Everyone Less Safe.* New York: Encounter.
Malone Gonzalez, S. 2019. "Making It Home: An Intersectional Analysis of the Police Talk." *Gender & Society* 33, 3: 363–386.
Neocleous, M. 2012. "'Don't Be Scared, Be Prepared' Trauma-Anxiety-Resilience." *Alternatives* 37, 3: 188–198.

Neocleous, M. 2015, June 5-6. Resisting Resilience. Resilience Discourse in Politics and in Aid. Tenth Anniversary of the Medico International Foundation and Symposium. www.youtube.com/watch?v=D_75mm_N7Vs

Neocleous, M. 2016. *The Universal Adversary: Security, Capital and "The Enemies of All Mankind."* London: Routledge.

Nowotny, Stefan and Gerald Raunig. 2008. "On Police Ghosts and Multitudinous Monsters." *European Institute for Progressive Cultural Policies.* http://eipcp.net/

Operation Ghost Rider: Police Riding in Unmarked Cars to Target Distracted Drivers on M-59. 2019. www.wxyz.com/

Park, L. 2019. "The Eternal Captive in Contemporary 'Lynching' Arrests: On the Uncanny and the Complex of Law's Perversion." *Theory & Event* 22, 3: 674-698.

Singh, N. P. 2014. "The Whiteness of Police." *American Quarterly* 66, 4: 1091-1099.

Turner, J. 2018. "'It All Started with Eddie': Thanatopolitics, Police Power, and the Murder of Edward Byrne." *Crime, Media, Culture.* 1741659018763898.

Von Hentig, H. 1919. *Fouché: ein Beitrag zur Technik der politischen Polizei in nachrevolutionären Perioden.* Mohr. Quoted in J. P. Brodeur. 2010. *The Policing Web.* Oxford: Oxford University Press, pp. 225-226.

Wall, Tyler and Travis Linnemann. Forthcoming. *No Chance: The Violence of Discretion, or the Secret of Police.* Social Justice.

Wilderson III, Frank B. 2014. "Irreconcilable Anti-blackness and Police Violence." Interview with Dr. Jared Ball.

8

"Dripping from Head to Toe with Blood"

Suffocation, Tentacles, Police, and Capital

BILL MCCLANAHAN

In what would go on to become the definitive popular takedown of conditions leading to the 2008 financial crisis, journalist Matt Taibbi once famously described the New York–based investment bank Goldman Sachs as "a great vampire squid wrapped around the face of humanity, relentlessly jamming its blood funnel into anything that smells like money" (Taibbi 2010, 90). The creature invoked by Taibbi is a real one: *Vampyroteuthis Infernalis*, translated literally as "vampire squid from hell," that was discovered in 1903 and given a taxonomical name inspired, somewhat disappointingly, by its cloaked appearance rather than any bloodsucking tendency.[1] Drawing on familiar and previously articulated visions of capitalist horror, including Marx's descriptions of capital as vampiric, Taibbi's phrase cut through the haze of the crisis, animating the moment with the specter of a menace both tentacled and bloodthirsty. Five years later, in 2014, New York City police choked and killed Eric Garner outside of a Staten Island bodega. The killing was captured in a video recording, and like Taibbi's cutting phrase, Garner's last words—"I can't breathe"—briefly captured a degree of public attention, finding salience for activists and everyday subjects of the policing of racial capitalism. What I want to suggest here is that the modes of sanguine and respiratory subjectivity illustrated in Taibbi's metaphor and made violently clear in Garner's murder—and other police killings—are not incidental but are instead dominant affective conditions of capitalist subjectivity.

First, though, a forewarning: in fidelity to The Weird as a frame of thinking, this chapter will itself be a bit weird, as my arguments will be made by way of a considerable number of somewhat disparate topics, including: octopus, police, blood, snakes, climate change, suffocation, ticks, capitalism, jellyfish, hauntology, hematology, and moose. In a nutshell, then, this is going to get weird. There is also a risk that requires discussion, though, in any Weird analysis of the violence of police and climate change and capitalism: the risk that things will be left to appear inadequately material, that things will be made to appear as a *fantasy* nightmare rather than a *lived* nightmare. I want to be clear before beginning, then, that I do not intend for the spectrality or immateriality of the Weird to supplant or somehow obscure the materiality of violence. There is, though, ample opportunity to read the subjectivities of capitalist police violence through the lenses offered by thinking in the mode of the Weird, which is what I aim to do.

Capital, Horror, the Tentacular, and the Weird

While Taibbi's witty and vivid naming of the institutions of late capitalism in such horrifyingly weird terms was certainly attention-grabbing, it was not the first time the writhing and reaching arms of squids, octopi, and deep-sea cephalopods had been called into cultural service in order to illustrate the suffocating conditions of capitalism. Prior to Taibbi, critics have, since at least the mid-nineteenth century, imagined, visualized, and metaphorized a diverse gallery of creatures lurking in the depths of social and economic relation, stretching across cultural and political landscapes as part of a campaign of terror threatening and portending the pains and horrors of ever-expanding capitalist subjectivities.

In these images, as in Taibbi's prose, capital finds its clearest form and articulation in the speculative materiality of the monsters of the unknown, with the uncertainty of the oceanic depths weaving itself into the precarity and unease that are so necessarily endemic to capitalist subjectivity. In these images we can locate early capitalist expansion avatarized as cephalopodic beasts: The tentacles of landlordism and rent systems, powerful monopolies, corporate greed, US capitalism, and colonial empire each take form as tentacles emanating from some sinister central power to reach nefariously across social, economic, and cartographic landscapes.[2] Just as the spider before it in gothic horror, these tentacled water animals quickly became the go-to monster of the age, conjured in order to communicate the horrifying conditions of the moment.

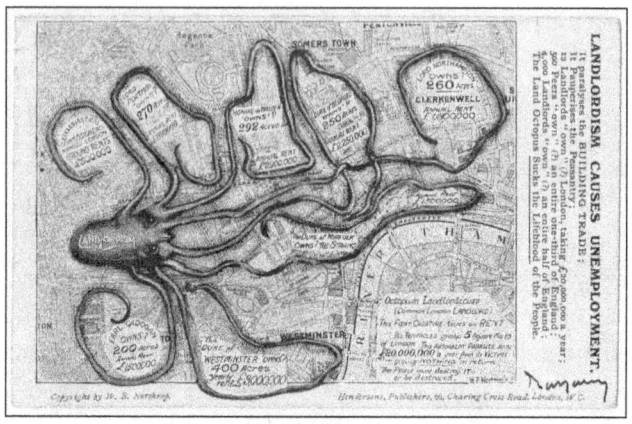

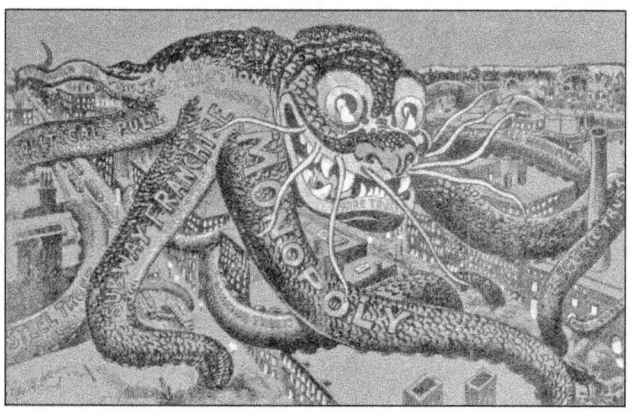

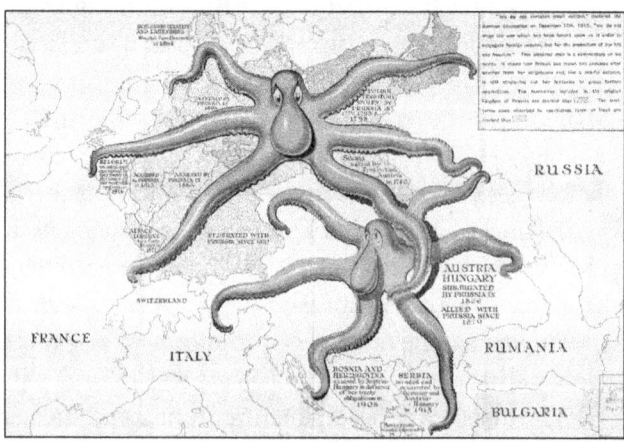

Figure 8.1a-c. Early Political Cartoons. Octopium Landlordicus, 1925. Credit: Public domain; The Menace of the Hour, 1899. Credit: Public domain; The Prussian Octopus, 1916. Credit: Wikimedia Commons.

The relevance and popularity of Taibbi's "vampire squid"—at the time, the phrase appeared to resonate uniquely over the din of the moment—serves as a reminder that the image of the tentacled capitalist monster did not lose its salience at the dawn of the twentieth century. Quite the contrary, in fact: The squid or octopus retained—and continues to retain, it would seem—its utility, with contemporary illustrations depicting everything from progressivism to President Donald Trump to the US Department of Education as a tentacled animal. Undead as ever, the monster squid had only been dormant, waiting in the shadows for the moment of its return, when it would again be given life on the visual registers of critique that arose, in part, in the wake of the 2008 financial crisis. There, it joined *ghost mortgages* and *zombie banks* and (re)*possessed homes* in a who's who of spectral metaphors drawing on a canonical lexicon of horror.

None of this is the least bit surprising considering that Mark Fisher, whose conceptualization of "the Weird" as a cultural mode, an affective condition, and a framework of analysis that scaffolds my arguments here, argued convincingly that capital is most fittingly analogized with the monstrous. Indeed, for Fisher (2009), the image and vocabulary of the monster is the "most accurate" mode in which to describe capital, which he called "an abstract parasite, an insatiable vampire and zombie-maker." Fisher, it is safe to assume, would likely have described the appearances of the squid or octopus in these historical images—and in more contemporary discourses of tentacled animality as avatar for the anxieties of capitalist subjectivity—as weird.[3] Moving forward, it is probably sufficient to simply note that the semiotic, linguistic, and visual forms that capital takes or is assigned are often monstrous or horrifying or weird or somehow wrong or repulsive (for an account of the relationship between the affective conditions of capitalist subjectivities and the modes and motifs of gore and blood that configure them, see Mark Steven's *Splatter Capital* [2017]). Tentacles, too, fit rather nicely into those same categories, likely owing to the ways in which their shape and movements suggest snakes, which humans have—according to research in experimental evolutionary psychology—a natural tendency to fear. The same mechanical dynamics of the tentacle—those relating to the number and movement of the tentacle limb—configure the image of the many-headed Hydra, a creature that, as Linebaugh and Rediker

(2013) describe, often stood in as a "symbol of disorder and resistance, a powerful threat to the building of state, empire, and capitalism" in the estimation of rulers and royalties from the empires of Greece and Rome on through to the dawn of capitalism and the foundation of the United States. The Hydra described by Linebaugh and Rediker is something like a fabular embodiment of Hobbes's state of nature, in that it stands opposed to the civilizing order of Leviathan. I will return to Hobbes later, but I want to note here that the many-headed, ungovernable Hydra of Linebaugh and Rediker, the sea-dwelling Leviathan, and the terrestrial Behemoth of both Hobbes and scripture are all, in their own ways, suggestive of tentacles.

It is, it would seem, largely its tentacled condition that gives the squid or octopus its salience, its essential position in our contemporary anxieties. As I have argued elsewhere (McClanahan 2019), horror—more than other cultural modes—offers the most suitable perspective for making sense of the conditions of contemporary capitalist subjectivity, and the octopus, the squid, or the otherwise tentacled are central and essential figures in the configuration of horror. This is most obviously clear if we turn to horror as genre rather than as affect. As Theodore Martin (2017) notes, "genre describes how aesthetic forms move cumulatively through history." Here we might think of the ways in which the tentacled constructs for itself its own genre, its limbs multiplying as it weaves its way in and out of anxious historical and contemporary expressions of the conditions of our relation.

Contrary to Martin, who describes the construction of "the contemporary" by genre as largely non-epochal, horror writer China Miéville (2009: 105) describes the tentacle as the "default monstrous appendage" signifying "the epochal shift to a Weird culture." Miéville's claims of epochal shift notwithstanding, he is, it would seem, entirely correct in identifying the centrality of the tentacle to the emergence of "the weird" as a popular mode of thinking the world. We might say, then, that it isn't so much that there has emerged a *new* cultural epoch, but rather that something that has always been there has arisen and awakened with a new salience and ferocity. That something, fittingly, is the tentacle.

Miéville, though, also goes to some length to understand the tentacle and the tentacled as fundamentally in conversation with "the ghost"— the chief concern of this volume, and a form I will return to, however briefly, later in this chapter. Miéville (2008: 128) notes that "Hauntology and Weird are two iterations of the same problematic." For Miéville, that problematic is precisely as described elsewhere by Fisher: that the conditions of modernity are such that each new crisis—and there is no shortage of new crises—is unquestionably new and old at once. The shadows of history are always cast onto the present, it seems. While the hauntological (or, to keep some thematic consistency and simplicity, the ghostly) and the Weird are always in opposition (as the former requires sameness and the latter demands difference), Miéville (2008: 128) nevertheless insists that "traces of the Weird are inevitably sensible in a hauntological work, and vice versa." The task at hand, then—to excavate the significance of the tentacle and to understand its salience in contemporary encounters with the violence of climate change and police—is at once weird and hauntological.

Because the Weird has also emerged as so central to horror, we might also take a moment to consider what, exactly, makes the tentacular horrifying. For me, it appears that the horror qualities of the tentacle are twofold. The first dimension concerns and implicates the Weird quite directly: The tentacle only reaches the crescendo of its horror when it appears out of place. Were we to encounter a tentacled animal at sea, it might mark a terrifying encounter with the nonhuman, but would be unlikely to rouse the sorts of dread that mark real horror. Conversely, if we were to encounter a tentacled animal on land—outside of what we imagine as its natural boundaries—we would be well and truly horrified. Such a scenario lies at the heart of any number of cinematic and literary productions. Take, for example, Netflix's runaway smash hit series *Stranger Things*, which features a tentacled monster that is rupturing expectations of a 1980s suburban tranquility unmolested by the Eldritch horrors of climate change. Or, to return to the first days of the 2008 crisis, we might recall *Cloverfield*, whose tentacled creature wreaks havoc on a New York City that, at the time of the film's release, was in the first days of the collapse of the financial system. Again, in *Cloverfield*, the tentacles—and the rest of the monster—clearly are things out of place. The second dimension of tentacled horror, every bit as important as this sense of *things out of place* and every bit as present in each of the examples above, is in the potential for us to be grasped, entangled, and suffocated by all of these tentacles.

Grasping, Entanglement, and Suffocation

Before turning to suffocation, we might make a proper start by simply asking from where, precisely, the tentacles of tentacular horror emerge. While the sorts of cephalopodic monsters most clearly and commonly associated with the tentacular skulked in the depths of antecedent authors like Victor Hugo, HG Wells, and Jules Verne, when the beast bears tentacles, we need look no further than Lovecraft, at once the father of modern horror and its offspring, "weird fiction." Writing in the early and mid-twentieth century, Lovecraft built a world and mythos that teased out the horrors of his own life as a destitute racist failure by mapping an unseen, unseeable, and psychosis-inducing realm of slumbering gods over the material cosmic landscapes of the world. His distinctly tentacled Cthulhu mythos, in particular, would endure, capturing the imagination of a wildly diverse constellation of authors including Stephen King, Joyce Carol Oates, William Burroughs, and Luis Borges, as well as philosophers and theorists including Timothy Morton, Eugene Thacker, Graham Harman and others working in the modes of speculative realism, object-oriented ontology, and dark ecology. One can hardly open a text of contemporary critical philosophy without finding Lovecraft lurking in its margins. Take, for example, Thacker's *Tentacles Longer than Night* (2015), or Donna Haraway's *Staying With the Trouble: Making Friends in the Cthulhucene* (2016) (Haraway's subtitle actually refers to a spider species, though is still plainly fashioned to make a somewhat cheeky call to those who prefer their philosophy tentacled). At the core of all of this, of course, is the weird, that mode of not-quite-rightness so thoroughly unpacked by Fisher and so necessary for horror. When we begin to see the world through the lens of the weird, we begin to notice that yes, in fact, things are *in the wrong places*, or even that things *are the wrong things*.

The tentacles deployed by Lovecraft and those who find in his work a fitting mode for thinking philosophy and social relation also, though, take on the other necessary dimension of tentacles-as-horror: the potential for our entanglement, for the tentacles to grasp and hold, leading ultimately to our suffocation. It seems to me that it is precisely the decentralized nature of the squid or octopus that makes it such a fitting avatar for capital and such a formidable foe: Its arms capable of touching everything at once, the seeming and unsettling autonomy of its limbs, and its position in the cultural imagination as a prehistoric or mythical throwback give the beast its horrifying quality. Though while the reach and autonomy of the tentacles are certainly unsettling, the real affective power of the tentacled is in its ability to suggest our entrapment and entanglement. As plenty of others (e.g., Hall 2012; Brown et al. 2019) have suggested—and, more immediately and importantly, as anyone who has spent even a single second as a capitalist subject already knows—capitalism is a trap. Here, then, in the image of the squid or octopus, is the enduring relation between the Real of capitalist subjectivity—the trap—and the Weird of contemporary conditions—the tentacle—as it is written into the scripts of contemporary life. We might also turn briefly to another version of entrapment and entanglement, Foucault's conceptualization of unfreedom, in which he described the ways in which human potentiality is strangled by the liberal state masquerading as in the service of human need, and which is often given tentacled form (Beiner 2014: 166–167).

In *Crowds and Power* (1984: 204), Elias Canetti describes the moment of predatory entanglement—that decisive moment when the pursued becomes prey—as "contain[ing] the oldest terrors," the horrors we "dream of" and that we take the greatest of pains to avoid through the protections supposedly afforded us by "civilization." This is, it should be clear, central to the fear of the tentacled that configures it as horrifying. Like the hands and teeth of power described by Canetti, the tentacles of the weird first grasp, then constrict, and finally incorporate into the whole. When the tentacles of weird horror take hold in the social imaginary, they do so precisely because the fear of this decisive moment is so strong, so primal. What I want to begin to develop here, though, is something that Canetti stops short of: Choking is a dominant affective mode of capitalist subjectivity. This is a point that, it seems to me, is inadequately theorized, despite its clear centrality to life in capitalism made evident by the ways in which we will offhandedly refer to being suffocated, choked, strangled, or otherwise made unable to breathe by the conditions of capitalism. Frantz Fanon (2008: 201) makes this relation strikingly clear, although without further theoretical development, by noting that "we revolt simply because, for many reasons, we can no longer breathe." Breath and breathing are also the evident site of what

Suvendrini Perera and Joseph Pugliese call the "strange intimacy of state violence" (2011: 1), a violence enacted in the killing of Eric Garner and other victims of police suffocation, to which I will return later. What I want to suggest, extending Fanon and Pugliese and Perera, is that beyond simply being ontologically generative, capitalism's "suffocation of flesh" is among the central modes and motifs of its subjectivity, the essential material respirationality of the suffocating trap.

The overwhelming but often-sublimated fear of suffocation so essential to the affective conditions of capital is aggravated most obviously, however, by the conditions of the global atmospheric climate. It is not only the fear of suffocation, though, that we can locate in our collective anxieties about climate change; while an atmospheric crisis certainly picks at the terrifying prospect of suffocation—how could it not?—we can also find the Weird once again emerging from the haze of the crises of a changing global ecology. Here we might follow those who insist that it is not so much *change* that is the issue—after all, if there is a failure of the vernacular of "climate change," as there was with "global warming" before it, it is that it leaves too much room for its own negation, as evidenced in any argument in which someone proposes that *of course the climate is changing, as that's something that climates do*—but that it is instead that the climate is changing *weirdly*. Responding to this observation, Canavan and Hageman (2016) call on us to think instead of global or climate "weirding." Because, as we've already established, the tentacled is essential to "the weird"—or at least to its articulation and formation both in and as genre—we must also try to understand the ways in which climate weirding takes a tentacular form in contemporary expressions of our eco-social fears, anxieties, and nightmares.

Climate weirding, it perhaps goes without saying, is the most contemporary, salient, and pressing horror of advanced capitalist political economy. As a problem of ecology, it is little wonder that changes to atmospheric planetary climate sometimes manifest in the cultural imagination in the form of the sentient nonhuman. Authors working in the modes of "the new Weird," most notably Miéville and Jeff Vandermeer, and those working in the broad literary milieu of "cli-fi," routinely call on "the monsters of climate change" in order to illustrate and make horror from ecological weirdness. Here, it is the montage chimera animals of the unknown, rising from the depths or descending from the sky, that offer the wrong dualities of weirdness. In *Area X* (2017), Vandermeer's trilogy of eco-horror, the horrors of contemporary ecological conditions take the form of an unknown tentacled creature, a Leviathan rolling forth at once from sky and sea. By appearing as notably leviathan-like, Vandermeer's beast gives embodied form not only to ecological crisis, but also to the capitalist political economy we call on to save us from that same crisis. Like other beasts before and since, Leviathan threatens us, first and foremost, with the "oldest terrors" described by Canetti: entanglement, suffocation, and consumption. And while it may be unnecessary here, I will nevertheless note that although Leviathan's origins in Hebrew mythology place it as a whale-like creature, the development of its image has seen it take on any number of traits associated with sea creatures, including tentacles.

Joel Wainwright and Geoff Mann, though, more clearly return the problem of climate weirding and disruption to fitting questions of Hobbes's *Leviathan* and its insistence on sovereignty, asking if the climate crisis is "fierce enough to rouse" the leviathan of a state power that has been largely rendered powerless in the face of climate change (Wainwright and Mann 2013: 3). What is most significant here, for my purposes, is not to respond to those questions, but to simply note that across literary, visual, and theoretical responses to contemporary climate conditions, the monster appears bearing tentacles, with all of the creeping and constricting limbs of earlier representations of precarity and crisis. Moreover, as climate change continues to affect sea levels, oceanic temperatures, and evolutionary biology, the likelihood increases that humans will encounter animals that were previously only speculative or mythic. Here, climate weirding arrives most clearly in the hyperstitial animality of the giant squid, a legend that has become real as warming seas and ocean acidification drive its return from the unexplored depths. While not a cephalopod—and not strictly tentacled—the hyperweird animality of the jellyfish joins the giant squid, proliferating and thriving in the new and weird oceanic geographies of climate disruption. In each, it seems to me, we can identify the centrality of tentacles and the tentacular to our contemporary capitalist subjectivities.

All that slithers and engulfs, though, is not tentacled, and all of the creatures that arrive or appear at the intersection of ecology, political economy, a changing climate, and culture—such as the hyperstitial giant squids noted previously—are not purely speculative. Here we can consider a "new" material monster, the Burmese python of the Florida everglades. After being introduced to the region as pets, Burmese pythons were soon released to the wild by owners not up to the task of keeping the snakes. Comfortable in Florida's rapidly changing climate, the snakes began to reproduce. Feeding on a variety of wild fauna—and the occasional house pet—the snake's numbers rapidly swelled to 300,000, and they were quickly classified as an invasive species, a move that allows the snakes to be hunted and killed year-round with no permit and no bag limit (Driggers et al. 2019). Here we should again consider the grotesque montage-animals of Vandermeer and others working in the broader New Weird literary movement, a form that suggests the wrongness of the Weird as it's described by Fisher: The snakes causing panic in Florida have rapidly evolved into a hybrid species, a weird genetic development brought about by climate change. Of course, because the Burmese pythons are a constricting snake, their position in the contemporary moment again picks up and picks at our collective fear of suffocation and entanglement. Here, police also begin to emerge as entangled in the tentacles of climate weirding, with local cops routinely called on to police pythons across the lawns and gardens of suburban Florida. Weird, no doubt, to see the familiar imagery of the police trophy shot take such a tentacled turn, but here we are.[4] The weird constricting snakes of climate change, then, operate effectively on the same plane of respiratory anxiety as capitalist and police subjectivities. To this list we might also add kudzu. A fast-growing "vine that ate the American South" after being introduced to help stop soil erosion, kudzu has also experienced a growth boom—particularly across the rapidly deindustrialized regions of the American South and central Appalachia—driven by changing climate conditions. If ever there were a suffocating and tentacular plant, kudzu is it, with loose vines that can grow up to one foot each day. Importantly, though, kudzu does not only suggest suffocation and entanglement by way of its woody tentacles: The plant also releases isoprene and nitric oxide which, when combined with nitrogen in the air, create surface ozone, a major pollutant that seriously degrades air quality and has significant negative human health effects (Hickman et al. 2010). Let's add kudzu, then, to the list of the tentacled monsters threatening suffocation. There are also, of course, constantly emerging non-tentacled threats to

Figure 8.2. Police officers posing with captured Burmese python, Pembroke Pines, Florida. Photo by P. Scicchitano, 2018.

respiration. From climate change, to constricting snakes, to "vaping disease" and the COVID-19 novel coronavirus, it seems that if modernity is liquid (Bauman 1999), it is a liquid we are drowning in.

Blood, Breath, Capital, and Climate Change

It is not only respiration with which capital—or, for that matter, the climate crisis—concerns itself. As Mark Neocleous convincingly argues, Marx's writing is consistently shot through with metaphors of blood. *Capital Volume I* alone contains no fewer than three direct mentions of the figure of the vampire, and Neocleous extends the count by situating "Marx's vampire metaphor . . . in the very heart of Marx's work: in his critique of political economy" (Neocleous 2003: 668). The relevance and significance of blood to capitalist political economy is also made clear in tendencies outside of Marx. In large part, it would seem, blood provides the central metaphor through which we understand capitalism and our position as its subjects. Various markets, products, and populations each take their turn as the *lifeblood* of the nation or, conversely, as *bloodsuckers* living off the labor of others or the generosity of the welfare state. Blood is also, of course, the prime divinatory object and site of the pseudo-biological construction of race. Here we can think of racist conventions such as the "one drop rule" of the antebellum south, which held that a single drop of "black blood" in an otherwise white person transfigured racial position from white to black, or "blood quantum" laws that police American Indian ancestry and ensure the reduction of tribal populations (Schmidt 2012).

Given this history, it is perhaps not surprising that contemporary right-wing politics so regularly employs blood as a key metaphorical category and, at times, political logic. Phillip Neel (2018) notes, for example, the ways in which right-wing politics—particularly the sort of rugged frontier conservative libertarianism that configures the political landscape of the contemporary American West, a politics most clearly exemplified by moments like the armed occupation of the Malheur nature preserve led by Cliven and Ammon Bundy—rely on what he calls "oaths of blood" to define the boundaries of their racial, economic, and political communities by way of exclusion. Neel, in naming blood as the key concept in the construction of certain political affinities (as he notes, in the American West the oaths of blood of the right are sometimes supplanted by "oaths of water" in the formulation and configuration of divergent political groups), joins Gil Anidjar (2018), who describes the ways in which "communities of blood" are formed only in the wake of an "insistent rhetoric of blood." We might also consider events at the Unite the Right rally in Charlottesville, Virginia, in August 2017, where a significant number of American white nationalists famously marched with torches while chanting "blood and soil," a slogan used by Germany's Nazi party that functioned to define a homeland (soil) as reserved for a racially defined national body (blood). In another illustrative intersection of blood and a distinctly anti-Jewish politics, "blood libel"—the ancient fiction that Jews murder Christian children in order to obtain their blood for ritual use—lays bare the ways in which the political body is one coursing with blood. Blood, then, is precisely as it is asserted to be by Anidjar: *Blood is politics and politics is blood*. In conjuring a distinctly bloodthirsty tentacled menace, then, Taibbi at once summons old political anxieties—the oldest terrors, to borrow again from Canetti—related to our respiratory and sanguine function. It is the interiority of this terrain, it seems to me, that makes its violation so horrifying; it indicates a constricting and invasive biopolitical power that can entangle, bruise, suffocate, and bleed until we are left without blood or breath.

Staying in pursuit of this second and more bloody thread, we might again turn to Taibbi by way of the climate crisis in reading contemporary capitalism as "giant *vampire* squid." Just as the contemporary conditions of our weirding climate indicate the wholesale and planetary constriction of respiration and the dawn of our suffocation, this turn to the bloodsucking also reveals the vampiric dimensions of contemporary ecological weirding. This relation is made most clear in the example of the moose ticks that, driven by climate disruption and changing conditions in the American Northeast, now present a grave risk to North American moose populations. Research (Rodenhouse et al. 2009) has described the voracity of the ticks, which now number so many that they often drain a moose calf of its total blood volume—3 to 4 gallons—in as little as two weeks of infestation. Shocking figures, no doubt, but less surprising when considering that, as of 2016, the average moose calf in the American northeast carried roughly 50,000 individual ticks, more than twice what a calf would have carried in 1990. The calves and cows affected by the ticks often rub their fur off in an effort to dislodge the parasites, resulting in a starkly mottled and pale figure that field biologists have dubbed "ghost moose."

Of course, climate change is a problem—indeed, an inevitable one—of capitalism, and the base market logics of capitalist exchange are also implicated in and by blood. Here we might consider "blood markets" that have emerged in some expanding capitalist economies. In Mexico, for example, those who cross the US border on short-term nonemployment visas are often targeted by US plasma sellers seeking to recruit Mexican donors who will sell for less than those formally participating in the US economy. China, meanwhile, has seen the rise of a rural "blood economy," where the sale of blood on the unregulated black market constitutes an "important source of household revenue." There is also ample cultural evidence for the foundational connection between blood and capitalist relations. Here we might consider contemporary reimaginings of the world of the vampire such as HBO's television series

True Blood, in which vampires and humans coexist through the bond of capitalist exchange, most often with fantastic cruelty, just as material relations with our climate (and with police and capital) are configured in and by violence.

Perhaps, then, the *vampire* of the capitalist vampire-squid has as much to tell us about climate weirding and the horrors of the unknowable future as the tentacled. It is not the distinction between these modes of horror— the vampiric, the ghostly, and the tentacular Weird—that matters here, just that horror is the most evident affective mode conditioning our social and economic relations and our ecological entanglement. We can also, though, turn to horror, the eerie, the hauntological, or the Weird in order to locate the affective mode of our subjective relations with police.

Bleeding, Gasping, Dying: Blood, Breath, and Police

Police is a killing power. This, of course, indicates that police asserts and exercises its power over the most essential functions of the body: the respiratory and the vascular. While this is made clear in every moment of police violence, it is perhaps most strikingly evident in those moments in which police undertake to murder a subject through strangulation, such as the killing of Eric Garner described briefly at the outset of this chapter. In the wake of Garner's murder, there was a moment of broad recognition of the suffocating conditions of capitalist subjectivity. His last words, captured in the footage of his murder—"I can't breathe," repeated eleven times as Garner pleaded for his life—briefly transcended the urgent somatic materiality of their original intent, capturing instead an affective condition endemic to capitalism, namely a capitalism enforced by the violence of police (Graeber 2015; Clover 2016; McClanahan et al. 2011; Correia and Wall 2018). Returning to the previous discussion of suffocation and its role in constituting the affective conditions of capitalist subjectivities, we might also read *I can't breathe* as an urgent articulation of Fanon's understanding of black revolt as tied to breath and respiration.

Here, however, I want to be absolutely clear that Garner's killing was not an aberration or a new twist in the exercise of police power, but that it was rather a single point along an uninterrupted line of police violence and terror. While the video of Garner's murder is horrifying—so

Figure 8.3. "We Can't Breathe." Photo by Fibonacci Blue.

much so that it compels one to wonder about the possibility of reading body camera footage of police violence and killing as its own emerging genre of something we might call *nonfiction found footage horror*—the particulars of his death are not in any way exceptional: A black man caught in the trap of capitalist subjectivity is made to not breathe, his heart made to not beat, by police violence. This is, of course, a quotidian constellation of events, not at all new or aberrant: The chokehold or the power to manually restrict oxygen is among the oldest items in the somatic toolbox of police violence, what David Correia and Tyler Wall (2018: 63) describe as "a central mode of police control." Garner's killing somewhat paradoxically illustrates, though, that it isn't only breath that police claims dominion over, it is also blood. The fact of Garner's killing and of each moment of police violence preceding it signals the ways in which police, like politics in Anidjar's claim, always implicates or is otherwise rooted in blood. Here we might usefully reformulate

Anidjar's assertion by noting that police finds its foundations in a sort of political hematology in which all paths are configured and conditioned largely by blood. We might also, though, go a step further in describing and thinking of police as being something like a *hemontological* power in that the very conditions of its being (and in particular its fabrication) are predicated on blood. When Marx described capital as coming into the world "dripping from head to toe, from every pore, with blood," he described its essential or metaphysical being, its ontological state. Marx, then, already named capital as having a hematological ontology, a fact made robustly clear in the countless articulations of vampiric or otherwise bloody capital made since. What I want to do here, though, is to map that same political *hemontology* onto police, which can never be thought of as somehow apart from capital. The police-blood relation is most clear in the material condition of victims of police violence, but also more subtly in the ways in which police controls the visuality of its bloody practice with less-than-lethal technologies designed to allow for the work of violence without the trouble of externalized blood.

Police also simultaneously configures itself as a brotherhood *built on blood*, or, conversely, as a community built by an *allegiance higher than blood*.

Tyler Wall (2019: 1) has argued that the "thin blue line" motif upon which these images draw, and that is essential in the cosmic mythology of police, offers an articulation of "police as the primary force which secures, or makes possible, all the things said to be at the core of 'human' existence: liberty, security, property, sociality, accumulation, law, civility, and even happiness." The police power to secure, however, is plainly predicated on the first and most essential police power: the ultimate authority over blood and breath. From whatever angle we might view it, then, the thin blue line is clearly a line drawn in blood, a line not only marking but *producing* the boundary between those left to breathe freely of the air of security and those made to suffocate. It is also telling—both of the real position of police as the protector of private property and its relations and of police's lack of self-awareness—that in these first two images, police has elected to present itself as "blue-blooded," a designation generally reserved not for police itself, but for the bourgeoisie class that enjoys the order produced and maintained by

Figure 8.4a-b. *Thin Blue Line* images illustrating the various relations between police and blood.

police. In its haste to assert an internal bond made in blood, then, police once again reveals its elemental relationship to capital and property.

In *Capital, Volume One*, Marx (1887: 522–523) describes the near-instant transformation of the unproductive workers created in the end of Feudalism into "beggars, robbers, [and] vagabonds" by "bloody

Figure 8.5. NYPD officers and supporters during a counterdemonstration in defense of NYPD, New York City, 2014.

legislation." Importantly, Marx is quite literal here with the image of blood, as is evident in his inclusion of the text of just such a piece of legislation enacted under Henry VIII in 1530, which makes reference to punishments in which "blood streams from [the] bodies" of the newly created criminal class. If, then, the law is necessarily "bloody," and if capital comes into the world, as Marx also claimed, covered in blood, so too does police. Here I want to assert that police and its violence, like capital, is always about the blood and the breath of both its practitioners and subjects. Police claims its own ontology as one of blood in its insistence that it is "built on blood," while at once claiming the blood of its subjects as within the ambit of its powers, evident across the spectrum of police violence from the power to compel a blood test to the power to fill a body with bullet holes. Similarly, police asserts the sanctity of its own respiration as ensured through violence while celebrating its right to take the last breaths of its subjects, as New York police did in the wake of the public outcry following Garner's murder, grotesquely asserting that, unlike Garner, NYPD officers *could* breathe.

Likewise, strangulation itself, at its biotic root, is about blood: The removal of respiratory function is really the negation of the capacity of blood to carry oxygen through the body. We should also keep in mind that police recognizes and regulates for itself two distinct forms of the chokehold: holds that restrict respiratory function via pressure to the windpipe, and holds that restrict vascular function via pressure to the carotid artery. Here, then, the fundamental connection between air and blood, and the ways that police claims its fundamental power over both, becomes strikingly clear.[5] I also want to attempt here to locate police in the broader landscape of the Weird. To that end, I think it is perhaps useful to consider the appearance of police in those places where *it should not be*, or of the chimeric merging of police with *that which is not police*. Here I am following Linnemann and Turner (2020), who—following Benjamin—describe the relative formlessness of police, and the ways in which police is often a power that is manifest when it is least needed, and absent when it is most needed. These authors mark police as a "ghostly presence" (Benjamin) or "eerie" (Linnemann and Turner). To this I wish to add that police is also *Weird*, a condition that is particularly evident in the entanglement of police with that which is already Weird, such as in the python trophy shot discussed above. Moreover, and as I have already outlined following Miéville, whatever boundaries exist between the Weird and the Spectral or Hauntological are already always so significantly blurred as to be meaningless. By being spectral and eerie and ghostly, police—like capital and like climate change—is already evidently a Weird violence that claims a penetrating territoriality over the internal vascular and respiratory functions of the body.

Nothing Out of the Ordinary, Nothing If Not Weird

All of what we have encountered here has been nothing if not weird. Not out of the ordinary, no: Killing members of working, racialized, and criminal classes is what police do, suffocating its subjects, either metaphorically or literally, is what capital does, changing in response to material conditions of industrial production is what climates do, and drinking blood is what ticks do. All quite ordinary, all quite weird. It seems true, then, that the weird emerges out of the familiar, not something unexpected but something *wrong*. All that we have encountered here has also, though, been far more united by sameness than divided by difference: Police and its violence, moose ticks, the climate crisis, zombie mortgages, blood markets, and every other specter raised here all emerge from the horror of capitalist relations. Weirdness and something-wrongness are nowhere more materially evident than in the ongoing climate crisis and the constricting, devouring, or exsanguinating power that I have argued here is so elemental not only to police power, but also to our subjectivities and the wise anxieties that configure them under capitalist modes of relation. Capitalism encourages us to imagine its force somatically, as an "invisible hand," one we are to assume is *natural* if not benevolent, while police and law are similarly metaphorized as a "long arm" whose reach we can never outrun. What I want to suggest is a reformulation of both, in which we instead imagine something like this: the long arm of the law, ending not with the hand but with the tentacle of capital, always wrapped around the throats of its subjects, the whole thing dripping in blood.

NOTES

1 For a dizzying and speculative look at *Vampyroteuthis Infernalis*, see the 2013 work of the same name by Villém Flusser and Louis Bec.
2 There is also a body of similar images in which those "sinister central powers" are plainly conceptualized in starkly antisemitic terms, highlighting further the ways in which the image of the tentacle plays various roles in configuring the contemporary political moment.
3 For Fisher, "the weird" is marked most significantly by things out of place, or the chimeric combination of two discordant parts into a single whole.
4 For a thorough discussion of the police trophy photo and the ways in which it is bound essentially to capital and accumulation, see Linnemann 2017.
5 It should be noted also that police is, as Linnemann and Turner have described, a "three-dimensional" power that asserts as its territory the total expanse of material space and atmosphere. For more on police as an atmospheric power, see McClanahan and South 2019; Kaplan and Miller 2019; Feigenbaum 2014, 2017.

REFERENCES

Anidjar, Gil. 2014. *Blood: A Critique of Christianity*. New York: Columbia University Press.

———. 2018. "BLOOD." In *Political Concepts: A Critical Lexicon*, edited by J. M. Bernstein, Adi Ophir, and Laura Ann Stoler, 25–44. New York: Fordham University Press.

Bauman, Z. 1999. *Liquid Modernity*. London: John Wiley & Sons.

Beiner, Ronald. 2014. *Political Philosophy: What It Is and Why It Matters*. New York: Cambridge University Press.
Brown, Michelle, Travis Linnemann, Jody Miller, and Vanessa Panfil. 2019. "Review Symposium: Jeff Ferrell, Drift: Illicit Mobility and Uncertain Knowledge." 1741659019847039.
Canavan, Gerry, and Andrew Hageman, eds. 2016. *Global Weirding*. Vashon Island: Paradoxa.
Canetti, Elias. 1984. *Crowds and Power*. New York: Farrar, Straus and Giroux.
Clover, Joshua. 2016. *Riot. Strike. Riot: The New Era of Uprisings*. New York: Verso.
Correia, David, and Tyler Wall. 2018. *Police: A Field Guide*. New York: Verso Books.
Dobbs, David. 2019. "Climate Change Has Entered Its Blood-Sucking Phase." *The Atlantic*, February 21.
Dodt, Stephanie, and Jan Strozyk. 2019. "Pharmaceutical Companies Are Luring Mexicans across the U.S. Border to Donate Blood Plasma." *Pro Publica*, October 4.
Driggers, Ronald, Orges Furxhi, Gonzalo Vaca, Veerle Reumers, Milad Vazimali, Robert Short, Prashant Agrawal et al. 2019. "Burmese Python Target Reflectivity Compared to Natural Florida Foliage Background Reflectivity." *Applied Optics* 58, no. 13: D98–D104.
Feigenbaum, Anna. 2014. "Resistant Matters: Tents, Tear Gas and the 'Other Media' of Occupy." *Communication and Critical/Cultural Studies* 11, no. 1: 15–24.
———. 2017. *Tear Gas: From the Battlefields of World War I to the Streets of Today*. New York: Verso Books.
Fisher, Mark. 2009. *Capitalist Realism: Is There No Alternative?*. Alresford: John Hunt Publishing.
Flusser, Vilém, and Louis Bec. 2012. *Vampyroteuthis Infernalis: A Treatise, with a Report by the Institut Scientifique de Recherche Paranaturaliste*. Minneapolis: University of Minnesota Press.
Graeber, David. 2015. *The Utopia of Rules: On Technology, Stupidity, and the Secret Joys of Bureaucracy*. New York: Melville House Publishing.
Hall, Steve. 2012. "The Solicitation of the Trap: On Transcendence and Transcendental Materialism in Advanced Consumer-Capitalism." *Human Studies* 35, no. 3: 365–381.
Haraway, Donna J. 2016. *Staying with the Trouble: Making Kin in the Chthulucene*. Durham, NC: Duke University Press.
Hickman, Jonathan E., Shiliang Wu, Loretta J. Mickley, and Manuel T. Lerdau. 2010. *Kudzu (Pueraria montana) Invasion Doubles Emissions of Nitric Oxide and Increases Ozone Pollution*. Proceedings of the National Academy of Sciences; DOI: 10.1073/pnas.0912279107
Kaplan, Caren, and Andrea Miller. 2019. "Drones as 'Atmospheric Policing': From US Border Enforcement to the LAPD." *Public Culture* 31, no. 3: 419–445.
Linebaugh, Peter, and Marcus Rediker. 2013. *The Many-Headed Hydra: Sailors, Slaves, Commoners, and the Hidden History of the Revolutionary Atlantic*. Boston: Beacon Press.
Linnemann, Travis. 2017. "Proof of Death: Police Power and the Visual Economies of Seizure, Accumulation and Trophy." *Theoretical Criminology* 21, no. 1: 57–77.

Linnemann, T., and Turner, J. 2020. "Three-Dimensional Policeman: Security, Sovereignty, and Volumetric Police Power." *Theoretical Criminology*. Advance online publication. https://journals.sagepub.com

Martin, Theodore. 2017. *Contemporary Drift: Genre, Historicism, and the Problem of the Present*. New York: Columbia University Press.

Marx, Karl. 1887. *Capital. A Critique of Political Economy. Volume I: Book One: The Process of Production of Capital*. Moscow: Progress Publishers.

McClanahan, Annie, Jasper Bernes, and Joshua Clover. 2011. "Percentages, Politics, and the Police." *Los Angeles Review of Books*, October 5.

McClanahan, Bill. 2019. "Earth–World–Planet: Rural Ecologies of Horror and Dark Green Criminology." *Theoretical Criminology* 24, no 4: 633–650.

McClanahan, Bill, and Nigel South. 2020. "'All Knowledge Begins with the Senses': Towards a Sensory Criminology." *British Journal of Criminology* 60, no. 1: 3–23.

Miéville, China. 2008. "MR James and the Quantum Vampire: Weird; Hauntological: Versus and/or and and/or or?" *Collapse IV*, 105–28.

Neel, Phil A. 2018. *Hinterland: America's New Landscape of Class and Conflict*. London: Reaktion Books.

Neocleous, Mark. 2003. "The Political Economy of the Dead Marx's Vampires." *History of Political Thought* 24, no. 4: 668–684.

Perera, Suvendrini, and Joseph Pugliese. 2011. "Introduction: Combat Breathing: State Violence and the Body in Question." *Somatechnics* 1, no. 1: 1–14.

Rodenhouse, Nicholas L., Lynn M. Christenson, Dylan Parry, and Linda E. Green. 2009. "Climate Change Effects on Native Fauna of Northeastern Forests." *Canadian Journal of Forest Research* 39, no. 2: 249–263.

Schmidt, Ryan W. 2012. "American Indian Identity and Blood Quantum in the 21st Century: A Critical Review." *Journal of Anthropology* vol. 2011, Article ID 549521, 9 pages.

Steven, Mark. 2017. *Splatter Capital*. London: Repeater Books.

Taibbi, Matt. 2010. *Griftopia: Bubble Machines, Vampire Squids, and the Long Con that Is Breaking America*. New York: Spiegel & Grau.

Thacker, Eugene. 2015. *Tentacles Longer than Night: Horror of Philosophy*. Alresford: John Hunt Publishing.

VanderMeer, Jeff. 2017. *The Southern Reach Trilogy*. London: Fourth Estate.

Wainwright, Joel, and Geoff Mann. 2013. "Climate Leviathan." *Antipode* 45, no. 1: 1–22.

Wall, Tyler. 2019. "The Police Invention of Humanity: Notes on the 'Thin Blue Line.'" *Crime, Media, Culture*. 1741659019873757.

PART III

Dead and Haunted Spaces

9

The Time of Ghosts

Sites of Violence, Environments of Memory

ALISON YOUNG

The landscape of a city is a cartography of violence: "all sites will at some point have been touched by violence" (Fiddler 2018: 9). Whether carried out by agents of the state, arising in interpersonal disputes, or merely the result of accident or chance, violence threads through urban spaces, sometimes rendered visible by official markers such as plaques and statues, but more likely occluded and all but forgotten, receding into the past. For all the social opprobrium directed at violence, its occurrence is rarely singled out for remembering within the everyday spaces of the city. It may be that violent crime is simply too commonplace (cities would be dotted by markers naming urban locations as crime scenes) or that it is too awful, forcing citizens to remember that which they might wish to repress.[1] As Nora suggests, "we speak so much of memory because there is so little of it left" (1989: 7). And although there is constant chatter in everyday life about crime and victimization, many are oblivious to the crime scenes through which they pass every day. But, sometimes, past violence can still be sensed in the present.

For some, this happens when they visit certain kinds of places. In the tunnels beneath a city, traces of characters written there by graffiti writers from decades earlier have engendered a frisson of connection to a culture now superseded by contemporary styles of writing and writers (Kindynis 2019). Others feel the emotional charge of a vanishing past in places of dereliction or ruin (Edensor 2008; Garrett 2013). In this almost archaeological form of engagement, a space that is drifting toward the past, evidenced through disrepair, crumbling masonry, and accumulation of dust, invites awareness of the layering of past lives and actions.

But what if, despite the absence of dust and dereliction, a site's past still seems to reach toward the present passerby? How can we account for the shivering moments of vertigo in which traces of past violence still seem to be felt in the present?

Attending to Ghosts

Such moments invite us to respond to the presence of a ghost. To speak of ghosts is not to make claims as to supernatural presence. Rather, "ghost," or "specter," is the name given by Derrida (1994) and numerous subsequent writers to the destabilization of certainty in the primacy of present existence, which is "replaced with the figure of the ghost which is neither present nor absent, neither dead nor alive" (Davis 2005: 373; and see, for example, Gordon 2008; Gunder 2008; Powell 2016; Zembylas 2013). This was named hauntology (*hauntologie*) by Derrida, playing on its near-homophone, ontology. To think hauntologically about places or events, then, is to attend to the usually overlooked or repressed Other, to acknowledge its "irrecuperable intrusion in our world, which is not compatible with our available intellectual frameworks, but whose Otherness we are responsible for preserving" (Davis 2005: 373).

The encounter with ghosts is always an uneasy one. As Gordon writes:

> Haunting is a frightening experience. It always registers the harm inflicted or the loss sustained by a social violence done in the past or in the present. But haunting, unlike trauma, is distinctive for producing a something-to-be-done. (2008: xvi)

In this chapter I pursue Gordon's comments on the productivity of haunting by thinking about memorialization after disaster. I do so in order to consider memorial practices after the Grenfell Tower fire in London in 2017, in which seventy-two people died. Since, as Gordon proposes, "to study social life one must confront the ghostly aspects of it" (2008: 7), I wish to consider what haunting might mean for criminological understanding of the aftermath of structural violence.

Locating Atrocity: Grenfell Tower

Grenfell Tower is a twenty-four-story building that is part of the Lancaster West Estate, built as "social housing" between 1972 and 1974. Social housing aims to make housing accessible and affordable for people who would struggle to pay rents in the private housing sector. Landlords are usually local councils, boroughs, or housing associations. Thanks to the discursive conjunction of poverty and crime, these laudable aims also generated associated stigmatization. While social housing is generally regarded with disadain, the tall buildings known as "tower blocks" have often been constructed as the prime locales of the social problems mapped onto social housing estates: Hanley notes: "there is one phrase in the English language that has come to be larded with more negative meaning than "council estate" and that is the "tower block"' (2012: 97, quoted in Shildrick 2018: 788). Grenfell Tower is a social housing tower block, a financial and social "problem," like the neighboring tower blocks and lower-level buildings, for the Royal Borough of Kensington and Chelsea, one of the wealthiest boroughs in London. Typical housing management practices have been criticized for being based on the assumption that social housing tenants did not merit the amenities, opportunities, and expenditure that come the way of private tenants or homeowners; rather, as Watt puts it, the "ordinary, working class multi-ethnic Londoners" who lived in towers such as Grenfell were treated as having "[d]isposable homes, disposable lives" (2017).[2]

That assumed disposability was made shockingly plain when, on June 14, 2017, a fire started in a fourth-floor apartment in Grenfell Tower, the result of a faulty part in a refrigerator. Its occupant, Behailu Kebede, reported the fire at 00:54 a.m. Emergency responders initially proceeded on an assumption that the fire would be easily contained within the building; however, it swiftly spread through the building (reaching the roof of the building by 1:26 a.m.), burning for more than sixty hours and resulting in an official death toll of seventy-two individuals. Surviving residents argued that this figure underestimates the likely total because the tower had residents, and temporary visitors, who were undocumented, often as a result of immigration status.[3] Even the probably too-low official figure makes the fire the worst in Britain since 1900.

The fire is the subject of a public inquiry, chaired by Sir Martin Moore-Bick. Phase 1 of the Inquiry took place in 2018, and a report on this initial phase (focusing upon the emergency services responses) was published on October 30, 2019; Phase 2 began in early 2020, with a final Report to be written at its conclusion.[4] The Inquiry will parse the minutiae of the fire's origins, the building's management, and the processes and decisions that led to the Royal Borough of Kensington and Chelsea opting to cover its outer façades with combustible aluminium composite cladding. The council had rejected a provider who would install fireproof cladding in favor of one whose cladding had failed fire tests, but which they believed would be cheaper (Booth 2018; Bulley 2019). The cladding was also intended to make an unattractive building (according to some denizens of the neighborhood) *look nicer*. As a result, the building's fire-readiness was woefully inadequate:

> The window frames were significantly smaller than the structural opening of the building whereas the space between frame and structure was filled by products, such as rigid foam insulation, that were not 30 minutes fire resistant. This allowed the fire to escape from the compartmentation zone of Flat 16 rapidly. The insulation used was flammable and carried no markings of the manufacturer. The front doors to many flats were not equipped with door closers, contrary to the demands of building regulations. . . . [T]here was not a wet riser and a sprinkler system installed in the building, and . . . the single stairwell was 8 cm too narrow. Lastly, the landscaping around the tower did not allow for more than one fire engine to attend at the base of the tower. (Zografos 2019: 145)

For years, residents had complained about the lack of fire safety in the building (Charles 2019: 173). Neither the Royal Borough of Kensington and Chelsea nor the Kensington and Chelsea Tenant Management Organization acted upon the residents' concerns. As Charles puts it, the tower's governance was organized by means of a "necropolitics (the politics of dictating how people live and die) that systematically dehumanizes, endangers and kills the very people the state (officials), through the premise of social housing, should protect" (2019: 168). The fire, therefore, should be conceptualized as resulting from an institutional, or structural, violence located within a tenant management organization that privileged profit margins and the continuing gentrification of the neighborhood, while disregarding complaints about neglect and fire risks from the people who lived in the tower (El-Enany 2019; Bulley 2019).

That the council's management of the tower, including the decision to use combustible aluminium composite cladding, might constitute a series of criminal acts has been confirmed by the Metropolitan Police announcement in June 2019 that they had interviewed under caution thirteen individuals with regard to possible corporate manslaughter charges. It should be noted, however, that the police have also said they will wait until the Inquiry has produced its final report; this means that charges, if any can be sustained, would not be likely to be laid before 2021 or 2022.[5]

Memorialization after Atrocity

I don't live in London, but I've known the city well for more than thirty years, and have family living there, so I'm a frequent visitor. The news of the fire was shocking, awful. That people had to continue to live and work in close proximity to what was in effect a mass grave (and a crime scene) reminded me of the after-effects of the World Trade Center attacks in New York City in 2001. Grenfell Tower's burned-out remains, however, constituted a shape that is the inverse of the enormous hole in the ground that the World Trade Center became, and where it was the towers' absence from New York's skyline that distressed many residents, in London it is the visibility of the burned-out tower that has caused visual trauma. I had previously researched and written about the processes of memorialization that emerged in New York City after 2001 (Young 2005), and I wondered what was happening, and what would happen, in West London.

Visiting London in September 2018, I went to see the tower and its environs. I went with caution. I did not wish to go there voyeuristically, as some were said to have done, and I did not wish to cause any distress to local residents or workers through my presence or conduct. I knew it would be a difficult place to be; I had not anticipated how difficult. As Edkins puts it, being there, without a personal connection to the tower or the area, you are an "interloper" (Edkins 2019a).[6]

That locals are aware of interlopers (a constant flow of journalists, "dark tourists," and other visitors no matter how well-intentioned) is made plain by signs at the local Underground station and on a nearby phone box, which state, "Respect the people of Grenfell Tower and Lancaster West Estate by avoiding the area around the estate wherever possible." A notice on a lamppost is addressed to journalists:

> Please treat the bereaved, survivors and the local community sensitively and with respect . . . Some people will want to tell you their stories, others will not . . . Please do not be intrusive, particularly in asking people to relive their experience, as this may place at risk their recovery from exposure to trauma.

All my experience as a researcher in public places seemed inadequate to the demands of being in the vicinity of the tower. There are a number of reasons for this. First, the tower's presence is monumental. The building is twenty-four stories tall, and, in the absence of taller buildings anywhere nearby, is starkly visible from most locations in the neighborhood. Whereas for a year it had remained unaltered in appearance since the immediate aftermath of the fire, it was now covered by plastic sheeting marked with a gigantic green heart and stating "GRENFELL FOREVER IN OUR HEARTS." For many local residents, the tower's visual appearance had been extremely traumatic; the sheeting reportedly assisted in the management of their trauma (discussed in Charles 2019: 184). (Although reducing the pain felt by those directly affected by the fire, the addition of the plastic sheeting echoed the borough's original impulse to renovate the tower's façade—to improve its appearance in the eyes of those who lived elsewhere in the borough—which led to the choice of flammable cladding as a cosmetic exterior surface.) As a visitor to the area, however, while the building was no doubt easier to look upon now that its burned shell was masked, the sheeting and its proclamation still drew my eye from wherever I walked or stood; the tower, covered or uncovered, was simply always there.

Second, while I had predicted the presence of numerous memorial markers, I was unprepared for the sheer pervasiveness of memorialization throughout the neighborhood. There were hundreds of different examples of memorials. "Documenting" them was impossible: It would

Figure 9.1. Grenfell Tower, September 2018. Photo by Alison Young.

have taken days to have done so. But beyond the sheer practicalities of that, it also seemed ethically impossible to even attempt to do so. The entire neighborhood was immersed in grief, and it had expressed this over and over again. So, instead, I walked quietly through the streets, pausing every now and again to take some notes, or to take an occasional, and discreet, photograph. I consciously tried not to stare, feeling aware of how a gawker might act, and trying not to perform those actions.

Although this practice (walking, thinking, looking, and trying to remember and absorb what I was seeing) seemed to be an acceptable means of being present, my entire time there felt imbued with discomfort and anxiety. Part of that related to a desire not to appear voyeuristic, but it was also a consequence of the affective atmosphere of the neighborhood. The hundreds of memorial markers and the looming tower made the fire a continually present aspect of the place, not in any way a memory that was located in the past. In the spatial manifestations of bereavement, sadness, and anger that surrounded me, I could sense the ghosts of the fire. The numerous memorial markers in the area made visible the dreadful absence of those who had died and those who had lost their homes.

When I was next in London, in July 2019, I wanted to return to the area. I visited a few weeks after the two-year anniversary of the fire. I spent a day walking, noting, absorbing, as I had done before, and I returned on a subsequent evening to take part in one of the area's memorial events. There is still awareness of interlopers, and notices at the station still chastise would-be voyeurs, but subtle changes are apparent in the neighborhood's manifestation of loss.

Walking through the area in 2019, it is still impossible not to think that the fire has reconfigured the entire neighborhood. As the Grime and hip-hop artist Lowkey puts it: "the area itself is kinda tinged by the event" (quoted in Charles 2019: 187). That "tinge," however, is not only grief (although that is still painfully gigantic and awful). The memorial markers around Grenfell Tower also include powerful exhortations to action, angry condemnatory statements of the government and local council, demands for change, and for justice. One large wall under the Westway, known as the "Wall of Truth" for its collation of information about the fire, proclaims that "THE TRUTH WILL NOT BE HIDDEN," naming the wall as a "People's Public Inquest." The

Figure 9.2. Memorial markers, September 2018. Photo by Alison Young.

called-for justice is expressed sometimes as "Justice for Grenfell" and sometimes in statements that "There is no justice, it's just us."

"Justice" might mean criminal prosecutions for corporate manslaughter, or for the inquiry to issue findings that acknowledge the residents' history of demands for change, or more adequate compensation, or suitable re-housing, or better housing for all members of the poor, or for the more than 300 buildings across Britain still covered in combustible cladding to be made safe.[7] "Just us" designates the isolation felt by residents and survivors as they struggle to obtain what would feel to them to be "justice," but also names the power of community in the area, and pays tribute to its self-organizing and indomitability in the face of the continued structural violence that led to the fire in the first place (see Charles 2019; Renwick 2019).

Since the fire, the neighborhood in which the tower stands and that is still home to numerous individuals who lost families and friends in the tower, has been the location for countless memorials and memorial acts. The tower building itself is inaccessible to survivors and relatives, sealed off due to safety concerns and for the duration of the inquiry. But many memorial practices have taken place, and there are dozens of distinctive memorials visible within the neighborhood. These include small crocheted hearts joined in strings that entwine around fences; notes pasted to hoardings or stuck to poles; children's toys (wrapped in plastic to protect them from rain) attached to railings; green hearts spray-painted onto bins, walls, and hoardings; green sashes tied around balconies, lampposts, and parked cars; candles and flowers placed next to messages mourning individuals; and numerous artworks painted on walls. In the area around the tower, there can be seen outward ripples of memorialization, in which different kinds of memorial markers have been made, and which have been installed at different times since the fire on the night of June 14, 2017. These are found in the greatest density in the area proximate to the tower, around the leisure center, the Maxilla Social Centre, the Notting Hill Methodist Church, and the nearby streets. If one walks even a short distance away from the area around the tower, the memorial markers start to diminish as the character of the district changes; by the time you reach the Portobello Road, only a few green hearts still appear on buildings and shops, easily overlooked.

Some memorial representations seek to remember individuals or take the form of individual devices: a drawing, a photograph, a handwritten note. Other memorials have been produced by specific groups: primary schoolchildren, for example, residents of neighboring buildings, or community groups. These tend to have common characteristics, such as the color green, or forms, such as a long green sash tied to railings or cars, or a heart shape, which appears in many drawings both large and small, and also as a three-dimensional object crocheted and tied together in strings or constructed from paper and wooden sticks, dozens of which are affixed to fences and hoardings around the neighborhood.

Finally, there are memorial acts and representations that are understood as authored by or representative of the whole neighborhood. These include the memorial garden, built under the Westway near the Maxilla Social Centre, the memorial mosaic created by community members and attached to a large hoarding near the base of the tower. And on the evening of the fourteenth day of every month since the fire, residents (and anyone else who wishes to) walk through the neighborhood in silence. Other whole-of-community memorials have a less direct relationship to place: They evoke the tower and its location, but their mediated form inserts a distance between the viewer or reader and the tower, the fire and its aftermath. These include the poem, *Grenfell Tower: 14 June 2017*, by Ben Okri, numerous documentaries and films made about the fire, and songs such as *Ghosts of Grenfell*, by Lowkey, with other musicians and residents of the area.[8]

Commissioning Memory

Absent thus far within the neighborhood is any kind of officially funded or commissioned memorial, but it is certain that one will come. One apparent proposal for a memorial, *Grenfell Tower: In Memoriam*, was made in August 2018 by architectural firm JAA Studio.[9] The proposal centered on the construction of a black "sarcophagus" formed by a shell of 224 concrete cladding panels, within which the burned shell of the tower would remain interred. The design proposed a light installation located within Apartment 16, where the fire started: "a small gilded beacon, a quiet nightly narrator of the tragic event" (Dunton 2018). At the base there would be a community center, and a viewing platform and garden would be located in a new twenty-fifth floor at the top of the structure.

But the proposal was not real. JAA director Alessio Cuozzo stated: "This is not a real project and should not be taken as such: it is a discussion piece to provoke conversation about what happens next." It was not intended "to be the answer to the difficult conditions found in the aftermath of Grenfell, but instead offers an alternative way of thinking about the site and its new-found sanctity through disaster" (Dunton 2018).

This provocative intention—to start a conversation rather than to constitute a formal design brief—was not well communicated in the media coverage that resulted, and initial responses were strongly negative. Local MP Emma Dent Coad said the proposal would turn the area into "a misery porn theme park" and stated: "The atrocity is but a year old. Think about those who live there. They have no wish to be reminded every day, for the benefit of others. This proposal is, frankly, macabre" (quoted in Jessel 2018).

The local community group Grenfell United also commented critically:

> What happens to the site is incredibly personal to all of us who used to live in the tower, lost loved ones in the fire or are part of the community . . . It will be survivors, bereaved families and the community that will make decisions together about what happens to the site and how we remember the loved ones we lost. (quoted in Dunton 2018)

JAA Studio staff hurried to reassure critics that the aim was to think through the significance of the site rather than to lobby for this one imagined design to be built. As Cuozzo put it:

> We feel the existing building has a significant level of importance following the fire, not just to those directly affected but also for the city. . . . We believe the tower will likely be demolished due to political pressure and a desire to forget, but we believe this is a mistake . . . We believe the building is important in helping us remember what happened and to improve how the industry procures construction projects . . . It would be a tragedy in itself to be left with a water fountain and a plaque as a memorial. (quoted in Kwun 2018)

Shortly after the JAA proposal was announced, Architects for Social Housing (ASH) announced a modified version, in which the names of "public and private individuals ostensibly responsible for the disaster" would be inscribed upon the black concrete façade (Morley 2018), in a move that inverts a dominant trope in memorialization practices, used at the Vietnam Memorial in Washington, DC, and at the World Trade Center Memorial in New York City, of writing the names of the dead on the surface of a memorial.

Perhaps it is coincidental that only weeks after these two "provocations" were published and discussed in the media, the British government announced its plans to develop proposals for a memorial, but perhaps JAA achieved its aim of starting the conversation. In September 2018, the Minister for Grenfell Victims announced the establishment of the Grenfell Tower Memorial Commission, with Terms of Reference framing its remit as the determination of "what happens to the Grenfell Tower site in the future, assumed to be a fitting memorial to remember those who lost their lives; and how the memorial site will be owned and sustainably managed for the long term."[10] The commission's membership is to comprise ten survivors and residents of North Kensington, along with representatives from the Ministry, the council, the NHS Trust, and the site management team, "structured to ensure the voice of the bereaved carries the most weight, equivalent to a 50% representative vote."[11] Extensive community consultation in North Kensington is envisaged, along with the *ex officio* involvement of figures such as the Inner West London Senior Coroner.

Whatever memorial is developed will be installed in an area undergoing numerous environmental and legal upheavals: frequent monitoring of air quality amid health concerns for residents, the transfer of the freehold of the site in mid-2019 from the council to the Ministry of Housing, Communities and Local Government, and continuous works to maintain the structural security of the site. The process of selecting a memorial is expected to last for a year, and comparisons, regarding the process of soliciting submissions and selecting a final design for a suitable memorial, are being made with the experiences of families and relatives of those killed in the 9/11 attacks. In New York City, this was a fraught and protracted process as a result of the stated need to redesign the site for a combination of commercial, community, and residential use. The competition for the site redevelopment was won by architect Daniel Libeskind, whose initial proposal was renamed the "Freedom Tower," after having been substantially revised to increase the space available for commercial use at the location (Young 2005). The site also includes a memorial, designed by Michael Arad and Peter Walker in 2004, and a museum.

Responses to the site development and memorial design in New York have been mixed. For some, the "touristification" of disaster has been deeply distressing (Kandell 2014), and others have noted the paradoxical way in which the museum and memorial have encouraged an active forgetting of the past. Edkins writes: "The world has been put back together, bigger and better. Trees planted, earth levelled, the past and its remains neatly boxed into museums and repositories that we can visit or not as we choose" (2019b: 121). Just as cities tend not to commemorate its crime scenes, forgetting disaster is enormously appealing: "you/we/they are entitled to concrete over the cracks, to reorient the city around new towers, to forget" (Edkins 2019b: 121). But the rewards of forgetting have a high cost. As Edkins notes of contemporary lower Manhattan, with words that might equally apply to any official memorial and redevelopment of the area around the burned tower, if "there are no echoes here of that time, of those dead" (2019b: 121), where do those memories go? If we are prevented from encountering the city's ghosts, then what have we lost? In the neighborhood around Grenfell Tower, it is possible to see numerous ways in which the community is *actively remembering*, in order to hold on to its ghosts.

Holding On: (i) Repetition

Memorials arrest time in a particular space. Any official, government-commissioned memorial will have to condense multiple narratives of loss into a singular location and form where the lapse of time will be halted in order for the work of memory to occur. The visitor to a memorial can be thought of as giving themselves up to the memorial's exhortation to remember, such that memory travels backwards toward the event of loss, despite the continual forward pull of temporality. Such is the conventional operation of memorial places and structures. But what of the memorial acts described in this chapter?

The acts of memorialization at and around Grenfell Tower in London demonstrate that effective memorialization needs certain conditions, specific to the place, community, and event, to be met. During the two years since the fire, the community has shown that it requires multiple memorials, taking place on different scales, sometimes singular and sometimes recurrent, and utilizing different formats and media. Around Grenfell, it is not so much that these numerous memorials manage successively to stop time so that the area's ghosts can be sensed, but rather it might be that the fire itself ruptured the community's history: Although, of course, time moves by as it ever did, the neighborhood may find that it is always the night of June 14, 2017. While some of the area's memorials fade or fall apart (some are replaced, some removed, and some simply deteriorate), others show the ways in which, for this community, time has been frozen in place.

Repetition is symptomatic both of the haunting of memory and haunting by memory. Poems and songs written after the fire feature recurrent phrases and ask questions that receive no answers. The name "Grenfell" or "Grenfell Tower" concentrates place, loss, and atrocity into one or two words: Ben Okri uses them, along with two temporal signifiers, as the title of a poem ("Grenfell Tower, June, 2017") that repeats the lines, "Those who were living are now dead / Those who were breathing are from the living earth fled," and exhorts the reader, again and again, "If you want to see how the poor die, come see Grenfell Tower / See the tower, and let a world-changing dream flower. Come see Grenfell Tower / See the tower, and let a world-changing act flower" (Okri 2019: xxviii, xxix, xx, xxi).

In "Ghosts of Grenfell," Lowkey asks over and over, "Did they die, or us?/ Did they die or us?/ Did they die, for us?"(2019: 75, 76, 77), acknowledging the indeterminacy of the border separating the living from those who have been lost, and the difficulties of living on after disaster. The song is structured around expressions of grief and sorrow: he mourns, first of all, the building's lost physical spaces:

> Rooms where, love was made and un-made in a flash of the night
> Rooms where, memories drowned in fumes of poison
> Rooms where, futures were planned and the imagination of children built castles in the sky

> Rooms where, both the extraordinary and the mundane were lived
> Become forever tortured graves of ash (Lowkey 2019: 75)

The song then narrates the disaster as it unfolded: "1:30 a.m. heard the shouting from my window/ People crying in the street/ Watchin' the burning of their kinfolk." In the song's final section, using the standard form of bureaucratic address, "to whom it may concern," he calls on the unnamed officials at "the Queen's royal borough of Kensington and Chelsea" to explain the whereabouts of the dead, as if they might still have presence, elsewhere:

> Where is Yasin El-Wahabi? Where is his brother Mehdi? Where is his sister Nur Huda? Where is their mother and father? Where is Nura Jamal and her husband Hashim? ... Tell us, where is Rania Ibrahim and her two daughters? (2019: 77–78)

The question is asked over and over, for all of the Grenfell dead: "Where is . . . ? Where is . . . ? Where are . . . ?" The song ends by using the second person pronoun to impute responsibility for the dead to the council:

> Where are all these people?
> Where are all these people?
> The blood is on your hands
> There will be ashes on your graves (Lowkey 2019: 78)

It would be easy to read the song as a simple litany of loss, a naming of the dead as the eponymous "ghosts of Grenfell." The lyrics, however, deliberately undercut the construction of a straightforward opposition between the living and the victims of the fire. Of the dead, Lowkey sings, "they are immortalized forever, the only ghosts are us" (2019: 77), and, as noted above, asks over and over "did they die or us? Did they die or us?" As Lowkey has also stated, for everyone in the area, "all of a sudden, their lives are ... Grenfellised" (quoted in Charles 2019: 186). Living on after the fire, in a neighborhood "tinged" with grief and anger, where residents "see Grenfell in [their] own future" (Lowkey quoted in Charles 2019: 180), the song makes clear that the distinction between living and dead, or between citizen and ghost, has dissolved.

Holding On: (ii) Invocations

Repetition is also an aspect of a different technique of memorialization, the monthly Silent Walk (on the walk, see further Charles 2019: 180–181). Occurring on the fourteenth evening of every month, the event is both a memorialization of loss and a performative demand for justice. I attended the twenty-fifth of these Walks, on July 14, 2019. On that evening, as with every other walk, people assembled at an advertised location, and then walked through the streets of the neighborhood, ending up at the Wall of Truth under the Westway. The Walk is a remarkable event, combining the characteristics of a funeral or memorial procession with those of a political protest. It is both melancholic and furious; it looks backwards to the fire and its devastating losses and also forward to a day when justice will be achieved for the survivors, local residents, and thousands of others in Britain who still live in buildings with combustible cladding or otherwise inadequate fire safety.

Walkers in the front row hold a lengthy banner that states "United for Grenfell," Others assemble behind them, filling the road. On the evening I attended, there were around 200 walkers: a small turnout, because the previous Walk, on the two-year anniversary of the fire, attracted more than 11,000 people to walk in silence through the streets. Some participants bring with them their own placards or banners. Others bring them to distribute for people to carry, so that the mass of people walking is punctuated by signs that state, JUSTICE FOR GRENFELL, Grenfell United, Unity, Peace + Love, Strength, Change, Clarity, Remembrance, Just Us, Peace, Respect, and more. Many walkers wear green; placards are often green and white with black text; some are heart-shaped and painted green. Green, which has always been the color associated with the community response to the fire, is the dominant color for the walk, a visible inflection that would communicate even if the words of the placards were illegible.

While people are assembling, there is a buzz of conversation and chatter, but as soon as they move into the road to commence the walk, the hubbub subsides and is gone. For the entire duration of the walk (around 30 minutes), no one speaks, no phones ring. The group is so quiet that footfalls on tarmac become the only noise made by participants. Police stop the traffic in the streets for the walk; people stand on

Figure 9.3. Grenfell Tower, Silent Walk, July 14, 2019. Photo by Alison Young.

the footpath and watch. The city is hushed; birds can be heard singing in the trees nearby. It is simultaneously a bearing witness to disaster and a demand for action.

That the walk has demands is made clear when it reaches the final point on its itinerary, the Wall of Truth and the recently constructed community Memorial Garden. A group of survivors and bereaved stand in front of the Wall, holding an enormous JUSTICE FOR GRENFELL banner. Each in turn reads the names of the dead, in groupings of about eight or ten at a time. After each group of names, the crowd murmurs, "Forever in our hearts" (the phrase that is printed on the sheeting covering the tower). Once all seventy-two names have been spoken, the crowd turns to face the tower, observing a silence that lasts seventy-two seconds. The weight of the lost is palpable; some members of the crowd are weeping.

But the mood shifts; a number of speakers address the crowd about the continuing struggle for answers, for involvement in various governmental processes, and in pressing for improvements in fire safety in other buildings. That the crowd is both remembering the lost and also substantively demanding something is made literal when we are asked to follow the speakers in another call-and-response exchange: "JUSTICE!" chant the speakers; "JUSTICE!" shouts the crowd in answer. Over and over, we call out the word. This echoing moment is extraordinarily powerful. What "justice" would involve is unspecified and is no doubt multiform (compensation, housing for those still displaced, better housing for all, an apology, criminal prosecution of responsible individuals, better building design, and more), but it is made to feel tangible, and the participants made active, just as the silent progression through the street gave embodiment to mourning and loss.

Holding On: (iii) Conservation

Memorialization requires effort and energy from those who enact it. One speaker at the Silent Walk on July 14 attempted to reassure those present who might feel anxious that the smaller number of participants indicated a dwindling of commitment or interest: "Not everyone can walk every time. We walked tonight for those who can't be here, and at other times they will walk for us," projecting a future in which the Walk will re-occur, ceaselessly, until the called-upon "Justice" will arrive.

The forward flow of time is punctuated with and interrupted by acts of memorialization; in that interruption, ghosts are made visible. Thanks to the abject status of crime and victimization, such visibility is uncomfortable; thus, time's forward movement is allowed to obscure the presence of ghosts. Memory after trauma both shies away from and requires repetition; and memorialization usually involves repetitive gestures or recurrent ceremonies. Repetition solves some of the tendency for memory to fade; however, time diminishes memorialization efforts in other ways as well. In 2018, I saw dozens of hearts crocheted by children and other local residents, which had been tied to lampposts, or strung around garden fences; returning ten months later, the bright hues of the hearts had faded, many looked damaged by rain, snow, and urban grime, and some had fallen to the ground. Where hearts had been tied to fences, some were now overgrown by ivy and other plants.

At numerous places around the neighborhood, drawings by children at the local primary school, made after the fire, were attached to fences or stuck to temporary hoardings. Although still brightly colored in September 2018, ten months later many were fading and others had had to be removed. A notice on one railing stated: "Exposure to the elements means [the drawings] have faded badly and some have fallen off and have been lost." In order to preserve remaining drawings, they have been "removed, cleaned, and stored safely." The notice had been posted by ACAVA (the Association for Cultural Advancement through Visual Art), a local organization responsible for numerous cultural activities in the aftermath of the fire. It also stated that the drawings will be taken elsewhere: "we plan to place them in an archive where the community can continue to have access to them. When that happens we will update this notice with details of where they have been placed." Time thus destroys memorial drawings made by traumatized local children; the understandable response is to salvage them so that they can be preserved. But such conservation necessarily detaches the drawings from a place deeply connected to the atrocity, and their subsequent display in a different setting risks an interruption of their affectiveness and an alteration in their communication of meaning and memory.

Other memorial acts have been preserved by virtue of their medium of expression. Some have been preserved in print (such as the collection of poetry, *Poems for Grenfell*) and on YouTube (such as the various iterations of *Ghosts of Grenfell*). The initial ad hoc hoardings placed around the tower have been replaced by a much more substantial one, where there can be found a mix of handwritten messages and memorial materials along with community-produced memorial images, such as large green hearts, and the Memorial Mosaic, a large flower shape created by residents working with ACAVA. Near the Wall of Truth, with its now-tattered and fading posters, is a memorial garden built by local residents. Together with the as yet unimagined memorial to be built by the government-sponsored Memorial Commission, these more recent acts of memorialization condense the multiplicity of memorial acts into a smaller number of expressions of loss and memory, many of which are characterized by the potential for longevity rather than the ephemerality of paper or wool. In the gradual shift from reliance on the repetition of temporary memorial acts to representational modes that offer greater capacity for permanence, what will happen to the ghosts that disrupt the surface of everyday life in the neighborhood?

Figure 9.4. Grenfell Tower memorial wall, July 2019. Photo by Alison Young.

Environments of Memory and Encounters with Ghosts

In his account of the tensions interconnecting history and memory, Pierre Nora draws a distinction between what he calls *lieux de mémoire*, or "sites of memory," and *milieux de mémoire*, which are "real environments of memory" (1989: 7). For Nora, memory is "in permanent evolution, open to the dialectic of remembering and forgetting, unconscious of its successive deformations, vulnerable to manipulation and appropriation, susceptible to being dormant and periodically revived" (1989: 8). It is "affective and magical" (7), and is to be distinguished from history, an "intellectual and secular production," relying on "analysis and criticism" (8). Nora is concerned that "environments of memory" are losing ground to "sites of memory," where remembrance "crystallizes and secretes itself" (7). Museums, monuments, and archives, for Nora, are sites of memory, destroying the possibilities of "spontaneous memory" and generating instead a "commemorative vigilance" (12) that concentrates the work of memory into a designated place and time.

The "commemorative vigilance" of the 9/11 Museum and Memorial in New York City confirms that sites of memory following disaster or atrocity paradoxically engender new kinds of loss: "you seemed to realise we all share a vulnerability ... but we find that you have thoroughly forgotten what that might have been and where that might have led" (Edkins 2019b: 121). It is not time that effects this loss (in the way that the image in a fading memorial drawing gradually becomes indistinct), but rather official exhortations to remember and their corralling of memory into narrowly defined (and confining) forms.

In West Kensington right now, it is evident that "memory is by nature multiple and yet specific; collective, plural and yet individual" (Nora 1989: 9). The area around Grenfell Tower is not a site of memory but is rather a *milieu de mémoire*—an environment of memory where "memory takes root in the concrete, in spaces, gestures, images and objects" (ibid.). The public, fugitive, transient, and fleeting moments, practices, and places of memorialization discussed in this chapter, whose drawings fade, and are replaced, whose subjects walk and walk again, month after month, whose songs are viewed on YouTube over and over[12]—these practices mediate our encounters with ghosts. Thinking of the ordinary places of the city as populated by ghosts asks its present inhabitants to imagine the possibilities of everyday violence, and, in that act of imagination, to desire a different landscape, to move past the vertigo of remembering the past and demand another future.

Fiddler writes that criminologists must "read city spaces for the shadows, the gaps and elisions of trauma, and ... fashion [a] creative response" (2018: 9)—that is, a haunted criminology has the potential to analyze the spaces of the present in light of the violence of the past in a way that will open us to a future time. The contours of that future are, however, not fixed: "spectres gesture towards a still-unformulated future" (Davis 2005: 379). The shape of that future time is neither static nor singular, and the "not-yet formulated possibilities of the future" (378–379) are uncertain. The residents of West Kensington and the survivors of the fire call for "justice," demanding prosecution of those responsible for corporate manslaughter, an end to unsafe building practices, and a making-safe of dangerous buildings.

But, as Shilliam points out, "whether justice will ultimately be served, or partially served, or betrayed, the aftermath already stretches on indefinitely" (2019: 196). The sense that past atrocity, present trauma, and aftermath have already merged is given voice in a comment by the singer Lowkey: "it's hard for us not to see Grenfell in our own future" (quoted in Charles 2019: 180). There is no simple linear progression from atrocity through memorialization to a future horizon when justice will be done. Instead, the fire can never not have taken place, the present can never not be tinged with grief, and although we may invoke justice, its advent cannot be guaranteed. The future holds simultaneously the possibility that justice will come to those who call for it along with the arrival of a time when all buildings have burned to ash or crumbled to dust. As Cairns and Jacobs put it, "all buildings must die" (2017) and, at certain moments, we are all, already, ghosts—for such is the present future for everyone, and every city.

NOTES

1. On visiting Holcomb, Kansas, Linnemann discovers that the town displays no markers commemorating the area's association with a number of infamous crimes (2015: 529).
2. To emphasize the diversity of "working class, multi-ethnic Londoners," the residents of Grenfell Tower were mainly social housing tenants, although some (12 out of 120 properties) had been purchased by their occupants under the government's Right To Buy scheme (Shildrick 2018: 788); some were unemployed, many were working (and some were working more than one job): "Grenfell was home to the young and the old, multiple generations of the same families, working-class Londoners who had lived there for decades, and those newly arrived, seeking sanctuary from their own war torn homes in places like Syria" (789); "many residents were British, or had secure immigration status, some did not" (Bradley 2019: 136).
3. For detailed consideration of the conjunctions between immigration status, social precarity, and vulnerability to violence, see El-Enany 2019; Keenan 2019.
4. The Phase 1 Report can be accessed online at www.grenfelltowerinquiry.org.uk.
5. Tuitt points out "the dissonance between law and justice [that] is emphasised whenever the question of justice is raised in the face of racism and other forms of exclusion" (2019: 119), and it is plain that the legal process in relation to the Grenfell fire, whether in the glacially slow criminal investigation or in the recourse to concepts such as "justiciability" in administrative law (120), may well be working in a manner antithetical to delivering outcomes that the survivors might consider to represent justice.
6. Away from the neighborhood, now writing this chapter, my interloper status remains, and animates a sense of caution in how I write about the fire and its aftermath, aware that, as Renwick points out, "Thousands now use Grenfell on

their CVs, there have been countless uses of its name" (2019: 37). And in writing about the aftermath of the fire, I must struggle to avoid what Shilliam calls "a cavalier treatment—or even abandonment—of locale" and to "proactively refine and redefine our terms of engagement with the communities that surround our institutions" (2019: 196, 197).

7   The same cladding is used in many other countries also. In Melbourne, Australia, for example, the State Government ordered an audit by the Victorian Cladding Taskforce of apartment buildings for fire safety after the implication of combustible cladding fires in Melbourne apartment buildings. Of the 2,227 apartment buildings audited for fire risk due to the use of aluminium composite cladding as of July 2019, 72 were rated as an extreme risk, 409 as a high risk, and 388 considered a moderate risk. These figures are likely to increase as the taskforce continues its survey. See Willingham (2019).

8   A recording of Okri reading his poem can be viewed on YouTube at www.youtube.com/watch?v=zC9Ni-IPnAc. Documentaries about the fire and its aftermath include *On the Ground at Grenfell* (Nendie Pinto-Duschinsky and Stowe Films, 2017) and *Searching for Grenfell's Lost Lives* (Reggie Yates for BBC2, 2018). Musical responses to the fire are discussed in Charles 2019.

9   Launched online at www.bdonline.co.uk.

10   See the Terms of Reference for the Grenfell Tower Memorial Commission, available online at www.grenfelltowermemorial.co.uk.

11   Commission membership is set out on its website, at www.grenfelltowermemorial.co.uk.

12   At the time of writing, the video *Ghosts of Grenfell*, by Lowkey featuring Mai Khalil, had been viewed 672,174 times. There are also videos of live performances of the song, such as a London performance with more than 33,000 views. Another version, *Ghosts of Grenfell 2*, by Lowkey featuring Kaia, which was filmed at the Wall of Truth a year after the fire, has been viewed 106,926 times.

REFERENCES

Booth, Robert. 2018. "Grenfell Tower: Fire-Resistant Cladding Plan was Dropped." www.theguardian.com/

Bradley, Gracie Mae. 2019. "From Grenfell to Windrush." In *After Grenfell: Violence, Resistance and Response*, edited by Dan Bulley, Jenny Edkins, and Nadine El-Enany, 135–142. London: Pluto Press.

Bulley, Dan. 2019. "Everyday Life and Death in the Global City." In *After Grenfell: Violence, Resistance and Response*, edited by Dan Bulley, Jenny Edkins, and Nadine El-Enany, 1–18. London: Pluto Press.

Cairns, Stephen and Jacobs, Jane M. 2017. *Buildings Must Die: A Perverse View of Architecture*. Boston, MA: MIT Press.

Charles, Monique. 2019. "Come Unity and Community in the Face of Impunity." In *After Grenfell: Violence, Resistance and Response*, edited by Dan Bulley, Jenny Edkins, and Nadine El-Enany, 167–192. London: Pluto Press.

Davis, Colin. 2005. "Hauntology, Spectres and Phantoms." *French Studies* 59, 3: 373–379.
Derrida, Jacques. 1994. *Specters of Marx: The State of the Debt, the Work of Mourning, and the New International*. London: Routledge.
Dunton, Tim. 2018. "JAA Floats Grenfell Tower Memorial Vision." www.bdonline.co.uk/
Edensor, Tim. 2008. "Mundane Hauntings: Commuting through the Phantasmagoric Working-Class Spaces of Manchester, England." *Cultural Geographies* 15: 313–333.
Edkins, Jenny. 2019a. "The Interloper." In *After Grenfell: Violence, Resistance and Response*, edited by Dan Bulley, Jenny Edkins, and Nadine El-Enany, 130–134. London: Pluto Press.
———. 2019b. "Loss of a Loss," in her *Change and the Politics of Certainty*. Manchester: Manchester University Press.
El-Enany, Nadine. 2019. "Before Grenfell: British Immigration Law and the Production of Colonial Spaces." In *After Grenfell: Violence, Resistance and Response*, edited by Dan Bulley, Jenny Edkins, and Nadine El-Enany, 50–61. London: Pluto Press.
Fiddler, Michael. 2018. "Ghosts of Other Stories: A Synthesis of Hauntology, Crime and Space." *Crime, Media, Culture*. DOI: 10.1177/1741659018788399.
Garrett, Bradley. 2013. *Explore Everything: Place-Hacking the City*. London: Verso.
Gordon, Avery. 2008. *Ghostly Matters: Haunting and the Sociological Imagination*. Minneapolis: University of Minnesota Press.
Gunder, Michael. 2008. "Ideologies of Certainty in a Risky Reality: Beyond the Hauntology of Planning." *Planning Theory* 7, 2: 186–206.
Hanley, Lynsey. 2012. *Estates: An Intimate History*. London: Granta.
Jessel, Ella. 2018. "MP Slams Architects' 'Misery Porn' Grenfell Tower Memorial Concept." www.architectsjournal.co.uk/
Kandell, Steve. 2014. "The Worst Day of My Life Is Now New York's Hottest Tourist Attraction." www.buzzfeednews.com/.
Keenan, Sarah. 2019. "A Border in Every Street: Grenfell and the Hostile Environment." In *After Grenfell: Violence, Resistance and Response*, edited by Dan Bulley, Jenny Edkins, and Nadine El-Enany, 79–91. London: Pluto Press.
Kindynis, Theo. 2019. "Excavating Ghosts: Urban Exploration as Graffiti Archaeology." *Crime, Media, Culture* 15, 1: 25–45.
Kwun, Aileen. 2018. "A Haunting Speculative Proposal for the Grenfell Tower Memorial." www.fastcompany.com
Linnemann, Travis. 2015. "Capote's Ghosts: Violence, Media and the Spectre of Suspicion." *British Journal of Criminology* 55, 3: 514–533.
Lowkey. "Ghosts of Grenfell." In *After Grenfell: Violence, Resistance and Response*, edited by Bulley Dan, Edkins Jenny, and El-Enany Nadine, 75–78. London: Pluto Press.
Morley, Jack Balderrama. 2018. "Alternative Grenfell Tower Memorial Design Calls Out Those Responsible." https://archpaper.com/
Nora, Pierre. 1989. "Between Memory and History: Les Lieux de Mémoire." *Representations* 26: 7–24.

Okri, Ben. 2019. "Grenfell Tower, June, 2017." In *After Grenfell: Violence, Resistance and Response*, edited by Dan Bulley, Jenny Edkins, and Nadine El-Enany, xxvii–xxxi. London: Pluto Press.

Powell, Kashif Jerome. 2016. "Making #BlackLivesMatter: Michael Brown, Eric Garner, and the Specters of Black Life—Toward a Hauntology of Blackness." *Cultural Studies ↔ Critical Methodologies* 16, 3: 253–260.

Renwick, Daniel. 2019. "Organising on Mute." In *After Grenfell: Violence, Resistance and Response*, edited by Dan Bulley, Jenny Edkins, and Nadine El-Enany, 19–46. London: Pluto Press.

Shildrick, Tracey. 2018. "Lessons from Grenfell: Poverty Propaganda, Stigma and Class Power." *Sociological Review* 66, 4: 783–798.

Shilliam, Robbie. 2019. "Afterword." In *After Grenfell: Violence, Resistance and Response*, edited by Dan Bulley, Jenny Edkins, and Nadine El-Enany, 195–197. London: Pluto Press.

Tuitt, Patricia. 2019. "Law, Justice and the Public Inquiry into the Grenfell Tower Fire." In *After Grenfell: Violence, Resistance and Response*, edited by Dan Bulley, Jenny Edkins, and Nadine El-Enany, 119–129. London: Pluto Press.

Watt, Paul. 2017. "'This place is post-something': London's Housing Crisis in the Wake of the Grenfell Tower Fire." www.city-analysis.net/

Willingham, Richard. 2019. "Flammable Cladding to Be Stripped from Buildings Under Victorian Government Plan." www.abc.net.au/

Young, Alison. 2005. *Judging the Image: Art, Value, Law*. London: Routledge.

Zembylas, Michalinos. 2013. "Pedagogies of Hauntology in History Education: Learning to Live with the Ghosts of Disappeared Victims of War and Dictatorship." *Educational Theory* 63, 1: 69–86.

Zografos, Stamatis. 2019. *Architecture and Fire: A Psychoanalytic Approach to Conservation*. London: UCL Press.

10

Dark Diffractions

A Performative Hauntology of 10 Rillington Place

ELAINE CAMPBELL

Mrs. Jessie Hide and cat look out from her first-floor window to the back garden of 10 Rillington Place (figure 10.1). Three days earlier, police had unearthed the skeletal remains of Ruth Fuerst and Muriel Eady from the corner of the garden, and three days before this, on March 24, 1953, the corpses of Kathleen Maloney, Rita Nelson, and Hectorina Maclennan were found secreted in a papered-over kitchen cupboard in John Christie's ground floor flat. On the same day, the remains of Mrs. Ethel Christie were discovered, wrapped in a blanket and entombed in rubble beneath the floorboards of the sitting room. It was not the first occasion that Mrs. Hide had cause to look across to the garden of 10 Rillington Place and pose for the press photographers. In December 1949, a police search of the outbuildings had uncovered the bodies of Beryl Evans and her thirteen-month-old daughter, Geraldine, in the wash house—Beryl Evans's body had been wrapped in a tablecloth, tied into a bundle, and stashed underneath the sink unit; Geraldine's unswathed body had been concealed behind the wash house door, hidden by a loose covering of timber shores and firewood. Between 1943 and 1953, eight murders were committed at this ordinary, drab, residential address; and one of its tenants, Timothy John Evans, was hung for a murder he did not commit.[1] Renamed as Ruston Close fourteen months after John Reginald Halliday Christie's arrest at Putney Bridge on March 31, 1953, demolished in 1970, flattened, and then built over in 1978 as part of a regeneration scheme, this house of horrors has been physically erased and cartographically deleted from the urban fabric of south west London.

According to Honeycombe (2011), more has been written on the murders at 10 Rillington Place than any other case investigated by the

Figure 10.1. "Mrs Jessie Hide and cat." Credit: Keystone Pictures USA/Alamy Stock Photo.

Metropolitan Police since the Whitechapel Murders of the late nineteenth century. It is a historiography that continually re-animates and enfolds the spectral shadows of unfinished business and unresolved mysteries, where questions of innocence and guilt—of the everyday and the exceptional, sanity and insanity, good and evil, fact and fiction, justice and injustice, known and unknown, rough and respectable—hover like ghosts, partial, incomplete, neither real nor imagined, actual nor virtual. The story of 10 Rillington Place is, arguably, the archetypical criminological form of the hauntological, and lends itself to theorizations of spectral life. Across the arts, humanities, and social sciences, "ghost thinking" has gathered apace in recent years to the extent that it would be fair to suggest a "spectral turn" in contemporary analyses that grapple with the sociopolitical uncertainties of twenty-first-century worlds. In the next section, the chapter offers a thumbnail sketch of contemporary "ghost work," paying particular attention to Derridean hauntology which has come to prominence within this burgeoning body of scholarship. Despite its pivotal contribution to "spectral studies," I argue that Derrida's analytic is ill-equipped to probe the ethical and political dynamics of haunting and provides little solid ground for responding to ghosts "in the name of *justice*" (Derrida 1994, xix; emphasis in original).

To address this lacuna, the chapter takes a "quantum turn" and sets out an alternative point of departure for hauntological thinking. It introduces the innovative work of Karen Barad (2003, 2007, 2010, 2014); a key thinker within feminist technoscience and the philosophy of science, Barad draws from quantum physics to elaborate a new materialist theory of agential realism that not only positions the hauntological within a performative and diffractive methodological framework, but does so in politically and ethically transformative ways—captured in Barad's triptych notion of the *onto-epistemo-ethical unity of practice*. Key Baradian concepts of material-discursive entanglements, indeterminacies, agential cuts, intra-actions, phenomena, and diffraction, are unpacked, and the remainder of the chapter offers (the beginnings of) a diffractive reading and a performative hauntology of 10 Rillington Place's principal occupant, John Reginald Halliday Christie. Though long since convicted and executed for multiple murders, this spectral figure is revisited and continually recreated through stage plays, books, film, television crime drama, press photography, archival documents, and museum exhibits. This cultural bricolage is also a space of ghostly encounters with Christie's multiplicity—as "an evil serial killer" (Root 2012); "a worried looking, insignificant mouse of a man" (*Sunday Times*, June 28, 1953); "the most respected person in the street" (Patricia Pichler [former neighbor] cited in Curnow 2017, 128); "a weird character" (*Evening Standard*, June 26, 1953), and "such a nice man" (National Archives [NA], MEPO2/9535). Through a Baradian lens, grappling with the haunting indeterminacies of Christie's being is not solely a question of mapping (his) difference as "evil monster"; rather, it also delineates the ethical ground within which matters of justice are always-already at stake. The chapter, then, makes an ontological, epistemological, and ethical contribution to the emerging subfield of "ghost criminology," introducing a mode of analysis that can grasp spectralities as performative enfoldings of matter and meaning that have politico-ethical form, content, significance, and power.

Ghost Work

Spectral thinking can be traced from Freud's (1919) thesis of the uncanny, through to Abraham and Torok's (1987[1978]) work on ancestral phantoms, and Gordon's (2008[1997]) sociological account of haunting as repressed/unresolved social violences. Yet, it is Derrida's (1994) hauntology that has become the main point of departure for an interdisciplinary field of contemporary spectral scholars—cultural geography (Buser 2017; Maddern 2008; Roberts 2012); political philosophy (Sprinker 1999); education studies (Peim 2005); literary studies (Davis 2005; Luckhurst 2002); and anthropology (Argyrou 2017) are all represented in this burgeoning literature. It is a framework that eschews the privileging of presence as the empirical touchstone of ontological thought and introduces the figure of the ghost as a deconstructive device and an ethical obligation (Davis 2005; Dixon 2007). To engage with ghosts is to grapple with the indeterminacy, uncertainty, and undecidability of the world (Roberts 2012); the spectral signifies a restlessness, "something unanswered, something incomplete" (Peim 2005, 76) that haunts our narratives of progress and enlightenment, of justice and democracy, not only unsettling our sense of their temporal unfolding and spatial patterning, but also disrupting the modes of thought and political imperatives that sustain them (Maddern 2008).

For all these reasons, encounters with ghosts demand both our attention and responsiveness—as Davis puts it, "(a)ttending to the ghost is an ethical injunction" (2005, 373). Moreover, if the spectral lingers as a signifier of unfinished projects, unresolved conflicts, and unrealized ambitions, and beckons to an uncertain future that is yet to come, it also stands as critique and opens up a critical space for politico-ethical engagements. That said, we need to ask how such engagements are mobilized when the ground for politico-ethical action is one of indeterminacy and undecidability, and when specters are always-already cast in shadowy excess, outside of discourse, and "impossible to exorcise through the securing categories that have often been created for them" (Holloway and Kneale 2008, 308). Indeed, Derrida's insistence that "(i)t is necessary to introduce haunting into the very construction of a concept" (1994, 161) undermines and overstretches the spectral's usefulness as a critical category—if everywhere and everything is haunted and haunting, including ourselves as researchers (Gordon 2008), then ghost work is rendered apolitical (Argyrou 2017), or is so generalized as to lose its ethico-political purchase and heuristic value (Holloway and Kneale 2008; Luckhurst 2002). Ultimately, Derrida has bequeathed a hauntological ethics (and politics) which, lacking in specific content, pivots on a somewhat vague engagement with spectral otherness, strangeness, and silence. Hauntologists, then, are left to grapple with uncertainty and indeterminacy with very little ethico-political guidance. If we are to listen to and speak with ghosts as a politico-ethical commitment, we need to find an alternative route through the impasse of undecidability, but in a way that does not betray the absent-presence of spectral power.

Taking a "Quantum Turn"

One fruitful way of displacing Derridean spectrology without losing sight of his hauntological orientation is to take a quantum turn and reposition our analyses within a theoretical framework more attentive to the politics and ethics of ghost work. I would not be the first to find resonances across Derridean hauntology and Karen Barad's (2007, 2010, 2014) quantum approach to entanglements, enfoldings, and space-time-mattering—see, for example, Blackman 2015; Crockett 2018. Indeed, in her agential realist account of "justice-to-come," Barad (2010) explicitly invokes the spirit of Derrida to unpack the hauntological relations of inheritance as a way of thinking with and through the dis/jointedness of time and space, the here and there, now and then of lived experience. Playfully mixing Derridean/Baradian concepts, Crockett's (2018) notion of "quantum Derrida" or "hauntological materialism" underlines the extent to which both theorists occupy common ground and share concerns for difference (and différance), traces, inconsistencies, absences, silenced narratives, displacements, and dis/continuities. Yet, it is in their dissimilarities that the added heuristic value and greater politico-ethical purchase of Barad's distinctive onto-epistemological framework shows up in sharp relief.

Where Derrida promotes an anti-foundationalist, non-essentialist philosophy, and prioritises deconstruction as epistemology and method, Barad (1999, 2003, 2007) argues for an agential realist prospectus which, as Lather puts it, "(marks) a return to materialism AFTER Derrida" (2016,

125; uppercase in original). This does not mean that Barad returns to an old-style Marxism, but that she questions the hitherto primacy of discourse over materiality, culture over nature, meaning over matter—an onto-epistemological commonplace perfectly exemplified by Derridean deconstructionism and its overprivileging of textual interpretation, its promotion of discursive idealism, its fixation on linguistic demystification, and reliance on representational logic (Livingstone 1998; Nealon 1992). Inspired by Bohr's advances in quantum theory,[2] Barad's new materialist approach has captured the attention (and imagination) of a transdisciplinary scholarship spanning fields as diverse as management studies (Orlikowski and Scott 2015), security studies (Aradau 2010), museology (Bergsdóttir 2017), social movement studies (Feigenbaum 2014), educational studies (Hultman and Taguchi 2010), and social media studies (Warfield 2016). As Hollin et al. (2017, 920) note, Barad's agential realist framework is not only theoretically innovative, but it also provides insightful analytical elaborations that resonate well with researchers working on issues of hybridity, mobility, relationality, assemblage and, importantly, hauntology. In the remainder of this section, I will unpack the key tenets of Barad's work—material-discursive entanglements, indeterminacies, agential cuts, intra-action, phenomena, and diffraction—using the spectral worlds of 10 Rillington Place to illustrate the nuanced contours of each concept. Where appropriate and helpful to the discussion, the quantum physics that underpin Barad's thesis will be adumbrated in footnotes.

Material-Discursive Entanglements

For Barad, discourse and materiality, words and things, should be thought together—matter is always-already entangled *with* discourse in the enactment of phenomena (more about this below). Her insistence on this pivotal ontological point is worth quoting at length:

> The relationship between the material and the discursive is one of mutual entailment. Neither is articulated/articulable in the absence of the other; matter and meaning are mutually articulated. Neither discursive practices nor material phenomena are ontologically or epistemologically prior. Neither can be explained in terms of the other. Neither has privileged status in determining the other. (Barad 2003, 822)

Though I have talked above of the "cultural bricolage" of 10 Rillington Place, it is more apt, perhaps, to figure this as "material-cultural bricolage." That is, entangled with the cultural outputs through which the "meaning" of 10 Rillington Place is generated is a wide array of materialities that come "to matter" in significant ways. Consider, for example, Betty Yang's review of the 2017 production of Howard Brenton's 1969 stage play, *Christie in Love*. Her headline reads, "not an experience for the faint-hearted" (Yang 2017), and she goes on to critically appraise the calibre of the acting, (dark) humor, characterization, and script, which animate an atmosphere of fearfulness, discomfort, and emotional disturbance. Importantly, however, Yang also reflects on the materialities of the play and how these are integral to the audience experience; she notes:

> The set consists of a large chicken wire cage that is half filled with scrunched up newspapers, the semi-visible headlines suggesting a world full of secrets and headlines to be unearthed. From this paper soil rises the haunting spectre of Christie (Rory Grant), born from this mass of media gossip and bearing his own body of secrets. He wears a huge, bulbous papier mâché mask on his head that is only made visible to the audience through flashing lights, creating a truly fearful and unnerving atmosphere. (Yang 2017)

Taking account of staging, lighting, sets, props, costumes, and other paraphernalia of theatrical production, is commonplace in performance studies and its associated genres of theater criticism (Schneider 2015; Sofer 2003). Even so, "taking account" entails more than simplistic assumptions that it is the director, playwright, set designer, choreographer, actors, and audiences who bring life to inanimate objects and infuse them with sociopolitical meaning, affective value, and cultural signification (Jones 2015). This is Barad's key point: There is no ontological distinction between artist and artwork, or scriptwriter and script; neither is there any separation of being from knowing and doing—artist, artwork, art criticism, and artistry are co-constitutive. *Christie in Love*— and more broadly, 10 Rillington Place—is an entanglement of human and nonhuman endeavors, all of which have agential capacity to effect and be effected in an ongoing and relational interplay of material-discursive becoming. How Barad theorizes this "becoming" opens up a number of innovative conceptual trajectories that re-orient Derridean hauntology in several important ways. It is to these that I now turn.

Indeterminacy, Agential Cuts, Intra-Actions

Barad builds from Bohr's principle of indeterminacy to argue that the world is always-already unknown and uncertain. On the face of it, there is an affinity here with the Derridean notion of "undecidability," but whereas Derrida invokes the spectral as an unsettling force that hybridizes previously stable categories, Barad insists that there are no preexisting entities with fixed properties (past/future; dead/alive) and essential attributes (innocent/guilty; sane/insane) that *can be* unsettled. She refers to this as ontic indeterminacy, and this is equally as true for subatomic particles as it is for a piece of wood, or *Christie in Love*.

So, while Yang pronounces on *Christie in Love* as "not for the fainthearted," Loxton's (2009) review of the play, staged at the Lion and Unicorn Theatre, Kentish Town, points out how the "scabrous limericks" had the audience laughing and "launch(ed) the play into a broad style of music hall." Both theater critics assign to the play particular properties, which not only sets (localized) boundaries around its reality, but also excludes others. Indeed, Yang (2017) also writes of the "emotional ambiguity and tonal complexity" of *Christie in Love*, noting how the play "works through the interplay between alienation and attraction, repulsion and fascination"; yet, and despite her "ambivalent feelings" (ibid.), she invokes what Barad refers to as an *agential cut*—a boundary-making practice that carves out from the indeterminacy of a multiplicity of material-discursive entanglements and a plethora of creative possibilities, a particular configuration of the play as "one for the fearless, for those who want to think without bounds" (ibid.).

For some, Yang's (or Loxton's) review of *Christie in Love* may be just a matter of opinion, a subjective reading that rests on their unique interpretations of the stage production. For Barad, however, far from being ideational constructs, such perspectives are the *effect* (not the cause) of *intra-active*, material-discursive practices, which include our "boundary-drawing practices" (2007, 140)—that is, our methods of analysis, modes of interpretation, writing styles, software programs, conceptual vocabularies, media of dissemination, empirical data, and research instruments. Contra *inter*-actions, which presuppose ontological distinctions between known (*Christie in Love*), knower (critic), and knowing (theater criticism), *intra*-actions signify the ontological-epistemological unity of practice, the "mutual constitution of entangled agencies," (2007, 33), and "*the ontological inseparability of agentially intra-acting 'components'*" (2003, 815; emphasis in original). Agency, in Baradian terms, is not located in either people or things; nor is it a capacity that someone or something *has*. Rather, agency is the enactment of an agential cut *within*-phenomena, a relational doing, a performative and *intra-active* practice of becoming—through intra-actions, "the boundaries and properties of components of phenomena become determinate and particular concepts (that is, particular material articulations) become meaningful" (Barad 2007, 139).

It is in the enactment of cuts, and through the intra-actions of boundary-making practices, that Barad's contribution to ethics is to be found. The making of exteriority, separability, Other, absence, and constitutive exclusion is the material-discursive effect of analysis itself and is an ethical and political moment of marking difference. Difference is *performative*, it *does* things, it is productive of marks on bodies, preferred meanings, hierarchies of value, spatial exclusions, temporal limits, taxonomies of being. The "cut," then, mobilizes an ethical obligation to be responsible and accountable for the differences we make. *Contra* Derrida, Barad's agential realist approach to hauntology grapples with and fosters an ethical awareness that has material-discursive form, content, significance, and power. Indeed, she insists that ontology, epistemology, and ethics should be thought together as a quantum entanglement (2007, 2010, 2011, 2012, 2014)—as the *onto-epistemo-ethical unity of practice*. Barad refers to this as an "ethics of worlding" (2007, 392), and reminds us:

> We are accountable for . . . (not only) the differential patterns of mattering of the world of which we are a part . . . (but also) the exclusions that we participate in enacting. Therefore accountability and responsibility must be thought in terms of what matters and what is excluded from mattering. (2007, 394)

Phenomena, Diffraction

The *phenomena* of 10 Rillington Place are constitutive of its reality—but what is meant by this concept within an agential realist framework? Phenomena are not things-in-themselves, nor are they observer-independent, fixed in time and space, or awaiting our discovery. As Barad explains, they are "ontologically primitive relations—relations without pre-existing relata" (2007, 333); as such, phenomena are "dynamic topological reconfigurings/entanglements/relationalities/(re)articulations of the world" (2007, 141) which are extensive, discontinuous, dispersed, and fragmented across time and space.

March 1953: Mrs. Jessie Hide and cat look out from the first-floor window of 216 Lancaster Road. *October 1966*: The Right Honourable Roy Jenkins signs a posthumous royal pardon in respect of Timothy Evans's conviction for the murder of his daughter, Geraldine. *May 1929*: In Almeric Road, Battersea, Maud Cole is assaulted with a cricket bat by John Christie, with whom she was living. *October 2014*: The Substance and Shadow Theatre, Exeter, presents Howard Brenton's 1969 play, *Christie in Love*. *November 2017*: A three-part television drama, *Rillington Place*, which aired on the BBC in December 2016, is nominated for a Satellite Award for Best Mini-Series. *January 1950*: Christie is called as a witness for the prosecution at the trial of Timothy John Evans. *April 2016*: The Museum of London's special exhibition, *Crime Museum Uncovered*, closes—it is the last opportunity for the public to see a display of evidential artifacts recovered from 10 Rillington Place. *July 1953*: The Islington Registrar records the death of John Reginald Halliday Christie, citing cause as "injuries to central nervous system following judicial hanging." *January 1971*: Based on Ludovic Kennedy's 1961 book of the same name, the film, *10 Rillington Place*, premieres in the United Kingdom. Each and all of these phenomena are the onto-epistemological "building blocks" of 10 Rillington Place "forever being reenfolded and reformed.... (as) intra-actions iteratively reconfigur(ing) what is possible and what is impossible" (Barad 2007, 177). There is no sense in writing the history of 10 Rillington Place here as a narrative journey of temporal unfolding; it is not a long-running saga that plays out across a linear trajectory of events that have their own time-space. Rather, 10 Rillington Place is a "quantum dis/continuity" (Barad 2010, 240) of hauntological and ghostly entanglements, spacetime enfoldings that *diffract* different times and places through one another in an ongoing process of material-discursive intra-activity. Mattering (material-discursive becoming), intra-actions, indeterminacy, agential cuts, and phenomena, not only recalibrate the embedded ontological battles and epistemological disputes that characterize social scientific endeavors, but also render problematic the conventional protocols and axioms that inform methodological practice. Barad's starting point is to question the optics of knowledge-generation, and in particular she rejects the central place of observational logic. The widespread reliance on representation, reflection, and reflexivity as standard bearers for mimetic, human-centered, exteriorized, "distance learning (research) practice" (Barad 2007, 90), is the legacy, she argues, of a representationalist paradigm that not only insists on the separation of knower and known—as if they were independent entities mediated by modes of signification (discourse, image, symbol, graph, map)—but also severs the cultural from the material, exposing a "deep mistrust of matter, holding it off at a distance, figuring it as passive, immutable and mute" (Barad 2007, 133; see also Barad 2007, chapter 2, for an extended discussion).

Given these suspicions, Barad borrows from quantum physics the optical metaphor of diffraction (see also Haraway 1991) which, contra reflection and reflexivity, is not concerned with mimesis and replication, and self-positionality, but with patterns of interference and intervention, with differences that *matter*. Diffraction is about "reading insights through one another in attending to and responding to the details and specificities of relations of difference and how they matter" (Barad 2007, 71).[3] As an analytical tool of inquiry, diffraction focuses attention not on differences per se, but on the *effects* of differences enacted through "agential cuts" that differentiate a co-emergent and co-constitutive material-discursive world, and anchor our political and ethical choices.

Diffraction is "attractive," suggest Kaiser and Thiele (2014, 16), not only as an "alternative vocabulary and different technology for critical inquiries," but also as "a praxis of analysis which foregrounds differentiality" (ibid.). De Schauwer et al. talk of diffractive work as opening up "an onto-epistemological space of *encounter*" (2018, 610; emphasis in original; see also Davies 2014); while Mazzei (2014) draws from Deleuze and Guattari's (1987) notion of "plugging in" to capture the idea of diffraction as a process of reading through multiple texts, ideas, theories, selves, affects, and data. It is in this spirit of praxis, encounter, and something other than thinking-as-usual, that I offer (the beginnings of) a diffractive reading and a *performative hauntology* of 10 Rillington Place's principal occupant, John Reginald Halliday Christie. In contrast to the Derridean analytic—which regards the hauntological as a troubling of preexisting categories—I reaffirm as ontologically primal the ghostly indeterminacies of this spectral figure. In so doing, I engage critically with the generative effects of intra-active becomings, those spaces of encounter through which the markers and boundaries of Christie's being, etched from a myriad of possibilities, come to matter and are made meaningful in politically and ethically significant ways.

A Performative Hauntology of John Christie

What are we to make of the mild-mannered man who made a mortuary of his ground-floor flat and garden? This rhetorical question—posed by Oates (2012, 183) in his concluding chapter—does not anticipate an answer, so much as invite us to challenge our presuppositions of the criminal Other, and problematize the trope of the serial killer as "evil monster." Oates is, perhaps, unusual in his treatment of Christie, neatly captured in his assertion that "(h)e was not all bad" (2012, 184). He is said to have been kind to children and animals; a good and supportive husband willing to run errands and undertake small DIY repairs around the house; an active trades union representative who also served as the workplace first aider; a man with commendations for military service (army and Royal Air Force [RAF]) in the First World War, and policework in the Second World War; a neighborly, friendly man, "quiet, well-dressed and respectable" (ibid.) who routinely exchanged greetings with the other residents of Rillington Place, was actively involved in community events as an amateur photographer, and was often invited around for get-togethers at Christmas (Curnow 2017, 128)—even as he was said to be "prudish and puritanical concerning sex and drink" (Oates 2012, 184), boastful, and known to seek out the company of prostitutes. None of this rehabilitates Christie—this is not Oates's intention; but it does remind us of the indeterminacies of our stabilizing categories—the necrophiliac murderer and the good neighbor, the family home and the burial ground, are neither signifiers of preexisting entities, nor do such terms denote a fixed, unified, "pure" presence or absence. Christie's trial, conviction, and execution in July 1953 may have sedimented his crimino-legal identity as murderer, but it did not settle the indeterminacies of his multiplicity—"a superposition/entanglement of (seemingly) disparate parts" (Barad 2014, 176)—nor did it exorcise the mysteries of 10 Rillington Place and those who lived and died there. In Baradian terms, the figure of respectability and the predatory killer—the domestic dwelling and the house of horrors—are not states of being, but intra-active becomings that come to matter in ways that (contingently) mark difference within multiplicities. The serial killer is born of modernity (Cameron and Frazer 1987; King 2006; Stratton 1996; Warwick 2006); this person is an invention that is rendered intelligible and made meaningful through a myriad of material-discursive practices that enact "exteriorit(ies)-within-phenomena" (Barad 2007, 140), and in so doing craft an ethics of inclusion/exclusion of what it means, and what it takes, to be the "killer among us" (Fisher 1997).

Interviewing Christie on remand in HMP Brixton, the Principal Medical Officer, Dr. John Matheson, concluded that: "(N)o evidence was found of the presence of insane delusions nor hallucinations" (NA PCOM9/1668 cited in Oates 2012, 143). It was an assessment shared by a relatively wide grouping of psychiatric experts asked to determine Christie's fitness for trial and evaluate the grounds for his intended plea of insanity. Without recourse to a diagnosis of psychopathy, Christie's monstrousness materializes from "a bizarre symptomatology" (Foucault 1978, 10) of the corporeal. With echoes of Lombrosian pathologism, it is a performative move that has partitioning effects; it not only expunges Christie's erstwhile "ordinariness" and stabilizes his identity as "evil monster," but also crystallizes what it is about him that matters, filters the judgments we (can) make of him, and reduces the multiplicities of his being to the sum of his "Frankensteinian" parts. Indeed, given the redundancy of psychiatric diagnostics, it is through narrativity, dramatization, cinematography, theatricalization, rumor and gossip, that Christie's body is rendered problematic and converted into a road map of Otherness; his somatic features, vocality, comportments, temperaments, penchants, and propensities, signpost a series of material-semiotic encounters that carve out a diffractive path to (his) difference,

Figure 10.2. John Reginald Halliday Christie and pets, in the back garden of 10 Rillington Place. Credit: Mirrorpix/Alamy Stock Photo.

and give flight to an ethical sensibility centered on embodied excess, surface aesthetics, and suspicion. I address each in turn.

An Ethics of Embodied Excess

Whether looking at family snapshots, the press photography of Christie's transit to court, or the waxwork displayed at Madame Tussaud's Chamber of Horrors, it is difficult to see anything other than a well-turned-out, bespectacled, balding, middle-aged, plain-looking man of slim build. Yet, Eddowes sees fit to describe Christie thus:

> For a famous and squalid mass murderer, he really did look the part, like a genteel Frankenstein's monster. His forehead, seen without headgear, ascended as if some other process of growth, perhaps mycological, had taken place: where a normal skull would start to curve back, his went up and even slightly outward. To make his appearance even more prim and sinister, he wore round spectacles. Some photographs show his eyes with an absurdly maniacal gleam. (1994, 5)

Monstering Christie's bespectacled head invents his Otherness, renders it externally visible and graspable, and marks his difference from "us." It is a conjuration that diffracts across variegated cultural media, from the sensationalist headlines of the time (Root 2012; Rowbotham et al. 2013) through to the latest dramatizations of the Rillington Place saga. This hyperbole takes material form in the stage props devised by the playwright Howard Brenton; first, as discussed above, the set of *Christie in Love* features a garden of crumpled newspapers as an allegory of the media frenzy and "hysterical uproar" (Yang 2017) that followed Christie's exposure; but, and second, even if Brenton intended to "disrupt the spectacle" (Dickson 2010) in Debordian style, he only amplifies the grotesque when the Christie actor emerges on stage (in Scene 3), rising from the detritus of news coverage wearing an over-sized, bulbous papier-mâché head. Other productions of the play—for example, at the Lion and Unicorn Theatre, Kentish Town in 2009—improvise with a gas mask (Loxton 2009); while the use of prosthetic balding caps, worn by both Richard Attenborough (*10 Rillington Place* 1970) and Tim Roth (*Rillington Place* 2016), casts a spotlight on the exaggerated shape and size of Christie's skull as though this singular corporeal feature encased the wellspring of his wickedness.[4]

An Ethics of Surface Aesthetics

Christie's persistent complaints of fibrositis and pain in walking, and his exposure to mustard gas in the 1914–18 war, which damaged his larynx and affected his speech, are a matter of medical and military record (Oates 2012); but it is how these physio-medical conditions are reworked as signifiers of a more clandestine persona that is of greater interest. As Curnow (2016) comments, despite being locally known for his brisk, upright, and somewhat military bearing, he materializes in *Rillington Place* as "stooping and shuffling," moving through the shadows of his neighborhood in a trilby hat, ill-fitting trousers, and grey trenchcoat like "an ocean of malevolence packed into one small, unassuming frame" (Mangan 2016). Similarly, while Eddowes's true crime investigation refers, rather benignly, to Christie's "prissy habits of speech" (1994, 5), Richard Attenborough talked of his "strange, soft, gentle, sort of seductive" vocality (*10 Rillington Place* DVD 1971, Special Features); but it is Tim Roth who explicitly channels Christie's malice through the prism of his voice. As Dickson notes of the actor's portrayal of the serial killer in *Rillington Place*:

> Roth plays Christie with precisely calibrated menace, turning the dial from pursed prissiness to full-on psychopathy without ever raising his voice. And it's the voice—soft, insistent, an instrument of absolute control—that is likely to live on in the heads of viewers. (Dickson 2016)

The exasperated figure of Brenton's Police Inspector asks Christie: "Why can't a pervert like you, already in the annals of nastiness, have fangs or something? Roll your eyes around, sprout horns" (*Christie in Love*, Scene 6). In the absence of such fantastical features, Christie's (latent) depravities are traced and traceable in the TV drama through movement, posture, costume, and speech, giving flight to a connective series of corporeal, sartorial, and vocal cues that signal Christie as peculiar and strange. It is not so much (or not solely) a question of what such cues "mean," but how they come to matter, that is more to the point. For example, in *Rillington Place* (2016), Christie's sinister *potential* is diffracted through an entanglement of material-semiotic-affective practices that draw on Gothic tropes and make use of a sensorium of filmic methodologies and expressionistic effects—mise-en-scène, dialogue, montage, sound, music, lighting—to generate a tense and brooding atmosphere of lingering, dark possibilities. As Mangan (2016) notes of the mini-series: "The sheer menace of the thing is extraordinary. The interiors are tiny, dark, oppressive. The script is minimal, elliptical. . . . the limning of the manipulation, the entrapment, the complicity without blame, the forced compromises, and the black misery spreading from one man's evil has surely rarely been better done." This *matters* because it enacts an ethical cut that not only shores up Christie's identity as serial killer, but also erases all trace of the goodly neighbor. Moreover, it is an ethics drawn across the surface aesthetics of his embodied idiosyncrasies—his "stooping, shuffling" gait, non-descript mode of dress, hushed (and menacing) tone of voice—and animated by the creative technologies of a cinematic/televisual suspense thriller. Like the Gothic dandy, Christie's secret life of deadly passions is made visible, and performatively assembled as an aesthetic spectacle of corporeal inscriptions, somatic comportments, and special effects. As Stratton has argued, in (post)modernity, the spectacularization of serial killing (and the serial killer) has transformed the nature of sociality to the extent that the ethical has been supplanted by the aesthetic as "the defining mode of experience" (1996, 79); see also Benjamin (1969); Black (1991); Featherstone (1990).

An Ethics of Suspicion

Anthropologists, such as Radhika Subramanian (1999), remind us that suspicion implies a "slightness" of knowing, born of mistrust, uncertainty, and unease rather than evidence-based, hypothesis-driven knowledgeability. Suspicion is spun from the threads of the mundane and the humdrum, forming an organic, interpretive web that marks difference by entrapping fragments of stories, fleeting glimpses, a disturbing memory, and chance encounters in its nebulous systems of matter and meaning. Suspicion, then, mobilizes an ethics etched from, and diffracted through, the material-discursive entanglements of everyday "knowingness" and practices that intra-actively produce Christie's "exteriority-within." Procured by journalists and investigators (police, prosecution, and defense) *after* his arrest in 1953, consider these several testimonies from those who knew or had come into contact with Christie:

> *Childhood friend, talking of their visits to the local cemetery to peer through the gaps in the children's vault*: "They (children's coffins) seemed to have a peculiar fascination for him." (NA CAB143/21 cited in Oates 2012, 5)
>
> *Former schoolmates*: "A queer lad; he never knocked about like the rest of us"; "He kept himself to himself. He was never popular." (NA CRIM1/2326 cited in Oates 2012, 6)
>
> *Clifford Spurling, work colleague and fellow First Aider, at the Post Office Savings Bank, Kew, 1947*: "He told me that if I should get a girl into trouble he could perform an abortion operation. He said he had done so before." (NA MEPO2/3147 cited in Oates 2012, 42)
>
> *John Girandot, neighbor, living at 220 Lancaster Road, 1940–41*: "I have had quite a lot of disagreements with him over various matters . . . (chiefly Christie's habit of throwing stones over the garden fence). . . . Whilst he was serving in the Police War Reserve, he offered to fight me, but when I went round to his address, he failed to open the door. (NA MEPO2/9535 cited in Oates 2012, 32–33)
>
> *Frederick Byers, detective inspector in the Police War Reserve*: "I didn't like him. I wouldn't like to put a finger on it, just one of those things, you either like or dislike." (NA MEPO2/9535 cited in Oates 2012, 31)
>
> *George Outram, Police War Reserve colleague*: "He used to go out picking up prostitutes.'" (NA MEPO3/3147 cited in Oates 2012, 31)
>
> *Mrs. McFadden of 3 Rillington Place, 1941*: "Often he tried to use his police authority to tell us to do what he wanted. He threatened to report practically everybody in the street for some lighting or other supposed irregularity.'" (NA PIN26/16679 cited in Oates 2012, 32)

These stray observations, passing thoughts, and personal memories come to matter in several ways. First, they authorize an ethics of exclusion premised on suspicion and a wariness of everyday peccadilloes and minor transgressions; an ethics that relies on rumor, anecdote, and intuition, and that responds only with feelings of misgiving, censure, and disapprobation.[5] Second, spurious recollections of Christie's curiosity with a burial vault, his solitary disposition, avuncular pretensions to medical expertise, quarrelsomeness, cowardice, petty authoritarianism, anti-social habits, and penchant for sex workers are redeployed as "explanatory variables" and converted into conditions of possibility for his serial killing. Third, they enfold Christie's Otherness through dispersed social relations (as acquaintance, friend, work colleague, neighbor), multiple cultural practices (playing, socializing, leisure pursuits, community involvement), and a plethora of materialities (coffins, stones, house lights, a garden fence, fights), diffractively weaving the notion of his "odd" character and disobliging temperament through nonlinear and discontinuous "scenes" (Barad 2010, 244). They assemble what might be described as a *cultural cartography* of Christie's journey to homicidal necrophilia across time and space—a narrative mapping of material-semiotic encounters with his *propensity* to murder.

Conclusion

Seltzer (1998), among others, has argued that the practice (and spaces) of serial killing blurs the boundaries between the individual and the collective body, private fantasy and public exhibition, fact and fiction, intimacy and publicity, and between internalized desire and externalized acts (see also Black 1991; Jenks 2003; Stratton 1996; Warwick 2006). Figuring the serial killer as a hybridizing force that unsettles (putatively) stable categories buys into a Derridean hauntological logic that locates the spectral in conditions of undecidability. It is not so much that this is "wrong," but to engage with spectral life as a realm of generalized uncertainty and irresolution removes the solid ground of ethical positioning and leads us into a politico-ethical vaccuum. This chapter has questioned the ontological and epistemological underpinnings of Derridean ghost work, arguing against an analytic that presupposes a world in which there is "no concept, no self-identity, no text, no writing, that is not haunted" (Luckhurst 2002, 535); and rejecting a deconstructionist approach where "(l)anguage has been granted too much power" (Barad 2003, 801). Informed by quantum physics and new materialist thinking, Barad's agential realist framework offers an alternative hauntology that involves three key theoretical moves, captured by the compound neologism of the *onto-epistemo-ethical unity of practice*.

First, for Barad, the world is ontologically and semantically fluid, uncertain, and indeterminate; it is a world that is always-already spectral, discontinuous, and dispersed, haunted by unmarked subjects and unknown entities. Who can say/know if John Christie is/was "the wickedest man in the world" (*Sunday Pictorial*, June 28, 1953) when we encounter him as a myriad of possibilities and an entanglement of different states of becoming? However, and second, Barad is less concerned with ghostly indeterminacies than with how determinacy is established. To put this another way, we should think (and do) ontology and epistemology together, and ask of each encounter with Christie, what is being made to matter here, how is (his) difference accomplished and performed? For Barad, and third, it is in the enactment of difference, and the constitutive effects of excluding some things (neighborliness, respectability) but not others (dark menace, monstrousness), that ethical choices about "good" and "evil" are made. This underpins the "radical potential" (Hollin et al. 2017, 932) of Barad's agential realism; it is through practices of boundary-making that we craft an "ethics of the outside" (ibid. 931) for which we should be fully accountable.

The events of Christie's arrest, trial, conviction, and execution generate specific encounters that not only enfold questions of being and knowing through a myriad of intra-acting socio-legal and criminal justice practices—from forensic technologies and evidential dossiers, to witness testimony, cross-examination, court exhibits, and psychiatric reports—but also enact an agential cut that marks Christie's difference as a serial murderer. Even so, this does not resolve the indeterminacy of Christie's being and, in this chapter, I have mapped out the onto-epistemo-ethical contours of our ongoing and extensive encounters with his multiplicity through the prism of books, films, drama series, stage plays, archival documents, press photography, and exhibitions. Endlessly recycled and re-imagined through diffractive practices of storytelling, display, testimonial, journalistic reportage, script-writing, cinematography, theatrical production, and a host of material-cultural performances, Christie's identity as a serial killer—an "evil monster" to boot—emerges from a cultural public sphere that trades in "pleasures and pains" (McGuigan 2005, 435) and works through a heteroglossia of expressive, material, aesthetic, affective, and performative modalities. In so doing, different options for ethical decision-making come into view and prefigure an alternative (though controversial) prospectus for "justice-to-come" (Barad 2010).

Barad insists that "ethics is an integral part of the diffraction (ongoing differentiating) patterns of worlding" (2010, 265), but she does not prescribe the ethical positioning such worlding involves. The diffractive analysis of the material-cultural bricolage examined in this chapter carves out an ethical space that is both difficult to defend and nigh on impossible to argue for. Each encounter with Christie has not only invited ethical judgments and evaluations based on matters of embodied excess, surface aesthetics, and suspicion, but also ushered us toward a mode of justice that is highly problematic. Feminist ethicist, Lynette Hunter, reminds us that "ethics is not a set of standards, it is about talking, discussing and negotiating over grounds we come to agree in order to make decisions and take action" (2001, 205). Grappling over dispositions of, for example, care, mutuality, compassion, empathy, tolerance, even retribution and condemnation, is integral to situated relational ethical practice; but it is difficult to envisage any serious discussion about an ethical orientation that marks difference through the superficialities of somatic features, personal traits and characteristics, and the vagaries of gossip, rumor, and anecdote. So, how might such a conversation proceed?

Borrowing from Primo Levi, Claudia Card reminds us of the "gray zones of practical ethics" (1999, 3) in which we may find ourselves complicit with regressive and ambiguous ethical positions; but through a Baradian lens, ethics is not about the "right response to a radically exterior/ized other, but about responsibility and accountabilities for the lively relationalities of becoming of which we are a part" (Barad 2007, 393). Our conversations, then, should focus on those moments of becoming when Christie stabilizes as a "serial killing monster," an enactment of difference that cuts through the multiplicities of his being and sets boundaries around what it is about him that matters. That this is ethically significant is not just that Christie could have been otherwise, and could have mattered differently—as the "postmodern self" of King's (2006) conception; or de Quincey's "fine artist" (Dobrée 1966); or Wilson's and Seaman's (1990) "resentment killer"—but that we are able to account for the material-discursive processes, methods, and practices through which (a specific configuration of) Christie's identity is accomplished and performed. If we are entertained, engaged, incensed, or even horrified by turning the pages of a book, watching a film in the comfort of our own homes, visiting a museum exhibition, or browsing a digital archive of crime scene photography, we are always-already entangled in a myriad of creative, intra-active possibilities of becoming, for which we should be ethically responsible.

NOTES

1 Timothy John Evans and his family lived in the top floor flat of 10 Rillington Place between 1948 and 1949. He was charged with the murders of his wife and child, but was only tried, convicted, and executed for the murder of his daughter, Geraldine. In 1966, Evans was posthumously granted a royal free pardon in relation to the latter; but the charge of murder relating to Beryl Evans remains on file.
2 Quantum theory underpins contemporary physics and explains the nature and behavior of energy and matter at the subatomic level—*quantum* is the Latin word for smallest amount. Referred to interchangeably as quantum physics and quantum mechanics, physicists working in this paradigm—such as Max Planck, Albert Einstein, Werner Heisenberg, Louis de Broglie, Nils Bohr, and Richard Feynman—revolutionized classical (Newtonian) physics, and significantly advanced our theoretical understanding of the nature of nature. The principle of wave-particle duality is, perhaps, emblematic of the quantum field. This theorem states that there is no difference in the makeup and behavior of energy and matter; both can take the form of, and act as if made of, particles *or* waves. Bohr theorized this duality as a *superposition*; that is, an entity exists in all possible states simultaneously until we attempt to measure it. Taking account of how the scientist and her methods of investigation are integral to the constitution of the phenomenon under study is, for Barad, Bohr's unique contribution for thinking the natural and social worlds together. Inspired by his philosophy-physics, Barad writes: "Bohr's naturalistic commitment to understanding both the nature of nature and the nature of science ... led him to what he took to be the heart of the lesson of quantum physics: *we are part of that nature that we seek to understand*" (2007, 67; emphasis in original).
3 In Newtonian and quantum physics, diffraction refers to patterns of overlap, interference, combination, diffusion, and distribution when waves of light (sound, water) encounter an obstruction. While particles of light "bounce off"

each other, colliding waves pass through one another; when waves overlap, their troughs and crests enfold within each other, and can disappear altogether; when light passes through a slit, it can appear to bend, and diffuse waves of light *within* and *through* regions of dark, and vice-versa. See Barad (2007, chapter 2) for a fuller discussion.

4 There are similarities here with Linnemann's (2015) critical reading of Capote's *In Cold Blood* (1993); as a way of marking difference, and rendering the bodies of murderers as abject, Linnemann notes how Capote describes the shape of Hickock's head, "(as though it) had been halved like an apple, then put together a fraction off center" (Capote 1993, 31, cited in Linnemann 2015, 524).

5 This is far from unusual and is commonplace during the early stages of police investigation. For example, in December 2010, a narrative of suspicion was cast around retired teacher, Christopher Jefferies, landlord and neighbor of the murdered architect, Joanna Yeates. Recycling anecdotes and students' stories from his teaching days, and with headlines such as "The Strange Mr. Jefferies" (*The Sun*, December 31, 2010), he was variously described as "creepy," "lewd," "weird," "a loner," "posh," a "peeping tom," "unkempt and dirty," and "having a strange walk." His love of poetry and high-brow reading matter was re-described as "eccentric behaviour," while his physical appearance, most notably his long, blue-tinged hair, was re-read as code for a "highly dubious character"—see Llewellyn 2018. In July 2011, Jefferies was awarded a six-figure sum in libel damages. Eight national newspapers were convicted of contempt of court and forced to issue a public apology (Greenslade 2011).

REFERENCES

Abraham, Nicolas and Torok, Maria. 1987[1978]. *L'Écorce et le Noyau*. Paris: Flammarion.

Aradau, Claudia. 2010. "Security That Matters: Critical Infrastructure and Objects of Protection." *Security Dialogue* 41, 5: 491–514.

Argyrou, Vassos. 2017. "Ontology, 'Hauntology' and the 'Turn' That Keeps Anthropology Turning." *History of the Human Sciences* 30, 1: 50–65.

Barad, Karen. 1999. "Agential Realism: Feminist Interventions in Understanding Scientific Practices." In *The Science Studies Reader*, edited by Mario Biagoli. New York: Routledge, pp. 1–11.

———. 2003. "Posthumanist Performativity: Toward an Understanding of How Matter Comes to Matter." *Signs* 28, 3: 801–831.

———. 2007. *Meeting the Universe Halfway: Quantum Physics and the Entanglement of Matter and Meaning*. Durham, NC: Duke University Press.

———. 2010. "Quantum Entanglements and Hauntological Relations of Inheritance: Dis/continuities, Spacetime Enfoldings, and Justice-To-Come." *Derrida Today* 3, 2: 240–268.

———. 2011. "Nature's Queer Performativity." *Qui Parle: Critical Humanities and Social Sciences* 19, 2: 121–158.

———. 2012. "On Touching—The Inhuman That Therefore I Am." *Differences* 23, 3: 206–223.
———. 2014. "Diffracting Diffraction: Cutting Together-Apart." *Parallax* 20, 3: 168–187.
Benjamin, Walter. 1969. *Illuminations*. New York: Schocken.
Bergsdóttir, Arndis. 2017. "Cyborgian Entanglements: Post-human Feminism, Diffraction and the Science Exhibition *Bundled-up in Blue*." *Museum Management and Curatorship* 32, 2: 108–122.
Black, Joel. 1991. *The Aesthetics of Murder: A Study in Romantic Literature and Contemporary Culture*. Baltimore, MD: Johns Hopkins University Press.
Blackman, Lisa. 2015. "Researching Affect and Embodied Hauntologies: Exploring an Analytics of Experimentation." In *Developing Cultural Research: Strategies for the Study of Affect*, edited by Britta Timm Knudsen and Carsten Stage. London: Palgrave, pp. 25–44.
Buser, Michael. 2017. "The Time Is Out of Joint: Atmosphere and Hauntology at Bodiam Castle." *Emotion, Space and Society* 25: 5–13.
Cameron, Deborah and Frazer, Elisabeth. 1987. *The Lust to Kill: A Feminist Investigation of Sexual Murder*. Cambridge: Polity.
Capote, Truman. 1993. *In Cold Blood: A True Account of a Multiple Murder and Its Consequences*. New York: Random House.
Card, Claudia. Ed. 1999. *On Feminist Ethics and Politics*. Lawrence: University Press of Kansas.
Crockett, Clayton. 2018. *Derrida After the End of Writing: Political Theology and New Materialism*. New York: Fordham University Press.
Curnow, John. 2016. "Rillington Place—Episode 3." *The Murders, Myths and Reality of 10 Rillington Place Blog*, blog.10-rillington-place.co.uk/
———. 2017. *The Murders, Myths and Reality of 10 Rillington Place*. E-book, www.10-rillington-place.co.uk
Davies, Bronwyn. 2014. *Listening to Children: Being and Becoming*. London: Routledge.
Davis, Colin. 2005. "Hauntology, Spectres and Phantoms." *French Studies* 59(3): 373–379.
Deleuze, Gilles and Guattari, Felix. 1987. *A Thousand Plateaus: Capitalism and Schizophrenia*. Translated by Brian Massumi. Minneapolis: University of Minnesota Press.
Derrida, Jacques. 1994. *Specters of Marx: The State of the Debt, the Work of Mourning, and the New International*. Translated by Peggy Kamuf. New York: Routledge.
De Schauwer, Elisabeth, Van de Putte, Inge, and Blockmans, Inge G. E. 2018. "The Intra-active Production of Normativity and Difference." *Gender and Education* 30(5): 607–622.
Dickson, Andrew. 2010. "A Life in Theatre." www.theguardian.com/
Dickson, E. Jane. 2016. "Rillington Place's Tim Roth on Playing Serial Killer John Christie: 'I thought My God, what have I got into?.'" www.radiotimes.com/
Dixon, Deborah. 2007. "A Benevolent and Sceptical Inquiry: Exploring "Fortean Geographies' with the Mothman." *Cultural Geographies* 14: 189–210.

Dobrée, Bonamy. Ed. 1966. *Thomas de Quincey*. New York: Schocken.
Eddowes, John. 1994. *The Two Killers of Rillington Place*. London: Little, Brown and Company.
Featherstone, Mike. 1990. "The Aestheticization of Everyday Life." In *Consumer Culture and Postmodernism*, edited by Mike Featherstone. London: Sage, 64–80.
Feigenbaum, Anna. 2014. "Resistant Matters: Tents, Tear Gas and the 'Other Media' of Occupy." *Communication and Critical/Cultural Studies* 11, 1: 15–24.
Fisher, Joseph C. 1997. *Killer Among Us: Public Reactions to Serial Murder*. Westport, CT: Praeger.
Foucault, Michel. 1978. "About the Concept of the 'Dangerous Individual' in 19th Century Legal Psychiatry." *International Journal of Law and Psychiatry* 1: 1–18.
Freud, Sigmund. 1919. "The Uncanny." Translated by James Stratchey. *The Standard Edition of the Complete Works of Sigmund Freud, Volume 17*. London: Hogarth Press and the Institute of Psycho-Analysis.
Gordon, Avery. 2008[1997]. *Ghostly Matters: Haunting and the Sociological Imagination*. Minneapolis: University of Minnesota Press.
Greenslade, Roy. 2011. "Eight Newspapers Pay Libel Damages to Retired Teacher." www.theguardian.com/
Haraway, Donna. 1991. *Simians, Cyborgs and Women: The Reinvention of Nature*. New York: Routledge.
Hollin, Gregory, Forsyth, Isla, Giraud, Eva, and Potts, Tracey. 2017. "(Dis)entangling Barad: Materialism and Ethics." *Social Studies of Science* 47, 6: 918–941.
Holloway, Julian and Kneale, James. 2008. "Locating Haunting: A Ghost-hunter's Guide." *Cultural Geographies* 15: 297–312.
Honeycombe, Gordon. 2011. *Murders of the Black Museum*. London: John Blake.
Hultman, Karin and Taguchi, Hillevi Lenz. 2010. "Challenging Anthropocentric Analysis of Visual Data: A Relational Materialist Methodological Approach to Educational Research." *International Journal of Qualitative Studies in Education* 23, 5: 525–542.
Hunter, Lynette. 2001. "Listening to Situated Textuality: Working on Differentiated Public Voices." *Feminist Theory* 2, 2: 205–217.
Jameson, Fredric. 1999. "Marx's Purloined Letter." In *Ghostly Demarcations: A Symposium on Jacques Derrida's Specters of Marx*, edited by Michael Sprinker. London: Verso, pp. 26–67.
Jenks, Chris. 2003. *Transgression*. London: Routledge.
Jones, Amelia. 2015. "Material Traces: Performativity, Artistic 'Work,' and New Conceptions of Agency." *Drama Review* 59, 4: 18–35.
Kaiser, Brigit Mara and Thiele, Kathrin. 2014. "Diffraction: Onto-Epistemology, Quantum Physics and the Critical Humanities." *Parallax* 20, 3: 165–167.
King, Anthony. 2006. "Serial Killing and the Postmodern Self." *History of the Human Sciences* 19, 3: 109–125.
Lather, Patti. 2016. "Top Ten+ List: (Re)thinking Ontology in (Post)qualitative Research." *Cultural Studies ↔ Critical Methodologies* 16, 2: 125–131.

Linnemann, Travis. 2015. "Capote's Ghosts: Violence, Media and the Spectre of Suspicion." *British Journal of Criminology* 55: 514–533.

Livingstone, David N. 1998. "Reproduction, Representation and Authenticity: A Rereading." *Transactions of the Institute of British Geographers* 23: 13–20.

Llewellyn, Mark. 2018. "Are All (Neo-)Victorians Murderers? Serials, Killers, and Other Historical Maniacs." *Literature Compass* 15, 7: 1–16.

Loxton, Howard. 2009. "Christie in Love." www.britishtheatreguide.info/

Luckhurst, Roger. 2002. "The Contemporary London Gothic and the Limits of the 'Spectral Turn.'" *Textual Practice* 16, 3: 527–546.

Maddern, Jo Frances. 2008. "Spectres of Migration and the Ghosts of Ellis Island." *Cultural Geographies* 15: 359–381.

Mangan, Lucy. 2016. "Rillington Place Review—There Are Nightmares Here, But They Are Real." www.theguardian.com/

Mazzei, Lisa A. 2014. "Beyond an Easy Sense: A Diffractive Analysis." *Qualitative Inquiry* 20, 6: 742–746.

McGuigan, Jim. 2005. "The Cultural Public Sphere." *European Journal of Cultural Studies* 8, 4: 427–443.

Nealon, Jeffery T. 1992. "The Discipline of Deconstruction." *Publications of the Modern Language Association* 107, 5: 1266–1279.

Oates, Jonathan. 2012. *John Christie of Rillington Place*. Barnsley: Pen and Sword Books.

Orlikowski, Wanda J. and Scott, Susan V. 2015. "Exploring Material-Discursive Practices." *Journal of Management Studies* 52, 5: 697–705.

Peim, Nick. 2005. "Spectral Bodies: Derrida and the Philosophy of the Photograph as Historical Document." *Journal of the Philosophy of Education* 39, 1: 68–84.

Roberts, Elisabeth. 2012. "Geography and the Visual Image: A Hauntological Approach." *Progress in Human Geography* 37, 3: 386–402.

Root, Neil. 2012. *Frenzy! Heath, Haigh and Christie*. London: Arrow Books.

Rowbotham, Judith, Stevenson, Kim, and Pegg, Samantha. 2013. *Crime News in Modern Britain*. Basingstoke: Palgrave Macmillan.

Schneider, Rebecca. 2015. "New Materialisms and Performance Studies." *Drama Review* 59, 4: 7–17.

Seltzer, Mark. 1998. *Serial Killers: Death and Life in America's Wound Culture*. New York: Routledge.

Sofer, Andrew. 2003. *The Stage Life of Props*. Ann Arbor: University of Michigan Press.

Sprinker, Michael. Ed. 1999. *Ghostly Demarcations: A Symposium on Jacques Derrida's Specters of Marx*. London: Verso.

Stratton, Jon. 1996. "Serial Killing and the Transformation of the Social." *Theory, Culture and Society* 13, 1: 77–98.

Subramanian, Radhika. 1999. "Culture of Suspicion: Riots and Rumour in Bombay, 1992–1993." *Transforming Anthropology* 8, 1 and 2: 97–110.

Warfield, Katie. 2016. "Making the Cut: An Agential Realist Examination of Selfies and Touch." *Social Media + Society* 2, 2: 1–10.

Warwick, Alexandra. 2006. "The Scene of the Crime: Inventing the Serial Killer." *Social and Legal Studies* 15, 4: 552–569.

Wilson, Colin and Seaman, David. 1990. *The Serial Killers: A Study in the Psychology of Violence*. London: W. H. Allen.

Yang, Betty, 2017. "Christie in Love: Not an Experience for the Faint-Hearted." http://oxfordstudent.com/

11

Who's Been Sleeping in My Bed?

Cheap Motel Rooms and Transgression

CAROLYN MCKAY

"It's going to feel like it's 100 per cent real but . . . it's just a dream."[1] In a series of preternatural sexual assaults that occurred in Sydney motel rooms between 2001 and 2008, this phrase was repeated to two female victims. Framed by the spectral, the circumstances that surrounded the sexual assaults were described in court appeal decisions as including the use of "mayia," a Greek word meaning magic and implying evil (Argyrou 1993)—fetishistic, voodoo-like objects, filled with one victim's hair and underwear, and small bones covered in fine writing. The so-called mastermind of these "black magic" and "red evil" sexual assaults paraded as a "holy man" with a reputation for being able to speak with angels (Arlington 2011). The two superstitious victims lived in fear of the "evil eye" and had been convinced that perceived curses could be removed by attending "prayer sessions" that were, in fact, disturbing ritualistic rape sessions orchestrated by the holy man and his co-offenders: another man ("AP") and that other man's wife ("FP").

One of the appeal decisions is well-known for its description of the extraordinary factual circumstances but also as a legal authority on the meaning of "in company" in aggravated sexual assaults. The woman, FP, had been convicted of a number of crimes regarding one of the victims, including three counts of aggravated sexual assault "in company," in which she assisted or encouraged others. The crimes had occurred in a motel room and FP had suggested that during the so-called prayer sessions, she had gone to the adjoining bathroom to say prayers. Nevertheless, it was held on appeal that the holy man and his male co-offender had sexual intercourse with the victim without consent and knowing that she was not consenting; FP shared a common purpose that this would occur; and FP's physical presence in the motel room was sufficiently proximate to either encourage the offenders or intimidate the victim. Moreover, FP had been present during the administration of an intoxicating substance to the victim before the sexual assaults. In these circumstances, her presence was sufficient for her to be "in company."[2]

Fine legal points aside, what particularly caught my eye was a judicial description of the setting for these offenses:

> The hotel/motel rooms
> It is appropriate to say something about the nature of the accommodation at the REDACTED hotel and the REDACTED Motor Inn. It is relevant to the submissions to which I will refer later concerning the "in company" element and the possibility that the applicant may have been in the bathroom at the time sexual assaults occurred. Photographs of rooms at each place were before the jury (Exhibits M and N). It is clear that the rooms were modest in both size and furnishings in relatively inexpensive establishments. They were hardly suites in a five-star hotel.[3] (my redactions)

While these violent crimes were occluded by faux mysticism, the chosen sites were in very ordinary suburban motels: utterly banal and unremarkable. Intrigued, I commenced a search for other criminal cases set in hotels, motels, and motor inns. And what began as a mere legal curiosity, with the aid of an online legal database search, was soon transformed into a flight of dark tourism (Bowman and Pezzullo 2009; Lennon and Foley 2000; Pascale 2018; Sharpley and Stone 2009; Stone 2009; Tennant 2018), visual criminology (Carrabine 2012; Brown 2014; Brown and Carrabine 2017), hauntology (Derrida 2012), and perhaps an excursion into a nascent ghost criminology, bringing me to a selection of motel crime scenes to textually and visually document the in/tangible. Through this theoretical, embodied, and visual arts–informed process, this chapter seeks to contribute to spatial understandings and representations of these hybrid private-but-shared rooms (Pritchard and Morgan 2006) as sites that have experienced sexual violence (Bachelard 1994; Bollnow 2011) and remain charged with the ghosts of criminal transgression. I propose that the haunting metaphor and methodology can be productively harnessed to analyze these supernatural sexual assaults and their spectral traces.

I begin with an overview of crime in the hospitality industry, a somewhat under-discussed site of criminal behavior given the industry's commercial interests. Nevertheless, my search has revealed the motel room as a rather typical crime scene, particularly for sexual violence and drug offenses. The motel room presents a conflation of intimacy, privacy, and anonymity with a world of transience and strangers, and even stranger events. In what follows, I place the motel crime scene in the context of this volume, drawing particular links to autoethnographic approaches, like those employed here. Given the volume's emphasis, my analysis centers topically on the supernatural and occult themes evident in the sex crimes referenced above. This flows to a discussion of the sexualized space of motel rooms and the interrelationship between hospitality, guests + hosts (ghosts), and ritual. Finally, I discuss the motel room through the lens of my visual arts practice, in which I photograph these sites in minute detail to document scenes of sexual violence and to capture a sense of the absent guests and lingering ghosts.

Some initial comments upfront. First, throughout this analysis, I have sought to preserve the anonymity of the various establishments out of respect to the victims and sensitivities involved, although the information is on public record through case law and media coverage. Second, I draw a distinction between "hotels" and "motels." "Hotel," a word that entered the English language around the 1760s, is derived from the French "hôtel," referring to a nobleman's residence (Sandoval-Strausz 2007a). Hotels have clung to this sense of exclusivity. But in this chapter, I generally use the word "motel" to refer to the establishments I identified in my criminal law research. The motel concept originated from the rise of the automobile that saw "motor hotels" springing up on cheap land along highways and wastelands (Sandoval-Strausz 2007a; Treadwell 2005). The "motor hotel" became the "mo-tel" (Eschner 2016) which captures an aura of cheapness that appeals to me, as well as the mobility and transience of guests who have come and gone from the places I visited. In this way, motels evoke a sense of vernacular and predetermined absence that resonates with the hauntological and the figure of the ghost.

The Motel Room as a Site for Strangers ... and Stranger Things

While there is considerable literature regarding tourists as victims of crime (Cohen 2019; Mansfeld and Pizam 2006), tourists' perceptions of risk, fear, and insecurity (Brunt et al. 2000; Hernández 2018; Mawby 2000; Ozascilar et al. 2019), as well as crime prevention and policing strategies for tourist destinations (Botterill and Jones 2010; Mawby et al. 2015), not much consideration has been given to crimes committed within the confines of the motel specifically. Publicizing crime in the hospitality industry, whether at resorts (Walmsley et al. 1983), in homestays or Airbnbs (Xu et al. 2017), on cruise ships (Little 2018; Myers 2007), or in hotels/motels or guest houses (Jones and Groenenboom 2002; Elliott 2007) is bad business, and operators are reluctant to discuss the issue (Botterill and Jones 2010; Jones and Groenenboom 2002; Xu et al. 2017). On this basis, it is not surprising that hospitality industry crime scenes, unlike other sites of trauma and violence (Tyner 2014), are rarely commemorated. Traces of crime are hidden or erased (Ambinder 1992; Boakye 2010) to protect material interests and operating performance (Hua and Yang 2017; Topham 2006), so these crime scenes often fly under the radar and generally remain a hushed secret.

However, my research of Australian criminal case law has uncovered the motel room as a common and significant site for a range of offenses, including murder, sexual assaults, drug offenses, robbery, even games of Russian roulette. Motel rooms are often used to avoid the police, and it is not surprising that fugitives often register at motels under false identities.[4] Knowing this, I have attempted to theorize the motel room as a site chosen *for* criminal transgression, asking: What is it about these private-but-shared spaces that enables, perhaps beckons, criminal behavior? And what tangible and intangible traces remain?

The motel room is well known as a site for overt romance and covert erotic encounters, a place of respite for tired tourists, business travelers, or itinerant workers. Motels represent leisure, fantasy (Braden 2018; Friedman 2003), and an escape from "real life" (Laurel 2016). They are a temporary utopia—an idealized version of life (Walsh 2015). In Australia, this ideal may have been transplanted from another country or culture: Ross (2019) notes that mid-century Australian motels, for instance, were seemingly shonky replicas inspired by US magazine images.

The resort establishment, in particular, is premised on "efficient organization, theatricality, romanticism, and deception" (Friedman 2003: 527), the last element referring to the concealment of housekeeping and maintenance circulation routes from the view of guests. Motel staff aim for seamless invisibility, like ghosts, in performing their functions, such as replenishment of towels and amenities (Walsh 2015). Put a sign "please make up the room" on the door handle and miraculously you return to fresh linen, and toilet paper with a neatly folded triangular edge. But just as the motel can conceal its inner workings from guests, guests can use the motel as concealment from the outside world. Industry professionals understand this and tread a fine line between monitoring and ignoring guests' activities and indiscretions (Sandoval-Strausz 2007a).

The inherent spatial contradictions of hospitality establishments are detailed in Sandoval-Strausz's (2007a, b) examination of the hotel: its distinctive arrangement, social constitution, and place in human geography and consumer capitalism. There is a distinctive spatial logic in hotels and motels evolving from the provision of bedding and sustenance, those essentials taken for granted at home (Sandoval-Strausz 2007a, b). Motel rooms are therefore simultaneously home-like, a home-away-from-home, and yet nothing, at all, like home. The rooms and their objects within are "familiar, but subtly rearranged, never the configuration one expects," and thus, a "home defamiliarized" (Koestenbaum 2007: 20, 116) where "homely and unhomely" are inextricably coiled together (Balanzategui 2016: 244). To stay in a motel room therefore is to be immersed in the uncanny (Freud 1964), *unheimlich*, "literally the 'unhomelike'" (Schwenger 2006: 65). There are furnishings and gadgets that may bear some resemblance to home except they are different, often hardwired and securely fixed to walls, given stringent health and safety regulations and the fact that, as a guest, you are assumed to be a thief (Walsh 2015). Moreover, motels "facilitate human mobility" and are therefore designed around transience, not residence (Sandoval-Strausz 2007b: 934): Guests may *stay*, not *live*, in these places (Walsh 2015). Motels hover in a state between "fixed address and vagrancy, between home and the car" (Treadwell 2005: 215), and occupation for the mobile subject is precarious. Of course it must be stated that material circumstances also make the motel a viable residential option for those experiencing financial hardships.

In addition to the quality of transience, as well as the uncertain balance between homeliness and unhomeliness, there is anonymity in the motel's concentration of "a world of strangers" (Sandoval-Strausz 2007b: 933, 957). Almost like a prison, motels house large groups of random people (Koestenbaum 2007; see Frearson 2012 regarding Berdaguer and Péjus' artwork transformation of a former prison to a "Gue(ho)st House"), providing a collective sort of anonymity (Trigg 2006, citing Kracauer 1995). "The stranger" developed as a central motif in literature as progressive human mobility (Sandoval-Strausz 2007b) and the increased affordability of the automobile (Linnemann 2015) meant that urban populations swelled and became increasingly anonymous. Drifters (Ferrell 2018) and "strangers on the road" (Linnemann 2015: 519) could shelter in cheap highway motels among "an arbitrary collection of human beings" thrown serendipitously together (Koestenbaum 2007: 12).

The resulting conflation of anonymity and strangerhood with transience, along with the mobility implicit in the "mo-tel" (Eschner 2016), creates "contradictory associations: traveler's haven and criminal hideout" (Sandoval-Strausz 2007a). In the wrong part of town, motels can become seedy microcosms of vice. Such is the industry's ongoing relationship with transgressive activities best kept secret: "sexual trespass" and the one-night stand (Koestenbaum 2007: 56, 114), drug use and sale, violence and deviancy (Treadwell 2005). As Wayne Koestenbaum puts it, motels are always "gaping, ajar" (2007: 154) and this welcoming openness invites the activities of rakes, grafters, and thieves, confidence men, tricksters, and hustlers (Sandoval-Strausz 2007a: 204) to an underworld emitting a "noir atmosphere: anonymity, shadow, knife, soullessness" (Koestenbaum 2007: 123). Would-be criminals can easily case the joint and, combined with the transience of strangers, they can "wander freely about the premises in a way that would generate suspicion in most other settings" and enjoy a quick escape (Sandoval-Strausz 2007a: 212). Of course, the surveillance of guests has evolved from a simple signature in a guest register, which nevertheless leaves the evidential trace of a spectral hand, to CCTV, key card entry, and credit card payment, all of which leave spectral traces of their own. Nevertheless, what goes on behind closed motel room doors largely remains secret.

Some have called the motel room a "passive, inert" setting (Adler 2008: 290) that sits there, waiting to offer up its innards to the next guests for them to do with the room as they will. But my contention here is that the spaces of the motel are far from inert. Following Fiddler (2018: 12), a "hauntologically-informed examination of space" reveals that these are sites that have been experienced and inhabited (Bachelard 1994; Bollnow 2011), albeit in churning transience. They are filled with accretions of human experience and with the ghosts of former guests, so much so that "guest" and "ghost" become almost interchangeable. Indeed, as Walsh (2015: 12) suggests, the motel is simultaneously a guest-house and *ghosthouse*. From this vantage, the motel room is never as inanimate or lifeless as its visible and physical emptiness may suggest.

Of Guests and Ghosts: Sleeping at Crime Scene Motels

There is a certain splendor to cheap motels (Koestenbaum 2007). As I embarked on this project, I decided to stay only at crime scene motels and motor inns that were decidedly run-down, basically seedy "dives" that reflected B-grade kitsch and nostalgia. I made a conscious decision not to stay at fancy, luxury, or "dream" hotels (Berger 2011: 1) where crimes had occurred. I ignored the usual irresistible attractions of extravagance and exclusivity of establishments that aspire to opulence (Koestenbaum 2007) and aristocratic and palatial designs, those "exaggerated representations of the aggrandized glory of capitalist production" (Berger 2011: 7). Instead, I favored ordinary establishments with drive-through ease, car parking right outside the door, and egalitarian access to budget accommodation. My co-guests have included large, multi-generational families crammed into bunk beds and family rooms, and armies of "hi-vis" clad tradespeople. There are always many single men who leave their motel room door open on hot summer nights, with the "footy" playing on the TV inside, while they sit outside on weather-worn plastic chairs and smoke. I speculate that some have cut deals with the motel for cheap, ongoing boarding arrangements. Maybe some are using the premises as a halfway house, that liminal space between incarceration and reintegration into the community. It's not uncommon for cheap motels to be used by Community Corrections.[5] One such motel was notorious as a place that is very close to where people who use and abuse illicit drugs congregate and attend a clinic to get help. It is a sad indictment of our community that when people are released from gaol they are placed in the only accommodation available but where there is a real risk old criminal contacts will be renewed. (*R v Wade* [2019] NSWDC 205, Haesler SC DCJ at [6])

The crime scene motels where I have stayed are sites in decline and, while still in use, they stand at the threshold of decay and ruination, entreating developers and bulldozers. I had no choice but to embrace the retro faded beigeness, shoddy workmanship, deterioration, corrosion, and mismatched bland furnishings that surely endured decades. In this way, these sites speak to the aesthetics of hauntology—some kind of ghostly nostalgia (Balanzategui 2016) for "lost futures" (Fisher 2012: 16), a projected utopia that was never realized, a kind of "presence of the past" that lingers (BBC 2019). Still filled with decades-old detritus, the motels are "architecture(s) of anachronism," analogue, and framed by time "out of joint" (Fisher 2012: 18, 20, citing Derrida 2012), and have conjured something of my own mid-century childhood and family holiday déjà-vus that I reimage and probably misremember (BBC 2019). These "out-of-time" (Fiddler 2018: 12; see also Kindynis 2019) rooms invite us to "hearken to the presence of the beforehand, the haunting" (Koestenbaum 2007: 42). More important, once attuned to these traces, one cannot help but read tired furnishings and general shabbiness as imbued with fragments of missing lives, residual human experience, obsolescence, temporality, and other-worldliness. These ghosts have not been exorcised by interior designers and refurbishment, but they remain nonetheless. Given the tired and utter mundanity of these motel rooms, it is somehow surprising to reckon them as traumascapes (Tumarkin 2015) and sites of violence.

Kindynis (2019: 25, 29) explains the spectral turn (Luckhurst 2002) in criminology and the emergent methodology of "ghost ethnography" as "an orientation which places an emphasis on absence and the interpretation of material and atmospheric traces." While the ghost can be seen as a metaphor or as part of daily phenomenological encounters, it invokes the criminological imagination to sense spectral residues that animate social space (Ferrell 2016; Kindynis 2019; Linnemann 2015; Trigg 2012).

I have co-opted this approach to study the accumulated absences and residual murmurs (Armstrong 2010) of the crime scene motel room. The motel rooms where I slept are "sites of haunted memory" where I can seek to interact "with the ghosts of lives lived" (Garrett 2013: 30). The motel room is not so much a lost ecology (Ferrell 2015; Kindynis 2019) but a completely overlooked and veiled crime site, so this research brings something "hidden to the fore" (Garrett 2013: 15, 30). The rooms are filled with "unacknowledged ghosts" (Batchen 2008: 10) of absent victims and perpetrators, and this ghost criminological perspective provides a means to understand the motel room as a social site with the potential to facilitate criminality.

In staying at the motels, my approach is autoethnographic (Armstrong 2010; Kindynis 2019). Autoethnography can be understood as the researcher's critical and reflexive engagement within a particular social context (Spry 2011) or as a conjoining of auto (self) with ethno (culture) to critique a particular cultural space (Neumann 1996; Gabor 2019). The research also draws broadly from scholarship underpinned by cultural criminology (Ferrell 1999), visual criminology (Carrabine 2012; Brown 2014; Brown and Carrabine 2017), and dark tourism (Bowman and Pezzullo 2009; Lennon and Foley 2000; Pascale 2018; Sharpley and Stone 2009; Stone 2009; Tennant 2018). In this entwining of critical perspectives, I seek to examine and construct meaning, through a reflexive, subjective, interpretative lens (Armstrong 2010), to understand the deviant behavior that has occurred in a specific social site (Ferrell 1999). This method represents a form of "criminological *verstehen*," that is, "a field researcher's subjective appreciation and empathic understanding of crime's situated meanings, symbolism, and emotions" (Ferrell 1999: 400; Kindynis 2017). That method recognizes the researcher's situated experience, deep immersion, and imagination in a particular criminal event (Ferrell 1999, 2016; Kindynis 2019). It also privileges attentiveness, and I attend, accost, or apprehend the crime scene through the camera's lens to produce images of what was seen, while hinting at what was unseen. In staying at crime scene motels, I focus on the motel room as a "dense site" of history and "social violence" (Gordon 2008: xvi, 8). There, I can take into my consciousness the "spatial 'unconscious'" (Kindynis 2019: 31, citing De Certeau, Giard, and Mayol 1998; see also Hayward 2012); the "sad and sunken couch

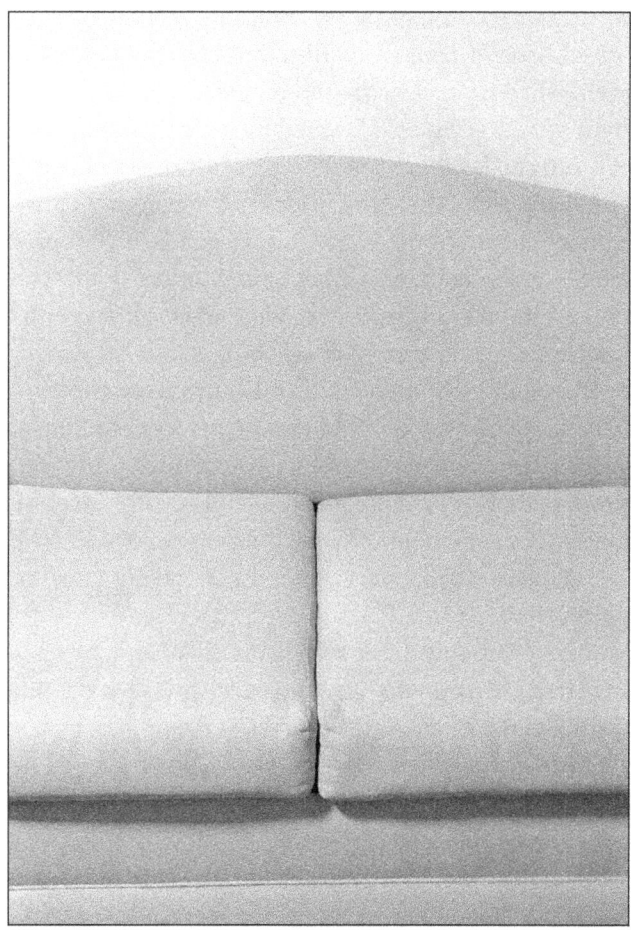

Figure 11.1. *Sofa*, 2019. Credit: Carolyn McKay.

that sags" from the collective weight of unremembered guests, the bed in a non-smoking room with burn holes on the quilt from long-gone cigarettes (Gordon 2008: xvi, 4). As I sleep on a mattress that has been used by many strangers, I can be attuned to the "ghostly presence of past violence" (Linnemann 2015: 520) that lingers in the present.

This mode of study can be understood as requiring a certain kind of "sensibility" (Kindynis 2019: 30), drawing from concepts of proprioception, that sense of body awareness, where the body is in space and how it relates and navigates spatial relationships (Callery 2015), as well as the notion of "space consciousness" (Bollnow 2011: 257). While ghosts and hauntings are not *temporally* fixed so that "the past can make its presence felt," they have clear *spatial* connections (Pile 2005: 137; see also Kindynis 2019; Trigg 2012). The tangible and intangible qualities of a motel room can be appreciated in the context of a phenomenological study of space, that is, a recognition that perception entwines haptic, optic, olfactory, auditory, and gustatory qualities with precognitive being-in-the-world encounters (Trigg 2012; Merleau-Ponty 1962, 1968). For instance, Pallasmaa suggests that every engagement with the built environment presents a panoply of sensorial cues and provides an experience of the building's "embodied and spiritual essence" (Pallasmaa 2012: 13). The motels I visited would hardly be recognized by most people as reflecting "memorable experiences of architecture" (76), yet their multi-sensorial attributes can be phenomenologically encountered and documented. An attunement to hauntings connects well with a "phenomenology of place" (Bell 1997: 813; see also Kindynis 2019; Linnemann 2015; Trigg 2012).

The resonances of any space or place are dependant on knowing. Kindynis (2019: 33) discusses criminologists who "seek out illicit atmospheres," while Gibson (2002: 1) talks about driving along a stretch of "immense, historical crime-scene," "a place you're warned not to go." Certainly, the crime scene motels are antithetical to Bachelard's poetic, happy, warm spaces (Bachelard 1994). Rather they are non-neutral "experienced spaces" with "rich content" (Bollnow 2011: 18–19) and, once you know their history, they become "menacing places that make us shudder with fear" (136). Our response to any space is contingent on knowledge, and the uncanniness of the motel room "signals that something unnatural has occurred"; there's a metaphysical creep of disturbance (Comaroff and Ong 2013: 15). With knowledge that sexual violence occurred somewhere on this site under the guise of spiritual healing and magic, my subjective spatial engagement is unsettled by my own imagination. What happened here? And why? There is something carnal lurking in the flesh of the room, and the visible physical space is overlaid with my own anxious and imaginative projections. "In reality all things are concretions of a setting," as Merleau-Ponty put it, and so, the motel room cannot be disentangled from my perceptions of it (Merleau-Ponty 1962: 374). Do ghosts haunt these rooms, or do they

Figure 11.2. *Lock*, 2019. Credit: Carolyn McKay

occupy my haunted mind? Am I the bringer of the weird and eerie? Of course, as Kociejowski (2014: 62) writes: "A ghost is not a ghost until it has a living audience." Here too, I am both audience and the medium who conjures forgotten violence. It is as Trigg (2012: 309) suggests, "the ghost expresses itself primarily through its native haunt, the human body."

I *do* know about these spaces, and there is an ineffable melancholia in the worn, utilitarian fixtures and fittings. The rooms and objects are steeped in a kind of animism from years of mortal handling, fleeting occupants, and the occasional crime. An archaeology exists of hair, fingerprints, carpet fibers, paint flakes, and bodily fluids that stand as mute witnesses to trauma, a type of "evidence that does not forget."[6] There are "tears of things" (Schwenger 2006: 1) and affective attributes (Young 2010) of objects that are not indifferent to the history that has tarnished them, left cigarette burn holes, and accretions of finger grime. In their connection with "metaphysical nonexistence" (Schwenger 2006: 174) these are spaces and objects that have experienced human ephemerality and they reek of meaning, a meaning that might be simultaneously profound and yet fugitive (Rugoff et al. 1997). Because I know the violence that has been committed on the site, I enter the motel room with a sense of some foreboding and unease, as if this project tempts fate and courts personal danger. It seems that cultural criminological fieldwork can be fraught with danger (Ferrell 1999: 400; Kindynis 2017, 2019) or, from my perspective, just an irrational tingling fear, especially as night falls. I arrive, close windows and curtains, and bolt the door. Or try to.

Motel Rooms, Sex, and Ritual

I have stayed at the two motels used in the supernatural sexual assault cases but, as the appeal court judgments do not identify the specific motel room numbers, I don't know if I'm in the actual room where the assaults were committed. Nevertheless, motels are essentially boxes containing smaller boxes, or cells (Koestenbaum 2007). There is a level of "seriality" in motel construction, and the rooms tend to be homogenous and interchangeable clones. From my perspective, it's enough that I'm in the actual establishment where I can revisit the details and allow my imagination to cooperate with my proprioception to feel unhinged from the present, to animate the surrounding space and furnishings. Making contact with motel room ghosts "refashions the social relations" I have with that location (Gordon 2008: 22), now and into the future. So, whenever I check into a motel, I cannot help but wonder: Who's been sleeping in my bed? More than a spot to rest your weary head, the motel bed is a focal point that establishes a "highly sexualized space" (Sandoval-Strausz 2007a: 211), a "site of tryst" and "submoral zone" (Koestenbaum 2007: 41, 98). The pay-per-view pornography television stations and brochures for a potpourri of in-room services; thoughts of illicit or immoral sexual activities that transpire or could, call forth ghosts of other kinds. Wayne

Koestenbaum (2007: 34) asks: "Isn't porn often filmed in hotel rooms? A flat pillow and quilted bedspread are not erotic, but they witness sex, attest to its flatness." Motels sell misbehavior (Walsh 2015); promiscuity is practically promoted. Indeed, the sexual assault cases in question mentioned "threesomes" and sex tapes as incidental to the proceedings. Cheap motels, at least in Nicaragua, provide "por rato" rent rooms for commercial and non-commercial sexual activities and are potential locations for the spread of sexually transmitted infections (Gorter et al. 1993: 1645). Foucault (1997: 355–356) suggests that motels are where "one enters with one's own vehicle and lover and where illicit sex is totally protected and totally concealed."

In addition to the central sexualized bed motif, motels can provide "a stage for numinous encounters" and can be places that "lend themselves to fugue states—to fits of dissociation and disembodiment" (Koestenbaum 2007: 21, 23, referencing W. G. Sebald's *Vertigo*). With

Figure 11.3. *Bed*, 2019. Credit: Carolyn McKay.

this understanding, it is interesting that the cases in question involved the drugging of the victims, highly ritualistic elements, voices from spectral entities, and faux sacred rituals performed in very non-sacred budget motel rooms. Dylan Trigg (2006) draws on Siegfried Kracauer's (1995) description of hotel lobbies as the antithesis of a collective place of worship—instead, they are transient spaces devoid of any god. This characterization, I contend, applies similarly to the non-numinous crime scene motel rooms:

> King Russell told MM that she must have sex with one of two people, either her father or AP. She said she was given instructions to go to the REDACTED motel, to invite AP to come and meet her at the hotel room, that when he arrived she was to knock on the back of her room door three times before she was to open it, naked. She was to say, "I want you to have sex with me" and, when he declined, she was to say, "If you don't I will scream, the neighbours will hear me and I will cause trouble for you." She was to have oral sex with AP, and was to pinch his nipples, and was told that if she knocked on the door three times as he arrived and left it would erase his memory.[7] (my redactions)

Between the two victims, there were certain similarities in the ritualistic steps taken by the offenders, the repeated phrase "it's going to feel like it's 100 per cent real but it's not, it's just a dream,"[8] and the non-consensual drug-induced fugue states. For instance:

> On each occasion MP was told to drink the orange juice after the applicant had prayed on it. She did so, and on each occasion, she said that she felt dizzy. MP gave evidence that on each occasion, she was sent to the bathroom, where she undressed, returned wearing a towel, and was sexually assaulted.[9] (my redactions)

These rooms bore witness to fake spirituality, perverse fantasy, and ritualized sexual subjugation. Perhaps unsurprisingly, there is a connection between ritual and hospitality, and hence the motel industry. Sacred rituals from many cultures, including ancient Greece, have underpinned the concept of hospitality, that "rite of incorporation" whereby a stranger is welcomed, hosted, assigned the role of a guest, and provided with "an intermediate status between outsider and insider" (Sandoval-Strausz 2007a: 137). That is, hospitality encompasses both welcome and suspicion to reflect "the right of a stranger . . . not to be treated with hostility" (Derrida 2000: 4). Nevertheless, the guest-host relationship is problematic, being premised upon both the trust and mistrust of the stranger and the difficulties of moderating the misbehavior of transients (Sandoval-Strausz 2007a; Graburn 1983). This returns us to the "ghosthouse" concept (Walsh 2015: 12), the Berdaguer and Péjus' "Ghe(ho)st House" (Frearson 2012), or in Marcel Duchamp's calculus: "A Guest + A Host = A Ghost." The combination of these paired but oppositional words, intrinsic to a symbiotic relationship (a host's hospitality is dependent on a guest receiving it) means that they cancel each other out (Gould 2000), so "a hotel is always haunted" (Koestenbaum 2007: 74). Graburn (1983), citing Hubert and Mauss (1964[1898]), also draws an interesting parallel between tourism and ritual behavior; In both there is something "sacred' in entrance and departure, a spatial displacement, and the experience of an out-of-the-ordinary or liminal state of being. Social norms disappear, behavior may be disinhibited in the motel room, and there is sexual license offering complete immersion within a ritual and/or a sex act (Graburn 1983). As I lie on the motel bed, I wonder if a "kind of sacred electric charge" (Bell 1997: 822) might have penetrated or possessed the mattress and remain potent.

Ghost Photography

I have taken more than 900 photographs of crime scene motel room interiors that seek to "accost" the site (Lee and Meyer 2008: 58, citing Greenberg 1964) to document the textures, fibers, stains, and spatters (sometimes identified using a blue light torch), a visual dissection of a particular spatial ecology. I take the room unawares (Schwenger 2006), as I find it, stepping over the threshold without any aesthetic rearrangement or intervention, although I recognize that my mere presence and intent mediate the scene. The images I have made are not explicit, voyeuristic, or ghoulish. Rather, they simply depict the same everyday objects and furnishings that you would find in any modest motel room. The three images reproduced in this chapter, *Sofa*, *Lock*, and *Bed* are typical of my body of work. While photographed in three separate crime scene motel rooms, they display a coherent palette of beigeness and the overt signs of human handling. The broken security bolt in *Lock* speaks to lax motel maintenance and reflects my trepidation in staying overnight in these rooms. I always shoved a chair against the door as an additional security measure. The seemingly neatly made *Bed* belies its accumulation of sleeping guests and sexual acts. While the quilt attempts to conceal the bed's archaeology of human experience, *Sofa* declares its history with imprints of former bodies on sagging cushions and stains from greasy heads. Photographing such ordinariness invites interpretation and the deciphering of evidence (Bond 2009). As Luc Sante (2006: 62) put it, there is a kind of "spectacle of ordinary things made immanent by proximity to violence" that recognizes the intersection of quotidian existence with deviance; the convergence of the uncanny, "the world-as-haunted," and everyday life (Trigg 2012: 325).

While not staged, the images are framed by an aesthetics of decay, and I capture the discoloration of these disintegrating rooms using everyday technology: my iPhone (occasionally a GoPro) that exudes "the aesthetics of banality" (Hjorth 2010: 34, citing Ilpo Koskinen). Harnessing the mobility and flexibility of this lightweight, compact device eschews notions of fine art photography; however, it offers high resolution images while being discreet in size. It is important to be unobtrusive, as I do not announce my documentary intentions to the motel proprietors, so my motel stays are a type of guerilla or covert shoot.[10] As Palmer (2012: 90) argues, iPhone photography is perhaps less about "*representation*" and more about "photographs as *information*" (emphasis in original) as it automatically stores locative data, generating a site-specific and geo-spatial connection. Other artists have used the iPhone in their art practices given that it is "the perfect collecting machine ... [that] can copy the world at will" (Palmer 2012: 93; Hjorth 2010). In using the iPhone, Palmer (2012: 95) concludes that the art of photography is conflated with "the mediation of individual identity in the psychic and social space of the mobile phone." I like the notion that I have documented the psychic and social space of motel rooms using my iPhone as medium, a device thoroughly haunted by my digital doppelgänger. By photographing these retro motel rooms with my iPhone, there is a clash of technologies: remnants of a "dead" analogue, material world are captured by the "living" digital and woven through the photographs are elements of strangeness, nostalgia, and the uncanny derived from the hauntological approach (Balanzategui 2016).

My work draws inspiration from Anne Ferran and her *Lost to Worlds* (2008) suite of images from Australian convict-era female factories. The photographs depict deserted and demolished sites of correction and the erasure of a particular female history. Ferran's photographs closely crop seemingly impassive and benign details that do not purport to present a truth of the past crime but, instead, evoke "a ghostly presence that still haunts" (Batchen 2008: 16). Of course, Sophie Calle's *L'Hôtel, Chambre 47* (1981) is right on point, adopting a "CSI" type "dispassionate" approach (Bond 2009: 23) to documenting the hotel rooms in which she worked as a chamber maid. Her modus operandi involved examining the personal belongings of the hotel guests and making observations about these strangers' lives (Calle 1999). While her photographs exploit the crime scene aesthetic and are coded with forensic objectivity, "they are evidence photos that *lack a crime*" (Bond 2009: 23; emphasis in original), perhaps reaffirming Benjamin's (1999) assertion that every inch of the city is a crime scene and every stranger, a culprit.

Like Calle's *L'Hôtel*, my body of work represents a mix of dispassionate or forensic chronicle (Lee and Meyer 2008) aspiring to be an "affectless" record that is nevertheless "pregnant with implication" (Sante 2006: 60–61). In appropriating the "aestheticization of the neutral document" (Wollen 1997: 32), my photographs, such as *Sofa, Lock,* and *Bed*, perhaps stand as a recreated archive. They are not real crime scene photographs, having been taken well over a decade since the violence, but as an ex post facto photographic collection, they may still have the power to haunt. In their compulsive quantity, the collected images attest to the fact that "every motel has already been occupied and the inhabitants and history cannot easily be forgotten" (Treadwell 2005: 221), although I'm certain that motel proprietors would prefer suppression and spatial amnesia regarding the crimes committed therein.

My photographic project of documenting the motel rooms also provides an alternative perspective on representations of scenes of sexual violence. The stereotypical "real" rape "occurs when a stranger attacks a woman in a public place," and sexual assaults that do not conform to this convention risk failure before the courts (Young 2010: 44). Yet the sexual assaults that occurred in the establishments where I slept involved parties known to one another and were committed in the privacy of motel rooms. On this basis, they were not "conventional" sexual assaults, especially in light of their preternatural context. While these scenes of past sexual violence invite spectatorship (Young 2010), I see my photographic documentation as a sensorial survey of the character of the motel room (Garrett 2013). This project is more than just looking—I'm after a "visceral reading of the site" (Kindynis and Garrett 2015: 10). It's about sleeping with, soaking up, and breathing in the motel room to commune with the ghosts overnight in the interstitial space (Gordon 2008) between the camera's lens and its peripheral blindness. Gordon (2008: 106–107) explains the animism—life force—of photographs and the relationship with haunting referring to Barthes's *studium/punctum*. The *studium* can be understood as the immediate interest of the photograph, while the *punctum* is the essence that "brings to life the life external" to the photograph (107). It is in the latter that the ghost is animated, and the back of the neck prickles as we see something that is perhaps not explicitly there. Of course, the relationship between photography with presence and absence, with life and death, and with temporal collapse is well understood. When photographing such sites, as Garrett (2013: 30) writes, "the snap of the camera shutter [is] like an exploding chemistry experiment where past, present and future are fused." The photographic process is about evidence-gathering, some verisimilitude of human trace (Gordon 2008), and a means to document those people and events that are no longer there (Ferrell 2015; Kindynis 2019). Photography is therefore undeniably a "house of spooks," a medium between the living and spirit worlds (Sante 2006: 61). Further, "the more empty the photograph, the more it will imply horror" (62). *Sofa*, *Lock*, and *Bed* provide such inklings and spectral traces of human encounters and transgression. It is through this process of documenting material elements and banal minutiae that I seek to commune with "the ghostly matter" (Gordon 2008: 134) of the immaterial that lingers in the motel rooms, while recognizing that something has happened here that cannot easily be grasped (Wollen 1997).

Conclusion

My overnight stays and research of legal databases have exposed the motel room as a significant crime site, a lawless space where, behind closed doors, wrongdoing is effortless. As a social site, the cheap motel, in particular, is "a transgressive architecture" that conflates "sour regrets, and nights of pleasure" (Treadwell 2005: 214–215) with transience and presents a unique spatial relationship with crime (Hayward 2012). Yet most motel guests who stay in these rooms would have no awareness or thought of the accretions of human experience. In examining the series of supernatural sexual assaults, I have applied a ghost criminological method to reveal how our understandings of any space are contingent: Knowledge of sexual violence evokes traces, shadows, and echoes in these banal, urban, and low-rise "commonplace geographies" (Linnemann 2015: 514). Through this approach, I have found that ghostly murmurs permeate the crime scene motel rooms and linger, waiting for acknowledgment. I have established that the motel rooms in which I slept are not inert but:

> carry traces of past occupancies that either painfully obtrude (the stray hair, marked surfaces) or must be imagined as blank sheet(s), clean and unoccupied, in an effort to erase knowledge of other bodies weighting the bed. (Treadwell 2005: 217)

Through a spectral lens, motel rooms are sites of the "abject and the uncanny" that may be "haunted by degradation and terror" (Wollen 1997: 24). Nevertheless, my deadpan photographs refrain from the morbid and instead seek to provide mundane clues of extramundane human experience.

This prompts a consideration of the ethics and outcomes of artistic intervention and interaction with these sites, and the larger issue of creative response to narratives of violence and trauma (Scott Bray 2014; Biber 2018; Bond 2009). But an understanding of the spectral may open doors to victimology and provide a means to understand "how memory and trauma become inscribed literally, symbolically, affectively and atmospherically in space and place" (Kindynis 2019: 39). Aesthetic responses entreat restitution and "encourage us to re-member" (Fiddler 2018:12). This is significant in sites, such as cheap motel rooms, that will never achieve memorialization and where the ghosts can only ever make themselves known to the knowing guest.

NOTES
1 *FP v R* [2012] NSWCCA 182, RA Hulme J at [30]; *Golossian v R* [2013] NSWCCA 311, [54]
2 *FP v R* [2012] NSWCCA 182, RA Hulme J at [126], [146], [150]. Hulme 2013: 16; *R v Button; R v Griffen* [2002] NSWCCA 159; (2002) 54 NSWLR 455; Bronitt and

McSherry 2017; see also Young's discussion of an English rape case regarding accessorial liability (2010: 52–53).
3 *FP v R* [2012] NSWCCA 182, R A Hulme J at [67].
4 Examples include: *The Queen v Griggs* [1999] FCA 1573; *Regina v Leanne Cassa* [1999] NSWSC 651; *R v Hammond* [2000] NSWCCA 540; *R v Lowrie & Ross* [2000] QCA 405; *R v Meyboom* [2001] FCA 861; *R v Hong Phuc Truong* [2002] VSCA 27; *R v Lyberopoulos* [2002] NSWCCA 268; *R v Su* [2003] VSC 473; *Golossian v R* [2013] NSWCCA 311.
5 For the US context, see Dum 2016.
6 *Harris v United States*, 331US145, 1947 cited in Houck 2001.
7 *Golossian v R* [2013] NSWCCA 311, Leeming JA at [55].
8 *FP v R* [2012] NSWCCA 182, [30]; *Golossian v R* [2013] NSWCCA 311, [54].
9 *Golossian v R* [2013] NSWCCA 311, Leeming JA at [38].
10 This is not the first time that I've generated a body of artistic work in this way. For instance, my 2012 solo exhibition *Covert* was a collection of video works filmed surreptitiously in Japan (McKay 2013).

REFERENCES

Case Law
FP v R [2012] NSWCCA 182
Golossian v R [2013] NSWCCA 311
Harris v United States, 331US145, 1947
R v Button; R v Griffen (2002) 54 NSWLR 455
R v Wade [2019] NSWDC 205

Primary Sources
Adler, Jeffrey S. 2008. Reviewed Work: The Hotel: An American History by A. K. Sandoval-Strausz, *Journal of Interdisciplinary History* 39, 2 (Autumn): 290–291.
Ambinder, E. 1992. "Urban Violence Raises Safety Fears." *Corporate Travel* 9, no. 6: 133–138.
Argyrou, Vassos. 1993. "Under a Spell: The Strategic Use of Magic in Greek Cypriot Society." *American Ethnologist* 20, no. 2: 256–271.
Arlington, Kim. 2011. "'Holy Man' Rapist Jailed for 20 Years." *Sydney Morning Herald*. May 6. www.smh.com.au
Armstrong, Justin. 2010. "On the Possibility of Spectral Ethnography." *Cultural Studies? Critical Methodologies* 10, no. 3: 243–250.
Bachelard, Gaston. 1994. *The Poetics of Space*. Translated by Maria Jolas. Boston: Beacon.
Balanzategui, Jessica. 2016. "Haunted Nostalgia and the Aesthetics of Technological Decay: Hauntology and Super 8 in Sinister." *Horror Studies* 7 (2): 235–251. doi:10.1386/host.7.2.235_1.
Batchen, Geoffrey. 2008. "'Evocations: The Art of Anne Ferran." In *Anne Ferran: The Ground, The Air*, ed. Craig Judd. Hobart: Tasmanian Museum and Art Gallery.

BBC. 2019. *What Is Hauntology? And Why Is It All Around Us?* March1. www.bbc.com
Bell, Michael Mayerfeld. 1997. "The Ghosts of Place." *Theory and Society* 26, no. 6: 813–836.
Benjamin, Walter. 1999. "Little History of Photography." *Selected Writings 2*, Part 2: 1931–1934.
Berger, Molly W. 2011. *Hotel Dreams: Luxury, Technology, and Urban Ambition in America, 1829–1929*. Baltimore, MD: Johns Hopkins University Press.
Biber, Katherine. 2018. *In Crime's Archive: The Cultural Afterlife of Evidence*. New York: Routledge.
Bishop, Elizabeth. 1983. *The Complete Poems, 1927–1979*. New York: Farrar, Straus & Giroux.
Boakye, Kwaku Adutwum. 2010. "Studying Tourists' Suitability as Crime Targets." *Annals of Tourism Research* 37, no. 3: 727–743.
Bollnow, Otto Friedrich. 2011. *Human Space*. London: Hyphen.
Bond, Henry. 2009. *Lacan at the Scene*. Cambridge, MA: MIT Press.
Botterill, David, and Trevor Jones, eds. 2010. *Tourism and Crime: Key Themes*. Oxford: Goodfellow Publishers.
Bowman, Michael S., and Phaedra C. Pezzullo. 2009. "What's So 'Dark'about 'Dark Tourism'?: Death, Tours, and Performance." *Tourist Studies* 9, no. 3: 187–202.
Braden, Susan R. 2018. *The Architecture of Leisure: The Florida Resort Hotels of Henry Flagler and Henry Plant*. Gainesville, FL: Library Press.
Bronitt, Simon and Bernadette McSherry. 2017. *Principles of Criminal Law*. Pyrmont: Thomson Reuters.
Brown, Michelle. 2014. "Visual Criminology and Carceral Studies: Counter-Images in the Carceral Age." *Theoretical Criminology* 18(2): 176–197.
Brown, Michelle, and Eamonn Carrabine, eds. 2017. *Routledge International Handbook of Visual Criminology*. London: Taylor & Francis.
Brunt, Paul, Rob Mawby, and Zoe Hambly. 2000. "Tourist Victimisation and the Fear of Crime on Holiday." *Tourism Management* 21, no. 4: 417–424.
Calle, Sophie. 1999. *Double Game*. London, Violette Editions.
Callery, Dymphna. 2015. *Through the Body: A Practical Guide to Physical Theatre*. London: Routledge.
Carrabine, Eamonn. 2012. "Just Images: Aesthetics, Ethics and Visual Criminology." *British Journal of Criminology* 52(3): 463–489.
Cohen, Erik. 2019. "Robbed: A Serial Autoethnography of a Tourism Researcher as a Robbery Victim." *Tourism Recreation Research* 1–9.
Comaroff, Joshua, and Ker-Shing Ong. 2013. *Horror in Architecture*. Novato: ORO Editions.
De Certeau, Michel, Giard, Luce and Pierre Mayol. 1998. *The Practice of Everyday Life: Living and Cooking. Volume 2*. Minneapolis: University of Minnesota Press.
Derrida, Jacques. 2000. "Hospitality." *Angelaki: Journal of Theoretical Humanities*5(3): 3–18.
———. 2012. *Specters of Marx: The State of the Debt, The Work of Mourning and the New International*. New York: Routledge.

Dum, Christopher P. 2016. *Exiled in America: Life on the Margins in a Residential Motel*. New York: Columbia University Press.
Elliott, Misty. 2007. *An Evaluation of Specialized Police Response Teams on Motel Crime*. Reno: University of Nevada.
Eschner, Kat. 2016. The World's First Motel Was a Luxury Establishment, Not a Dive. *Smithsonian*, December 12. www.smithsonianmag.com
Ferrell, Jeff. 1999. "Cultural Criminology." *Annual Review of Sociology* 25, no. 1: 395–418.
———. 2012. "Anarchy, Geography and Drift." *Antipode* 44, no. 5: 1687–1704.
———. 2015. "Ghost Ethnography: On Crimes Against Reality and Their Excavation." *Crimes Against Reality Common Session*, University of Hamburg, Germany. https://lecture2go.
———. 2016. "Postscript: Under the Slab." *Liquid Criminology: Doing Imaginative Criminological Research*. London: Routledge, 221–229.
———. 2018. *Drift: Illicit Mobility and Uncertain Knowledge*. Berkeley: University of California Press.
Fiddler, Michael. 2018. "Ghosts of Other Stories: A Synthesis of Hauntology, Crime and Space." *Crime, Media, Culture*. doi: 1741659018788399.
Fisher, Mark. 2012. "What Is Hauntology?." *FILM QUART* 66, no. 1: 16–24.
Foucault, Michel. 1997. Of Other Spaces: Utopias and Heterotopias. In N. Leach (Ed.), *Rethinking Architecture: A Reader in Cultural Theory*, pp. 350–356. London: Routledge.
Frearson, Amy. 2012. "Gue(ho)st House by Berdaguer & Péjus." *de zeen*. October 1. www.dezeen.com
Freud, Sigmund. 1964. Trans. James Ed Strachey. "The Uncanny." In *The Standard Edition of the Complete Psychological Works of Sigmund Freud*. London: Hogarth Press and the Institute of Psychoanalysis.
Friedman, Alice T. 2003. "The Architecture of Leisure: The Resort Hotels of Henry Flagler and Henry Plant by Susan R. Braden." *Journal of the Society of Architectural Historians* 62, 4 (December): 526–528.
Gabor, Georgina Oana. 2019. "The Autoethnographic Undertaking: A Day in Ron Pelias' Life." *Qualitative Inquiry*. doi: 1077800419868501.
Garrett, Bradley L. 2013. *Explore Everything: Place-Hacking the City*. London: Verso Trade.
Gibson, Ross. 2002. *Seven Versions of an Australian Badland*. Brisbane: University of Queensland Press.
Gordon, Avery F. 2008. *Ghostly Matters: Haunting and the Sociological Imagination*. Minneapolis: University of Minnesota Press.
Gorter, Anna, Esperanza Miranda, George Davey Smith, Pascual Ortells, and Nicola Low. 1993. "How Many People Actually Use Condoms? An Investigation of Motel Clients in Managua." *Social Science & Medicine* 36, no. 12: 1645–1647.

Gould, Stephen Jay. 2000. "The Substantial Ghost: Towards a General Exegesis of Duchamp's Artful Wordplays." *Tout-fait. The Marcel Duchamp Studies Online Journal* 1, 2 (May). www.toutfait.com
Graburn, Nelson H. H. 1983. "The Anthropology of Tourism." *Annals of Tourism Research* 10, no. 1: 9–33.
Greenberg, Clement. 1991. "Four Photographers: A Reprinted Review (1964)." *History of Photography* 15, no. 2: 131–132.
Hayward, Keith J. 2012. "Five Spaces of Cultural Criminology." *British Journal of Criminology* 52, no. 3: 441–462.
Hernández, Lopéz. 2018. "Tourism and Fear of Crime-Violence. The Case of the Historical City of Guanajuato, México." *Estudios y Perspectivas en Turismo* 27, no. 4: 805–830.
Hjorth, Larissa. 2010. "Photoshifting: Art Practice, Camera Phones and Social Media." *Photofile* 89: 32–37.
Houck, Max M., ed. 2001. *Mute Witnesses: Trace Evidence Analysis*. Cambridge, MA: Academic Press.
Hua, Nan, and Yang Yang. 2017. "Systematic Effects of Crime on Hotel Operating Performance." *Tourism Management* 60: 257–269.
Hubert, Henri and Marcel Mauss. 1964[1898]. *Sacrifice: Its Nature and Functions*, trans. W. D. Halls. Chicago: University of Chicago Press.
Hulme, The Honourable Justice RA, 2013. Local Court of NSW Annual Conference 2013: Criminal Law Update. A Year of Legislative Activity and Appellate Decisions Concerning the Criminal Law Relevant to the Local Court. www.supremecourt.justice.nsw.gov.au
Jones, Peter, and Karen Groenenboom. 2002. "Crime in London hotels." *Tourism and Hospitality Research* 4, no. 1: 21–35.
Kindynis, Theo. 2016. "Urban Exploration: From Subterranea to Spectacle." *British Journal of Criminology* 57, no. 4: 982–1001.
———. 2019. "Excavating Ghosts: Urban Exploration as Graffiti Archaeology." *Crime, Media, Culture* 15, 1: 25–45.
Kindynis, Theo, and Bradley L. Garrett. 2015. "Entering the Maze: Space, Time and Exclusion in an Abandoned Northern Ireland Prison." *Crime, Media, Culture* 11, 1: 5–20.
Kociejowski, M. 2014. *The Pebble Chance: Feuilletons & Other Prose*. Windsor: Biblioasis.
Koestenbaum, Wayne. 2007. *Hotel Theory: 8 Dossiers; Hotel Women: 18 Chapters*. New York: Soft Skull Press.
Kracauer, Siegfried. 1995. *The Mass Ornament*, trans. Thomas Levin. Cambridge, MA: Harvard University Press.
Laurel, Brenda. 2016. "What Is Virtual Reality?" *Medium*, June 15. https://medium.com
Lee, Anthony W., and Richard Meyer. 2008. *Weegee and Naked City*. Vol. 3. Berkeley: University of California Press.

Lennon, J. John, and Malcolm Foley. 2000. *Dark Tourism*. Andover: Cengage Learning EMEA.

Linnemann, Travis. 2015. "Capote's Ghosts: Violence, Media and the Spectre of Suspicion." *British Journal of Criminology* 55, no. 3: 514–533.

Little, Janine. 2018. "'Not Available on the Evidence': Australian Narratives of Violence Against Women in Legal and Media Texts." *Ethical Space: The International Journal of Communication Ethics*, 1–25.

Luckhurst, Roger. 2002. "The Contemporary London Gothic and the Limits of the 'Spectral Turn.'" *Textual Practice* 16, no. 3: 527–546.

Mansfeld, Yoel, and Abraham Pizam, eds. 2006. *Tourism, Security and Safety: From Theory to Practice*. Oxford: Elsevier Butterworth-Heinemann.

Mawby, Rob. 2000. "Tourists' Perceptions of Security: The Risk–Fear Paradox." *Tourism Economics* 6, no. 2: 109–121.

Mawby, Rob, Kwaku Boakye, and Carol Jones. 2015. "Policing Tourism: The Emergence of Specialist Units." *Policing and Society* 25, no. 4: 378–392.

McKay, Carolyn. 2013. "Covert: The Artist as Voyeur." *Surveillance & Society* 11, 3: 334–353. www.surveillance-and-society.org

Merleau-Ponty, Maurice. 1962. *Phenomenology of Perception*. London: Routledge, 182.

———. 1968. *The Visible and the Invisible: Followed by Working Notes*. Evanston, IL: Northwestern University Press.

Morris, Meaghan. 1988. "At Henry Parkes Motel." *Cultural Studies* 2, no. 1: 1–47.

Myers, Rosie. 2007. "Cruise Industry Regulation: What Happens on Vacation Stays on Vacation." *Australian and New Zealand Maritime Law Journal* 21: 106.

Neumann, Mark. 1996. "Collecting Ourselves at the End of the Century." *Composing Ethnography: Alternative Forms of Qualitative Writing* 1: 172–198.

Ozascilar, Mine, Rob I. Mawby, and N. Ziyalar. 2019. "Perceptions of Risk on Vacation Among Visitors to Istanbul." *Safer Communities* 18, no. 1: 16–29.

Pallasmaa, Juhani. 2012. *The Eyes of the Skin: Architecture and the Senses*. Chichester: John Wiley & Sons.

Palmer, Daniel. 2012. "iPhone Photography: Mediating Visions of Social Space." In *Studying Mobile Media: Cultural Technologies, Mobile Communication, and the iPhone*, edited by Larissa Hjorth, Jean Burgess, and Ingrid Richardson. New York: Taylor and Francis, 85–97.

Pascale, Marius A. 2018. "Morality and Morbidity: Semantics and the Moral Status of Macabre Fascination." *Journal of Value Inquiry*, 1–27.

Pile, Steve. 2005. *Real Cities: Modernity, Space and the Phantasmagorias of City Life*. London: Sage.

Pritchard, Annette, and Nigel Morgan. 2006. "Hotel Babylon? Exploring Hotels as Liminal Sites of Transition and Transgression." *Tourism Management* 27, 5: 762–772.

Richon, Olivier. 2003. "Thinking Things." In Ute Eskildsen, ed., *Real Allegories*. Göttingen: Steidl.

Ross, Tim. 2019. *Motel: Images of Australia on Holidays*. Hunters Hill: Modernister Books.
Rugoff, Ralph, Anthony Vidler, and Peter Wollen. 1997. *Scene of the Crime*. Cambridge, MA: MIT Press.
Salzani, Carlo. 2007. "The City as Crime Scene: Walter Benjamin and the Traces of the Detective." *New German Critique* 100: 165–187.
Sandoval-Strausz, Andrew K. 2007a. *Hotel: An American History*. New Haven, CT: Yale University Press.
———. 2007b. "Homes for a World of Strangers: Hospitality and the Origins of Multiple Dwellings in Urban America." *Journal of Urban History* 33, 6: 933–964.
Sante, Luc. 2006. *Evidence: NYPD Crime Scene Photographs: 1914–1918*. New York: Barnes & Noble.
Schwenger, Peter. 2006. *The Tears of Things: Melancholy and Physical Objects*. Minneapolis: University of Minnesota Press.
Scott Bray, Rebecca. 2014. "Rotten Prettiness? The Forensic Aesthetic and Crime as Art." *Australian Feminist Law Journal* 40, no. 1: 69–95.
Sebald, Winfried Georg. 2000. *Vertigo* 12, 3. New York: New Directions Publishing.
Sharpley, Richard, and Philip R. Stone, eds. 2009. *The Darker Side of Travel: The Theory and Practice of Dark Tourism*. Bristol: Channel View Publications.
Spry, Tami. 2011. "Performative Autoethnography: Critical Embodiments and Possibilities." In N. Denzin and Y. Lincoln (Eds.), *The Sage Handbook of Qualitative Research*, 4: 497–512.
Stone, Philip. 2009. "Dark Tourism and New Moral Spaces." In R. Sharpley and P. Stone (Eds.), *The Darker Side of Travel: The Theory and Practice of Dark Tourism*, 56–72. Bristol: Channel View Publications.
Tennant, M. 2018. *Prison History and the Ethics of Public Engagement*. Presented at Difficult Heritage Conference, April 13, York.
Topham, Gwyn. 2006. *Overboard: The Stories Cruise Lines Don't Want Told*. Sydney: Random House.
Treadwell, Sarah. 2005. "The Motel: An Image of Elsewhere." *Space and Culture* 8, no. 2: 214–224.
Trigg, Dylan. 2006. *The Aesthetics of Decay: Nothingness, Nostalgia, and the Absence of Reason*, Vol. 37. New York: Peter Lang.
———. 2012. *The Memory of Place: A Phenomenology of the Uncanny*. Athens: Ohio University Press.
Tumarkin, Maria. 2015. "Traumascapes Revisited." *Artlink* 35.1: 32–37.
Tyner, James A. 2014. "Violent Erasures and Erasing Violence: Contesting Cambodia's Landscapes of Violence." In *Space and the Memories of Violence*, pp. 21–33. London: Palgrave Macmillan.
Virgil, *The Aeneid*. 29–19 BC. 1961. Translated by C. Day Lewis. London: Hogarth.
Walmsley, D. James, Rudiger M. Boskovic, and John J. Pigram. 1983. "Tourism and Crime: An Australian Perspective." *Journal of Leisure Research* 15, no. 2: 136–155.
Walsh, Joanna. 2015. *Hotel*. London: Bloomsbury.

Wollen, P. 1997. "Vectors of Melancholy." In Ralph Rugoff et al., *Scene of the Crime*. Cambridge, MA: MIT Press.

Xu, Yu-Hua, Kim, Jin-won, and Lori Pennington-Gray. 2017. "Explore the Spatial Relationship Between Airbnb Rental and Crime." Travel and Tourism Research Association: Advancing Tourism Research Globally. https://scholarworks.umass.edu/

Young, Alison. 2010. *The Scene of Violence: Cinema, Crime, Affect*. Oxfordshire, UK: Routledge-Cavendish.

12

Excavating Ghosts

Urban Exploration as Graffiti Archaeology

THEO KINDYNIS

Yes! It's only a couple of names . . . but it's also memories, a story of identity, distant screams for recognition frozen in time then fleetingly glanced before they are "finally" consigned to history. Shit like this isn't everyone's cup of tea but for those of us that give a fuck this is our archaeology. This is OUR fucking history. (Drax WD 2014)

We skulk down a side street, out of view of the evening traffic and swivelling CCTV cameras; quickly wriggling into scratchy orange hi-vis vests and donning hard hats. It is a deceptively simple disguise: the anonymous uniform of construction and maintenance workers confers an aura of plausibility that allows the wearer to transgress spatial boundaries unquestioned. I pull on a pair of work gloves, snapping their elasticated cuffs against my wrists as we saunter back across the main road. After a quick glance up and down the street—(no police, or, for that matter, actual workmen, who might call our bluff)—I heave open a hatch in the middle of the pavement as passers-by gaze oblivious into their smartphones. Once Andy is at the bottom of the ladder, I pass our rucksacks down, before squeezing into the manhole. Hunching my shoulders, I slowly lower the hatch over my head, pulling it shut with a resounding CL-UNKKK that reverberates through the darkness.
    The air is thick with a sour mouldy smell. I turn on my headtorch with a click and the darkness yields a volume. Our torch beams sweep through a haze of dust that hangs suspended in the air. We are stood on a grilled metal gantry platform at the top of a twenty-or-so-metre-deep circular shaft that plunges downward beneath our feet. Silently, we descend into the void. Layers of crust crunch and break away from the rungs of the access ladders as I grab at them. At the bottom of the shaft water pools on the floor, reflecting our torch lights and the dirty yellow ember of a burnt

out fluorescent strip light in the distance—somehow still electrified. We catch our breath and begin to take in our surroundings as the adrenaline subsides. At our feet: dead leaves, crumbled polystyrene cups, empty crisp packets and a discarded copy of the *London Evening Standard*. A white tiled corridor—the walls covered in decades of grime—snakes off in front of us, and the slow rumble of Underground trains—somewhere above or below—thunders through the tunnels.

We creep slowly forward. On one wall a tattered, faded poster depicts a beaming housewife, advertising a long-forgotten brand of soap. Andy's camera clicks and whirrs. A pale glow spills across the floor. Tentatively, I poke my head into an adjacent stretch of tunnel, illuminated at intervals by bulkhead lights. Glistening calcium stalactites hang suspended from rusting cast iron tunnel segments that stretch out into the distance. In a cross passage, streaks and bursts of spray-paint crisscross back and forth over the brickwork, blistered and worn, spelling out the names of those who once also stalked this sprawling subterranean labyrinth, but are now no longer here:

ZOMBY TOX03 FUME DDS
OZONE SHAM COSA BOSH
SUBONE SCARE89

I am struck by the realisation that this place is haunted by a secret past: one unwritten in the annals of history yet inscribed into its very materiality; silent assertions of absent presences—identities etched into place.

This chapter seeks to connect crime (vandalism), media (material inscriptions), and culture (subcultural history and geography). The chapter considers the criminological implications of discovering decades-old residual traces of graffiti—or "ghosts," in graffiti parlance—while exploring and documenting London's disused, forgotten, non-public, and otherwise off-limits spaces. The chapter proceeds in four parts. The first part reflects on three sources of methodological inspiration: unauthorized urban exploration and documentation; more-or-less formal archaeological studies of graffiti; and "ghost ethnography," an emergent methodological orientation that places an emphasis on *absence* and the interpretation of material and atmospheric traces. The second part of the chapter considers recent theoretical work associated with the "spectral turn." Here, *ghosts* and *haunting* provide useful conceptual metaphors for thinking about lingering material and atmospheric traces of the past. The third part of the chapter offers some methodological caveats and reflections. The fourth and final part of the chapter brings together theory and method, and asks: What significance can be drawn from unauthorized encounters with graffiti "ghosts"?

An Exploratory Method: Three Sources of Inspiration
Urban Exploration: "Lost Ecologies"

During the past four years, I have conducted extensive ethnographic research into London's graffiti subculture, as well as in-depth semi-structured interviews with some of the city's most prolific graffiti vandals from past and present (Kindynis 2017a). Although this research certainly informs the approach taken here, the present chapter is based primarily on my own ongoing research into, and exploration and documentation of, London's abandoned, disused, forgotten, non-public, and otherwise off-limits spaces (Kindynis 2017b). As such, the present chapter can be read as a kind of criminological by-product of several years of near-nightly excursions into these urban and infrastructural interstices.[1] I have discussed this research—along with its legal and ethical implications—in detail elsewhere (ibid.). Here, I want to connect this work with an ethnographic excavation of the material traces of graffiti found in these sites, via a discussion of method and a theoretical engagement with the spectral.

Many of the places with which the present chapter is concerned can be thought of as architectural glitches where, as the city is continually retrofitted, renovated, and reconfigured, the stacked superimposition of successive (infra)structural elements traps the intervening spaces—holes (Deleuze and Guattari 1987) or bubbles (Sloterdijk 2011)—between the rigidly rectilinear planes of late capitalist urbanism. In urban planning terminology, they are "space left over after planning" (SLOAPs)—a kind of negative intervening space between the city's "official zones of use and occupation": with no commercial or residential value, they quickly become disused or ignored; retained only as service areas, with access preserved in anticipation of future maintenance work (Papastergiadis 2002: 48).[2]

Entombed behind façades of sterile stainless-steel cladding, bricked up or buried, these in-between spaces also function as time capsules: a kind of accidental, historic cache of material culture. They are, to use Jeff Ferrell's term, "lost ecologies": spatially and temporally interstitial urban "ruins" (2004: 258; 2015). While exploring these places, in addition to finding newspapers, posters, and other ephemera dating as far back as the 1950s, I have frequently encountered remaining tags and "throw-ups"[3] left by graffiti writers, some of which are recognizable as many years or even decades old. Within the graffiti-writing subculture, such traces—either unsuccessfully removed, or simply worn and weathered by the elements—are known as "ghosts." In these hidden spaces, sheltered from the elements and spared from "the buff" (graffiti removal by local authorities), these enduring traces of paint and ink reveal a counter-history to what are typically thought of as "non-places" (Augé 1995): anonymous, asocial, and utilitarian spaces of circulation, characterized by an ostensible absence of history, sociality, and identity. Moreover, since we can trace the genesis of subcultural graffiti in London back to the early 1980s,[4] I would argue that these early surviving residues are not insignificant contemporary subcultural-historical artifacts—all the more remarkable since only a relatively small amount of the graffiti produced during this period was ever documented (Drax 1993).

The research method employed herein can, accordingly, be positioned as a form of "urban exploration": the practice of researching, gaining access to, and documenting forbidden, forgotten, or otherwise off-limits places (Edensor 2005; Garrett 2013; Kindynis 2017b; Ninjalicious 2005). In recent years, an emergent global subculture has coalesced around this activity. Although the motivations behind urban exploration are, in general, multiple, diverse, and shifting (Kindynis 2017b), of particular relevance to the present chapter, it remains a practice "intensely interested in locating sites of haunted memory, seeking interaction with the ghosts of lives lived" (Garrett 2013: 30).

While the term "exploration" connotes voyages of discovery and remote scientific expeditions, the deployment of exploration as a research method within an urban context is not without precedent. Indeed, if we conceive of "urban exploration" more broadly as the "adoption of the practices and discourse of exploration in the context of cities" (Castree et al. 2013: 540; Pinder 2005), we might position the approach taken here within a methodological lineage spanning the investigations of nineteenth-century social reformers Henry Mayhew (1862) and William Booth (1890), the urban ethnographies of the Chicago School sociologists (Park et al. 1925), and the inner-city "expeditions" of the radical geographer Bill Bunge (1977).[5][6] Moreover, and as I have suggested elsewhere, criminologists would do well to exploit the potential of urban wandering, exploration, and infiltration—in their various forms—as immersive spatial research methods, capable of producing a Geertzian (1973) "thick description" of place (Kindynis and Garrett 2015).[7]

In addition to deploying urban exploration as a research method, the approach taken here draws on two further sources of methodological inspiration: more-or-less formal archaeological analyses of graffiti; and ghost ethnography—an emergent methodological orientation that foregrounds an attentiveness to absence and the interpretation of material and atmospheric traces. In the remainder of this section, I discuss each of these methodological influences in turn.

Archaeological Excavation

The second source of methodological influence for the present chapter is archaeological excavation: the study of human cultures through the exposure, recording, analysis, and interpretation of their material traces. Significantly, archaeologists have in recent years "begun to turn their attention away from symbols of authority and towards the daubed, painted and scratched writings of the disadvantaged, the excluded or the subversive in society" (Oliver and Neal 2010: 15). Accordingly, several more-or-less formal archaeological analyses of graffiti have been undertaken to date, with ancient (Baird and Taylor 2010), medieval religious (Champion 2015), military (Merrill and Hack 2013), and convict graffiti (Casella 2014) having all been shown to reveal a myriad of insights into past societies and their material culture.[8][9] Notably absent from this body of work, however, is any archaeological analysis of subcultural (i.e., tag-based) graffiti (Castleman 1982; Ferrell 1996; Macdonald 2001).[10]

Arguably of closest relevance to the present study is a chapter recording and interpreting graffiti by members of the notorious 1970s punk band, the Sex Pistols (Graves-Brown and Schofield 2011). Appearing in the usually conservative archaeological journal, *Antiquity*, the article's publication was met with widespread controversy (see, for example, Jones 2011). However, if we are willing to look beyond the pompous dismissal of "low" culture, and consider contemporary graffiti "more broadly as a marking practice—as a form of trace and a manner of performing one's presence and place in the world" that has been practiced for millennia (Frederick 2009: 213)—there seems little reason why we should not approach it with the same seriousness as that from thousands of years earlier (Graves-Brown and Schofield 2011).

As Graves-Brown and Schofield (2011: 1399) note, the interpretation and analysis of graffiti can reveal "feelings and relationships, personal and political," it can inform us of its social and spatial context and can present us with "a layering of time and of changing relationships over time." Perhaps most important, although some of this information might be gleaned from other (sub)cultural-historical documents—such as (auto) biographies, photographs, books, fanzines, films, and documentaries—graffiti's materiality offers something uniquely visceral, immediate, and affective (Graves-Brown and Schofield 2011). However, while graffiti is certainly amenable to more conventional archaeological analyses, here I want to advance a more processual and reflexive approach; an exploratory mode of inquiry as much to do with the search as with the find. With this in mind, a third source of inspiration can be drawn from an emergent methodological orientation: ghost ethnography.

Ghost Ethnography

Recent years have seen an increasing interest in ghosts and haunting as conceptual metaphors within the humanities and social sciences. This "spectral turn" (Luckhurst 2002) has thus far been a largely theoretical enterprise (and discussion is therefore reserved for the following section). However, in attempting to think through how we might find, research, and "listen" to social "ghosts"—the disjointed, uncanny, other, no-longer, or not-quite-there absent presences that "haunt" the margins of everyday life—at least two commentators have proposed an attendant methodological orientation or sensibility. First, the cultural anthropologist Justin Armstrong (2010) has reflected on the possibility of undertaking a "spectral" ethnography: the application of (auto)ethnographic methods in studying absence. Spectral ethnography constitutes "an anthropology of people, and places and things that have been removed . . . or abandoned to the flows of time and space'" (Armstrong 2010: 243). Armstrong's approach is one that shares archaeology's concern with excavating the material traces of human culture, but that also, crucially, cultivates an awareness of the affective and atmospheric "resonances" left behind in places now abandoned, isolated, or forgotten: "the spectral presences of people" no longer there (245, 246).

Of particular relevance to this chapter, spectral ethnography is concerned with those unseen, abandoned, isolated, disused, transient, peripheral, or "hollowed-out" spaces that are frequently thought of as "non-places" (Armstrong 2010; Augé 1995). This method of inquiry asks:

> What significance can be drawn from the multiple layers of time and materiality that have accumulated in these places and what type of haunted narratives can emerge from the discarded remnants of human occupation? How can ethnography excavate the lives-once-lived from the space of abandonment? (Armstrong 2010: 243)

In order to answer these questions, Armstrong advocates a highly subjective, reflective, imaginative (even speculative) form of (auto)ethnography that "allow[s] these spaces and their associated material cultures to speak for themselves . . . through the lens of the ethnographer's positionality" (2010: 246). The resulting "reading" is inevitably highly interpretative and impressionistic.

Taking influence from Armstrong, the cultural criminologist Jeff Ferrell has recently discussed the possibility of engaging the social and cultural "spectres" or "apparitions" that *haunt* the margins of everyday life, through what he terms "ghost ethnography" (2015, 2016). Ferrell connects the conceptual metaphors of ghosts and haunting (discussed below) with the notion of "social death": a term used to describe the condition of marginalized groups who are denied a social or political identity, or who are perceived as less-than-fully human (see, for example, Cacho 2012; Patterson 1985). These groups—among which Ferrell counts refugees, the homeless, struggling addicts, and registered sex offenders—must "learn to live as ghosts, as apparitions, as spectres: on the edge of social life, but never quite visible within it" (Ferrell 2015).

Whereas much sociological and criminological research necessitates careful observation of the often ephemeral or barely perceptible details *present* in social life, studying such social, cultural, and spatial ghosts requires, Ferrell suggests, an ability to "excavate absence" in order to be "able to see who is not there" and "who is no longer there" (Ferrell, 2015). Ghost ethnography thus "invoke[s] the criminological imagination" to look "beyond the present instant" in order "to search for what is now gone or never was" (Ferrell 2016: 227). In "trac[ing] the ghosts of exclusion, the women or immigrants or homeless folks never allowed in," in "record[ing] those . . . who have drifted away and those arrangements that have been lost to historical change," and in "accounting for the ghostly presence of these losses that lingers in our lives," ghost ethnography also engages a "politics of absence" (ibid.). Of particular relevance to the present discussion, ghost ethnography also engages the city's abandoned, interstitial, and in-between spaces or "ruins." Thus, it is also a form of what we might call "*interstitial ethnography*": one that "promotes a sensitivity to spaces that exist in between and around the edges" (ibid.; emphasis in original). Such an approach asks: "In any city, what constitutes the ruins of that city? And where, among those ruins, would we hope to find the ghosts of urban life?" (Ferrell 2015).

One foreseeable criticism of a proposed "ghost ethnography" is that ethnography *proper* entails communicating with, and gathering data from, (living!) human subjects—through observation, interviews, and so on. To what extent can ghost ethnography really be considered an ethnographic method, if ethnography, at least as it has conventionally been practiced, has fundamentally to do with studying *ways of living*—or is the term simply a misnomer? I consider some of the inherent epistemological challenges presented by an ethnography of *absence* in the final part of the chapter. At this juncture, however, I want to suggest that the "ethnography" in ghost ethnography might denote an assumed *sensibility* over and above any prescribed set of methodological practices (e.g., participant observation; see Schatz 2009). Accordingly, ghost ethnography denotes an exploratory, situated, immersive, reflective, impressionistic, and imaginative approach to the study of space and place: an ethnographic "*way of seeing*" the material traces and affective residues of social worlds (Wolcott 2008).

Within criminology, such an approach might draw on cultural criminology's experimental use of new forms of scholarship—such as narrative, vignettes, "true fiction," photography, and documentary filmmaking (Ferrell et al. 2008). However, this approach can of course be supplemented with more traditional qualitative methods. Indeed, Armstrong suggests that this "holistic and reflexive exercise in cultural analysis" can complement, or be complemented by, "more established approaches to ethnographic fieldwork, such as face-to-face interviewing and participant observation" (Armstrong 2010: 246).

Ghosts in the City

Alongside the methodological approaches proposed by Armstrong and Ferrell, in recent years there has been an increasing interest in ghosts as a conceptual metaphor—a *theoretical motif*—within the humanities and social sciences (Pilar Blanco and Peeren 2013).[11] The origins of this "spectral turn" (Luckhurst 2002) are often traced to the publication of Jacques Derrida's *Spectres de Marx* in 1993 (and its English translation, *Spectres of Marx*, the following year; see Derrida 1994). However, a pertinent and seemingly overlooked earlier use of this theoretical trope can be found in a 1998 essay, entitled "Ghosts in the city," by the French cultural theorist Michel De Certeau. In this essay, De Certeau addresses the contemporary redevelopment of Paris in language surprisingly evocative of the speculative "regeneration" of large areas of London today, describing the systematic "elimination" of urban places steeped in history in favor of a homogenous "city of glass" (De Certeau 1998: 133).[12]

For De Certeau, urban planners' conceptions of the city as a "tabula rasa" for urban renewal are "disrupted"—or rather, "*haunted*"—by "'resistances' from a stubborn past," the "ruins of an unknown, strange city": the ghosts of the "already there" (1998: 133; emphasis added). The material traces of the past—historical façades, derelict buildings, old cobblestone streets and, indeed, graffiti—articulate a kind of spatial "unconscious": an often indecipherable, opaque, and ambivalent antipode to the unambiguous functionalism of modernist planning (ibid.:

133–135, inter alia; see Hayward 2012). Scathing formal heritage practices, De Certeau (1998: 141), declares that such "gestures"—the minutiae and ephemera of everyday life—"are the true archives of the city." "They remake the urban landscape every day. They sculpt a thousand pasts that are perhaps no longer nameable," yet "structure no less [the] experience of the city" (141–142). It is interesting that, for De Certeau, these scattered fragments "are witness to a history that, unlike that of museums or books, no longer has a language . . . Their histories . . . are no longer 'pacified,' nor colonized by semantics," but rather are "wild, delinquent" (135). In drawing our attention to this ineffable, pre-linguistic quality of "haunting," De Certeau anticipates the emphasis later accounts would place on its *affective* and *atmospheric* qualities (see below). Perhaps most important, however, De Certeau suggests that it is the "opaque ambivalence" of these residual "oddities that makes the city liveable" (134).

We can read De Certeau's essay as an early approximation of what Derrida (1994) terms "hauntology." In its original formulation, this concept, or "puncept"—hauntology sounding very similar to ontology in Derrida's native French—refers to "the way in which nothing enjoys a purely positive existence. Everything that exists is possible only on the basis of a whole series of absences, which precede and surround it" (Derrida 1994; Fisher 2014: 17–18). Accordingly, hauntology replaces the priority of "being and presence with the figure of the ghost as that which is neither present nor absent, neither dead nor alive" (Davis 2005: 373). In recent years, several critical theorists—notably Mark Fisher (2012, 2014)—have broadened and developed Derrida's definition. Though hauntology, for Fisher, remains concerned with the dialectical interplay of absence/presence, it has to do primarily with a sense of *temporal dislocation* or "time out of joint." Haunting, for Fisher, "happens when a place is *stained by time*, or when a particular place becomes the site for *an encounter with broken time*" (Fisher 2012: 19, emphasis added). The kind of ineffable and ambiguous affective impressions, evoked by De Certeau, formed in encounters with residual material traces of the past ("ghosts") are clearly one such example of this. Indeed, Fisher is keen to point out that "hauntology concerns a crisis of space as well as time: (ibid.). Specifically, although the "erosion of spatiality" characteristic of capitalist globalization "has been amplified by the rise of what Marc Augé calls the 'non-place,'" haunting "can be seen as intrinsically resistant" to this "contraction and homogenization of time and space" (ibid.).

The cultural geographer Steve Pile (2005) has also evoked both the figure of the ghost and the notion of haunting, in arguing that we should take seriously the imaginary, fantastic, and emotional aspects of city life. "Haunting," for Pile, reveals "the significance of time and memory in the production of urban space. Haunting is closely associated with place": "ghosts" "haunt places, spaces or locations" (Pile 2005: 131). Interestingly, Pile anticipates Fisher's (2012: 19) suggestion that haunting has to do with "broken time." For Pile (2005: 131), "ghosts destabilise the flow of time of a place. They change a place's relationship to the passage of time." "Ghosts are figures that disrupt the linear procession of time that leads from the past, through the present, to the future" (Pile 2005: 139). Moreover, haunting, for Pile, is an encounter with "fractured and fragmented" time (148): a kind of temporal dissonance, where "suddenly, the past can make its presence felt" (137). Such encounters "bring to light the heterogeneity of temporalities in modern city life" (136) and reveal the simultaneous co-existence of "innumerable pasts" (143). These histories and memories are multiple, often irreconcilable, and contradictory: "Ghosts are not coherent. They do not have one story to tell, or have one relationship to the living" (162; see Kindynis and Garrett 2015). "The city is marked, then, by its multitude of ghosts; heterogeneous ghosts; a density of ghosts" (Pile 2005: 162). Furthermore, evoking Ferrell's discussion of ghost ethnography, Pile suggests that to be "alert . . . to the presence of ghosts" "requires a particular kind of seeing" (139).

It seems that at least part of what De Certeau, Fisher, and Pile are concerned with in their discussions of haunting is "the phenomenology of place," particularly how memory and materiality inform or inflect our lived experience of place (Bell 1997: 813). For Bell, ghosts "give a space social meaning and thereby make it a place" (820). Of particular interest, Bell alludes to the "kind of sacred electric *charge* about [a] place" precipitated by "the imagined presence of those who are not physically there" (822; emphasis added). In doing so, Bell evokes the *atmospheric* aspects of haunting. In everyday speech, the term "atmosphere" is used interchangeably with "mood," "feeling," "ambience," "tone," and other ways of naming collective affects, yet until relatively recently such phenomena have rarely been explicitly theorized

(Anderson 2009: 78). Such ineffable *auras*—a "strange tissue of space and time" (Benjamin 1991, quoted in Böhme,1993: 117)—are of patent relevance to criminology. Consider, for instance, the palpable "lull" in the moments before a riot breaks out: "that heavy atmospheric threat of something about to burst," the "strange tension in the air, a feeling of excitement and vague expectant fear" (Horowitz 2001: 89). Fear of crime is frequently attributed to an unpleasant and hostile atmosphere, yet the precise nature of this peculiar malaise is rarely, if ever, interrogated. My own research has also suggested that recreational trespassers and others engaged in "edgework" activities seek out the illicit atmospheres to be experienced in off-limits places (Kindynis 2017b; Lyng 1990, 2004). Intriguing work from outside criminology has shown how atmospheres are now actively engineered as a novel and insidious modality of social control (see, for example, Adey 2008; Bissell 2010). Yet criminologists have paid scant attention to the character or constitution of atmospheric effects.

Talking to Ghosts? Reflections on Method

Before continuing, I want to offer two brief reflections on method. The first has to do with the informal, impromptu nature of the research under discussion. As noted earlier, the graffiti "ghosts" that constitute the focus of the present chapter were inadvertently encountered during the course of (auto)ethnographic research into another subcultural practice: recreational trespass, or "urban exploration" (see Kindynis 2017b). As with former exploratory incursions (Kindynis and Garrett 2015), the idea that my encounters with these residual traces might comprise "data" for criminological research was, to be frank, an afterthought. Furthermore, the extent to which my own recreational trespassing can be said to constitute (auto)ethnographic "research" is itself something of an open question. My motivations for engaging in this practice are multiple and diverse but, I confess, personal enjoyment, architectural and historical geekery, thrill-seeking and one-upmanship all, frankly, eclipse any strictly academic interest in urban exploration. Accordingly, my own trespassing—and, it follows, the "method" for the present chapter—lies somewhere between autoethnography, embracing what Ferrell (1997) has termed "criminological *verstehen*"—the idea that in order to fully understand criminality, we have to immerse ourselves in the "criminal moment"—and a form of "post-methodological" criminology, "that has moved beyond method as a formal procedure and toward more fluid, holistic, and personal forms of inquiry" (Ferrell 2012: 227; 2009).

The reflections that follow thus derive from an opportunist, partial, fragmentary, and sketched early approximation of criminological ghost ethnography. Ethnography is, after all, an inevitably "fluid and idiosyncratic undertaking" (Ferrell 2009: 13). Future iterations of this methodological approach might well involve a more sustained, purposive, and formalized approach—perhaps experimenting with the transposition of visual ethnographic or audio documentary methods. However, as Ferrell (2009) notes, we should be wary of reifying the ethnographic method. As "all good ethnographers know," he writes:

> the field researcher's deep engagement with subjects and settings renders any preordained methodological prescriptions provisional at best. Ethnographic research techniques are in reality not deployed; they are negotiated . . . invented or reinvented on the spot and not infrequently discarded in the dangerous, ambiguous, interactive process of field research. (Ferrell 2009: 12–13; Ferrell and Hamm 1998)

Second, I want to reflect on the challenges inherent in "talking" to "ghosts" in the present context. Put another way, to what extent "is it possible to gain empirical knowledge of culture without the presence of its usual sources" (Armstrong 2010: 248)—perhaps first and foremost among which are living people? According to conventional, empiricist ethnographic approaches, many of the sites with which ghost ethnography is concerned are marked by a notable "*absence* of immediately apparent," observable, "and quantifiable ethnographic data" (ibid., emphasis added). Armstrong's response is that:

> Put simply, it is not empiricism that [ghost] ethnography seeks; rather, it moves toward an understanding of subjectivity and reflection in ethnographic practice and presents linkages [with] spatial, ideological, and material resonances in the abandoned and isolated spaces of cultural production. (2010: 248)

The task of ghost ethnography is thus to excavate the traces of past lives and cultures that have been inscribed into the materiality of place, and to allow these "ghost texts"—"haunted" spaces and objects—to speak for themselves (Armstrong 2010: 246). In light of this, prospective ghost ethnographers would do well to engage with recent methodological developments inspired by so-called non-representational theory (see, for example, Thrift 2008).[13] "Although complex," non-representational theory can essentially be understood as:

> an attempt to move beyond static geographic accounts of landscape in a bid to create an alternative approach that actively incorporates the experiential, affective, and inter-material aspects of space that rarely feature in traditional representational geography (or, for that matter, in most criminology). (Hayward 2012: 449)

Accordingly, the emergent methodological orientation of *non-representational ethnography* emphasizes the materiality, atmospheres, and backgrounds of everyday life, foregrounding the relationships between people, objects, and the built environment (Vannini 2015). Furthermore, traditional, empiricist, or "realist" ethnographic writing posits the representation of its research subject(s) as a more-or-less faithful rendition of the world based on observable data. Such approaches are inevitably problematic when trying to account for the precognitive, non-discursive, atmospheric, affective, and indeed spectral dimensions of everyday life. Non-representational ethnography, by contrast, does not attempt to report such experiences in an impersonal, neutral, or "reliable" manner (Vannini 2015: 318). Rather, although inspired by ethnographers' lived experiences in the field, non-representational ethnography is impressionistic and creative (Vannini 2015). Non-representational ethnographic styles "strive to animate rather than simply mimic, to rupture rather than merely account, to evoke rather than just report, and to reverberate instead of more modestly resonating" (ibid.: 318). Perhaps most important, non-representational research "advocates resolute experimentalism" (Dewsbury 2009: 321). And in much the same manner, I would like to suggest that prospective "ethnographers" of the spectral—whatever ethnography might come to mean in this context—experiment determinedly with new permutations of research settings, objects, methods, and writing styles.

Places Stained by Time

People want to inscribe marks and find traces in the city, like the stories they used to tell about the stars and constellations, in order to feel more at home in an indifferent universe. (Baker 2012: 280)

What significance, then, can be drawn from unauthorized encounters with residual traces of decades-old tags and "throw-ups" left by graffiti writers in London's hidden, disused, forgotten, off-limits, and interstitial spaces? At a fundamental level, these "ghosts" reveal how bygone illicit visitors saturated such sites with subcultural significance and mythopoeic meaning. As I have written elsewhere (Kindynis 2017a), tags are read by graffiti writers as physical extensions of their peers' individual or group personas, and thus have an inherent sociality. Moreover, for those familiar with the chirographic conventions of graffiti, the "flow" or "style" of a tag can denote all kinds of information about its author's subcultural credentials and competence (Kindynis 2017a; see below). It also follows that an accumulation of tags on a wall can indicate who's been where with who, and when. A wall with numerous tags and throw-ups on it provides graffiti writers with an:

> opportunity to tell stories about the exploits of their peers . . . to narrate a scenario; not only who was here, but who was here first, who has beef with whom, who's more talented, who's in from out of town . . . whose tags are getting better, and whose are getting worse. (Snyder 2009: 69)

Thus, a wall or door with "heavy layers of graffiti reveals a history to its viewers in the same way that the sedimentary layers of ancient ruins inspire archaeologists to tell tales of past civilizations" (Snyder 2009: 70). On occasion, while exploring these sites, a veritable *stratigraphy* of graffiti revealed itself:[14] a palimpsest of blistering and faded paintwork, crumbling brick and rusted iron revealing successive layers of

Figure 12.1. Graffiti stratigraphy: Layered tags spanning more than two decades, in a now-disused deep-level stabling sidings tunnel in the London Underground. Reproduced with permission. Credit: Luther Blissett.

subcultural history—a rich historical cache of accumulated material culture requiring interpretation (see figure 12.1). In several instances, I have been fortunate enough to have been accompanied by graffiti writers during such unauthorized expeditions. Upon uncovering some surviving tag or throw-up, these writers would often narrate second- or third-hand accounts, passed-down stories—oral histories, perhaps even subcultural myths—about their predecessors' escapades.[15] Sometimes, as a way of reaching back through history and connecting with their own subcultural ancestry—the desire to inscribe themselves into this venerated place becoming unbearable (Garrett 2013: 67)—they would add their own tag before we passed on: a kind of spray-painted séance. On other occasions, having inquired within the graffiti-writing community as to the provenance of some discovered ghost tags, I have been able to speak directly with the authors of such inscriptions. Photographs of surviving tags can evoke nostalgic memories, emotions, experiences, and sensations, and elicit anecdotes of bygone antics, loyalties, and rivalries. Viewed in this light, these spectral traces of paint and ink—often hidden from view, or otherwise barely perceptible or unintelligible to the untrained eye—reveal a hidden counter-history to what are typically thought of as "non-places" (Augé 1995) and challenge the assumption that these spaces are "ageless" or "static" (Oliver and Neal 2010: 20).

Related to the subcultural significance that can be read from graffiti are the more properly *hauntological* qualities of graffiti ghosts. Many of the old tags encountered while exploring disused, interstitial, and off-limits spaces are identifiable as such since they are followed by a year (for example, SCARE 89 or TOX 03). What is most striking, however, is that such inscriptions—even when they are not accompanied by a year—are immediately recognizable (to those familiar with the chirographic conventions of subcultural graffiti) as hailing from another era. This is because the "handstyle"—the spacing, skew, and calligraphic flare or "flow"—of these tags is noticeably consistent with that of earlier generations of the graffiti subculture in London (and, thus, an earlier stage in its stylistic evolution) (see figure 12.2).[16]

Additional clues can be deduced from other aspects of graffiti's physical form. The "skinny" appearance of some tags suggests that they were painted

Figure 12.2. "THE SUPREME TEEM"—1980s handstyles in a disused tunnel under central London. Reproduced with permission. Credit: Luther Blissett.

using "stock" caps—the standard-issue nozzles with which auto and radiator spray paints are sold—and thus perhaps pre-date the development of specialist graffiti paint and caps. Other media (such as glass etchant fluid) and tools (such as chisel-tipped permanent markers) have become more or less widely available and used over time and can thus provide further hints regarding the provenance of a given piece of graffiti. As one graffiti writer I spoke to remarked: "Even the paint has a history! You see certain colours and [think], 'Man, that's a Buntlack black' or 'That's a Japlac red,' 'That's a Smoothrite' or 'They stopped making that colour.'" Thus, particular colors or palettes can also connote certain periods in time.

For these reasons and more, the experience of happening upon surviving graffiti "ghosts"—an "encounter with broken time" (Fisher 2012: 19)—is often an arresting one. There is something jarringly *uncanny* about this experience, in the Freudian sense of the word: ghostly, "strangely familiar," out of place—or, rather, out of time.[17] While such inscriptions adhere to the familiar aesthetic logic of subcultural graffiti, their specific styles, colors, names, and so on appear somehow "out of joint." "It is like the eruption of dreams or unconscious thoughts into consciousness. As in dreams, the fixity of space and the linearity of time give way" (Pinder 2001: 11). Moreover, these fragments of broken time invite us to imagine an-other era—evoking an altogether different city: perhaps a kind of simulacratic nostalgia for the London of the 1970s, 1980s, and 1990s, experienced—imagined?—vicariously through popular (sub)cultural representations such as Bob Mazzer's analogue photographs of the London Underground, "jungle" drum and bass or early London graffiti videos such as *Steel Injection* (1994), *Londonz White Trash* (2001), and *London Tonight* (2010).

Discovering or excavating—*exhuming? exorcising?*—these ghosts also entails retracing the steps of those who left their marks, as well as inhabiting, however momentarily, the same spaces and places in which they left them. This process of discovery takes on an additional layer of significance for at least two reasons. First, if our aim is indeed to direct an ethnographic approach toward an analysis of space and place, in order that we might excavate hidden meaning from found material traces of human (sub)cultures, then we should substitute or supplement "deep hanging out" (Geertz 1998) with *deep loitering*. Ghost ethnography necessitates lingering: soaking up smells, soundscapes, textures and, indeed, atmospheres. In the present instance, this is important not least because the affective, emotional, visceral, and sensorial dimensions of graffiti writing are central to the experience of, and motivations for, engaging in the practice (see, for example, Halsey and Young 2006; Scannell 2002). Furthermore, it is through this kind of attentive engagement with the textures and atmospheres of urban space that one is made aware of the lingering "spectral traces"—the absent presences—of those "who were apparently" here "earlier but who have now moved on or are missing" (Pinder 2001: 9). In forgotten recesses, deep below the cacophony of the metropolis, we find traces of bygone others, "etched visually" into "the materiality of the place itself" (Turner and Peters 2015: 319). Here, a haunting tension between past and present, absence and present, makes itself felt.

In our relationship with conventional sites of historical and cultural importance, we often "rely on the voice of a guide, a narrator or an expert to mediate our relationship and to explain why the place is significant. Less often do we let places speak to us directly" (Garrett 2016: 81). The time-worn materiality of graffiti ghosts, by contrast, reveals a hidden history, sociality, and (sub)cultural significance to places in a uniquely immediate, visceral, and affective manner. Traditionally, graffiti "has been a very private and insular scene with very public"—albeit often esoteric, incomprehensible, and ephemeral—"output" (Payne 2005: 161). Graffiti's illegality, secrecy, rivalry, and egotism have ensured that historical accounts of the subculture have tended to consist of conflicting narratives, self-promotion, and misinformation as much as they have resembled "faithful" historical documents. Graffiti, accordingly, does not lend itself to a singular, authoritative, historical interpretation. Rather, in undertaking "unguided tours, without permission" or "formal elucidation" (73, 75), we encounter a multiplicity of "embedded"—literally, *inscribed*—"narratives" (Armstrong 2010: 245; see Kindynis and Garrett 2015). Foreknowledge plucked from internet forums and blogposts; the stories of friends who have been there before; subcultural folklore, myths, and rumors; and our own speculation and imagination "all contribute to the types of spectralities we might encounter" therein (Garrett 2016: 78). If the furtive exploration of such places can indeed be considered a kind of "rogue archaeology" (87), it is one that adopts an approach "that *listens, gathers* and *assembles* rather than coheres and orders," privileging the sensory, affective, and atmospheric (Dobraszczyk et al. 2015: S29; emphasis in original).

Second, the embodied experience of retracing the steps of early generations of London graffiti writers is also significant in and of itself. Graffiti writers traverse the city and its interstitial spaces in a transversal and capillary manner: slipping down back alleys, stalking through fire escape corridors and stairwells, descending ventilation shafts, squeezing through service ducts and prying open the city's cracks in order to reach the "spots" they choose to paint—such as the depots ("yards") and sidings ("layups") in which rolling stock is stabled overnight (see Ferrell and Weide 2010). Details of how to access such locations are passed down through successive generations of writers—a kind of illicit,[18] arcane, cumulative, embodied knowledge:

> It was about secrets, hiding spots . . . skeleton keys, folklore . . . How to get on to what line and where. How to get into certain yards. This knowledge could only be earned or passed on once respect had been gained by other (better) writers. (Payne 2005: 161)

Graffiti writing, then, comprises a set of esoteric "spatial practices" (Lefebvre 1991), including both the act of writing graffiti as well as these enduring routes and pathways, by means of which the subculture is reproduced. "Excavating" these "pathways" (Pinder 2001: 11)—or "get ons" as they are known in graffiti parlance—thus taps into a kind of kinaesthetic tradition. Accordingly, accessing and lingering in disused, non-public, hidden, and otherwise off-limits spaces can be thought of as a form of criminological *verstehen*: an "immersion in the situated logic and emotion that define criminal experience" otherwise unavailable to the researcher (Ferrell 1997: 3).

Conclusion: Toward a Ghost Criminology

As Jeff Ferrell (2015) has recently remarked, graffiti "is entirely almost a kind of ghostly activity":

> Aggressive urban surveillance, environmental design and broken windows policing . . . limit available locations for painting . . . graffiti, and

promote the legal destruction of existing work. All of this is of course backed up by the daily endeavours of countless anti-graffiti contractors and graffiti clean-up crews, who busily go about buffing . . . and painting over tags and throw-ups. The result is counter-intuitive but it would seem, indisputable: as pervasively visible as we take . . . graffiti to be, the vast majority executed over the past half century is now distinctly and decidedly invisible. The . . . graffiti that we see so widely today is but a small portion of that which has been lost or is currently hidden away, and in any case only the latest layer in an urban palimpsest of spray paint and whitewash. Graffiti . . . hide[s its] own history; [its] very visibility enacts [its] ongoing invisibility. (Ferrell 2017: 33)

Graffiti, for Ferrell, thus resembles a "ghost in the machinery of the contemporary city" (Ferrell 2017). A "spectral presence," graffiti is simultaneously "there and not there, made to appear and disappear 'while you were sleeping' . . . Coming and going as a series of urban apparitions" (ibid.). In this chapter, I hope to have shown that the spectral atmospheric resonances that "flow forth" (Böhme 1993: 117) or "seep" from (Turner and Peters 2015: 315) the material traces of graffiti endure long after their authors have departed. In this way, as Mark Fisher so evocatively put it, place becomes stained by time.

Beyond graffiti, how and why might criminology seek to engage with "ghosts" and "haunting"? We need not look far for suggestions. Travis Linnemann (2015) has recently invoked the spectral in his study of the murders that form the subject of Truman Capote's *In Cold Blood*. For Linnemann, violence, terror, and horror *haunt* both the social imaginary and specific locations, "animat[ing] social space with spectral power" (ibid., 517). In London's Whitechapel district, at the site of the concentration camp at Auschwitz, and the site of the former World Trade Center buildings, *ghosts*—atmospheric resonances, traces, or afterimages of "people, places and things"—"linger" in the collective conscience (ibid.). Moreover, evoking these kinds of sites, notions of haunting might also contribute to a *cultural victimology of place* (Walklate et al. 2011). Writing on so-called dark tourism at sites of imprisonment, murder, and genocide has already engaged with the spectral (Hughes 2008; Wilbert and Hansen 2009; Kindynis and Garrett 2015). However, work from within victimology also stands to benefit from the conceptual metaphors—*images to think with*—offered by notions of haunting and the spectral. Such motifs furnish us with the theoretical language necessary to explicate how memory and trauma become inscribed literally, symbolically, affectively, and atmospherically in space and place.

Keith Hayward, drawing on the work of the postmodern theorist Frederic Jameson, has argued that we "now inhabit a world of simultaneity" in which the past and future are flattened "into an incessant and uninterrupted present" (Hayward 2004: 64, 66; Jameson 1991). While Hayward is concerned with the (criminogenic) implications of this temporal collapse at the level of individual subjectivity, Simon Hallsworth has pointed toward the broader political ramifications of late capitalism's "culture of now." "To grow up in a neoliberal capitalist culture is to find yourself in an anomic space," Hallsworth (2013: 174) writes, "where historical memories and any connection to a past history of struggle have been utterly attenuated. It is to inhabit a present wholly disconnected from the past that determined it." It is this social and cultural amnesia that Franco Berardi (2011: 18) has described as "the slow cancellation of the future." One prospect is that a critical criminological engagement with *haunting*—the (re)connection of the past, through the present, with "lost futures"—could perhaps provide an antidote to this cultural dyschronia.

Perhaps most important, an attentiveness to spectral resonances—the ghostly atmospheric and material traces of the past—connects criminology's renewed interest in the lived experience of (urban) space with a visceral apprehension of (sub)cultural history, and an appreciation of the discontinuous, distorted, and multiple temporalities of the city. Many cities are currently undergoing an era of unprecedented change. The urban landscape is being dramatically reconfigured in ways that both reflect and perpetuate grotesque socioeconomic inequalities. In London, at the same time as vast swathes of urban space steeped in history are being lost to speculative "redevelopment," archaeological excavations undertaken during the construction of the Crossrail subway line have unearthed seventeenth-century plague pits, Roman roads, and Bronze Age artefacts—peeling back layers of time buried beneath the asphalt. Once the archaeologists have conducted their hurried surveys and withdrawn to the surface, tunnel boring machines chew and churn their way through the urban substrata, consigning countless other fragments of broken time to the spoil tip. Perhaps in decades or centuries to come, others will stalk these tunnels—future ruins of subterranean London—asking questions of discarded hi-vis vests, tags dated "2020," the scrawlings of bored track workers preserved in the dust and the detritus of a capitalist metropolis. In the meantime, more quotidian encounters with the past can be sought throughout the city—above and below. Scattered fragments of the past—residual anomalies—haunt the homogenous "city of glass" in spite of planners' desires for an urban "tabula rasa" (De Certeau 1998: 133).

NOTES

1 The present work may, accordingly, be read as an instance of what Ferrell has termed *interstitial ethnography*: a methodological orientation that "promotes a sensitivity to spaces that exist in between and around the edges; it suggests a way of seeing the world glancingly, out of the corner of one's eye, with an awareness that the most important action may take place out of frame and out of focus" (Ferrell 2016: 227).

2 These types of spaces have been conceptualized as "parafunctional" (Hayward 2012; Papastergiadis 2002). Often perceived as "abandoned, empty or derelict," parafunctional spaces are "blind spots in the urban landscape"; they exist in the "white space" on the map (48). However, such spaces "never remain purely empty": rather, they are the site of "counter-narrative[s] for urban life" (48, 45).

3 Whereas tags are broadly analogous to a signature, throw-ups consist of quickly executed one- or two-color bubble- or block-letter words.

4 See, for example, Ashford (2013: 150–151, inter alia). That subcultural graffiti in London originated during this period is also widely corroborated by interviewees: "London graf goes back to about '81, '82 . . . Graffiti had obviously kicked off in New York in the '70s and cousins and family friends and that would send letters back to London, or Londoners would go out there to see family and they'd see this stuff [and so] it started to spread very slowly [to the UK]."

5 For critiques of the problematic imperial, colonial, and exclusionary discourses and visual regimes that span this methodological lineage, see Pinder (2005) and Mott and Roberts (2014a). The normative, privileged, and exclusionary facets of urban exploration in particular can, should, and have been acknowledged and challenged (see Bennett 2011; Garrett and Hawkins 2014; High and Lewis 2007; Kindynis 2017b; Mott and Roberts 2014b).

6 See also Walter Benjamin on the "art of straying" and his own "fantasies" of the Paris Metro's "maze . . . of tunnels . . . opening their hundreds of shafts all over the city" (Benjamin 1979[1932]: 298–299).

7 The direction of an ethnographic approach toward the analysis of space and place is not without precedent (see, for example, Aoki and Yoshimizu 2015; Corsín Jiménez 2003; Mayne and Lawrence 1999; Pink 2008).

8   In 2014, "graffiti archaeology" also earned an entry in the *Encyclopedia of Global Archaeology* (Ralph 2014).
9   In Cesare Lombroso's early study of prison graffiti (1888), the criminal anthropologist positions himself "as a kind of archaeologist," comparing "his study of the 'prison palimpsests' to those of antiquity and prehistory, his own project the assembly of a 'codex' of these inscriptions of foreignness" (Spector 2016: 33–34).
10 Although see Merrill (2015) for a discussion of subcultural graffiti as heritage.
11 Readers are directed to the edited collection by Pilar Blanco and Peeren (2013), as well as to the special issue of *Cultural Geographies* 2008, 15(3) on "spectro-geographies."
12 It is interesting that, in a temporal reversal of De Certeau's hauntology, the growing number of "buy-to-leave" residential properties now being built in global cities such as London—bought as assets by wealthy foreign investors, and "intentionally and permanently left unoccupied until they appreciate and are sold at some later date" (Norwood 2016)—threatens to turn large swathes of these cities into "ghost-towns of the super-rich" (Herrmann 2014).
13 As Campbell (2012: 401) has noted, NRT has a "considerable resonance" with a cultural criminological approach that "emphasizes the subjective, affective, embodied, aesthetic, material, performative, textual, symbolic, and visual relations of space."
14 Stratigraphy in archaeology refers to the layered accumulation of material culture over time.
15 Such narratives (as well as first-hand accounts) can be found in abundance on the kind of digitally driven, informal archives of graffiti history that have proliferated in recent years on photo-sharing websites such as Flickr (Cianci and Schutt 2014; Schutt 2017). Readers are encouraged to peruse, for example, the groups Old School London Graffiti (www.flickr.com/groups/oldschoollondongraffiti/pool/) and British Train Graffiti 85–93 (www.flickr.com/groups/britishtraingraffiti85-93/pool/). These online images, like their counterparts in physical space, slowly erode and fade according to a process of digital degradation, whereby each time a JPEG is compressed, "something of the original image is lost, and the anomalies and imperfections hiding beneath" the surface "are slowly revealed" (Meier 2013).
16 "Style" is governed by an esoteric and unspoken set of principles, foremost among which, and "hardest to understand," is the "mystical quality" known as "flow" (Siege 52, 2009: 68). "It seems straightforward in concept—it's how the piece flows, rolls, travels from left to right. But there's a practiced science to it, one that every writer who cares about style has studied . . . It's how [the letters] overlap and touch, how a letter holds itself up against the one next to it . . . the shapes of the spaces in between the letters, are as important as the letters themselves" (Siege 52, 2009: 68).
17 The uncanny, "uncannily enough," writes Fiddler (2007: 196), "is a slippery concept," one difficult to pin down. As described by Freud in his essay, "Das Unheimlich," the uncanny refers more to a constellation of ideas than a strict theory

as such (Fiddler 2007). Nevertheless, central themes in Freud's writing on the uncanny are the ghostly, the "strangely familiar," and that which seems out of place, or out of time. Moreover, the uncanny is that which is normally "concealed and kept out of sight" (Freud 1919: 224–225). Of particular significance to the present discussion, the notion of the uncanny has attracted interest in both architectural theory and urban studies (see, for example, Vidler 1992, and the edited collection by Huskinson 2016a). Huskinson (2016b: 1) suggests that the city can be described as uncanny "when it reveals itself in a new and unexpected light . . . its familiar streets and buildings suddenly appear strange"—evoking De Certeau's (1998: 133) notion of an urban "unconscious," articulated by 'resistances' from a stubborn past."

18 Foucault referred to such insights of deviant, criminal, and outsider groups as "subjugated," "disqualified," or "insurrectionary knowledges" (Foucault 2003: 7–8). De Certeau's notion of "tactics" is also instructive in conceiving of illicit spatial practices. De Certeau uses the term to designate those "innumerable practices by means of which users reappropriate space" (De Certeau 1984: xiv). A tactic is "determined by the absence of a proper locus . . . it must play on and with a terrain imposed on it and organized by the law of a foreign power . . . it is a maneuver within enemy territory" (De Certeau, 1984: 37).

REFERENCES

Adey, P. 2008. "Airports, mobility and the calculative architecture of affective control." *Geoforum* 39(1): 438–451.

Anderson, B. 2009. "Affective atmospheres." *Emotion, Space and Society* 2(2): 77–81.

Aoki, J. and Yoshimizu, A. 2015. "Walking histories un/making places: Walking tours as ethnography of place." *Space and Culture* 18(3): 273–284.

Armstrong, J. 2010. "On the possibility of a spectral ethnography." *Cultural Studies ↔ Critical Methodologies* 10(3): 243–250.

Ashford, D. 2013. *London Underground: A Cultural Geography*. Liverpool: Liverpool University Press.

Augé, M. 1995. *Non-Places: Introduction to an Anthropology of Supermodernity*. London: Verso.

Baird, J. A. and Taylor, C. (eds). 2010. *Ancient Graffiti in Context*. London: Routledge.

Baker, P. 2012. "Secret city: Psychogeography and the end of London." In *London from Punk to Blair*, edited by J. Kerr and A. Gibson, 277–291, 2nd ed. London: Reaktion.

Bell, M. M. 1997. "The ghosts of place." *Theory and Society* 26(6): 813–836.

Benjamin, W. 1979 [1932]. "A Berlin chronicle." In *One Way Street and Other Writings*, edited by W. Benjamin and translated by E. Jephcott and K. Shorter, 293–346. London: NLB.

———. 1991. *Gesammelte Schriften*. Frankfurt: Suhrkamp.

Bennett, L. 2011. "Bunkerology—A case study in the theory and practice of urban exploration." *Environment and Planning D: Society and Space* 29(3): 421–434.

Berardi, F. 2011. *After the Future*. Edinburgh: AK Press.

Bissell, D. 2010. "Passenger mobilities: Affective atmospheres and the sociality of public transport." *Environment and Planning D: Society and Space* 28(2): 270–289.

Böhme, G. 1993. "Atmosphere as the fundamental concept of a new aesthetics." *Thesis Eleven* 36: 113–126.

Booth, W. 1890. *In Darkest England and the Way Out*. London: Salvation Army.

Bunge, B. 1977. "The first years of the Detroit Geographical Expedition." In *Radical Geography*, edited by R. Peet, 31–39. Chicago, IL: Maaroufa Press.

Cacho, L. M. 2012. *Social Death: Racialized Rightlessness and the Criminalization of the Unprotected*. New York: New York University Press.

Campbell, E. 2012. "Landscapes of performance: Stalking as choreography." *Environment and Planning D* 30(3): 400–417.

Casella, E. C. 2014. "Enmeshed inscriptions: Reading the graffiti of Australia's convict past." *Australian Archaeology* 78(1): 108–112.

Castleman, C. 1982. *Getting Up: Subway Graffiti in New York*. Cambridge, MA: MIT Press.

Castree, N., Kitchin, R., and Rogers, A. 2013. *A Dictionary of Human Geography*. Oxford: Oxford University Press.

Champion, M. 2015. *Medieval Graffiti: The Lost Voices of England's Churches*. London: Ebury Press.

Cianci, L. and Schutt, S. 2014. "Keepers of ghosts: Old signs, new media and the age of archival flux." *Archives and Manuscripts* 42(1): 19–32.

Corsín Jiménez, A. 2003. "On space as a capacity." *Journal of the Royal Anthropological Institute* 9: 137–153.

Davis, C. 2005. "Hauntology, spectres and phantoms." *French Studies* 59(3): 373–379.

De Certeau, M. 1984. *The Practice of Everyday Life*. Berkeley: University of California Press.

———. 1998. *The Practice of Everyday Life. Vol 2: Living and Cooking*. Minneapolis: University of Minnesota Press.

Deleuze, G. and Guattari, F. 1987. *A Thousand Plateaus: Capitalism and Schizophrenia*, translated by B. Massumi. London: Bloomsbury.

Derrida, J. 1994. *Spectres of Marx: The State of the Debt, the Work of Mourning and the New International*, translated by P. Kamuf. New York: Routledge.

Dewsbury, J. D. 2009. "Performative, non-representational and affect-based research: Seven injunctions." In *The SAGE Handbook of Qualitative Geography*, edited D. DeLyser, S. Herbert, S. Aitken, et al., 321–334. London: SAGE.

Dobraszczyk, P., Lopez-Galviz, C. and Garrett, B. L. 2015. "Digging up and digging down: Urban undergrounds." *Journal of Contemporary Archaeology* 2(2): S26–S30.

Drax. 1993. "Maybe it's because I'm a Londoner." *Graphotism* 3: 7–10.

Drax, W. D. 2014. *Scattered pictures*. Flickr. Available at www.flickr.com/photos/draxwd/13335190603/.

Edensor, T. 2005. *Industrial Ruins: Spaces, Aesthetics, and Materiality*. Oxford: Berg Publishers.

Ferrell, J. 1996. *Crimes of Style: Urban Graffiti and the Politics of Criminality*. Boston, MA: Northeastern University Press.

———. 1997. "Criminological verstehen: Inside the immediacy of crime." *Justice Quarterly* 14(1): 3–23.

———. 2004. "Speed kills." In*Cultural Criminology Unleashed*, edited by J. Ferrell, K. Hayward, and W. Morrisson, 251–262. London: GlassHouse.

———. 2009. "Kill method: A provocation." *Journal of Theoretical and Philosophical Criminology* 1(1): 1–22.

———. 2012. "Autoethnography." In *The SAGE Handbook of Criminological Research Methods*, edited by D. Gadd, S. Karstedt, and S. F. Messner, 218–230. London: SAGE.

———. 2015. "Ghost ethnography: On crimes against reality and their excavation." Paper presented at Crimes Against Reality common session, University of Hamburg, Germany, May 4. https://lec-ture2go.uni-hamburg.de.

———. 2016. "Postscript: Under the slab." In *Liquid Criminology: Doing Imaginative Criminological Research*, edited by M. H. Jacobsen and S. Walklate, 221–229. London: Routledge.

———. 2017. "Graffiti, street art and the dialectics of the city." In *Graffiti and Street Art: Reading, Writing and Representing the City*, edited by K. Avramidis and M. Tsilimpounidi, 27–38. London Routledge.

Ferrell, J. and Hamm, M. (eds.). 1998. *Ethnography at the Edge*. Boston, MA: Northeastern University Press.

Ferrell J., Hayward, K., and Young, J. 2008. *Cultural Criminology: An Invitation*. London: SAGE.

Ferrell, J. and Weide, R. D. 2010. "Spot theory." *City* 14(1–2): 48–62.

Fiddler, M. 2007. "Projecting the prison: The depiction of the uncanny in *The Shawshank Redemption*." *Crime Media Culture* 3(2): 192–206.

Fisher, M. 2012. "What is hauntology?" *Film Quarterly* 66(1): 16–24.

———. 2014. *Ghosts of My Life: Writings on Depression, Hauntology and Lost Futures*. Winchester: Zero Books.

Foucault, M. 2003. *Society Must Be Defended. Lectures at the Collège de France 1975–1976*. Translated by D Macey. New York: Picador.

Frederick, U. K. 2009. "Revolution is the new black: Graffiti/art and mark-making practices." *Archaeologies* 5(2): 210–317.

Freud, S. 1919. *The Complete Psychological Works of Sigmund Freud, Vol. 17 (1917–1919)*. London: Hogarth Press.

Garrett, B. L. 2013. *Explore Everything: Place-Hacking the City*. London: Verso.

———. 2016. "Urban exploration as heritage placemaking." In *Reanimating Industrial Spaces: Conducting Memory Work in Post-Industrial Societies*, edited by H. Orange, 72–91. London: Routledge.

Garrett, B. L. and Hawkins, H. 2014. "And now for something completely different . . . thinking through explorer subject-bodies: A response to Mott and Roberts." AntipodeFoundation.org. https://radicalan-tipode.files.wordpress.com.

Geertz, C. 1973. "Thick description: Toward an interpretive theory of culture." In *The Interpretation of Cultures*, edited by C. Geertz, 3–30. New York: Basic Books.

———. 1998. "Deep hanging out." *New York Review of Books*, October 22. www.ny books.com/.
Graves-Brown, P. and Schofield, J. 2011. "The filth and the fury: 6 Denmark Street (London) and the Sex Pistols." *Antiquity* 85(330): 1385–1401.
Hallsworth, S. 2013. *The Gang and Beyond: Interpreting Violent Street Worlds*. London: Palgrave Macmillan.
Halsey, M. and Young, A. 2006. "'Our desires are ungovernable': Writing graffiti in urban space." *Theoretical Criminology* 10(3): 275–306.
Hayward, K. 2004. *City Limits: Crime, Consumer Culture and the Urban Experience*. London: GlassHouse.
———. 2012. "Five spaces of cultural criminology." *British Journal of Criminology* 52(3): 441–462.
Herrmann, J. 2014. "The ghost town of the super-rich: Kensington and Chelsea's 'buy-to-leave' phenomenon." *Evening Standard*, March 21. www.standard.co.uk.
High, S. and Lewis, D. W. 2007. *Corporate Wasteland: The Landscape and Memory of Deindustrialization*. Ithaca, NY: Cornell University Press.
Horowitz, D. L. 2001. *The Deadly Ethnic Riot*. Berkeley: University of California Press.
Hughes, R. 2008. "Dutiful tourism: Encountering the Cambodian genocide." *Asia Pacific Viewpoint* 49(3): 318–220.
Huskinson, L. (ed.). 2016a. *The Urban Uncanny: A Collection of Interdisciplinary Studies*. London: Routledge.
———. 2016b. "Introduction: The urban uncanny." In *The Urban Uncanny: A Collection of Interdisciplinary Studies*, edited by L. Huskinson, 1–17. London: Routledge.
Jameson, F. 1991. *Postmodernism, or, the Cultural Logic of Late Capitalism*. London: Verso.
Jones, J. 2011. "Preserving the Sex Pistols' graffiti is an archaeological swindle." *The Guardian*, November 22. www.theguardian.com.
Kindynis, T. 2017a. "Bomb alert: Graffiti writing and urban space in London." *British Journal of Criminology*. doi:10.1093/bjc/azx040.
———. 2017b. "Urban exploration: From subterranea to spectacle." *British Journal of Criminology* 57(4): 982–1001.
Kindynis, T. and Garrett, B. L. 2015. "Entering the Maze: Space, time and exclusion in an abandoned Northern Ireland prison." *Crime Media Culture* 11(1): 5–20.
Lefebvre, H. 1991. *The Production of Space.*, translated by D. Nicholson-Smith. Oxford: Blackwell.
Linnemann, T. 2015. "Capote's ghosts: Violence, media and the spectre of suspicion." *British Journal of Criminology* 55(3): 514–533.
Lombroso, C. 1888. *Palimsesti del Carcere: Raccolta Unicamente Destinata Agli Uomini di Scienza*. Turin: Bocca.
Luckhurst, R. 2002. "The contemporary London gothic and the limits of the 'spectral turn.'" *Textual Practice* 16(3): 527–546.
Lyng, S. 1990. "Edgework: A social psychological analysis of voluntary risk taking." *American Journal of Sociology* 95: 851–886.

———. 2004. "Crime, edgework and corporeal transaction." *Theoretical Criminology* 8(3): 359–375.
Macdonald, N. 2001. *The Graffiti Subculture: Youth, Masculinity and Identity in London and New York*. Basingstoke: Palgrave Macmillan.
Mayhew, H. 1862. *London Labour and the London Poor*. London: Griffin, Bohn & Co.
Mayne, A. and Lawrence, S. 1999. "Ethnographies of place: A new urban research agenda." *Urban History* 26(3): 325–48.
Meier. 2013. "Documenting the digital degradation of images in Project LOSS." *Hyperallergic*, December 5. www.hyperallergic.com.
Merrill, S. 2015. "Keeping it real? Subcultural graffiti, street art, heritage and authenticity." *International Journal of Heritage Studies* 21(4): 369–389.
Merrill, S. O. C. and Hack, H. 2013. "Exploring hidden narratives: Conscript graffiti at the former military base 'Kummersdorf.'" *Journal of Social Archaeology* 13(1): 101–121.
Mott, C. and Roberts, S. 2014a. "Not everyone has (the) balls: Urban exploration and the persistence of masculinist geography." *Antipode: A Radical Journal of Geography* 46(1): 229–245.
———. 2014b. "Difference really does matter: A reply to Garrett and Hawkins." AntipodeFoundation.org. https://radicalantipode.files.wordpress.com.
Ninjalicious. 2005. *Access All Areas: A User's Guide to the Art of Urban Exploration*. Toronto, Canada: Infilpress.
Norwood, G. 2016. "The impact of 'buy to leave' on prime London's housing market." *Financial Times*, February 12. www.ft.com.
Oliver, J. and Neal, T. 2010. "Elbow grease and time to spare: The place of tree carving." In *Wild Signs: Graffiti in Archaeology and History*, edited by J. Oliver and T. Neal, 15–22. Oxford: Archaeopress.
Papastergiadis, N. 2002. "Traces left in cities." *Architectural Design* 156: 45–51.
Park, R. E., Burgess, E. W. and McKenzie, D. 1925. *The City*. Chicago: University of Chicago Press.
Patterson, O. 1985. *Slavery and Social Death: A Comparative Study*. Cambridge, MA: Harvard University Press.
Payne, O. 2005. "Our yards." In *Oliver Payne and Nick Relph*, edited by O. Payne and N. Relph, 158–169. London: Serpentine Gallery.
Pilar Blanco, M. and Peeren, E. (eds.). 2013. *The Spectralities Reader: Ghosts and Haunting in Contemporary Cultural Theory*. London: Bloomsbury.
Pile, S. 2005. *Real Cities: Modernity, Space and the Phantasmagoria of City Life*. London: SAGE.
Pinder, D. 2001. "Ghostly footsteps: Voices, memories and walks in the city." *Ecumene* 8(1): 1–19.
———. 2005. "Arts of urban exploration." *Cultural Geographies* 12(4): 383–411.
Pink, S. 2008. "An urban tour: The sensory sociality of ethnographic place-making." *Ethnography* 9(2): 175–196.
Ralph, J. 2014. "Graffiti archaeology." In *Encyclopedia of Global Archaeology*, edited by C. Smith, 3102–3107. New York: Springer.

Scannell, J. 2002. "Becoming-city: Why graffiti writers love the city more than you ever will." *M/C Journal5(2)*. www.journal.media-culture.org.au.
Schatz, E. 2009. "Ethnographic immersion and the study of politics." In *Political Ethnography: What Immersion Contributes to the Study of Power*, edited by E. Schatz, 1–22. Chicago: University of Chicago Press.
Schutt, S. 2017 "Rewriting the book of the city: On old signs, new technologies and reinventing Adelaide." *Urban Geography* 38(1): 47–65.
Siege 52. 2009. "The psychology of optimal stylistic experience." In *Crack & Shine*, edited by F. Forsyth, 68–73. London: FFF.
Sloterdijk, P. 2011. *Bubbles*. New York: Semiotext(e).
Snyder, G. 2009. *Graffiti Lives*. New York: New York University Press.
Spector, S. 2016. *Violent Sensations: Sex, Crime, and Utopia in Vienna and Berlin, 1860–1914*. Chicago: University of Chicago Press.
Thrift, N. 2008. *Non-Representational Theory: Space, Politics, Affect*. London: Routledge.
Turner, J. and Peters, K. 2015. "Unlocking carceral atmospheres: Designing visual/material encounters at the prison museum." *Visual Communication* 14(3): 309–330.
Vannini, P. 2015. "Non-representational ethnography: New ways of animating lifeworlds." *Cultural Geographies* 22(2): 317–327.
Vidler, A. 1992. *The Architectural Uncanny: Essays in the Modern Unhomely*. Cambridge, MA: MIT Press.
Walklate, S., Mythen, G. and McGarry, R. 2011. "Witnessing Wootton Bassett: An exploration in cultural victimology." *Crime Media Culture* 7(2): 149–165.
Wilbert, C. and Hansen, R. 2009. "Walks in spectral space: East London crime scene tourism." In *Strange Spaces: Explorations into Mediated Obscurity*, edited by A. Jansen and A. Lagerkvist, 187–203. Aldershot: Ashgate.
Wolcott, H. 2008. *Ethnography: A Way of Seeing*. 2nd ed. Plymouth: AltaMira Press.

Ghost Criminology

A Requiem

MICHAEL FIDDLER, THEO KINDYNIS, AND
TRAVIS LINNEMANN

If the reader were to look at the frontispiece of Thomas Hobbes's (1651) *Leviathan*, they would see the familiar figure of the Sovereign King looming over a pastoral landscape. This colossus holds out a sword in one hand and a crozier in the other. These are symbols of force and office. In front of the rolling hillsides there is a walled city in the foreground. If we look closer, we notice that the city's streets are curiously quiet. There are, however, two small figures by the cathedral toward the right of the image. Their distinctive beak-like masks mark them as plague doctors. The empty streets take on an eerie resonance. This is a city in quarantine.

As with all texts, reading is an act of mediumship. The reader is channeling ideas shaped months, years, or centuries in the past. As you are reading this, you are joining with a text that was written during the closing months of 2020. At the time of writing, many of the contributors to this volume are in a lockdown due to a global pandemic. Globally, 1.33 million people have died, with many more expected to pass in the coming months. Australia's "black summer" bushfires and the Western United States' wildfires have caused untold damage to ecosystems while acting as harbingers of a climate catastrophe. The Summer of 2020 saw global protests and demonstrations following the murders of George Floyd and Breonna Taylor, and the shooting of Jacob Blake. This has been a year that has felt especially laden with temporal dis-ease. It feels heavy with the inheritances of the passed/past. Derrida spoke of the "visor effect"—another reference to Hamlet's encounter with his father-as-specter—as a way of describing the way in which we stand before the dead and are regarded by them without being able to look back. The inequalities exacerbated by the COVID-19 pandemic, the racial injustice brought to vivid focus by camera phone footage of lethal state violence, and the fires that have scoured continents evoke a gaze that is difficult to return. If we are to truly consider time as non-linear, that past-present-future can exist as a constellation and not as a straight line, the "present moment" feels especially connected. This temporal assemblage appears dendritic. The massed points of connection are deeply knotted and tied. We are at a point charged with both the past and future. *And* possibility. We feel the gaze of the past/passed bore into us. There is the heaviness of the "no longer" about these events. As Wendy Brown phrased it, this is the sense that we do not inherit "'what really happened' to the dead, but what lives on from that happening." We are living that which has lived on. There is also the weight of the "not yet." Where the fires that coursed across California turned the skies above San Francisco an other-wordly orange, we have been visited by the ghosts of the Anthropocene. This is a vision of the (or—generously—a *possible*) future. These are demands for ethical and liberating actions. These debts to the dead and to the ghosts of the future must be repaid.

This takes us to the current project of Ghost Criminology. As we have stated, our analytical focus is upon the ghost(ed) and a need to attend to those figures and groups, spaces and concepts that have been disappeared, the harms of the past that have persistent afterlives, as well as the haunting presence of the future. Our goal in this text was to mark the spectral turn in the discipline, in addition to gathering texts that point toward a method to interrogate the "things behind the things." As such, if ours is a gaze from a "past" in which this text was written, we must also turn that hauntological "look" inward upon ourselves. To what extent have we absented others? What debts must we repay?

In order to address this, it is helpful to group these thoughts by theme and offer a sense of where a Ghost Criminology might lead. They also offer a sense of future avenues for Ghost Criminology. First, we will briefly direct the reader toward work being carried out in parallel to the project outlined here. These texts also speak to the haunting impact of the current moment. Then we will touch upon non-Western understandings of the ghost before turning to Achille Mbembé's (2003, 2019) notion of "necropolitics" and its applicability to the ideas raised here.

This then is our attempt to attend to voices of the past/passed, while looking to this particular sub-discipline's "not yet."

The footage of the murder of George Floyd joins a growing archive. This record of black lives extinguished by a death-dealing state is not simply the horrifying collection of ghostly imprints of deaths in the moment. Rather, it speaks to a constellation of the past-present that places the history and practice of racialized violence into an ever-present now. This is something that is explored in this collection by both Michelle Brown and Bill McClanahan, as well as Travis Linnemann and Justin Turner. But it is important to also highlight the work of others—outside of the discipline of criminology—who have been working in a similar space. Christine Sharpe's (2016) *In the Wake: On Blackness and Being* engages with the different registers of the word "wake." For our purposes, there is the closest resonance with the project outlined here by her discussion of wake as a convening with or remembrance of the dead. Sharpe (2016, 5) uses this to highlight the "precarities of the afterlives of the dead." Further, Michelle M. Wright (2015) in her book *Physics of Blackness: Beyond the Middle Passage Epistemology* draws upon—as we also saw in Elaine Campbell's chapter in this collection—quantum physics to unpack the sociological within a non-linear temporality. Here, Wright (2015) "cautions against over-reliance on the exclusive use of linear progress narratives to define Blackness." Instead, Wright (2015, 14) states that

> [t]he only way to produce a definition of Blackness that is wholly inclusive and nonhierarchical is to understand Blackness as the *intersection* of constructs that locate the Black collective in *history* and in the *specific moment* in which Blackness is being imagined—the "now" through which all imaginings of Blackness will be mediated.

In short, writers are utilizing this hauntological literature—indeed, pushing at its boundaries—to convene with the dead, to attend to their voices and consider their afterlives. Perhaps it is this particular moment within the ongoing crisis of racialized violence that sees hauntology as well-positioned to attend to these voices and consider that heavy burden of debt that is owed.

It is important that we also acknowledge that the literature we refer to here, both academic and literary, is steeped in a particular Western tradition. The language of hauntology refers to a peculiarly Western understanding of the ghost and spectrality. It relies upon psychoanalytic understandings of trauma and philosophical approaches that look to a particularly Anglo-European experience. In this regard, Saleh-Hanna (2015) provides perceptive commentary on the ghosts within Derrida's work. Specifically, there are those spectral traces of "Derrida's own personal, colonizing history" that can be traced within his own texts. Our next task must be to reach out to authors of the global South—notwithstanding our gratitude to our Australian contributors—to take on a hauntology that speaks to non-Western traditions of haunting. This is not to replicate colonizing or appropriating practices (of the sort Saleh-Hanna highlights), but to provide space for such voices to be heard in the closed academic networks of the global North (inter alia Carrington, Hogg, and Sozzo, 2016). To give shape to this, it is helpful to turn to Lincoln and Lincoln's (2014) approach to a "critical hauntology" as applied, in their case, to the ghosts of Vietnam. They provide a critique of Avery Gordon's work in *Ghostly Matters* that, in many respects, applies to our thinking here as well. Lincoln and Lincoln (2014, 194) point toward Gordon's use of a

> trope of haunting as a means to encompass disparate liberatory projects that invoke the historic imagination to compel a reckoning with violence, suffering and injustice.

This is a goal that aligns with our own and which we elaborated upon in the introduction to this collection. What is key for Lincoln and Lincoln is that Gordon's (and by extension *our*) approach is to diminish the importance of *the ghost* within the ghostly. You will recall that we dismiss the actual presence—as it were—of the ghost in the introduction. Rather, we—and many of the contributors here—focus our analytical attention upon "'ghostly' signals, matter, and traces" (Lincoln and Lincoln 2014, 195). This is to ignore "[g]hosts *qua* ghosts" (ibid.). This is to fail to attend to "individuals or social groups who experience haunting as something consistent with, and rooted in, their cosmology, ontology, and psychology" (ibid.). As such, as Lincoln and Lincoln (2014, 196) describe it, finding traces of the specter in texts and spaces locates them inside the consciousness of those they "visit," rather than on the borders of the physical and metaphysical, thereby rationalizing, simplifying, and perhaps also distorting aspects of the phenomena it claims as its object of study.

So, to recognize the "ontological status" of the ghost is to respond to the lived experiences of those that encounter them. They highlight the Confucian and Buddhist traditions in Asia that "supply elaborate supporting cosmologies" for the ghost as a social presence, figure, and actor (ibid., 197). In Vietnam, they point toward work that explores "the virtual epidemic of unsettled, intrusive and angry ghosts, afflicting postwar Vietnam" (ibid.). They argue for a separation between primary and secondary haunting. Primary haunting would refer to the traumatic and traumatizing encounter of a small number of individuals with such a ghost. This would lead to the living paying their debt to the dead by taking on and sharing the pain that has caused the dead to return, thereby prompting a "moral action so that the living and dead can share a righteous peace" (ibid., 210). A secondary haunting is, in part, more akin to the analysis of the spectral outlined here. This attends to traumas at a broader scale. Within Lincoln and Lincoln's (ibid.) framing, this is "not with the hope of putting anyone to rest, but to mobilize a moral community to prevent such atrocities in the future." We would argue that the project outlined in this collection offers a more nuanced approach to dealing with the harms of the past, as well as considerations of the future's role in the present. That said, attending to "the ghost" as an active social force could lead this project into challenging new avenues of inquiry. Similarly, Siegel (2006), in the introduction to his anthropological study of witchcraft in East Java, draws upon Steve Biko's (of the African National Congress) notion of witchcraft as a superstition, one that is "part of the mystery of our cultural heritage." As Siegel (2006, 13) frames it,

> Witchcraft can and even should form a part of public life, at least in Africa [. . .] Witchcraft should be a part of public life in order to defend against the fears that it brings. To whites, superstition brings fear; to eliminate it is to eliminate fear. To Biko, "witchcraft," as superstition and as an element of tradition, means bringing fear to light.

As criminologists, well attuned to the language of fear, we would do well to attend to that which illuminates it.

Tangential to these analytical frames for trauma and temporality is Achille Mbembé's (2003a, 2003b, 2019) notion of necropolitics. Mbembé's (2003b) necropolitics is best considered as an adjunct to the Foucauldian notion of biopower. Biopower is concerned with the "explosion of numerous and diverse techniques for achieving the subjugations of bodies and the contral of populations" (Foucault 1990, 140). If we take Foucault's notion of sovereign power as being centrally concerned with the right to kill, Mbembé extends this to consider populations *"let die"* (2003a, 40; emphasis in original). Necropower itself then is concerned with the "subjugation of life to the power of death" (ibid., 39). To put this differently, rather than being put to death, these are groups that are "kept alive, but in a *state of injury*, in a phantom-like world of horrors and intense cruelty and profanity" (Mbembé 2003b, 21). They exist in *death-worlds*:

> forms of social existence in which vast populations are subjected to conditions of life that confer upon them the status of living dead (ghosts). (Mbembé 2003a, 1; emphasis in original)

It is difficult not to see the responses of many countries to the current pandemic as being examples of precisely these kinds of death-worlds and of populations "let die." As Mbembé (2003a, 22) describes it, those who have been "let die" "maintain alternative perspectives towards time." The body itself is a marker of forces that transcend and expand beyond human timescales. This is an analysis that can be wedded to a non-linear temporality where harms persist, extend, and fold back on one another through time. Further, a growing number of criminologists have turned to this framework to explore necropolitical governmentality (Estévez 2020), necropolitics, and sex offenders (Higgins and Rolfe 2017), as well as the policing of young people (Flacks 2020).

An analysis informed by the spectral and hauntological can reveal much about the complexity of lived experiences. Further, it opens up the necessity for an ethical response to the passed/past while also making demands for praxis for the future. The framework outlined here allows us to confront Avery Gordon's "repressed or unresolved social violence," as well as opening up spaces for imaginative responses to future harms. The contributors to this volume have drawn upon a diverse array of spectral phenomena to illustrate the lingering absence/presence of the "no longer" within the social world. This collection has then, we hope, begun to capture something of the spectral turn within the discipline of Criminology while also shaping what may follow.

Wendy Brown (2001) spoke of the past and future acting as a "force" upon the present. Similarly, Mark Fisher (2014) described the "no longer" and "not yet" as acting as a "virtuality." This takes us back to one of the ghosts we used to illustrate haunting in the introduction. The afterlives of slavery and colonial oppression act as a force in the present and continue to haunt the future. In a May 1969 appearance on *The Dick Cavett Show*, James Baldwin, the essayist, novelist, and civil rights activist, reflected on the afterlives of slavery, stating that: "[a]ll your buried corpses are now beginning to speak." Between 1619, 1968, and 2020, the corpses are speaking. They've never stopped. We need to listen.

We opened with a "spirit guide" and now we close with a requiem. Why refer to it like that? It speaks, once more, to the importance of time and of remembering. And of *justice*. A requiem seeks to ensure the repose of the dead. Having sought out ways to heed their voices, what steps are there to ensure a sense of peace for the departed? This brings us back to the looming figure from the frontispiece of *Leviathan*. In heeding the voices of the dead and seeking out points of intervention to achieve justice for them, we must imagine a state that does not wield a symbol of force, of *death*. This "moment" demands radical praxis to ensure justice in the intersecting crises of racial injustice, structural imbalance, and climate catastrophe. In listening to the ghosts of the future, we must shape the "not yet." We must imagine a state that does not see its most vulnerable members "let die" through climate catastrophe or pandemic. We must imagine a state that is not death-dealing. We must imagine a state that does not use the techniques and technologies of war to "police" its citizens. Rather than using the "language and rituals" of violence,[1] we must imagine communities that operate through non-violence, through *empathy*. This could be the force that we feel in the present. It may be one tentative step in listening to those voices of the dead calling out to us.

NOTE

1 We are taking this phrasing from a discussion between Ta-Nehisi Coates and Ezra Klein (*The Ezra Klein Show*, June 2020).

REFERENCES

Brown, Wendy. 2001. *Politics Out of History*. Princeton, NJ: Princeton University Press.
Carrington, Kerry, Hogg, Russell, and Sozzo, Máximo. 2016. "Southern Criminology." *British Journal of Criminology* 56, 1: 1–20.
Estévez, Ariadna. 2020. "Mexican Necropolitical Governmentality and the Management of Suffering Through Human Rights Technologies." *Critical Criminology* 28: 27–42.
Fisher, Mark. 2014. *Ghosts of My Life: Writings on Depression, Hauntology and Lost Futures*. Winchester: Zero Books.
Flacks, Simon. 2020. "Law, Necropolitics and the Stop and Search of Young People." *Theoretical Criminology* 24, 2: 387–405.
Foucault, Michel. 1990. *The History of Sexuality, Vol. 1*. New York: Vintage Books.
Higgins, Ethan M. and Rolfe, Shawn M. 2017. "'The Sleeping Army': Necropolitics and the Collateral Consequences of Being a Sex Offender." *Deviant Behavior* 38, 9: 975–990.
Lincoln, Martha and Lincoln, Bruce. 2014. "Toward a Critical Hauntology: Bare Afterlife and the Ghosts of Ba Chúc." *Comparative Studies in Society and History* 57, 1: 191–220.
Mbembé, Achille. 2003a. "Life, Sovereignty, and Terror in the Fiction of Amos Tutuola." *Research in African Literature* 34, 4: 1–26.
——. 2003b. "Necropolitics." *Public Culture* 15, 1: 11–40.
——. 2019. *Necropolitics*. Durham, NC: Duke University Press.
Saleh-Hanna, Viviane. 2015. "Black Feminist Hauntology: Rememory the Ghosts of Abolition?" *Penal Field*. https://journals.openedition.org/
Sharpe, Christine. 2016. *In the Wake: On Blackness and Being*. Durham, NC: Duke University Press.
Siegel, James. 2006. *Naming the Witch*. Stanford, CA: Stanford University Press.
Wright, Michelle M. (2015) *Physics of Blackness: Beyond the Middle Passage Epistemology*. Minneapolis: University of Minnesota Press.

ABOUT THE CONTRIBUTORS

KATHERINE BIBER is Professor of Law at the University of Technology–Sydney and a legal scholar, historian, and criminologist. Her work examines the laws of evidence as they confront photographs, visual culture, and documentation. She is author of *Captive Images: Race, Crime, Photography* (2007) and *In Crime's Archive: The Cultural Afterlife of Evidence* (2018).

MICHELLE BROWN is Associate Professor of Sociology at the University of Tennessee. Her research explores the lived and cultural life of carceral regimes; forms of premature and slow death and dying in US criminal justice; visual criminology; and emergent forms of political organizing and alternative justice in response to mass incarceration. She is the author of *The Culture of Punishment* (2009), co-author of *Criminology Goes to the Movies* (with Nicole Rafter, 2011), and co-editor of *Media Representations of September 11* (2003), *The Routledge International Handbook of Visual Criminology* (2017), The Palgrave Macmillan Crime, Media and Culture Book Series, and the Sage journal, *Crime Media Culture*. She is senior editor for the *Oxford Research Encyclopedia on Crime, Media, and Popular Culture* (2018), and is currently working on a book manuscript examining the transformation of American criminal justice through abolition and alternative justice movements.

ELAINE CAMPBELL is Professor of Criminology at Newcastle University in the UK and an interdisciplinary criminologist working across criminology, sociology, cultural studies, and cultural geographies. She researches and publishes on the spatial, affective, and performative dynamics of crime, policing, surveillance, and security, with a focus on how these are visually, materially, and discursively constitutive of urban environments.

EAMONN CARRABINE is a Professor in the Department of Sociology at the University of Essex. He has published widely on media criminology, the sociology of punishment, and cultural theory. He currently holds a Leverhulme Trust Major Research Fellowship to research his project, *The Iconography of Punishment: From Renaissance to Modernity*, which will be published as a book. Since 2015, he has been co-editing the journal *Crime, Media, Culture* with Michelle Brown (University of Tennessee) and they have recently edited the *Routledge International Handbook of Visual Criminology* (2017). With Avi Brisman (Eastern Kentucky University) and Nigel South (University of Essex) he has also co-edited the *Routledge Companion to Criminological Theory and Concepts* (2017).

JEFF FERRELL is Professor of Sociology at Texas Christian University, USA, and Visiting Professor of Criminology at the University of Kent, UK. He is author of the books *Crimes of Style (1993)*, *Tearing Down the Streets (2001/2)*, *Empire of Scrounge (2006)*, and, with Keith Hayward and Jock Young, the first and second editions of *Cultural Criminology: An Invitation (2008, 2015)*, winner of the 2009 Distinguished Book Award from the American Society of Criminology's Division of International Criminology. He is co-editor of the books *Cultural Criminology (1995)*, *Ethnography at the Edge (1998)*, *Making Trouble (1999)*, *Cultural Criminology Unleashed (2004)*, and *Cultural Criminology: Theories of Crime (2011)*. Ferrell is founding and current editor of the New York University Press book series Alternative Criminology, and one of the founding editors of *Crime, Media, Culture: An International Journal*, winner of the ALPSP 2006 Charlesworth Award for Best New Journal. In 1998, Ferrell received the Critical Criminologist of the Year Award from the Critical Criminology Division of the American Society of Criminology. His latest book is *Drift: Illicit Mobility and Uncertain Knowledge (2018)*.

BILL MCCLANAHAN is Assistant Professor of Justice Studies at Eastern Kentucky University. Writing at the intersections of sociology, geography, justice studies, cultural ecocriticism, and environmental humanities, his research focuses on ecology, memory, visual and literary cultures, and environmental justice. He is co-author, along with Reece

Walters, Avi Brisman, and Nigel South, of *Water, Crime, and Security in the Twenty First Century: Too Dirty, Too Little, Too Much* (2018), and his work has been published in academic journals including *Crime, Media, Culture, Deviant Behavior, Critical Criminology*, and *Contemporary Justice Review*, among others. He is currently completing a monograph on cultural ecocriticism, memorialization, resource extraction, and haunted geographies of horror.

CAROLYN MCKAY is a Senior Lecturer at the University of Sydney Law School, where she teaches Criminal Law, Civil & Criminal Procedure and Digital Criminology, and is co-Deputy Director of the Sydney Institute of Criminology. She is the author of *The Pixelated Prisoner: Prison Video Links, Court "Appearance" and the Justice Matrix* (2018). McKay has served on the 2019 NSW Law Society Legal Technologies Committee and was appointed to the 2019–2020 NSW Bar Association Innovation & Technology Committee. She has been a Visiting Scholar at the Centre for Socio-Legal Studies, University of Oxford 2019 and for three months at the Oñati International Institute for the Sociology of Law, Spain 2013–14. She has previously consulted on anti-dumping trade disputes and indirect taxation, working in both Sydney and Tokyo, and she also has a digital media/visual arts practice.

DANIEL ROBINS is a Doctoral Researcher at the University of York. His research focuses on the parts of the corpse that can be considered as "waste," otherwise known as "necro-waste."

JUSTIN TURNER is a faculty member in the Criminal Justice Studies department at Bellarmine University. His research explores the complex interplay between state power, violence, and everyday life, and how these forces tend to collide under the auspices of criminal justice. His work has been published in academic journals including *Crime, Media, and Culture, Social Justice*, and *Critical Criminology*.

ALISON YOUNG is the Francine V. McNiff Professor of Criminology in the School of Social and Political Sciences at the University of Melbourne. She is the founder of the Urban Environments Research Network, an interdisciplinary and international group of academics, artists, architects, and activists interested in cities, social change, and urban governance. At the University of Melbourne, she is a Research Convenor in the Future Cities Research Cluster, Melbourne Sustainable Societies Institute. She is currently researching the relationship between the built environment and urban governance in Australia and Japan, in respect of issues such as graffiti and urban creativity, homelessness, and the night-time economy and street crime.

ABOUT THE EDITORS

MICHAEL FIDDLER is Associate Professor of Criminology at the University of Greenwich in London. His research has explored the spaces and architecture associated with crime and punishment.

THEO KINDYNIS a criminologist and lecturer at Goldsmiths, University of London. His primary research interest is the nexus between urban space, crime, and social control. To date his research has focused on graffiti writing, "urban exploration" (recreational trespass), and consumer spaces.

TRAVIS LINNEMANN is Associate Professor of Sociology in the Department of Sociology, Anthropology and Social Work at Kansas State University. He is the author of *Meth Wars: Police, Media, Power* also published by the New York University Press, Alternative Criminology series.

INDEX

Abedi, Salman, 144, 146
abject, 139, 245, 275, 299
abolition, 31, 54, 92, 100, 103, 105, 109, 344–345
Abraham, Nicolas, 6–7, 9, 29, 46, 63, 256, 275, 304
aesthetics, 11, 16, 25, 30, 36, 47, 55–56, 60, 78, 106, 131, 154, 160, 172, 206, 269, 273, 295, 297, 299, 305, 324, 330, 332
affect, 141, 206, 211, 276, 306, 336
agency, 31, 113–114, 156–158, 188, 192. *See also* agency of the virtual
agency of the virtual, 23, 180, 184
agential, 25, 33, 255, 257–263, 265–271, 272, 275, 278, 280, 283
Anderson, Nels, 80, 85
Anidjar, Gil, 214, 222
animality, 205, 211
anthropocene, 30, 128–130, 338
anthropology, 42, 116, 224, 256, 275, 278, 303, 313, 331, 349
anti-black, 93, 101, 105–108, 200, 202, 205
anti-graffiti, 69, 74, 327
anti-security, 194–196
Appadurai, Arjun 81, 85
apparition, apparitional, 1, 11, 39, 67, 70, 81, 116, 121, 135, 160, 185, 188
archaeological, 227, 308, 311–312, 328, 334
archaeology, 30, 56, 65, 251, 291, 296, 303, 307, 325, 330, 332, 335
archival, 92–92, 112, 159, 255, 272, 332
archive, 20, 29, 31, 92–95, 131, 167, 171, 177–178, 246, 276, 297, 301, 316, 330, 332, 339, 345

Ashworth High Security Psychiatric Prison, 135–138, 144–146
assemblage, 24, 80, 258, 338
atmosphere, 19, 31, 110, 128, 139, 222, 234, 259, 269, 276, 285, 290, 317–318, 325, 331–332, 336
Augé, Mark, 310, 313, 316, 323, 331
autoethnography, 282, 288, 301, 302, 305, 318, 333

Bachelard, Gaston, 281, 286, 290, 300
Baer, Ulrich, 54–57, 62–63
Baldwin, James, 54, 63, 343
Barad, Karen, 25, 255, 257–258, 260–263, 265, 271–275, 277
Bedlam (The Royal Bethlem Hospital), 2, 5–6, 26
Bell, Michael M., 73–74, 76,
Beloved (Morrison), 53–54, 108
Benjamin, Walter, 3, 5, 8, 13, 16, 21, 22, 27, 29, 56–57, 63, 103, 121–123, 125, 129, 131, 155, 177, 181, 184, 200, 221, 269, 276, 301, 305, 318, 329, 331
Bentham, Jeremy, 10, 12
Biber, Katherine, 20, 23, 119
Biko, Agozino, 13, 29, 341
biohazardous, 157, 160, 167
biopolitical, 17, 98, 109, 215
biopower, 98, 342
Black Lives Matter, 100, 185, 186–188, 190
Blackness, 90, 106, 109, 190, 194, 252, 339, 344
Blanco, Pilar, 18, 26, 28–30, 36, 63, 113, 130, 315, 330, 335
Blue Lives Matter, 24, 185–186, 188–192

351

Bohr, Nils, 258, 260, 274
Brady, Ian, 31, 135–138, 141–151, 153
Brenton, Howard, 259, 262, 268
bricolage, 25, 81, 255, 259, 273
Brighenti, Andrea Mubi, 84–85, 87
Brisman, Avi, 160, 177, 346–347
Brown, Michelle, 22, 31, 88, 90, 92, 94, 96, 98, 100–108, 131, 223, 301, 339, 344–346
Brown, Wendy, 4, 6, 8–9, 29, 338, 343–344
Buck-Morss, Susan, 111, 114, 129
Buse, Peter, 8, 27, 29
Butler, Judith, 17, 40
Byrne, Edward, 187, 201

Cacho, Lisa Marie, 98, 106, 314, 332
Campbell, Elaine, 24–25, 30, 339
Canetti, Elias, 209, 211, 215, 223
Carlson, Jennifer, 193
Carrabine, Eamonn, 6, 344
The Castle of Otranto (Walpole), 14, 46
CCTV, 20–21, 30, 285, 307
Charlottesville, 18, 183, 214
Chernobyl, 110, 118–119, 121, 127
Christie, John, 24–25, 253–276
CIA, 5, 62, 173
Clark, Edmund, 2, 23, 173
Clarke, David, 187–188, 190
Class Struggles in France (Marx), 39
colonization, 53, 91, 97
The Communist Manifesto (Marx and Engels), 8–9, 39
Conty, Arianne, 123
Correia, David, 192, 217,
counter-visual, 111, 118–119, 129
criminological *verstehen*, 288, 318, 326
criminology: cultural, 19, 288, 315; Gothic, 14–16; visual, 281, 288
crypt, 6–7, 20
Cunningham, Nijah, 188, 190

dark tourism, 281, 288, 327
Davies, Thom, 120–121
Davis, Angela, 90, 198

Davis, Colin, 3, 8, 256, 316
death-worlds, 98, 121, 342
De Certeau, Michel, 315–317, 331–332
déchiqueteuse, the, 162, 164. *See also* Tallgren, Immi
deconstruction, 40, 51–52, 159, 257–258, 278
Deleuze, Gilles, 85, 263
Denzin, Noman, 71,
Derrida, Jacques, 4–10, 21, 24, 36, 40, 46, 51–52, 61, 113, 117, 119, 121, 123, 126, 129, 155, 160, 166, 228, 256–261, 315, 316, 337, 340; *Specters of Marx*, 8–11, 36, 315
DeSilvey, Caitlin, 78,
dialectical image, 30–31 111, 114, 117–118, 121 125–129
Doherty, Willie 66–67
Dracula, 4, 16
drift, criminology of, 68–71, 75–76, 80–82, 86,
Duchamp, Marcel, 295
Dupin, Auguste, 49–52
Durkheim, Emile, 37–38

Edkins, Jenny, 231, 240
"The Eighteenth Brumaire of Louis Napoleon." *See* Marx, Karl
Engels, Friedrich, 39–40, 160
Enlightenment, 14–15, 43, 116, 256
ethnography: ghost, 19, 25, 28, 287, 308, 311–319, 352; instant, 71; liquid, 71; spectral, 73, 75, 313
exorcism, 17–18, 95

Fanon, Franz, 88, 90, 209–210, 216
Ferguson, Missouri, 99, 101
Ferrell, Jeff, 19, 22, 25, 30, 285, 302, 313–319, 326–329
fetishized, 71, 89, 93
Fiddler, Michael, 20, 22, 286
Fisher, Mark, 4, 9, 23–24, 112–114, 126, 130, 180, 183, 197–200, 205, 207–208, 212, 277, 316–317, 327, 343–344

Floyd, George, 2, 88, 337, 339
Foucault, Michel, 11, 40, 155, 209
Freud, Sigmund, 22, 35–36, 50, 52, 197, 256, 324
Fukushima, 110–112, 126–127
Fukuyama, Francis, 8–9

Galton, Francis, 10–13, 116–117, 125–126
Garner, Eric, 88, 202, 210, 216–220
Garrett, Bradley, 298, 302–303
Ghani, Mariam, 169–171
ghost. *See* ethnography
Gibson, Kristina, 69
Gordon, Avery, 3, 5, 13, 21, 35–36, 44, 52–54, 61, 94, 105, 165–166, 228, 256–257, 288–289, 292, 298, 302, 340, 343
gothic, 7, 14–16, 20–21, 35, 45–49, 61–62, 114–116, 126, 203, 269, 304, 334. *See also* criminology
graffiti, 19–20, 22–25, 67–69, 74, 80, 227, 307–349
Graham, Paul, 59–61
Grenfell Tower, 24, 228–252
Grixti, Joseph, 141, 146
Guattari, Felix, 85–86, 263
Guterl, Matthew, 97–98

Hallsworth, Simon, 85–86, 328
Hamlet, 3, 9, 45–46, 155, 166, 175–176
Hamm, Mark, 74, 76
Hand mit Ringen (X-ray) 123, *124*, 126–128
Haraway, Donna, 125, 129–130, 208
Hartman, Saidiya, 89, 92–94, 100–101
hauntology/ hauntological, 4, 8–9, 16, 21, 25, 40, 46, 52, 111–113, 126, 160, 180, 203, 207, 228, 260–261, 264, 272, 281, 316, 323, 338–340, 342
Hayward, Keith, 80, 320
Hetherington, Kevin, 143–144, 151
Hindley, Myra, 135–136
Hirvonen, Ari, 166
Hobbes, Thomas, 185, 206, 337
Holland, Sharon Patricia, 98

Holocaust, 7, 54–55
Holzer, Jenny, 172
Hooker, Juliet, 96
Hutchings, Peter, 11–12, 30, 95

interstitial, 25, 80–82, 84, 298, 310, 314, 321, 323, 326, 329
in-visible, 113, 117, 119, 126

Jenkins, Roy, 262
Johnson, Barbara, 52
Johnson, Micah, 187

Kalb, Margery, 7
Kerouac, Jack, 68, 79
Kindynis, Theo, 1, 19, 25, 287, 290
Koestenbaum, Wayne, 285, 292
Kuchinskaya, Olga, 119–120

Lacan, 17, 22, 46, 50–52, 61, 301
Lacanian Real, the, 17
Lange, Dorothea, 76–77, 80
Lederer, David, 42–43
Le Goff, Jacques, 41
Lennard, Natasha, 186
Leviathan (Hobbes), 85, 206, 211, 337, 343
Lincoln, Martha and Bruce, 8, 16, 340–341
Linebaugh, Peter, 205–206
Linnemann, Travis, 19, 23–24, 66, 68, 94, 98, 160, 168–169, 213, 327
Little, Janine Mary, 28
Lombroso, Cesare, 18, 20–24, 133–134
Lowkey (hip-hop artist), 242, 245, 249–250, 257
Lyman, Stanford, 22
lynchings, 56, 104, 109, 204–205

MacDonald, Heather, 188
Malone-Gonzales, Shannon, 194
Mangan, Lucy, 268–269
Martin, Theodore, 206
Martin, Trayvon, 88, 185,
Martinot, Steve, 93, 97, 99

Marx, Karl, 9–11, 38–39, 46, 62, 160, 202, 213, 218–220; *Class Struggles in France*, 39; "The Eighteenth Brumaire of Louis Napoleon," 27n24, 39. See also *Specters of Marx (Derrida)*
Marxism, 39–40, 258
Masco, Joseph, 118
material-cultural, 259, 273
material-discursive, 25, 255, 258–261, 263, 265, 269
materialism: historical, 39; hauntological, 257
materialist, new, 255, 258, 272
materialities, 259, 271
materiality, 77, 82, 105, 118, 122, 203, 216, 258, 308, 312–313, 317, 320, 325; marw
Mbembé, Achille, 98–99, 108, 125, 130, 342, 344
McClanahan, Bill, 24, 119, 128, 339
McDonogh, Gary, 72, 74
McKay, Carolyn, 25
McVeigh, Timothy, 74, 76, 79
Meagher, Jill, 20–21
Merleau-Ponty, Maurice, 290
metaphysical, 218, 290, 292
Miéville, China, 24, 206–207, 210, 221
Mirzoeff, Nicholas, 90–91
Mitchell, Don, 81, 84
mobility, 62, 145, 258, 282, 284–285, 296
modernity, 15, 37, 49, 56, 67, 91, 104–105, 207, 213, 265, 269
monstrosity, 138, 142–144, 146, 152
mourning, 6, 38, 40–41, 55–56, 88–89, 93, 101–102, 116, 176, 236, 245
Munro, Rolland, 138, 142

necropolitics, 90, 98, 230, 338, 342
Neel, Phillip, 214
Neocleous, Mark, 185, 195, 213
neoliberalism, 70, 79, 168, 191, 194, 328
Nixon, Rob 117, 119–121, 131
nonhuman, 207, 210, 259

non-representational theory, 320
NYPD, 185, 187, 189–191, 220

Obrist, Hans Ulrich, 167
Okri, Ben, 237, 241
Olson, Philip, 138–139
ontological, 96, 210, 218, 255–256, 258–259, 261, 263, 264, 271, 272, 341
ontology, 8, 12, 40, 52, 113, 208, 218, 220, 228, 261, 272, 316, 340
optical, 11, 115–116, 121–122, 126, 263
optogram, 113–115, 117, 120–121, 125–127

Paglen, Trevor, 110–112, 125–127
Pallasmaa, Juhani, 290
Palmer, Daniel, 296
pandemic, 337–338, 342–343
Park, Robert, 15
Parker, Cornelia, 23, 164–166
Peeren, Esther, 18, 36, 130
Penfold-Mounce, Ruth, 137, 146
Perera, Suvendreni, 210
phantasmagoria, phantasmagoric, 14, 92, 97, 113–120, 123
phantom, 4, 6–9, 11–12, 16, 40, 46, 54, 97, 105, 112, 251, 256, 342
phenomenology, 17, 74, 290, 317
Picart, Joan, 14
plague, 4, 126, 328, 337
Pócs, Eva, 42
Poe, 7, 14, 22, 48–50, 52, 64–65, 115
police, 2, 23–24, 30, 50–51, 63, 92–93, 96–100, 102–103, 139, 140, 168–169, 180–198, 202, 212–214, 216–222, 231, 243, 253–254, 268, 270, 275, 283, 307, 343
possession, 15, 42, 190
postmodern, 274, 328
praxis, 18, 263–264, 343
precarity, 83, 92, 96, 101, 203, 211
premodern, 43, 49, 58
presence, absence, 3–8, 12, 21, 23, 35, 70, 73, 75, 113, 129, 141, 152, 180, 182, 240, 257, 265, 298, 312, 314, 316, 325, 343

psychoanalysis, 3, 6–7, 20, 35, 50, 52, 56, 111, 165, 340
Pugliese, Joseph, 98, 210

quantum, 24–25, 214, 255, 257–258, 261–263, 272, 274

race, 7, 13, 21, 48, 90–91, 96–99, 101, 147, 189–190, 214
racecraft, 189–190
racial: capitalism, 53, 104, 197, 202; colonialism, 11, 21–22; difference, 189, 214, 338, 343; politics, 89–97; slavery, 61, 197; violence, 6–7, 338–339, 343
racism, 18, 54, 61, 90, 99, 189–190, 194, 196–197; anti-racism, 89, 91
Racz, Imogen, 166
Rafter, Nicole, 15–16, 115
Rankine, Claudia, 88–89, 98–99, 102
Rashkin, Esther, 7, 46
realism: agential, 255, 257–258, 261–262, 272; magical, 53; speculative, 208
Rediker, Marcus, 205–206
Reid, Julian, 195
Reid, Tiana, 188
remembrance, 55, 74, 100, 243, 247
representation, 36, 38, 44, 45, 55–56, 58, 61, 96, 116, 119–121, 211, 237, 246, 258, 263, 281, 286, 296
repressed, 5, 35, 52, 57, 94, 166, 197, 228, 256, 343
revenant, revenants, 3, 42, 45, 94, 197
Robinson, Cedric, 90–91
Roth, Tim, 267–268

sacred and profane, 37–38
Saddleworth Moor, 135–136, 140, 150
Saleh-Hanna, Viviane, 21–22, 93, 104, 340
Sandoval-Strausz, Andrew, 284–285
Sante, Luc, 296–298
Schutz, Dana, 95, 108
security, politics of, 181, 185, 194, 195, 218
Sekula, Allan, 11, 116

Seltzer, Mark, 271
sensorial, 19, 290, 298, 325
sensory, 118, 326
Sharpe, Christina, 89, 94–95, 99–104, 339
Shilliam, Robbie, 248
Siegel, James, 341
Simon, Taryn, 167–168
slavery, 2, 18, 47, 53–54, 61, 89, 101, 104–105, 196, 198, 343
Smith, Danez, 88
Sontag, Susan, 168
Sothcott, Keir, 15
sovereign, sovereignty, 155–156, 166, 169, 171, 173, 175, 185, 211, 337, 342
spatial, spatiality, 17, 19, 25, 56, 68, 72, 76, 79, 82, 85, 120, 128, 187, 234, 256, 261, 281, 284, 288–290, 295, 297, 299, 311–312, 314–316, 319, 326
spectacle, 11, 88–91, 93, 95, 98–99, 101, 103, 155, 159, 168–169, 175, 267, 269
Specters of Marx (Derrida), 8–11, 36, 315
specter, spectre, 1, 4, 7, 9–11, 27, 30, 46, 88–89, 91–93, 95, 97–103, 105, 107, 109, 111, 114–115, 123, 125–126, 129, 135, 160, 164–166, 169, 187–188, 191, 202, 222, 228, 340. See also *Specters of Marx*
spectral, 1, 3–8, 10–12, 15–21, 23, 25–26, 35–36, 54, 56–57, 59, 65, 67–68, 73, 75–76, 81, 91, 93, 96–98, 103, 110–111, 113, 118, 125–126, 129, 155–156, 164, 166, 169, 171, 176, 181, 184–185, 192, 197, 205, 221, 254–258, 260, 264, 271–272, 280, 282, 285, 287, 294, 298–300, 309, 312–313, 315, 320, 322, 325, 327–328, 331, 338, 340–343
spectralization, spectralized, 114, 118, 125–126, 129
spiritualism, 10–12, 180
Stasi, 23, 162–164
supernatural, 1, 3, 12, 15, 36, 38, 41–43, 46, 49, 53, 70, 114, 146–147, 228, 282, 292, 299
surveillance, 67, 90, 127, 163, 181, 285, 326, 345

Taibbi, Matt, 202–203, 214–215, 224
Tallgren, Immi, 162–163
Tarlow, Sarah, 136
Taylor, Breonna, 88, 337
Taylor, Leila, 14
Taylor, Paul, 76, 79
temporalities, 5, 15, 62, 240, 287, 317, 328, 339, 342
Till, Emmett, 84, 87
trauma, 1, 3, 5–7, 9, 16, 19–20, 24, 46, 54, 56, 58, 111–112, 123, 193–196, 228, 231–232, 245, 248–249, 283, 292, 299, 298, 328, 340, 342
Trigg, Dylan, 294
Troyer, John, 136–137, 145
Tunnell, Ken, 73, 78, 87
Turner, Justin, 23–24, 187, 221, 339

uncanny, 19, 23–25, 35–36, 45, 56, 93, 118, 120, 197, 120, 256, 284, 290, 296, 299, 312, 324
unconscious, 165, 197, 247, 288, 315, 324
undead, 7, 146, 205
unheimlich, 22, 36, 284
unhomely, 36, 284

vampire, 202, 205, 213, 215–216
Vampyroteuthis infernalis, 202
Vandermeer, Jeff, 210, 212
Vidler, Anthony, 56, 66, 305, 331, 336
violence, anti-black, 93, 192
Vismann, Cornelia, 161, 174
visuality, 23, 89–91, 97, 101, 113, 117–118, 121, 125, 218

Wall, Tyler, 192, 117–118
weird 4, 5, 23, 24, 180–197, 202–222, 291
whiteness, 61, 88, 91–92, 95–96, 98, 103
Wilderson, Frank, 192, 194
Wright, Michelle, 339

X-ray, 110–111, 113, 115, 117, 119, 121, 123, 125–127, 129, 131, 172

Yang, Betty 259–260
Young, Alison, 19, 24
Ystehede, Per, 15–16, 115

zombie, 62, 68, 70, 205, 222
zombification, 15, 98

www.ingramcontent.com/pod-product-compliance
Lightning Source LLC
Chambersburg PA
CBHW020240030426
42336CB00010B/557